European Communication Research and Education Association (ECREA)

This series consists of books arising from the intellectual work of ECREA members. Books address themes relevant to the ECREA's interests; make a major contribution to the theory, research, practice and/or policy literature; are European in scope; and represent a diversity of perspectives. Book proposals are refereed.

Series Editors
Nico Carpentier
François Heinderyckx

Series Advisory Board
Denis McQuail
Robert Picard
Jan Servaes

The aims of the ECREA are

a) To provide a forum where researchers and others involved in communication and information research can meet and exchange information and documentation about their work. Its disciplinary focus will include media, (tele)communications and informatics research, including relevant approaches of human and social sciences;
b) To encourage the development of research and systematic study, especially on subjects and areas where such work is not well developed;
c) To stimulate academic and intellectual interest in media and communication research, and to promote communication and cooperation between members of the Association;
d) To co-ordinate the circulation of information on communications research in Europe, with a view to establishing a database of ongoing research;
e) To encourage, support and, where possible, publish the work of young researchers in Europe;
f) To take into account the desirability of different languages and cultures in Europe;
g) To develop links with relevant national and international communication organizations and with professional communication researchers working for commercial organizations and regulatory institutions, both public and private;
h) To promote the interests of communication research within and among the Member States of the Council of Europe and the European Union;
i) To collect and disseminate information concerning the professional position of communication researchers in the European region; and
j) To develop, improve and promote communication and media education.

Trends in Communication Policy Research: New Theories, Methods and Subjects

Trends in Communication Policy Research: New Theories, Methods and Subjects

Edited by Natascha Just and Manuel Puppis

intellect Bristol, UK / Chicago, USA

First published in the UK in 2012 by
Intellect, The Mill, Parnall Road, Fishponds, Bristol, BS16 3JG, UK

First published in the USA in 2012 by
Intellect, The University of Chicago Press, 1427 E. 60th Street,
Chicago, IL 60637, USA

A catalogue record for this book is available from the
British Library.

Cover designer: Persephone Coelho
Copy-editor: MPS Technologies
Production manager: Tim Mitchell
Typesetting: Planman Technologies

ISBN 978-1-84150-674-6
ECREA Series ISSN: 1753-0342

Printed and bound by Hobbs, UK

Contents

Introduction

Natascha Just & Manuel Puppis

Trends in Communication Policy Research

Technological, economic and social trends are changing the context of communication policy. Convergence, liberalization, commercialization, new media (e.g. the Internet and mobile communication), audience fragmentation and globalization are only a few of the more notable terms that describe this change. The question of how *communication policy* copes with these changes is not only of interest to academics but also of the highest societal relevance. Scholars are well aware of current and imminent changes; options for reforming communication policies and regulation are the subject of lively debates in the field.

In this volume, we are not just interested in what the above-mentioned changes mean for communication policy but foremost and more importantly in what the challenges and implications are for *communication policy research*. As the insights of communication policy research are fundamental to understanding and shaping media landscapes and thus for safeguarding the existence of the media necessary for democratic societies, a thorough analysis of how we undertake this research is needed. Although communication policy research traditionally proves to be a self-critical as well as self-conscious (and not always self-confident) area of research, it has been a while since new directions for communication policy research in Europe were discussed.

Trends in Communication Policy Research aims to revive and foster such a discussion by offering an overview of and insights into current and future areas of inquiry in this contested policy field. This unique volume is a compilation of articles that were mostly presented at the 2009 workshop of the European Communication Research and Education Association's (ECREA) Communication Law and Policy Section in Zurich (Switzerland). The original call for papers solicited work that deals with questions of how to approach new communication policy issues theoretically and methodologically, of understanding what insights can be gained from the application of theories and methods of cognate areas and of identifying what policy challenges are emerging.

However, some chapters were added, as conference proceedings – no matter how thoroughly planned conceptually – always risk not doing justice to the overall field, and omissions are almost inevitable. The volume for the most part offers perspectives from European scholars on communication policy research. However, neither is it a book about European communication policies, nor is its use confined to this geographical context alone. Particularly those contributions dealing with questions of what theories and methods may be appropriate for furthering communication policy research are of wider significance. Whereas several contributions highlight the trend to apply various strands of new institutionalism to communication policy, demonstrating the potentials and limitations of such approaches, other theoretical perspectives are reflected as well. Despite technological convergence, most articles focus on traditional mass media. Nevertheless, this volume also emphasizes the trend of increasing research into the Internet, communication infrastructures and telecommunications regulation.

Thus, with the help of scholars from a variety of countries who contributed with their specific expertise, *Trends in Communication Policy Research* succeeds in offering thorough analyses of a wide range of communication policy subjects and addresses various methodological and theoretical challenges that face this field of research.

Overview of the Book

The introductory chapter by Natascha Just and Manuel Puppis (Universität Zürich) looks into the history of communication policy research and its contribution to policy-making. It shows that our research field is often highly self-conscious and not too self-confident, bemoaning the state of research as well as the perceived lack of influence and recognition. The authors argue, however, that communication policy research is instead a meaningful and mature sub-division, which is capable of making itself heard. Nevertheless, in order to cope with changing society and changing communication policy and to gain new insights into policy and regulation, scholars also need to apply theories that have previously not been considered. Furthermore, research methods need to be more thoroughly discussed and scrutinized so as to increase awareness of their benefits and challenges. And finally, it is pertinent to keep an open mind regarding new research subjects.

Consequently, it is necessary to discuss new or rarely employed theoretical and methodological ways of analysing communication policy issues and to identify changes in communication policy that require scholarly attention. *Trends in Communication Policy Research* is thus divided into three parts: new theories, new methods and new subjects.

New Theories

Scholars in communication policy research apply a wide variety of different theoretical approaches to their subjects. Articles in this part of the book apply theories that have previously been considered only marginally in communication policy research to different subjects. Specifically, institutions (different forms of new institutionalism), interests (actor-centred approaches) as well as ideas are used in order to gain new insights into policy and regulation.

Jan Loisen (Vrije Universiteit Brussel) builds upon Douglass North's new institutionalism in order to analyse the audio-visual dossier of the World Trade Organization. He argues that this framework makes it possible to map the complexity of the issue and to analyse institutional change. The analysis indicates that the audio-visual dossier is on a path-dependent course to liberalization. However, there is scope to include non-economic concerns.

Matthias Künzler (Universität Zürich) is interested in liberalization as well. Looking at the introduction of private broadcasting in three small European states, Künzler uses an ideas-based approach to explain differences in regulation. Based on Berger and Luckmann's sociology of knowledge, he develops a theoretical model that can be empirically tested in order to show how ideas are able to shape media policy decisions.

Regulatory agencies have become key actors in communication policy-making. Manuel Puppis (Universität Zürich) and Martino Maggetti (Universität Zürich and Université de Lausanne) focus on their contested accountability and legitimacy. By drawing on policy diffusion theory and new institutionalism in organization studies, they argue that both the participation in regulatory networks and the political communication of regulators may enhance their accountability and legitimacy.

Avshalom Ginosar (Emek Yezreel Academic College and University of Haifa) looks into regulatory regimes of product-placement regulation in the European Union, Canada and Israel. New institutionalism is employed in order to understand the similarities and differences between these regimes. The theory reveals the path dependency of the policy discourse and of the stakeholders' positions and thus of the outcome of the political process.

Using a different institutional theory, Christian Katzenbach (Freie Universität Berlin) attempts to link approaches and insights from science and technology studies with a governance perspective. He argues that conceiving of technology as an institution is necessary in order to take the politics of information and communication technologies into account as well as to overcome a determinist view on technology.

With veto-player theory, Ulrike Klinger (Universität Zürich) applies a theoretical concept of political science to media ownership regulation. She argues that veto-player theory connects well with actor-centred approaches and can open the 'black box' of political decision-making. As an example, she compares reforms of ownership regulation in very different political systems – Mexico and Italy.

New Methods

The articles in the second part of the book on the one hand analyse often used but rarely discussed methods of communication policy research like comparative methods and document analysis. On the other hand, the potential of new approaches focusing on networks and coalitions is dealt with. By focusing on methods, these articles establish a basis for scrutinizing and advancing communication policy research in this area.

Peter Humphreys (University of Manchester) discusses the existing comparative communication policy research. After dealing with the development of approaches to comparing media systems, he specifically focuses on Hallin and Mancini's seminal typology. His argument is that insights from historical institutionalism are needed to explain national divergences.

Focusing on a widely used method of communication policy research, Kari Karppinen (Helsingin Yliopisto) and Hallvard Moe (Universitetet i Bergen) talk about document analysis. The authors argue that it is necessary to explicate the process from data gathering to actual analysis in order to increase the impact of communication policy research both in academic and policy debates.

The use of qualitative network analysis as a research method for communication policy research is discussed by Maria Löblich and Senta Pfaff-Rüdiger (Ludwig-Maximilians-Universität München). This approach offers an opportunity to empirically investigate how interactions produce network structures and how actors are shaped by their networks. The merits and pitfalls of applying interviews and network cards are discussed using the example of the protection of minors in Germany.

Similarly, Hilde Van den Bulck (Universiteit Antwerpen) is also interested in the main policy-making stakeholders. The starting point of her article is the fact that researchers often face blind spots in their understanding of the political process, hence missing out on key documents and actors. She develops a process model for the analysis of media policy and discusses its methodological implications.

New Subjects

New policy challenges arising from media change are manifold and widespread in communication policy research. The theoretical and empirical articles in this section analyse specific new and emerging policy challenges and give an overview of current communication policy research and future fields of inquiry where research is still being developed or scholarly attention is called for.

The collection in this part of the book includes various overlapping issues that share a common topic or problem, yet they approach and analyse it from various angles and points of view. These articles have several links with articles not only in this part, but also in other parts of the book. The issue of convergence, for example, is explicitly or implicitly acknowledged as a major driving force of many current and future changes in communication policy and thus in communication policy research. The analysis by Just, Latzer and Saurwein is closely linked with *New Methods*, as it presents a novel research approach that methodologically furthers online research in the fields of data collection, online content and link analyses. The article by Sarikakis connects with *New Theories*, as it calls for a wider theoretical recognition of human and gender aspects in communication policy-making and provides guidelines for a human-centred policy approach.

The articles are arranged according to the three sub-sections, *Convergence*, *State Aid* and *Participation, Power & the Role of Gender*.

Convergence is the motor of change in communication policy and consequently sets the framework for much current research. Karol Jakubowicz (Warsaw, Poland) analyses how technological change impacts the conceptual framework of media and communication policy by analysing changes in the object ('the media') and objectives of communication policy as well as shifts in communication policy paradigms.

With convergence and digitization, new topics are emerging and others are becoming more prominent. Andrew T. Kenyon (University of Melbourne), Julian Thomas (Swinburne University of Technology) and Jason Bosland (University of Melbourne) analyse policy challenges resulting from digital content management and show how there are shifting conceptions of public interest and regulation in relation to audio-visual content.

The online activities of public service broadcasters are disputed throughout Europe and the Internet is evoking various challenges for the monitoring and control of such activities. Natascha Just, Michael Latzer and Florian Saurwein (Universität Zürich) discuss regulatory responses to and regulatory implications of online activities of public service broadcasters, based on the first large-scale study assessing the compliance of the Swiss PSB's online service with regulations.

With the increasing disputes surrounding PSB's online activities, European *state-aid policy* and the role of the European Commission have become more important in communication policy-making.

Jo Bardoel (Universiteit van Amsterdam and Radboud Universiteit Nijmegen) and Marit Vochteloo (Dutch Ministry of Education, Culture and Sciences) examine the struggle over how to balance cultural and economic interests in European public service broadcasting policy. They review European state-aid policy, its effect on Dutch broadcasting regulation and infer from their analysis how the current direction of PSB policy may depoliticize the definition of the role and remit of PSBs while in turn politicizing their actual editorial strategy.

European state-aid policy and the controversies over the cultural and economic nature of communication goods play a determining role in the field of cinematographic work as well. Lucia Bellucci (Università degli Studi di Milano) identifies these controversies as a source of conflict within and between the European Commission and EU member states and discusses attendant challenges that may determine the future of developments in this policy area.

State-aid policy to broadband and next-generation networks is another thus-far under-addressed, yet emerging, research area. Seamus Simpson (University of Salford) reasons that the neo-liberal character of EU telecommunications policy is being continued in this area and consequently jeopardizes and restrains the extent of state intervention for social policy reasons, despite official rhetoric to the contrary.

Finally, the sub-section on *Participation, Power & the Role of Gender* brings together three articles that focus on various contexts of changes in media and media governance, the role of civil society and the claim for a wider theoretical attention of gender in policy research.

Although the place of PSB as one of the key pillars of national media systems has been secured in western Europe for many decades, such a historical legacy is absent in post-communist east and central European countries. Peter Bajomi-Lazar (University of Oxford), Vaclav Stetka (University of Oxford) and Miklós Sükösd (University of Hong Kong) analyse these PSB systems comparatively with regard to trends in audience share, changes in funding schemes, supervision and political influence. They conclude by asserting that public service media need broad public support in order to guarantee its autonomy and independence.

Pietro Rossi and Werner Meier (Universität Zürich) outline how the involvement of civil society is paramount in governance processes. Based on results of case studies of advertising regulation, they argue how a participatory media governance approach, with its emphasis on conferring decision-making power on the public, may result in a reinvigoration of the democratic legitimacy of the mass media.

Finally, Katharine Sarikakis (Universität Wien) argues for the need for a gender-conscious agenda in communication policy analysis in order to adequately contribute theoretically and practically to understanding the complex power relations of social and political worlds. Such a perspective would seek to integrate a gender perspective, among other things, in the evaluation and analysis of policy objectives and of the effects of policy implementation.

Words of Thanks

It would not have been possible to organize the 2009 workshop of the ECREA's Communication Law and Policy Section in Zurich without the substantial financial support of the Association of Non-Professorial Academic Staff at the University of Zurich (VAUZ), the University of Zurich's *Hochschulstiftung* and the University of Zurich's Institute of Mass Communication and Media Research (IPMZ), whose generous support we gratefully acknowledge.

We would also like to thank ECREA for selecting this volume to be published in the ECREA Book Series and for subsidizing its publication. Moreover, the *Zürcher Universitätsverein* (ZUNIV) and the IPMZ generously co-financed the proof reading of the manuscript. Last but not least, our thanks go to David Westacott (Vienna) for copy-editing and to Florian Schmitz (Zurich) for supporting us in the production of this volume.

Chapter 2

Communication Policy Research: Looking Back, Moving Forward

Natascha Just & Manuel Puppis

Old paint on a canvas, as it ages, sometimes becomes transparent. When that happens it is possible, in some pictures, to see the original lines: a tree will show through a woman's dress, a child makes way for a dog, a large boat is no longer on an open sea. That is called pentimento because the painter 'repented,' changed his mind. Perhaps it would be as well to say that the old conception, replaced by a later choice, is a way of seeing and then seeing again. (Hellman 1973: 3)

Introduction

Communication policy research evolved from the outset as a multi-disciplinary field and domain of various academic disciplines from sociology and political science to law and economics, resulting in the coverage of a myriad of multi-faceted topics. The choice of subjects in communication policy research is affected by sociocultural, political, economic and technological forces that determine the overall framework for communication policy and regulation as well as by the many regulatory objectives in communication. This makes it almost impossible to sort out, identify and categorize all of the scholarship in this area. As Rowland (1984: 423) noted:

> [...] [there is] no central, uniformly recognized body of literature and instruction [that] qualifies as communication policy studies, and there is no singularly comprehensive forum for its discussion. [...] while the topic is treated [...] as if it were a recognizable whole, it is in fact a widely disparate body of work about whose dimensions there is relatively little agreement.

Despite its 'exceptional and deeply rooted difficulties' (McQuail 1994: 39), the study of communication policy 'is a meaningful area of research and theory in communication studies' (Reinard and Ortiz 2005: 594). It is generally argued, however, that the peculiarities of communication policy pose unique challenges to communication policy analysis, 'a particularly daunting set of questions' (Bauer et al. 2005: 1) and 'an analytical burden more complex than analysis in other policy areas' (Napoli 1999: 568). Communication policy decisions can directly affect political and social beliefs and values that are central to the democratic process and often involve both economic and social value objectives (Napoli 1999: 566, 570). Decisions have far-reaching effects on society and affect the creation, processing, dissemination and use of information – in other words the processes that create shared meaning among members of a society (Bauer et al. 2005: 1; Krieger 1971: 306). Quite ironically, however, communication policy issues are low profile, and do not receive the same attention as nuclear power plants, inflation or balancing the budget (Havick 1983: 15). In addition, under the pretence of press freedom, it is often argued that communication policy is unwarranted. As a consequence, the very idea of policy for communication as well as of researching such policies has been regarded with suspicion (McQuail 1994: 39; Rowland 1984: 427).

This article does not intend to offer a cohesive review of all scholarship let alone to account for the whole history of communication policy research. The outcome of such an endeavour would always be 'incomprehensive and incomplete' (Sarikakis 2008: 294).[1] Instead, in attempting to understand the state of communication policy research, it recalls some narratives that have had a lasting influence on it and continue to shape its current status. This is characterized by self-analysis of epistemological matters, applied theories and methods, and similarly by a history of debate and fundamental criticism about its actual contributions to theory development and practice. This is mirrored in the questions of the general role of communication research in communication policy-making with its endless discussions over administrative versus critical research as well as in communication scholars' liking for self-castigation with regard to their assumed failure to actively inform and contribute to policy processes or to realize social objectives effectively. In essence, it is argued here, however, that communication scholars should move from self-consciousness to self-confidence about their work and that there are sufficient grounds to do so.

In what follows, this article first discusses the origins and legacies of communication policy research and, second, the role of research in communication policy-making. After this look back, the final section discusses options of moving communication policy research forward.

Origins, Legacies, Controversies

An important and founding impetus for communication policy research came from Harold D. Lasswell, who also figures prominently as a founding father of communication science and policy science (Rogers 1994). He argued that future advances in communication study depended upon the development of a policy focus and upon being a third voice supplying 'a competing appraisal of the images spread by self-serving sources' (Lasswell 1972: 307).

> It is not enough for communication specialists to acquire skill in surveying, content analysis, or other technical operations. A genuine profession can be said to complement skill with enlightenment. In the case of communication, this implies a common map of

the trends, conditions, and projections of the entire process. It also implies the capacity to invent and evaluate policies for the accomplishment of postulated goals. (Lasswell 1972: 306)

In his writings on the policy sciences, which Lasswell began in the 1950s, he identified various key requirements for the policy sciences: that they be multi-disciplinary (multi-method approach), have a problem-oriented, contextual outlook and be explicitly normative (Lasswell 1951, 1970). Furthermore, he stipulated the need for a democratic, distinctly human policy science by emphasizing 'the policy sciences of democracy [...] directed toward providing the knowledge needed to improve the practice of democracy' (Lasswell 1951: 15).

The extent and impact of Lasswell's legacy and the appraisals of his commitment to democracy, morals and policy are disputed, however (e.g., Brunner 2008; Farr et al. 2006; 2008). Lasswell is characterized as 'a contradictory figure, at once positivist and value-laden, elitist and democratic, heroic and implausible' (Farr et al. 2006: 579). His work and contribution is seen by critics such as Rowland (1984) as the epitome of positivism, of formal policy science neglecting wider democratic concerns and social responsibilities. Critical scholars argue that the question 'why' should be added to Lasswell's five-question formula (who says what in which channel to whom with what effect?), which broadly frames the subject matter of communication studies, and also for an emphasis on the context in which communication occurs (Olson 1989: 73). Supporters of his work, on the other hand, stress that others misconstrue Lasswell's conception of policy sciences, with its emphasis on contextual orientation, and thereby obscure precisely those dimensions of his work that counter the positivist logic (Torgerson 1985). Although the controversies of legacy are not resolvable here, these historical narratives set the terms of discussion regarding the status of communication policy research and also regarding the relationship of mainstream communication science and policy research. The debates on administrative and critical research have become prime examples of this ongoing conflict (see later).

The Development of Communication Policy-Making and Policy Research

Determining the precise beginning of communication policy-making and the attendant idea of researching it systematically is difficult. It is often said to have begun with the emergence of telegraphy, telephony and wireless communication and not with the traditional mass media. Van Cuilenburg and McQuail (2003: 182), for example, identify three consecutives phases of communication policy-making and argue that 'it would be anachronistic to speak of communications policies before the series of electronic inventions beginning with the electric telegraph in the mid-19th century'. This is also when the *idea* of a systematic study of policy-making started. Braman (2003c) traces this idea back to the birth of the bureaucratic welfare state in the late nineteenth century, with the telegraph and postal service serving as prime examples. This first phase (from the mid-19th century until the start of World War II) was marked by ad hoc measures aimed at facilitating and regulating innovations with the intent of protecting the national interest and fostering the development of communication systems. However, during this phase the lines for the future regulation of other media were laid down as well. Of particular importance here is the development of the distinction between policy regimes on the basis of technologies and distribution networks during the later years of this phase (van Cuilenburg and McQuail 2003: 186f). This resulted in what Pool (1983: 2) termed a 'trifurcated communications system' with the three domains of communication (print, broadcasting and common carriage) subject to different regulatory regimes. This characteristic would later unsettle communication policy research, especially with regard to the definition and demarcation of its research object, because of its mostly narrow focus on mass media with a concurrent neglect of telecommunications.

Policy-related research in general flowered noticeably in the period following World War II (Braman 2003c: 38; McQuail 1994: 40). One reason for this, as Rowland (1984: 424) states, is that the experience of the war contributed to an interest in applying science in the service of transforming society. Nonetheless, to the extent that the history of communication policy is characterized as 'a story of inertia and incrementalism' (Bar and Sandvig 2008: 532), this similarly holds true for communication policy research.

As a consequence, the beginning of an institutionalized and more systematic communication policy research is often dated later than its idea, namely around the 1970s, at a time when both communication science and the policy sciences took off (Harms 1977; 1980) and national communication policy-making widely emerged (Schiller 1975).

> Ten years ago few communications practitioners thought in terms of any overall communication policy, and few communications researchers would have recognized policy research as an established category. All that has changed. Communication policy has emerged as a field of research. (Pool 1974: 31)

A factor that also influenced this late development was that relatively stable market structures with monopoly regulation and national protectionism generally led to there being little interest in political analysis of broadcasting and telecommunications.[2]

The political decision for liberalization was then an important step in the surge of communication policy research. Yet, the greatest impetus for the acceleration and development of communication policy research is most frequently attributed to *technological change*. It is seen as the key driver for the rise of and for changes in communication policy-making and hence research into it (e.g., Krieger 1971; Pool 1974; Rowland 1984; Reinard and Ortiz 2005). As Rowland (1984: 426) states, an overwhelming amount of communication policy literature has been dominated by problems of technological change. As a result, 'most of the discussions of public policy for the mass media during the past fifteen years have been driven by questions about the role and promises of the "new technologies"' (Rowland 1984: 426). These statements are very similar to the bulk of more recent discussions of convergence of media, telecommunications and information technologies, which yet again have spurred increased communication policy research. The scholarly interest in communication policy issues has since become the domain of various academic disciplines from law to sociology, economics and communication science (Latzer 2009). Technological change alone is not enough, however, for changes in policies and research. Instead, technology should be viewed as an enabler of such change. Latzer (2009: 415) views these processes as *co-evolutionary*, which means that the direction and speed of change is 'shaped by the reciprocal interplay of technological innovations, corporate strategies, political–legal reforms as well as changes of media reception patterns.' Such a view also transcends the dichotomy between technological and social determinism.

Nonetheless, technology has had a strong fixing influence on many of the parameters that define communication policy research: the above-mentioned technology-oriented sub-division into media and telecommunications and into mass/individual communication, which are in turn also reflected in the respective regulatory structures and the research agendas (Latzer 2009). With convergence then 'the search for a new communications policy paradigm' began (van Cuilenburg and McQuail 2003: 181), and communication scholars (particularly in Europe) started to get a grip on their field of research, especially by trying to incorporate telecommunications, which had long been ignored in favour of mass-media research with an emphasis on public communication. Mueller (1995: 465) in fact argues that 'telecommunications has been interpreted as outside the purview of [the] field' and that in order to achieve policy relevance it is essential 'to jettison "mass communication" as a label for the field or program of research.' Similarly, van Cuilenburg and Slaa (1993: 173) conclude that by ignoring such issues, communication science will damage the political and policy relevance of its work and run the risk of not being able to play an adequate role in public debates. This dispute then also resonates in the discussions of how to define communication policy research, which is dealt with in the next section.

Defining Communication Policy Research

Lasswell (1970: 3), who not only discussed key requirements but also brought forward a definition of policy sciences as knowledge *of* the policy process and knowledge *in* the process, emphasizes that communication policy research encompasses two tasks: on the one hand, it is *research about communication policy*; on the other hand it also *informs communication policy-makers* (Harms 1980: 5).[3] The former concerns the subject(s) of communication policy research; the latter touches upon the role of communication policy research in communication policy-making and will be dealt with in the next section.

But what exactly does research about communication policy entail? By and large, there is a lack of concrete definitions of communication policy research or its subjects. The definitions run from generic to more specific to enumerations of research topics. For example, Rowland (1984: 423) describes communication policy research as the 'investigation of those issues centering around the way in which – and why – societies and governments make choices they do regarding the purposes, ownership, control, support and guidance of their media institutions and services.' In a similar vein, Kunkel and Farinola (2001: 413) state that research into communication policy traditionally means studying the policy-making process as well as examining the patterns and trends in communication policy over the years. Van Cuilenburg and McQuail (2003: 183f) identify precise elements of interest to communication policy research:

> [...] the goals or objectives to be pursued; the values and criteria by which goals are defined or recognized; the various content and communication services to which policy applies; the different distribution services (mainly print publishing, cable, satellite and broadcast dissemination and telecommunications); and finally the appropriate policy measures and means of implementation (mainly embodied in law, regulation, self-regulation or market practices).

Other approaches to circumscribing the field of communication policy research focus on the analytical distinctions commonly applied in political science, namely the distinctions between *polity*, *politics* and *policy* (e.g., Puppis et al. 2010: 276f). This allows for the analysis of the institutional setting, the process and actors of communication policy as well as of the content of actual decisions. Yet others categorize communication policy research by way of different disciplinary perspectives. Vowe (2003), for example, distinguishes between a *historical school of thought* that analyses communication policy chronologically with an emphasis on reconstructing developments; a *law perspective* with a focus on communication freedom; a *social science approach* centring on democratic and social functions, and an *economic approach* concerned with issues of state intervention in communication markets.

The Role of Research in Communication Policy-Making

As already outlined, Lasswell's (1970: 3) definition of policy sciences as knowledge *of* the policy process as well as knowledge *in* this process suggests that communication policy research also involves making information available to decision-makers. It aims at providing 'policymakers with pragmatic, action-oriented recommendations' (Majchrzak 1984: 12).

This view of communication policy research directly ties in with the fierce debates on the role that communication research should play in communication policy-making. Lasswell (1972: 303ff) was quite specific about the potential influence of communication research at the various stages of the policy-making process. An important question that comes to mind here is whether communication scholars care enough to contribute to policy-making effectively (Docherty et al. 1993: 231) and what kind of conditions influence or restrain their attitude towards involvement. It is argued here that restraints are in part home-made, 'institutionalized' by the endless debates over administrative versus critical research and communication scholars' love of self-castigation. As the conditions for involvement have recently been enhanced because of convergence and attendant changes in governance patterns, scholars should strive for increased participation, paying particular attention, however, to the context in which such involvement occurs.

The Endless Struggle over Administrative Versus Critical Research

The distinction between the critical and administrative, originally introduced by Paul Lazarsfeld (1941) in the early 1940s, has been a focal point and a curse in the debate over the role of communication research in general and of communication policy research in particular. In its strictest sense, *administrative research* is understood as research 'carried through in the service of some kind of administrative agency' (Lazarsfeld 1941: 8) or 'carried along on the strength of industrial or government grants' (Rowland 1986: 170). It is quite often associated with positivist, behavioural analytical methods that promise great mathematical precision and objectivity or is defined as applied (market) research devoid of any wider theoretical considerations of pressing social and economic issues (Martin 1976: 19). This is also why 'research, in its applied, administrative, policy-related variety, became identified with the would-be manipulators of a capitalist or bureaucratic order [...]' (McQuail 1994: 41). Or as Rowland (1986: 170) puts it:

> There is little analysis that is deeply social, political or cultural, and most of the discussions of domestic and international policy problems are presented from perspectives that, whether conscious or not, are ultimately protective of the fundamental structures and global status of the American corporate welfare state [...].

What distinguishes *critical research* from administrative research then is that the former 'develops a theory of the prevailing social trends of our times [...] and [...] seems to imply ideas of basic human values according to which all actual or desired effects should be appraised' (Lazarsfeld 1941: 9).

The distinction between administrative and critical research can be traced back to a time when different research traditions met in the US, i.e., when European social theory as articulated by the *Frankfurt School* encountered US communication scholarship, with US research showing more of a tendency towards assessing media systems within the given policy parameters and European research emphasizing the importance of critique (Corner et al. 1997: 4; Rowland 1986: 165). By now, researchers identifying themselves with either tradition or both can be found on both sides of the pond. Yet, the struggle over deliberate disengagement and engagement is still continuously voiced (Docherty et al. 1993: 231).

In essence, administrative research is criticized for yielding to the temptation of simply solving short-term problems and maintaining the status quo rather than investigating more basic questions of existing political and economic power relations (Martin 1976: 19; Melody and Mansell 1983: 104; Rowland 1986: 178). The contribution of critical research lies in scrutinizing the taken-for-grantedness of societal structures and of communication policy. It can reveal that the way things are is not an objective necessity and that communication policy can be imagined and constructed otherwise (Streeter 1990: 61). Yet, critical research too often contents itself with documenting weaknesses and failures in existing institutions (as well as in administrative research) instead of analysing institutional structures and presenting solutions (Melody and Mansell 1983: 110).

This struggle over administrative versus critical research has been revisited many times. Often it is presented as an unresolved dispute about the nature of research as *either* favouring the positivist nature of quantitative analysis and evidence-based decision-making by simultaneously eschewing normative and value judgements *or* acknowledging explicitly that communication policy research is value-laden, occurs within specific social and political contexts and involves subjective judgement (Just 2009). However, it is of utmost importance to recognize that the distinction is not one between empirical and non-empirical research. Lazarsfeld himself assumed empirical work to be part of both traditions (Braman 2003b: 12). The debate is not about rejecting empirical research but about asking what 'empirical social research could and should do *within* a theoretical framework' (Hardt 1976: 94f). Moreover, both traditions can perform applied policy research (Katz 1979: 83) and hence *do research about policy* and also *inform the policy process.* 'The fundamental distinctions lie not in the realm of abstract theory and methodology. [...] The real basis for the dichotomy between critical and administrative traditions lies in the allegiance of researchers to the status quo versus change [...]' (Melody and Mansell 1983: 109f).

Administrative and critical researchers thus differ in the selection of relevant real-world problems. This context of discovery, as Max Weber (1968) called it, simply cannot be objective and value-free. As a consequence, even though Lazarsfeld believed that both traditions could be integrated (Braman 2003d: 422; Melody and Mansell 1983: 105), such attempts seem to be doomed from the very beginning (Docherty et al. 1993: 232). But again, both traditions can produce knowledge of the policy process as well as inform the policy process.

Communication Policy Scholars' Love of Self-Castigation

For many years, however, scholars self-critically complained that communication studies had failed to inform communication policy-making significantly and that other disciplines 'have filled the policy research gaps left vacant by communications research' (Napoli and Gillis 2006: 671). Communication scholars regularly complain about the inability of the field to define itself, its lack of recognition from the outside world and, most importantly, a lack of influence (Kunkel and Farinola 2001: 411f). Noam (1993: 199f, 1999: 424), for instance, criticizes the fact that communication science has played only a marginal role in communication policy and has thus lacked a real-world role. Mueller (1995: 457) agrees, stating that communication scholarship has failed to have a noticeable impact upon policy responses to the changing communication environment. 'The closer we get to ideas which have directly shaped public policy, the more communication scholarship recedes from the picture' (Mueller 1995: 459). Economics and law seem to make themselves heard more efficiently (Bauer et al. 2005: 22; Mueller 1995: 459f; Noam 1999: 424).

Several reasons have been advanced for this failure to play a more prominent role in policy-making. Firstly, it has been argued that communication scholarship and public policy had long been operating out of sync. 'Not until recently has research served mutual needs. Media researchers have gained legitimacy and, indeed, importance, and regulators have gained a sympathetic support group armed with "the facts"' (Reeves and Baughman 1983: 40). Secondly, communication science has developed rather slowly as an academic discipline (Reeves and Baughman 1983: 40). Thirdly, policy-makers' predominant professional background in law and economics leads them to pay less attention to the main issues raised by communication research. As a consequence, communication scholars have 'faced a steeper hill to climb in terms of receiving consideration from policy-makers' (Napoli and Gillis 2006: 672). And finally, everyone has his or her own experience of the media, thus feeling confident enough to comment critically on our field of research (Reeves and Baughman 1983: 40f). Moreover, communication researchers are themselves often criticized for their unwillingness to become engaged in the communication policy-making process (Napoli and Gillis 2006: 686). To make a contribution to communication policy, this obviously needs to change.

It seems that the time has come to repaint this bleak picture of a lack of recognition. Arguably, the opportunities for communication scholars to contribute to communication policy-making have improved significantly. The demand for research in communication policy-making is greater than ever. 'This is due to the changing nature of the questions being asked by policymakers [...] and a growing recognition within the policymaking community of the limitations of economic analysis in answering important communications policy questions' (Napoli and Gillis 2006: 672; see also Ang 2008; Verhulst and Price 2008). Further, with convergence the regulatory regime for the communication sector as it had been taught and practised for several decades is crumbling and a new pattern of governance is emerging. Some characteristics of this transformation also affect the relationship between communication research and policy-making.

> With convergence, not only is the economization of the convergent sector increasing, but the importance of the often overlooked interaction of social and economic implications in the mediamatics sector is also growing. Because of increasingly application- and effect-dependent regulation in the new governance model, communications research may gain momentum and growing relevance in the shaping of policy making [...]. (Latzer 2009: 423)

Regardless of whether communication policy research did indeed fail in playing a role in communication policy-making in the past or whether the self-consciousness of the field mutated into some kind of self-castigation, at least today communication policy research is anything but absent from the policy process. 'It is our position that communication policy research is a vital element of the field that is contributing significant knowledge to help inform and influence public policy, despite persistent concern to the contrary' (Kunkel and Farinola 2001: 412).[4] The problem, Kunkel and Farinola (2001: 426) claim, is not that our research fails to reach the policy arena but that the field receives no credit. It is difficult to make a conclusive assessment of this claim, however, as there are no detailed studies of participation.

Be that as it may, there is good reason to share a more confident view. Although this does not mean that scholars should overestimate their influence, moving from self-consciousness to self-confidence seems appropriate, as continuous complaining seems counter-productive, hindering more than contributing to any advance. Generally, it seems that there is good reason for communication scholars to be able to join the chorus of disciplines that inform communication policy-making.

After all, communication policy research has a lot to offer. It can help in interpreting situations and selecting a course of action, in deciding how to address a policy problem and in designing specific policy measures (Bauer et al. 2005: 5). There are consequences for society when the knowledge represented by researchers is not used. Thus, there are *good reasons for informing the policy process*. First of all, communication policy research contributes to an improvement in decision-making. Policy needs and the effects of policies in place can only be made visible by research (Braman 2003a: 6). Without research, policy decisions are not as informed as they should and could be. Scholars can raise the knowledge level of policy debates and guide them in the direction of the most relevant issues (Melody 1990: 33, 37; Pool 1974: 40). Moreover, due to its greater independence from vested interests,[5] academic research is both less subject to pressures to deliver preordained outcomes (Frieden 2008: 424) and in a unique position to focus on issues that go beyond the normal short-term horizons of policy-makers (Melody 1990: 33).

Certainly, convenient ideas will attract more interest than threatening ones. Good research is not necessarily the one that helps regulators do a better job (Reeves and Baughman 1983: 41) and policy-makers are less interested in analyses that are too far outside the range of what they deem politically feasible (Haight 1983: 230f). Yet, ideas matter. They need to be expressed in the policy process and can be used 'to illuminate, legitimate, and do battle' (Noam 1993: 200). By informing the policy process, communication policy researchers expand the range of possibilities contemplated by policy-makers and may assist them in understanding the choices available (Bauer et al. 2005: 2; Braman 2003a: 6; 2003c: 39; 2008: 434). If research is to have an effective bearing on substantial problems of modern societies, then scholars need to embrace a social responsibility that goes beyond fostering their own careers:

If the central purpose of our work is only to further career, to preen, to seek the security of tenure or some prestigious chair, to find pleasure in seeing one's name in print, or to find comfort in disengaged radical certainty as to the inequities of the ages; if this is all we are about, is it not an extraordinarily shabby form of narcissism, and a basic betrayal of a public trust and a public need to know? (Docherty et al. 1993: 237)

To inform policy effectively and to receive a successful hearing, however, it is also important to take into consideration the wider context in which policy-making happens.

Beware of the Context

Publishing research is not enough to be noticed – let alone to be taken into consideration – by politicians (Bauer et al. 2005: 20). Theories and research results need to be translated into a form that will be easily understood by those involved in policy-making (Braman 2003c: 47f; 2008: 434; Melody 1990: 37; Owen 1975). But the influence of research on political decisions is rarely that direct. On the one hand, more indirect methods, such as circulating relevant work to stakeholders, are important (Napoli and Gillis 2006: 686). On the other hand, research is influential at a more abstract level, 'impacting which issues policymakers choose to focus their attention on, or perhaps influencing how a particular policy issue is framed' (Napoli and Seaton 2007: 302).

As a matter of course, informing the policy process also involves serious *pitfalls*. First of all, one danger arises 'from the hubris of scholars who would prefer to play philosopher-king rather than be factual researchers' (Pool 1974: 40). It can be very tempting to be involved in the big questions of public policy. Katz (1979: 85) even suggests that some researchers are not satisfied with sitting next to the driver but want to drive themselves. Secondly, because critical analyses are not always welcome, scholars may be inclined to narrow their analysis to the politically feasible. In order to meet the perceived needs of policy-makers, researchers might feel the need to limit themselves to a more pragmatic selection of subjects and approaches (Corner et al. 1997: 7f; Freedman 2008: 102; Haight 1983: 231). On a related note, policy-making institutions are not interested in funding research that might undermine their power (Haight 1983: 232; Melody and Mansell 1983: 111). Thirdly, some commentators see the trend towards a greater reliance on research and empirical evidence as a mechanism for marginalizing citizens' input into policy-making as well as insulating policy-making from 'biased' opinions and values. It is, however, similarly dubious whether this so-called evidence-based approach is devoid of political interests (Freedman 2008: 99; Napoli and Seaton 2007: 299). Finally, a common concern is that policy-makers use research to legitimize decisions that have already been taken (Braman 2008: 433; Haight 1983: 228; Napoli and Seaton 2007: 300). 'It is not hard to think of situations in which evidence is adduced *after* a policy decision has already been made; or in which decisions are made regardless of the evidence, and the evidence is "spun" in order to support a predetermined course of action' (Buckingham 2009: 204). It is indeed inevitable that research findings will be used by vested interests. No matter what scholars would like to see happen to their work, once they bring it into political debates politicians will use it to serve their own ends (Braman 2003c: 44; Melody and Mansell 1983: 112).

Despite these potential problems of informing the policy process, scholars should not avoid the dialogue with political actors and bury their heads in the sand (Pool 1974: 42). Rather, they should try to make themselves aware of the vested interests involved (Melody and Mansell 1983: 112) and bring in their views 'in a pragmatic and humble fashion' (Bauer et al. 2005: 21f). As Melody and Mansell (1983: 133) put it, the crucible of communication policy research is the advocacy of policy in the direction indicated by research results.

In the end, it should not be expected that research 'is going to yield magic answers' (Melody 1990: 37). The contribution of research to policy-making will always be limited but 'the capacity of research has improved in other respects and the relationships among researchers, media communicators, and those concerned with policy are now less abrasive' (McQuail 1994: 49).

Theories, Methods and Subjects for Future Communication Policy Research

After this review of the role of research in communication policy-making in general and the role of communication science in it in particular, one may finally ask what communication policy research needs to do in order to be of lasting relevance.

Scholars need to *choose topical subjects* for their research – subjects that are of societal relevance. This involves the difficult task of anticipating pressing issues facing policy-makers (Bauer et al. 2005: 21; Buckingham 2009: 204) by understanding the overall framework for communication policy and regulation as well as the many objectives of communication regulation that are in turn affected by political, economic, sociocultural and technological changes.

In their attempt to identify communication policy and law research, Reinard and Ortiz (2005: 601) state that the 'most frequent area of scholarship has been on issues of regulation of mass media [...] followed by scholarship related to the Internet and attempts to regulate it, freedom of expression issues, intellectual property rights, behavior of the press, and communication in the legal setting, television and children's issues.'[6] Additionally, across Europe there seems to be a convergence over the objects of study, as the attention of regulators also influences the attention of policy scholars (Sarikakis 2008: 295). Thus, it can be criticized that most studies focus on regulatory details at the expense of the broad structure of regulation (Streeter 1990: 44). Moreover, although scholars have generated an impressive amount of knowledge about a wide range of policy uses, much less attention has been paid to the policy-making process itself: 'In other words, we know quite a lot about the intricacies of each policy question [...] but relatively little about the underlying forces shaping actual policy outcomes' (Galperin 2004: 159).

When it comes to suggestions for future subjects of communication policy research, there is a feeling that it can play a central role 'if it identifies its subject matter broadly enough' (Rowland 1984: 431). Firstly, there is a widespread call for what Burgelman (1997: 125) called 'scientific convergence.' As argued earlier, communication policy research should keep pace with the convergence of the broadcasting and telecommunications industries and thus move beyond traditional mass media (Mueller 1995: 465; Noam 1999: 428). Secondly, communication policy research is not only affected by convergence but also by Europeanization and globalization. Accordingly, there is a need to look into the tensions between the national, the European and the global levels in communication policy (Burgelman 1997: 141). Thirdly, moving from individual policies to politics and analysing the political process and the actors involved seems to be a promising and necessary undertaking as well (e.g. Freedman 2008; 2010).

Doing research on subjects that matter, however, is not enough. There is also the need to *advance our theoretical foundations and methodological skills.*

With respect to *theories*, much of communication policy research to date has been problem-driven. Most studies are topically and empirically specific. Although this can also be a strength and reflects a high degree of technical expertise, it mostly means that research is only loosely related to theory (Reinard and Ortiz 2005: 621; Rowland 1984: 424, 428). The tendency to react to industry and government demands often results in more descriptive than theoretically grounded and analytical work (Mosco 1988: 107; Mosco and Rideout 1997: 154; Reinard and Ortiz 2005: 621; Rowland 1984: 428). Rowland (1984: 426) argues that this is a legacy of the formative phase of communication policy research:

> To the extent that both the broader fields of communication research and policy science eschewed epistemologically serious theoretical discourse, communication policy studies began to develop without reliable guidance as to all the facets of its own origins and the consequences of the skewed, proadministrative research orientation of that history.

Regardless of whether one shares this interpretation, more theoretically grounded work is needed. Otherwise, communication policy research is limited to reactions to changes in law and technology, involving a large degree of tautological reasoning and technology-driven assumptions (Burgelman 1997: 125, 142; Reinard and Ortiz 2005: 621). The key issues of communication policy cannot be handled solely with media-centred theories. Rather, it is pertinent to include more 'conceptual work that connects communication with the larger body of social and political theory' (McQuail 1994: 46). Significant improvements and accomplishments in this respect can be noted. Firstly, studies that explain regulation by drawing on theories that deal with interests, institutions and ideas are blossoming (see, for instance, the contributions in this volume). Secondly, there are attempts to integrate innovation, evolution and complexity theories in order to better incorporate the co-evolutionary relationship between technical, economic, political and cultural change and its consequences for communication policies (Latzer 2010). Thirdly, the so-called governance concept as a means of describing, explaining and criticizing the entirety of forms of regulation is attracting growing interest (d'Haenens et al. 2010; Latzer et al. 2003; Puppis 2010; Raboy and Padovani 2010). Ironically, it is argued that it is in this 'theoretically much more self-conscious vein that communication policy research will most likely offer something of lasting intellectual value' (Rowland 1984: 432). Theory-based research is thus particularly invited (Reinard and Ortiz 2005: 621).

As for *methods*, it is jarring that methodological approaches to communication policy studies are seldom explicated. Despite its self-conscious and self-critical stance, discussion of methodological questions is virtually non-existent in most overviews of the field. Reinard and Ortiz (2005: 601) show, for one thing, that studies of various countries and comparisons of regulatory models from different countries dominate and, for another, that there is not a great diversity in approach. The problem is not so much that there is no empirical work and no comparison – far from it. However, mostly neither the methods of comparison nor the empirical methods of data collection and data analysis are explained, let alone critically discussed. Yet, in order to be credible in academia and beyond, it is imperative for communication policy scholars to go into methodological debates. Firstly, given the increasing importance of comparative research in reforming regulation (Verhulst and Price 2008), it is necessary to deal more thoroughly with the question of what exactly comparing media systems and regulation means (Puppis and d'Haenens 2011). Secondly, the empirical methods employed need to be disclosed and scrutinized. Qualitative document analysis and qualitative interviews with experts and elites are among the most common methods in communication policy research. It is high time that scholars took notice of and participated more widely in the joint methodological debates of all social sciences.

Communication policy research in Europe and beyond is enormously rich. Without falling into the trap of *pentimento* (to continue the former analogy to painting) and starting a new round of self-castigation, one has to be aware that there 'still lingers an ambivalence […] in respect of policy research' (McQuail 1994: 49) among researchers and practitioners alike. At the same time, richness also implies that policy scholarship in Europe is fragmented across languages, disciplines and national traditions (Sarikakis 2008: 308). It is thus worth reiterating that there is a need for theoretical groundwork and development, for methodological rigour, and for expanding the range of subjects. Such advance helps to reinforce the basis of communication policy research and to preserve a position of relevance.

Acknowledgements

We would like to thank Michael Latzer for his valuable comments. The usual disclaimer applies.

References

Ang, P. H. (2008), 'The Academic and the Policy Maker', *International Journal of Communication*, 2, pp. 450–453.

Bar, F. and Sandvig, C. (2008), 'US Communication Policy After Convergence', *Media, Culture & Society*, 30: 4, pp. 531–550.

Bauer, J. M., Kim, S., Mody, B. and Wildman, S. S. (2005), 'The Role of Research in Communications Policy: Theory and Evidence', *Paper presented at the 55th Annual Conference of the International Communications Association*, New York, USA, 26–30 May.

Braman, S. (2003a), 'Introduction', in S. Braman (ed.), *Communication Researchers and Policy-Making*, Cambridge and London: MIT Press, pp. 1–9.

—— (2003b), 'The Long View', in S. Braman (ed.), *Communication Researchers and Policy-Making*, Cambridge and London: MIT Press, pp. 10–31.

—— (2003c), 'Policy as a Research Context', in S. Braman (ed.), *Communication Researchers and Policy-Making*, Cambridge and London: MIT Press, pp. 35–58.

—— (2003d), 'Facing In: Researchers and Academia', in S. Braman (ed.), *Communication Researchers and Policy-Making*, Cambridge and London: MIT Press, pp. 415–434.

—— (2008), 'Policy Research in an Evidence-Averse Environment', *International Journal of Communication*, 2, pp. 433–449.

Brunner, R. D. (2008), 'The Policy Scientist of Democracy Revisited', *Policy Sciences*, 41: 1, pp. 3–19.

Buckingham, D. (2009), 'The Appliance of Science: The Role of Evidence in the Making of Regulatory Policy on Children and Food Advertising in the UK', *International Journal of Cultural Policy*, 15: 2, pp. 201–215.

Burgelman, J.-C. (1997), 'Issues and Assumptions in Communications Policy and Research in Western Europe: A Critical Analysis', in J. Corner, P. Schlesinger and R. Silverstone (eds.), *International Media Research. A Critical Survey*, London and New York: Routledge, pp. 123–153.

Corner, J., Schlesinger, P. and Silverstone, R. (1997), 'Editor's Introduction', in J. Corner, P. Schlesinger and R. Silverstone (eds.), *International Media Research. A Critical Survey*, London and New York: Routledge, pp. 1–17.

d'Haenens, L., Mansell, R. and Sarikakis, K. (2010), 'Editor's Introduction', *Communication, Culture & Critique*, 3: 2, pp. 131–133.

Docherty, D., Morrison, D. and Tracey, M. (1993), 'Scholarship as Silence', *Journal of Communication*, 43: 3, pp. 230–238.

Farr, J. Hacker, J. S. and Kazee, N. (2006), 'The Policy Scientist of Democracy: The Discipline of Harold D. Lasswell', *American Political Science Review*, 100: 4, pp. 579–587.

—— (2008), 'Revisiting Lasswell', *Policy Sciences*, 41: 1, pp. 21–32.

Freedman, D. (2008), *The Politics of Media Policy*, Cambridge and Malden: Polity Press.

—— (2010), 'Media Policy Silences: The Hidden Face of Communications Decision Making', *The International Journal of Press/Politics*, 15: 3, pp. 344–361.

Frieden, R. (2008), 'Academic Research and its Limited Impact on Telecommunications Policymaking', *International Journal of Communication*, 2, pp. 421–428.

Galperin, H. (2004), 'Beyond Interests, Ideas, and Technology: An Institutional Approach to Communication and Information Policy', *The Information Society*, 20: 3, pp. 159–168.

Haight, T. R. (1983), 'The Critical Researcher's Dilemma', *Journal of Communication*, 33: 3, pp. 226–236.

Hardt, H. (1976): 'The Rise and Problems of Media Research in Germany', *Journal of Communication*, 76: 3, pp. 90–95.

Harms, L. S. (1977), 'Toward a Shared Paradigm for Communication: An Emerging Foundation for the New Communication Policy and Communication Planning Sciences', in S. A. Rahim and J. Middleton (eds.), *Perspectives in Communication Policy and Planning*, Honolulu: East-West Center, pp. 77–99.

—— (1980), 'Appropriate Methods for Communication Policy Science: Some Preliminary Considerations', *Human Communication Research*, 7: 1, pp. 3–13.

Havick, J. J. (1983), 'Introduction', in J. J. Havick (ed.), *Communications Policy and the Political Process*, Westport and London: Greenwood Press, pp. 3–23.

Hellman, L. (1973), *Pentimento*, Boston and Toronto: Little, Brown and Company.

Katz, E. (1979), 'Get Out of the Car. A Case Study of the Organization of Policy Research', *International Communication Gazette*, 25: 2, pp. 75–86.

Krieger, S. (1971), 'Prospects for Communication Policy', *Policy Sciences*, 2: 3, pp. 305–319.

Kunkel, D. and Farinola, W. J. M. (2001), 'Underestimating Our Own Weight? The Scope and Impact of Communication Research on Public Policy', in W. B. Gudykunst (ed.), *Communication Yearbook 24*, Thousand Oaks, London and New Delhi: Sage, pp. 411–431.

Just, N. (2009), 'Measuring Media Concentration and Diversity: New Approaches and Instruments in Europe and the US', *Media, Culture & Society*, 31: 1, pp. 97–117.

Lasswell, H. D. (1951), 'The Policy Orientation', in D. Lerner and H. D. Lasswell (eds.), *The Policy Sciences. Recent Developments in Scope and Method*, Stanford: Stanford University Press, pp. 3–15.

—— (1970), 'The Emerging Conception of the Policy Sciences', *Policy Sciences*, 1: 1, pp. 3–14.

—— (1972), 'Communication Research and Public Policy', *Public Opinion Quarterly*, 36: 3, pp. 301–310.

Latzer, M. (1999), 'Transformation der Staatlichkeit im Kommunikationssektor: Regulierungsansätze für die Mediamatik', in K. Imhof, O. Jarren and R. Blum (eds.), *Steuerungs- und Regelungsprobleme in der Informationsgesellschaft*, Opladen: Westdeutscher Verlag, pp. 282–296.

—— (2009), 'Convergence Revisited: Toward a Modified Pattern of Communications Governance', *Convergence – The International Journal of Research into New Media Technologies*, 15: 4, pp. 411–426.

—— (2010), *Medienwandel durch Innovation: Konvergenz, Ko-Evolution, Komplexität. Working Paper*, Zurich: IPMZ.

Latzer, M., Just, N., Saurwein, F. and Slominski, P. (2003), 'Regulation Remixed: Institutional Change through Self- and Co-Regulation in the Mediamatics Sector', *Communications and Strategies*, 50: 2, pp. 127–157.

Lazarsfeld, P. F. (1941), 'Remarks on Administrative and Critical Communication Research', *Studies in Philosophy and Science*, 9, pp. 2–16.

Majchrzak, A. (1984), *Methods for Policy Research*, Newbury Park: Sage.

Manheim, J. B. (1980), 'Communication Policy: A Selected Bibliography', *Policy Studies Journal*, 9: 1, pp.132–145.

Martin, G. M. (1976), 'The Social Component in Communications Policy Research', *International Communication Gazette*, 22: 1, pp. 18–25.

McQuail, D. (1994), 'Media Policy Research: Conditions for Progress', in C. J. Hamelink and O. Linné (eds.), *Mass Communication Research: On Problems and Policies. The Art of Asking the Right Questions*, Norwood: Ablex, pp. 39–51.

Melody, W. H. (1990), 'Communication Policy in the Global Information Economy: Whither the Public Interest?', in M. Ferguson (ed.), *Public Communication. The New Imperatives. Future Directions for Media Research*, London, Newbury Park and New Delhi: Sage, pp. 16–39.

Melody, W. H. and Mansell, R. (1983), 'The Debate over Critical vs. Administrative Research: Circularity or Challenge', *Journal of Communication*, 33: 3, pp. 103–116.

Mosco, V. (1988), 'Toward a Theory of the State and Telecommunications Policy', *Journal of Communication*, 38: 1, pp. 107–124.

Mosco, V. and Rideout, V. (1997), 'Media Policy in North America', in J. Corner, P. Schlesinger and R. Silverstone (eds.), *International Media Research. A Critical Survey*, London and New York: Routledge, pp. 154–183.

Mueller, M. (1995), 'Why Communications Policy is Passing "Mass Communication" by: Political Economy as the Missing Link', *Critical Studies in Mass Communication*, 12: 4, pp. 457–472.

Napoli, P. M. (1999), 'The Unique Nature of Communications Regulation: Evidence and Implications for Communications Policy Analysis', *Journal of Broadcasting & Electronic Media*, 43: 4, pp. 565–581.

Napoli, P. M. and Gillis, N. (2006), 'Reassessing the Potential Contribution of Communications Research to Communications Policy: The Case of Media Ownership', *Journal of Broadcasting & Electronic Media*, 50: 4, pp. 671–691.

Napoli, P. M. and Seaton, M. (2007), 'Necessary Knowledge for Communications Policy: Information Asymmetries and Commercial Data Access and Usage in the Policymaking Process', *Federal Communication Law Journal*, 59: 2, pp. 295–330.

Noam, E. (1993), 'Reconnecting Communications Studies with Communications Policy', *Journal of Communication*, 43: 3, pp. 199–206.

———— (1999), 'Information and Communications Policy Research – More Important, More Neglected', in B. M. Compaine and W. H. Read (eds.), *The Information Resources Policy Handbook. Research for the Information Age*, Cambridge and London: MIT Press, pp. 423–429.

Olson, S. R. (1989), 'Mass Media: A Bricolage of Paradigms', in S. Sanderson King (ed.), *Human Communication as a Field of Study: Selected Contemporary Views*, Albany: State University of New York Press, pp. 57–83.

Owen, B. M. (ed.) (1975), *Telecommunications Policy Research. Report on the 1975 Conference Proceedings*, Palo Alto: Aspen Institute Program on Communications and Society.

Pool, I. d. S. (1974), 'The Rise of Communications Policy Research', *Journal of Communication*, 24: 2, pp. 31–42.

—— (1983), *Technologies of Freedom. On Free Speech in an Electronic Age*, Cambridge: Harvard University Press.

Puppis, M. (2010), 'Media Governance: A New Concept for the Analysis of Media Policy and Regulation', *Communication, Culture & Critique*, 3: 2, pp. 134–149.

Puppis, M. and d'Haenens, L. (2011), 'Media Policy, Regulation and Governance', in F. Esser and T. Hanitzsch (eds.), *Handbook of Comparative Communication Research*, London and New York: Routledge.

Puppis, M., Latzer, M. and Jarren, O. (2010), 'Medien- und Telekommunikationspolitik', in H. Bonfadelli, O. Jarren and G. Siegert (eds.), *Einführung in die Publizistikwissenschaft. 3rd Edition*, Bern, Stuttgart and Vienna: Haupt, pp. 271–306.

Raboy, M. and Padovani, C. (2010), 'Mapping Global Media Policy: Concepts, Frameworks, Methods', *Communication, Culture & Critique*, 3: 2, pp. 150–169.

Reeves, B. and Baughman, J. L. (1983), '"Fraught with Such Great Possibilities". The Historical Relationship of Communication Research to Mass Media Regulation', in O. H. Gandy Jr., P. Espinosa and J. A. Ordover (eds.), *Proceedings from the Tenth Annual Telecommunications Policy Research Conference*, Norwood: Ablex, pp. 19–52.

Reinard, J. C. and Ortiz, S. M. (2005), 'Communication Law and Policy: The State of Research and Theory', *Journal of Communication*, 55: 3, pp. 594–631.

Rogers, E. M. (1994), *A History of Communication Study. A Biographical Approach*, New York: The Free Press.

Rowland, W. D. (1984), 'Deconstructing American Communications Policy Literature', *Critical Studies in Media Communication*, 1: 4, pp. 423–435.

—— (1986), 'American Telecommunications Policy Research: Its Contradictory Origins and Influences', *Media, Culture & Society*, 8: 2, pp. 159–182.

Sarikakis, K. (2008), 'Communication and Cultural Policy Research in Europe: A Review of Recent Scholarship', in I. Fernández Alonso and M. d. Moragas i Spà (eds.), *Communication and Cultural Policies in Europe*, Barcelona: Generalitat de Catalunya, pp. 293–315.

Schiller, H. I. (1975), 'The Appearance of National-Communications Policies: A New Arena for Social Struggle', *International Communication Gazette*, 21: 2, pp. 82–94.

Streeter, T. (1990), 'Beyond Freedom of Speech and the Public Interest: The Relevance of Critical Legal Studies to Communications Policy', *Journal of Communication*, 40: 2, pp. 43–63.

Torgerson, D. (1985), 'Contextual Orientation in Policy Analysis: The Contribution of Harold D. Lasswell', *Policy Sciences*, 18: 3, pp. 241–261.

van Cuilenburg, J. and McQuail, D. (2003), 'Media Policy Paradigm Shifts. Towards a New Communications Policy Paradigm', *European Journal of Communication*, 18: 2, pp. 181–207.

van Cuilenburg, J. and Slaa, P. (1993), 'From Media Policy Towards a National Communications Policy: Broadening the Scope', *European Journal of Communication*, 8: 2, pp. 149–176.

Verhulst, S. G. and Price, M. E. (2008), 'Comparative Media Law Research and its Impact on Policy', *International Journal of Communication*, 2, pp. 406–420.

Vowe, G. (2003), 'Medienpolitik – Regulierung der medialen öffentlichen Kommunikation', in G. Bentele, H-B. Brosius and O. Jarren (eds.), *Öffentliche Kommunikation*, Wiesbaden: Westdeutscher Verlag, pp. 210–227.

Weber, M. (1968), 'Die "Objektivität" sozialwissenschaftlicher und sozialpolitischer Erkenntnis', in M. Weber (ed.), *Gesammelte Aufsätze zur Wissenschaftslehre. Herausgegeben von Johannes Winckelmann. 3rd Edition*, Tübingen: Mohr Siebeck, pp. 146–214.

Notes

1   For overviews on communication policy research see, for example, Manheim (1980); Reinard and Ortiz (2005) and Sarikakis (2008).

2   For European communication research, it is in fact argued that as such it did not exist until the 1980s when the EU articulated its plan for a common market in broadcasting and telecommunications. Before that 'one could (at the most) speak of a common intellectual approach in different countries' (Burgelman 1997: 123), which also resulted from the fact that a stable pattern of state regulation into communication had established itself in western economies (Latzer 1999).

3   Kunkel and Farinola (2001: 413) contest this prevalent view and argue that communication policy research may include any study with findings that inform communication policy-makers and not just studies examining communication policy-making: 'From this perspective, one can see that communication policy research may encompass virtually any subdivision or interest area within the field [of communication studies].' Their view is, however, not shared here.

4   One has to note, however, that Kunkel and Farinola's (2001) statement might be influenced by their very wide understanding of communication policy research. As mentioned earlier, they identify all studies in communication science that inform communication policy-makers as communication policy research.

5   The increasingly evident tendency in academia to pledge scholars to acquire third-party funds is in part undermining this independence.

6   However, the authors confined themselves to an analysis of papers presented at the ICA's Communication Law and Policy Division and articles published in the US journal *Communication Law & Policy*.

PART I

NEW THEORIES

Chapter 3

Prospects and Pitfalls of Douglass North's New Institutional
Economics Approach for Global Media Policy Research

Jan Loisen

Introduction

This article aims to respond to the goal of this edited volume to discuss new or rarely employed theoretical and methodological ways of analysing communication policy. More specifically, attention is devoted to the search for adequate frameworks and methodologies in the emerging but under-theorized field of global media policy (GMP) (Raboy and Padovani 2010: 150, 152, 155). Specifically, the article will present the new institutional economics approach by its most important proponent and theoretician, Douglass C. North (Hira and Hira 2000: 269), and we discuss its relevance for the analysis of GMP and of global audio-visual policy in particular. This issue will be used throughout the article to illustrate and tentatively apply the theoretical elaboration.

North's aspiration is to develop a political-economic framework to explore long-term institutional change and economic performance. To attain this goal, he has combined insights from research in economics, history, sociology, political science, technological studies and psychology. He has developed an analytical framework that not only integrates the analysis of institutions into economics but also re-examines social-science theories in general in order to improve our understanding of historical change (North 1990: 3). Not only did this eclectic endeavour earn him the Nobel Prize for economics (1993), it also inspired many theorists and scholars. On the one hand, many researchers integrate his insights into contemporary social research on economic, historical, political or sociological shifts. On the other hand, his work has triggered critical scrutiny – and rejection – of the ideas, concepts and general analytical framework he puts forward (Vandenberg 2002).

Although long-term change can cover several centuries, the exploration of North's work has also been proposed for research on the relatively young multi-lateral trading system (e.g. Blackhurst 1997: 542), which seems particularly salient for the research topic of audio-visual policy in the World Trade Organization (WTO). Although different strands of institutionalism and related domains are being put to the test in media policy research, North's approach has regrettably been left largely unexplored. This article aims to fill this gap by presenting and critically discussing North's ideas in order to develop an analytical framework that will be applied to the audio-visual dossier in the WTO. The article ends with conclusions on the usefulness of North's institutionalist approach for studying GMP.

North's Theoretical Framework in a Nutshell

North's political–economic theory begins with the individual (1990: 5). He takes issue however with behaviouralist assumptions underlying the rational choice framework in neoclassical economy. Initially requiring their modification in terms of bounded rationality (Milonakis and Fine 2007: 30), North (2005: 23f) increasingly rejects the assumptions that actors have stable preferences and cognitive systems that supply them with true models of how the world works. On the contrary, he argues (1990: 17) that actors and individuals make choices on the basis of subjectively derived models, which in most cases will ultimately not converge into economic equilibrium. Moreover, individual behaviour often deviates from a quest for profit maximization as a consequence of other motivations. In addition, actors usually decipher their environment on the basis of existing mental constructs, ideology and subjectivity – and with incomplete information. Instead of neoclassical economic equilibrium and harmony, multiple equilibria can exist (North 1990: 24). A similar tension in views can be observed in the audio-visual dossier in the WTO, where the United-States-driven 'culture as commodity' view is often opposed to a 'culture as dialogue' perspective (Sauvé and Steinfatt 2003). Whereas the former stresses free trade and opposes protectionism in order for consumers to maximize their preferences, the latter aims to legitimize government intervention on the basis of market failures in the audio-visual sector that may deny citizens a qualitatively pluralist and culturally diverse audio-visual offer.

A related and key element of North's theory of institutions is assigned to the role of transaction costs. These consist of measurement costs (i.e. the costs of measuring the value of what is being transacted/traded) and enforcement costs (i.e. the costs of protecting property rights and monitoring and enforcing agreements). It is clear that with regard to trade in audio-visual goods and services, which not only have economic value but also convey meaning and cultural values that are not (easily) quantifiable, measurement and enforcement will be very problematic. Moreover, due to the increasing complexity of society, transaction costs are not only high and rising but also asymmetrical (North 1990: 27–31). In this respect, North contends (1990: 30, 35,) that social, political and economic institutions have been developed to somehow manage transaction costs that may enhance cooperation. This is not an automatic process, however, nor is it necessarily socially productive (North 1990: 23).

Constituting Elements of an Institutional Framework

North identifies:

(1) Informal constraints
(2) Formal rules
(3) Enforcement mechanisms

as the fundamental institutions of an institutional framework. It is important to acknowledge that North's concept of institutions is very different from the common understanding of institutions as organizations such as the WTO. For North, institutions are the rules of the game in a society, i.e. the humanly devised constraints that shape human interaction (North 1990: 3). A corollary of North's institution concept is indeed that he (1990: 7f) explicitly distinguishes institutions from organizations, i.e. the players that play the game (e.g. nation states in their capacity as WTO members, the WTO itself, multi-national corporations, civil society groupings). The goal of the rules is to define how the game will be played. Regulated by the institutional framework, the players try to win the game through aptitude, strategy, coordination or even foul play (North 1990: 30, 108). The interaction between the organizations that engage with this framework shapes changes in the institutional matrix in a particular direction (North 1990: 5). Understanding these institutions and the process of institutional change is therefore key to understanding historical change (North 1990: 3–7), or in our case the development of the audio-visual dossier in the WTO.

Informal Constraints

In the modern western world, the structure of the economy and society is usually formulated in terms of formal rules and property rights. Informal constraints, however, are more pervasive with regard to choices actors make in negotiation, cooperation and social or economic organization. Examples of these are (internally applied) codes of conduct, (socially sanctioned) norms of behaviour, standards and conventions (North 1990: 36). According to North (1990: 37), these informal constraints are the result of socially transmitted information and cultural heritage, i.e. knowledge, values, ideology and other elements that influence behaviour from one generation to the next by means of learning processes and imitation. This cultural filter offers a conceptual framework for encoding and interpreting the information we are confronted with and provides for the continuation of informal solutions to deal with past, present and future problems. Consequently, informal constraints are important sources for the continuity of long-term societal change – or in the case of the debate on cultural diversity, the continuity of stagnation, because the opposing views of culture as commodity and culture as dialogue have led to a 'dialogue of the deaf' (Roy 2005). Informal constraints are difficult to identify, however, as is the explanation of their origins, persistence or demise (North 1990: 37, 44f).

Formal Constraints

Formal constraints can complement or increase the effectiveness of informal constraints. Alternatively, they can alter the pervasiveness of informal constraints, although this is more difficult because of the latter's persistence. The hierarchy of rules is spread from general rules to particular specifications, with the former usually being more costly to change (North 1990: 46f). The economic and political diversity of interests and associated relative (negotiating) power will influence the structure of the rules. Numerous interests imply that negotiating processes and decision-making will be more difficult. Consequently, a structuring of negotiating mechanisms to facilitate the negotiating process can be expected. As the rules are designed largely on the basis of the (im)balance of power, they first and foremost serve dominant interests and not necessarily general social welfare. Nonetheless, in complex institutional structures where many different interest groups interact, compromises are often needed. In order to manage the associated transaction costs, the institutional framework will be developed to allow for political *ex ante* agreements on cooperation and the reduction of uncertainty. This implies difficult and costly measurement and enforcement. Globalization and convergence in the media sector, as well as the increasing multi-level governance nature of audio-visual policy, clearly make policy-making and measurement and monitoring of audio-visual trade-related issues (e.g. measurement and monitoring of flows, piracy, dumping) a difficult and contentious endeavour. The dual nature of the audio-visual sector, requiring a balance in achieving both economic and non-economic goals of audio-visual policy, furthermore amplifies tensions: who is responsible, and at which policy level, for developing, monitoring and enforcing agreements? Moreover, efficiency in political markets is not analogous to efficient economic markets, and incomplete information and subjective perceptions become more important in making political choices (North 1990: 47–51).

Enforcement

As a consequence of the increasing complexity in negotiations, decision-making and society at large, enforcement mechanisms have a fundamental role in the institutional framework. Nevertheless, they too are imperfect. On the one hand, third parties that have enough information to assess whether a party is complying with an agreement and have the means at their disposal to penalize non-compliance should be established. It is extremely costly, however, to fully map and understand all aspects of an agreement and to know when it is being violated. Transaction costs may be too high to assure that non-compliance is penalized. Moreover, a particular agenda of the enforcement actors may influence the enforcement process (North 1990: 54). For example, in a case concerning Canada's magazine policy (Neil 2006: 41–44) the WTO dispute-settlement bodies have been accused of practising judicial activism (Krikorian 2005: 957), favouring a free-trade ideology over cultural concerns.

Interrelations within an Institutional Framework

In sum, the institutional constraints that define the available choices for actors in negotiation and decision-making are part of a connected web of different combinations in formal and informal constraints and enforcement mechanisms. On the one hand, the web is relatively stable, as important changes in the institutional architecture lead to possibly unintended changes that other actors will resist. This is reinforced by the persistence of informal constraints and the cultural filter upon which actors enter into debate and decision-making. On the other hand, other groups try to restructure the institutional framework. Change is therefore usually incremental, but the interrelation between the different elements of the institutional structure will gradually alter the institutional framework and produce margins for change (North 1990: 67f).

Change of an Institutional Framework

Elements Contributing to Change

Three interrelated sources of change in the institutional matrix can be discerned. Firstly, institutional frameworks shape the direction of acquiring knowledge and skills that actors pursue in order to achieve their goals. This is not necessarily an efficient process. Some institutions reward restrictions on output whereas others reward productive activity (North 1990: 73–78). Alternatively, spending resources on changing the institutional constraints can induce change. Incremental institutional change, for example, occurs by means of changing the formal rules. An even stronger impact would be to create or buttress public support for investment in the type of knowledge that contributes to economic growth. Essential in this process is the concept of adaptive efficiency, which refers to society's will to acquire knowledge and to learn, and to encourage decentralized decision-making processes that allow societies to explore alternative ways of solving problems (North 1990: 79ff). This is not at all easy 'because organizational errors may not only be probabilistic, but also systematic, due to ideologies that may give people preferences for the kinds of solutions that are not oriented to adaptive efficiency' (North 1990: 81). Thirdly, institutions also change as a consequence of incremental changes to their underlying structure. Changes in the relative prices (of information, skills, knowledge, technology, etc.) could lead to the perception among one or several parties to an agreement that they would be better off with a new deal. Renegotiation is therefore put on the agenda. But because agreements are embedded in a hierarchy of rules, renegotiation may only be possible by restructuring a higher set of rules or by violating certain codes of conduct that are at the core of the existing institutional framework. Change in a certain institutional constraint will consequently lead to a reconfiguration of the institutional structure and in changes in other institutional constraints. For example, changing the formal rules can have consequences for informal norms and conventions. However, the latter change more slowly than formal rules. Hence, there is no formal cultural exception in the WTO, as audio-visual services have been included in the General Agreement on Trade in Services (GATS). But by not adopting any liberalization commitments and exempting many of its support mechanisms from the application of the most-favoured-nation (MFN) principle, the European Union has nonetheless largely retained its traditional approach, which is now defended in the name of cultural diversity (Pauwels and Loisen 2003). In other words, change is seldom revolutionary but usually incremental (North 1990: 83–90).

The Path of Institutional Change

The way institutional change effectively occurs is not straightforward. The creation of institutions is accompanied by high initial set-up costs. The main question initially is whether the benefits of their creation outweigh the costs. Subsequently, learning, coordination effects and adaptive expectations occur with regard to the functioning of the institutional framework and the opportunities or constraints it sets. The path of institutional change, then, is on the one hand the result of the increasing returns that the interdependent web of institutions will generate. On the other hand, imperfect markets characterized by high transaction costs also shape the development path of the economy and society. Because markets seldom function perfectly and transaction costs remain high, fragmentary information and the actors' subjective models play a decisive role. Once a certain path is taken, actors, institutions and (marginal) processes of change act on and reinforce each other (North 1990: 95–104). Such path dependency is not necessarily efficient, however, nor is it socially productive or conducive to cultural diversity for that matter. At the same time, the idea of path dependency does not close out the prospect of change altogether:

> At every step along the way there were choices – political and economic – that provided real alternatives. Path dependence is a way to narrow conceptually the choice set and link decision making through time. It is not a story of inevitability in which the past neatly predicts the future. (North 1990: 98f)

Fundamental to the development of institutions is to try as far as possible to work towards adaptively efficient paths. This means policy trajectories in which the necessary space is left to respond to uncertain choices by making possible a maximum number of choices, allowing trial and error and the creation of efficient feedback mechanisms in order to eliminate inefficient choices. Changes to an institutional framework are possible as a consequence of the margins that its dynamic character continually produces. The (negotiating) power of actors is an essential factor that influences these margins. However, this does not mean that a successful or detrimental path can simply be overturned. The institutional framework only changes incrementally. Moreover, policy developments and adjustments that are made in the margins of the institutional framework will not have a uniform impact but possibly different implications in different policy contexts (multiple equilibria). A one-size-fits-all approach is therefore undesirable. Policy based on adaptive efficiency offers more opportunities to tailored policy development that takes into account the specific context it acts upon (North 1990: 99–104).

To sum up, modifications to the constituent elements can make changes to history but they cannot change its course altogether. Opportunities for policy change are set at the margins. Notwithstanding incremental change, the underlying institutional framework remains relatively robust, locked in and path dependent. In the final analysis, policy change therefore is partially unpredictable but largely irreversible at the same time (North 1990: 104). Before testing whether this hypothesis also applies for the WTO's interference with audio-visual policy, the next section will scrutinize several elements in North's theoretical elaboration.

Criticisms and Additions for the Study of Global Media Policy

To start with, 'institutions' is a contested concept. North aims to understand long-term structural constraints and margins for change regarding economic transactions, markets and policies predominantly at the national level. Our case, however, targets the treatment of media policy within the relatively young global multi-lateral trade regime. Simply transposing North's framework may therefore lead to a number of blind spots.

Institutions and Organizations

Firstly, the analytical separation between institutions and organizations may create such a blind spot. As North is primarily interested in explaining long-term macro aspects of institutional change, organizations – in our case, for example, WTO members, i.e. nation states – are abstracted as a unitary and autonomous actor (Hira and Hira 2000: 271). When dealing with contemporary policy issues, the different ideas and power among individuals and sub-groups of an organization, as well as potential conflicts within the organization (e.g. nation states, 'the' EU or 'the' WTO) may assume a more direct relationship with the evolution of the institutional framework. In this respect, Hodgson (2006: 10) considers organizations themselves to be generally regarded as institutions and in some circumstances as actors – i.e. in encompassing systems, indicating the existence of different levels of an institutional framework.

Multiple Levels

A second addition or modification vis-à-vis North's approach therefore is to take into account multiple levels or interrelated institutional frameworks influencing the audio-visual dossier in the WTO. From an analytical point of view, a distinction must be made between at least three interrelated levels in the institutional framework. Firstly, the global institutional framework, in which the WTO is one of the actors involved in a game structured by such general institutions as state sovereignty, international treaties, the different cultural background or the identity of the actors involved, etc. Secondly, the institutional framework of the global trading system can be depicted as an intermediate institutional framework. Thirdly, the institutional framework for the audio-visual dossier involves actors that interact on the basis of the rules of the game that apply to this specific, audio-visual, institutional framework. For the purpose of the analysis, which will take these three frameworks into account but will focus predominantly on the 'audio-visual' institutional framework, the link between actors and institutions may be expected to be more direct. In a similar vein, as Hodgson argues, the actors simultaneously have institution-like characteristics (e.g. the EU as an actor provides institutional rules for its members and individuals but acts like an organization in WTO negotiations) and are therefore included explicitly in the analytical framework alongside informal, formal and enforcement institutions.

Culture

The third and problematic issue in North's development of the theoretical framework is his account of culture – predominantly the cultural filter underlying informal constraints. According to Heydemann (2008: 29), North's conception is flawed, as it relies on an essentialist conception of culture, which is historically inaccurate and analytically misleading. North's approach resonates with a functionalist paradigm that emphasizes a somehow pre-configured culture with stable and orderly characteristics (Martin and Nakayama 1999: 4). It dismisses critical research approaches to culture that emphasize the processual, conflictual and unstable aspects of culture and society and in which culture is seen as a site of struggle for various meanings. As a result, the pace and degree of institutional change is underestimated and the variety of institutional forms and economic performance is poorly taken into account (Heydemann 2008: 29).

North has been receptive to such criticisms, narrowing down the cultural filter to existing (individual) mental models (Heydemann 2008: 31) and by engaging strongly in cognitive science (North 2005). Nonetheless, the general thrust of culture as constituting and constraining economic behaviour is still simmering. Instead of discarding the culture concept altogether, the framework would benefit from a dialectical and processual approach to culture, integrating the simultaneous stability-supporting and conflict-provoking features of culture as a site of struggle (Martin and Nakayama 1999). In other words, the variation in and persistence of institutions is very much culturally as well as politically determined and is also dependent on the distributional advantages they confer upon powerful actors within a society (Heydemann 2008: 30ff).

Power

In a similar vein, the fourth topic up for discussion concerns power. Although North acknowledges that power processes play their part in bargaining and policy-making, they take a secondary role in his approach (Peukert 2001: 114). The concept of power is largely left implicit and under-conceptualized. When dealing with GMP, especially in an anarchic international setting, power dynamics need to be included in a political–economic framework that tries to work out the interplay between ideas, interests and institutions shaping policies (Bhagwati 1993: 17). Moreover, the underlying operating mechanisms of power processes should ideally be clarified to allow for a political–economic holistic view of research issues pertaining to GMP (Toboso 1995: 73) and to explore the transformation of existing power relations for the democratization of global media governance. Although such an endeavour is difficult (Raboy and Padovani 2010: 151, 162) and could not be adequately treated within the scope of this article, a useful starting point for a firmer inclusion of the concept of power is Barnett and Duvall's discussion (2005) of various intertwined forms of power in international politics.

The first, traditional concept of power is coercive or compulsory power: A has the power to let B do what B otherwise would not do – e.g. Korea relaxing its screen quota when pressured by the US in exchange for negotiations on a bilateral investment treaty. Secondly, institutional power refers to formal and informal institutions that mediate between A and B and by which a party structures and constrains the actions of the other party through the rules, norms and decision-making procedures that define institutions. A party however does not 'own' institutions, and the parties are socially distant from each other as a consequence of these mediating elements. Institutions themselves can therefore generate unforeseen effects. In the example mentioned earlier, Korea long applied institutional power, as Article IV of the General Agreement on Tariffs and Trade (GATT) legitimizes the use of screen quotas, much to the disgruntlement of the US. Thirdly, structural power refers to a direct constitutive relationship in which structural position A only exists as a consequence of its relation to structural position B (e.g. centre-periphery models in a world systems approach or, for that matter, in the global audio-visual sector characterized by very uneven trade flows). Productive power, finally, is associated with discourse, social processes and knowledge systems through which meaning is produced and transformed. The concept of productive power refers then to a socially diffuse production of subjectivity in systems of meaning and signification (e.g. processes related to the switch in discourse from cultural exception to cultural diversity) (Barnett and Duvall 2005: 48–57).

Transaction Costs and Adaptive Efficiency

Fifthly, North's intermediate position between mainstream economics and 'a fundamental recasting of the way we think' (North 2005: vii) comes to the fore in his discussion of transaction costs and adaptive efficiency. Although he acknowledges that political markets do not work like economic markets (North 2005: 56), the repercussions regarding both concepts are not entirely clear and are still predominantly explained from a traditional economic viewpoint (Milonakis and Fine 2007: 49f). But how can the concept of transaction costs be used, for example, in the negotiation of audio-visual policy-related matters in the WTO? Surely, the identification of measurement and enforcement costs in terms of their price would only reveal a very partial and one-sided economic aspect of the issue. Although interesting work is being done on defining and measuring cultural diversity in media markets (e.g. Ranaivoson 2007), the intangible but crucial aspects of audio-visual services – such as their contribution to cultural diversity, pluralism and democracy – remain elusive for North's transaction cost approach.

A similar line of reasoning applies to the concept of (adaptive) efficiency. What would the most adaptively efficient system to realize cultural diversity in the global media market be? If assessed only in terms of a cost/price framework or economic growth, the dual nature of media policy would not adequately be taken into account, and policy responses based on such a partial account would be imbalanced. This, however, raises the question of balance, which in the case of GMP and the audio-visual issue in the WTO has been the controversial issue since the trade regime's inception. In other words, adaptive efficiency in the context of global governance is value-laden and essentially a question of politics. Interestingly, this tension is similar to a current debate on the legitimacy and institutional crisis of the WTO. Some argue for the 'constitutionalization' of the trade regime. They want to solve the WTO's crisis by reinforcing the technocratic character of the trade regime and to eliminate politics as much as possible (see for a discussion Dunoff 2006). This implicit rejection of more political debate has led others to argue for alternative paths out of the WTO crisis (e.g. Howse and Nicolaïdis 2003). In analogy with adaptive efficiency for economic markets – i.e. to provide 'the incentives to encourage the development of decentralized decision-making processes that will allow societies to maximize the efforts required to explore alternative ways of solving problems' (North 1990: 81) – these authors subscribe to a global subsidiarity model in international (trade) politics, which aims to reinvent the concept of embedded liberalism, i.e. 'to devise a form of multilateralism that is compatible with the requirements of domestic stability' (Ruggie 1982: 399). Such a model of global subsidiarity rests on the principles of institutional sensitivity, political inclusiveness and top-down empowerment (Howse and Nicolaïdis 2003: 73), which can be translated loosely into: (partial) deference of policy-making from the WTO to other institutions and policy levels in the case of non-exclusively trade-related policy issues (e.g. to UNESCO or the state level in the case of policies aimed at promoting cultural diversity); the inclusion of varied stakeholders with differing perspectives on such issues (e.g. civil society networks on cultural diversity or cultural ministers); and room for adjusting to obligations, especially for developing countries (Howse and Nicolaïdis 2003: 86–90).

Change

The final issue concerns the contradictory notions of change that North derives from his theoretical framework. The sources of change, although interrelated, can be found in the margins produced by the institutional framework's dynamics – when actors exploit openings within the institutional system (e.g. large developing countries such as India and Brazil are increasingly demanding to be heard in the audio-visual dossier, introducing new perspectives on the issue in the process) (Pauwels et al. 2006) – and if there are contextual changes (e.g. in relation to technological developments in media). The last two are exogenous to the model however. Moreover, North's long-term historical approach dismisses exogenous shocks, is relatively ignorant of power or individual personalities in policy-making and disregards the multi-faceted nature of culture. The ambiguous and largely unexplained relationship between actors and the institutional framework also ultimately leads to insufficient consideration of the dynamic processes related to the institutional framework's development. Consequently, North overly relies on a static explanation of institutions in terms of (multiple) equilibria and path dependency. One can therefore conclude that institutions are only proximate sources of change, which suggests the need for a direct study of the factors that change institutions, i.e. culture, ideology, technology, power, etc. (Hira and Hira 2002: 272, 275–278).

Towards an Analytical Framework for Global Media Policy Research

Although some of North's critics call for an entirely new and dynamic model that focuses on culture, ideas and social practice as the drivers of institutional change (Hira and Hira 2000: 279f; Milonakis and Fine 2007: 54), we would argue along with Daunton (2010: 156) that 'North's book should start a dialogue and not lead to silence.' North's work contains great potential to (theoretically) explore GMP.

Firstly, it offers a framework, albeit in need of modification and critical elaboration, for approaching the complexity of GMP. In this respect, Bhagwati argues (1993: 17) that 'profound commitments to policies are generally due to a mix of ideological factors (in the form of ideas and example), interests (as defined by politics and economics), and institutions (as they shape constraints and opportunities).' Following North's institutional approach, and taking into account the previous discussion on culture (related to ideas) and power (related to interests), the concept of institutions (including actors that can be both an institution and an organization) provides a link (or trade-off) between the interrelated spheres of ideas and interests, culture and power or agency and structure. In this 'I, I & I mix,' the sphere of institutions is, on the one hand, a corollary of the other spheres. The various ideas and power dynamics shape institutions, aiming to reduce uncertainty and to structure interaction. On the other hand, the institutional framework is also a determinant of what perceptions will matter and how these are translated into transforming the environment (North 2005: 6). In other words, studying institutions as sites of struggle – influenced by actors, their varied cultural backgrounds and different power dynamics, and influencing these factors simultaneously as the institutional framework develops – might be beneficial for gaining insights into the complexities and ambivalences of GMP (see Figure 1)

In addition, North's conceptual framework is open for discussion and provides several (conceptual) entry points for scholars to improve their analytical frameworks in the light of their research. Finally, the framework he has developed allows a comprehensive mapping of the many dimensions, actors and factors involved in the development of GMP issues. In case of the audio-visual dossier in the WTO, Figure 2 shows a map of its multiplicity. It indicates that the audio-visual institutional framework is one level embedded in a broader

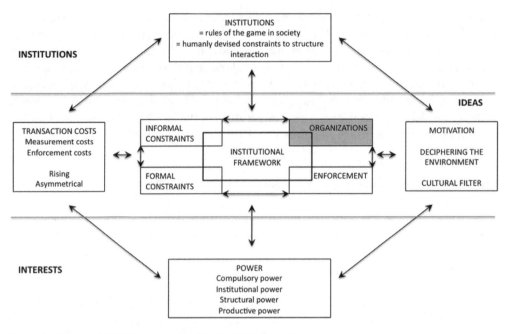

Figure 1: From the 'I, I & I mix' to an Institutional Framework.

context. It is therefore placed at the centre and is enclosed by two more general institutional frameworks. Each level is divided into four quadrants, referring to:

(1) Informal constraints
(2) Formal rules
(3) Enforcement
(4) Actors

No quadrant is isolated and a certain overlap is unavoidable within a particular institutional framework and between different quadrants. This overlap is important. Firstly, it indicates the interrelation between the audio-visual dossier and the functioning of the WTO and broader discussions on international policy. Changes within both encompassing frameworks undoubtedly have consequences for the further development of the audio-visual institutional framework. Secondly, it points out that changes in one of the domains of an institutional framework will have repercussions for other domains.

In operational terms, informal constraints (quadrant 1) are the most difficult category. We have identified different policy traditions, norms and values related to three fields of tension, i.e. the relationship between culture and economics, sector-specific audio-visual and multi-sectoral information policy, and the preferred policy levels for defining and implementing audio-visual policies. In the encompassing institutional frameworks, informal constraints have also been incorporated in the analysis by discussing ideological and cultural tensions (e.g. between the norms of reciprocity and non-discrimination). Regarding formal rules and enforcement (quadrants 2 and 3), the analysis focused on the WTO regulatory framework and relevant case law. In terms of actors (quadrant 4), the main focus was on the WTO and UNESCO as international organizations and on a set of powerful WTO members (the US, the EU, Japan, Canada, Brazil, India, Australia and China). Naturally, other organizations (e.g. other international organizations and countries, corporations, civil society) can be included in the analysis as well if required.

Concretely, each set of institutions within the audio-visual institutional framework has been studied on the basis of different methods (literature study, document analysis and expert interviews) and with input from different insights from media studies, the political economy of communication, international relations, (media) economics and law. This is not the place, nor is there space, to give a full account of this study (Loisen 2009). To provide just one example of the use of the analytical framework presented in Figure 2, we consider the status of audio-visual services trade liberalization in the GATS (quadrant 2).

Proponents of a further liberalization of trade in audio-visual services stress the flexibility that governments find within the GATS. They can engage in commitments while simultaneously maintaining policy instruments to realize cultural objectives (Roy 2005: 951). On the other hand, it has been argued that the WTO has 'the potential to rock the foundations of media regulation in western democracies, bringing about highly commercialized media landscapes and subordinating cultural objectives to competition. Regulatory measures implemented for social, political or cultural reasons may be incompatible with the GATS' (Puppis 2008: 408).

An analysis along the lines set out in our analytical framework might result in a narrative that allows competing evaluations to be tied together and explored further. When applying the different elements of the analytical framework, the first observation is that GATS rules do indeed provide for flexibility. Countries may choose not to take on commitments. They can comply with progressive liberalization by taking on commitments in other GATS sectors. Moreover, if exemptions from the MFN principle for audio-visual policy have been taken up they can be continued. As a result, the scope to retain a locally or nationally defined audio-visual policy that makes use of trade barriers can be maintained. Furthermore, convergence in the media has so far not led to successful attempts to dismantle the audio-visual protective measures via other WTO agreements that impose more rigorous rules (e.g. the GATT). Notwithstanding the pressure of the US, it seems that the position not to engage in further liberalization is relatively easy to uphold, as the institutional power provided by the GATS, which is a young and 'work-in-progress' agreement, is considerable (Loisen 2009: 523).

However, the flexibility observed in the GATS agreement can also be seen as negative flexibility. Whereas the goal of the post-war compromise in the spirit of embedded liberalism

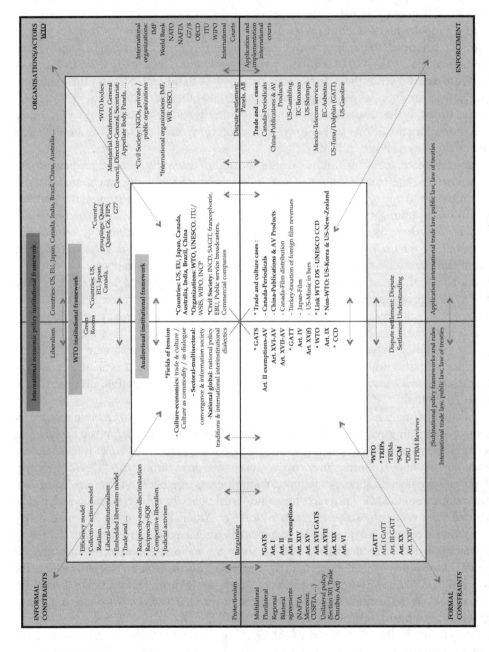

Figure 2: The Audio-Visual Institutional Framework within its Broader Institutional Context.

was to support liberalization, albeit with space for domestic public policy, as a second point, we can observe that the current flexibility does not support the development of both at the same time. It provides hardly any clarity, legal certainty or strengthened support for cultural diversity. The rules with regard to subsidies for service sectors still need to be fleshed out and the WTO agreements' exception clauses may only indirectly, if at all, be applicable to audio-visual policy. This is a long way from a stable compromise that links progressive liberalization to the allowance of specific supporting mechanisms at appropriate policy levels. Nor is there space for adaptively efficient instruments. Once a liberalization commitment is taken it is very difficult and costly to reverse. Furthermore, there has only been limited action in the WTO to turn this negative flexibility into positive flexibility or an adaptively efficient environment – including possibly deference to outside expertise (Loisen 2009: 586f).

Hence changes in WTO members' ability to uphold protective cultural measures have, on the one hand, been relatively minor since the conclusion of the GATS framework. On the other hand, the path (dependency) set out since the Uruguay Round has added to the dilution of the embedded post-war liberalism compromise to the benefit of a liberal, pro-trade bias. This more nuanced evaluation of the status of trade in audio-visual services within the GATS can, in addition, also be analysed in relation to the other quadrants and levels of the analytical framework.

Firstly, in terms of enforcement, the Canada Periodicals case has been used as a prime example to highlight the WTO's neglect of cultural considerations. Not only did the Appellate Body disregard the cultural goals of Canadian magazine policy, which was under attack by the US (Neil 2006: 41–44), but it is even thought to have applied judicial activism (Krikorian 2005: 957), suggesting a reinforcement of the commodification of culture in the WTO. On the other hand, WTO dispute settlement can only work with the instruments made available by the members. Because there are no negotiated rules for an exceptional treatment of cultural products, an outcome acknowledging the specificity of the sector being scrutinized would be unlikely. Moreover, the judgement in Canada Periodicals was important but did not necessarily set a precedent for other cases. Finally, when looking at enforcement in encompassing levels, i.e. other cases involving a balancing act between trade and non-trade environmental concerns, the WTO dispute-settlement system has, tentatively, interpreted provisions taking non-economic concerns into account. Whether a balanced approach can be expected for future trade and culture cases remains unpredictable however (Loisen 2009: 638f).

Secondly, the framework's formal weakness in enabling positive action for cultural diversity is related to tensions in informal norms, e.g. with regard to reciprocity. According to Herrmann-Pillath (2006) the post-war norm of general reciprocity – i.e. mutual benefits for trading partners, including the necessary leeway for sensitive issues on the domestic level – has since the 1980s increasingly degenerated into an unequal form of reciprocity stripped of its political dimension and restraining domestic adjustment policies. This observation brings us to the tensions within the WTO regarding a way out of its current crisis and the above-mentioned debate on constitutionalization and global subsidiarity.

The latter model envisages a WTO that is cautious vis-à-vis issues requiring a balance between trade and other policy concerns, that aims for a greater political contesting of these issues and on such sensitive matters argues for stronger ties with other organizations and policy levels outside the WTO. Such a shift in the current WTO path is unpredictable and may be improbable. But it is not inconceivable, as it would reconnect with the remnants of embedded liberalism, albeit in a changed context.

Interestingly, and finally, important developments outside (but related to) the WTO can indeed be discerned. Unease with the ambivalent formal rules and audio-visual institutional framework for audio-visual policy in the WTO has led actors to search for other avenues to pursue their interests. Firstly, exploiting its structural power, the US increasingly seeks to realize its objectives in regional and bilateral trade agreements. The EU has recently followed a similar strategy to tie countries to its position in the inter-institutional dialectics between the WTO and UNESCO, with the negotiation of protocols on cultural cooperation in bilateral trade agreements (Loisen and De Ville 2010). Secondly, UNESCO has indeed re-entered the debate. Although the cultural diversity convention's legal impact is minimal for the time being, it is seen as an important political signal that global cultural diversity cannot be catered to from an exclusively economic perspective. An embryonic epistemic community seems to be under construction to reflect upon ideas and policy options for a more balanced treatment of audio-visual policy and the link between liberalization and (national) margins for manoeuvre. It remains to be seen, however, whether the instrument can be a vehicle for channelling productive power to create more balanced cultural and audio-visual policies and trade flows (Loisen 2009: 685). Thirdly, in light of a possible reproduction of the 'dialogue of the deaf' between the US and Canada and the EU, the introduction of new voices into the debate is important. For the time being, it seems that countries can withstand further liberalization as long as they have nothing to gain by doing so. However, positions could switch relatively quickly when the audio-visual sector has growth potential and if political and economic negotiating power rises (Pauwels et al. 2006: 156). Notably, Brazil and India can place other (neglected) issues on the policy agenda and have the dominant trading blocs make a stronger case as to what cultural diversity is, why it is important and how it can be attained.

In summary, the example briefly outlined earlier shows that the different elements of an institutional framework, including its underlying ambivalences, are deeply interrelated. If changes occur in one of the quadrants or levels, these may influence institutions and levels elsewhere, even if change will probably be of an incremental nature. In this respect, the general analysis of the audio-visual dossier in the WTO has shown that, on the one hand, a path (dependency) is developing in the WTO that favours the liberalization of the sector over cultural concerns. But on the other hand, the innumerable interrelations within the institutional framework make it a dynamic but relatively slowly developing path, which nonetheless produces margins for change. Whether these margins are exploited and whether they will contribute to re-adjusting or aggravating the current imbalance in the global audio-visual sector remains an open question and is dependent on several actors, factors and processes, not least the political choices WTO members make within the WTO or elsewhere.

Conclusion

Although North focuses on long-term historical change, the analytical framework he has developed has been useful for looking into the complexity and ambivalence of a particular and relatively young GMP issue. Also, taking into account the criticisms targeted at North, which have revealed various pitfalls in need of further elaboration, several prospects for GMP research come to the fore.

Firstly, the analytical framework we have developed on the basis of this discussion is in essence a heuristic device to map complex GMP issues, which is a necessary first 'step toward understanding the interactions, competing interests, and alternative perspectives involved in global media and communication policy' (Raboy and Padovani 2010: 163).

Secondly, North's ideas have provoked social-science scholars to articulate conceptual improvements, theoretical alternatives and methodological and normative challenges vis-à-vis his theory of institutions and views on cooperation, change and path dependency. The theory provides for many entry points for other disciplines to engage in theoretical reflection and scrutiny. In addition, it supports multi-methodological approaches necessary to come to grips with complex research issues like GMP.

Thirdly, the application of the analytical framework derived from the discussion of North's work gives a multi-faceted account of the audio-visual services issue in the WTO. Its mapping has been an essential step to account for the many interrelated actors, factors and processes involved. Moreover, North's emphasis on path dependency, incremental change and margins for action seems to be applicable to the issue under investigation. The analysis has provided insights and substance to the idea that the WTO's interference in audio-visual policy is to some extent irreversible but remains unpredictable (Pauwels and Loisen 2003).

Finally, the analytical framework we have developed may be useful to apply to other GMP cases as well. Granted, our understanding of the dynamics between an institutional framework and the 'I, I & I mix' necessitates further elaboration. A similar argument holds with regard to the normative basis we refer to in evaluating the path of (institutional) change in the audio-visual institutional framework. Both the relationship between ideas, interests and institutions and the concept of global subsidiarity have been presented in general terms and need to be fleshed out and articulated more specifically. In this sense, this article hopes to have contributed to the research agenda of the emerging field of GMP – an agenda on the basis of which, yet again, new or rarely employed theoretical and methodological ways of analysing communication policy issues will be deployed and used to improve the analytical framework presented in this contribution.

Acknowledgements

I wish to thank professors Robin Mansell, Caroline Pauwels and Karen Donders for extensive, critical and constructive comments. Naturally, the remaining errors and gaps in this theoretical work-in-progress are my responsibility.

References

Barnett, M. and Duvall, R. (2005), 'Power in International Politics', *International Organization*, 59: 1, pp. 39–75.

Bhagwati, J. (1993), *Protectionism*, Cambridge and London: The MIT Press.

Blackhurst, R. (1997), 'The WTO and the Global Economy', *The World Economy*, 20: 5, pp. 527–544.

Daunton, M. (2010), 'Rationality and Institutions: Reflections on Douglass North', *Structural Change and Economic Dynamics*, 21: 2, pp. 147–156.

Dunoff, J. L. (2006), 'Constitutional Conceits: The WTO's "Constitution" and the Discipline of International Law', *European Journal of International Law*, 17: 3, pp. 647–675.

Herrmann-Pillath, C. (2006), 'Reciprocity and the Hidden Constitution of World Trade', *Constitutional Political Economy*, 17: 3, pp. 133–163.

Heydemann, S. (2008), 'Institutions and Economic Performance: The Use and Abuse of Culture in New Institutional Economics', *Studies in Comparative International Development*, 43: 1, pp. 27–52.

Hira, A. and Hira, R. (2000), 'The New Institutionalism: Contradictory Notions of Change', *American Journal of Economics and Sociology*, 59: 2, pp. 267–282.

Hodgson, G. M. (2006), 'What Are Institutions?', *Journal of Economic Issues*, 40: 1, pp. 1–25.

Howse, R. and Nicolaïdis, K. (2003), 'Enhancing WTO Legitimacy: Constitutionalization or Global Subsidiarity?', *Governance: An International Journal of Policy, Administration, and Institutions*, 16: 1, pp. 73–94.

Krikorian, J. D. (2005), 'Planes, Trains and Automobiles. The Impact of the WTO "Court" on Canada in Its First Ten Years', *Journal of International Economic Law*, 8: 4, pp. 921–975.

Loisen, J. (2009), 'The Audio-Visual Dossier on the Agenda of the World Trade Organization', unpublished Ph.D. thesis (in Dutch), Brussels: Vrije Universiteit Brussel.

Loisen, J. and De Ville, F. (2010), 'The European Commission and the Protocol on Cultural Cooperation in EU Free Trade Agreements', in ISA (International Studies Association), *Annual Convention 2010. Theory vs. Policy? Connecting Scholars and Practitioners*, New Orleans, USA, 17–20 February 2010, ISA: Tucson.

Martin, J. N. and Nakayama, T. K. (1999), 'Thinking Dialectically About Culture and Communication', *Communication Theory*, 9: 1, pp. 1–25.

Milonakis, D. and Fine, B. (2007), 'Douglass North's Remaking of Economic History: A Critical Appraisal', *Review of Radical Political Economics*, 39: 1, pp. 27–57.

Neil, G. (2006), 'The Convention as a Response to the Cultural Challenges of Economic Globalisation', in N. Obuljen and J. Smiers (eds.), *UNESCO's Convention on the Protection and Promotion of the Diversity of Cultural Expressions: Making It Work*, Zagreb: Institute for International Relations, pp. 41–70.

North, D. C. (1990), *Institutions, Institutional Change and Economic Performance*, Cambridge: Cambridge University Press.

—— (2005), *Understanding the Process of Economic Change*, Princeton and Oxford: Princeton University Press.

Pauwels, C. and Loisen, J. (2003), 'The WTO and the Audiovisual Sector: Economic Free Trade vs Cultural Horse Trading?', *European Journal of Communication*, 18: 3, pp. 291–313.

Pauwels, C., Loisen, J. and Donders, K. (2006), 'Culture Incorporated; or Trade Revisited?', in N. Obuljen and J. Smiers (eds.), *UNESCO's Convention on the Protection and Promotion of the Diversity of Cultural Expressions: Making It Work*, Zagreb: Institute for International Relations, pp. 125–156.

Peukert, H. (2001), 'Bridging Old and New Institutional Economics: Gustav Schmoller and Douglass C. North, Seen with Oldinstitutionalists' Eyes', *European Journal of Law and Economics*, 11: 2, pp. 91–130.

Puppis, M. (2008), 'National Media Regulation in the Era of Free Trade'. The Role of Global Media Governance', *European Journal of Communication*, 23: 4, pp. 405–424.

Raboy, M. and Padovani, C. (2010), 'Mapping Global Media Policy: Concepts, Frameworks, Methods', *Communication, Culture & Critique*, 3: 2, pp. 150–169.

Ranaivoson, H. (2007), *Measuring Cultural Diversity: A Review of Existing Definitions. Working Paper*, Paris: UNESCO.

Roy, M. (2005), 'Audiovisual Services in the Doha Round: Dialogue de Sourds, the Sequel?', *Journal of World Investment and Trade*, 6: 6, pp. 923–952.

Ruggie, J. G. (1982), 'International Regimes, Transactions, and Change: Embedded Liberalism and the Post-War Economic Order', *International Organization*, 36: 2, pp. 379–415.

Sauvé, P. and Steinfatt, K. (2003), 'Towards Multilateral Rules on Trade and Culture: Protective Regulation or Efficient Protection?', in P. Sauvé (ed.), *Trade Rules Behind Borders: Essays on Services, Investment and the New Trade Agenda*, London: Cameron May, pp. 323–346.

Toboso, F. (1995), 'Explaining the Process of Change Taking Place in Legal Rules and Social Norms: The Cases of Institutional Economics and New Institutional Economics', *European Journal of Law and Economics*, 2: 1, pp. 63–84.

Vandenberg, P. (2002), 'North's Institutionalism and the Prospect of Combining Theoretical Approaches', *Cambridge Journal of Economics*, 26: 2, pp. 217–235.

Chapter 4

'It's the Idea, Stupid!' How Ideas Challenge
Broadcasting Liberalization

Matthias Künzler

Introduction: The Role of Ideas in Explaining Media Policy

The policy decision to liberalize the broadcasting sector in most western European countries during the 1980s has had enormous consequences for public service broadcasters, publishers, advertisers, journalists and the audience (Theis-Berglmair 1994). Admittedly, even countries with similar market structures (e.g. small states) have introduced and regulated private broadcasting in different ways. This focuses attention on the question of the reasons for different ways of regulating the media.

(Media) policy research has developed three approaches to explaining regulation: the interest approach, the institutional approach and the force-of-ideas approach (Baldwin and Cave 1999: 18–33; Jarren et al. 2002: 56–73; Poteete 2003: 527). Interest theories engage both in the question of whose purposes regulation suits and in a cost-benefit analysis of regulation. There is a broad distinction among 'public', 'group' and 'private' versions of interest theories. These different strands of theory were also adopted in some significant studies of media policy, such as McQuail's classical study of the public interest in communication (McQuail 1992) or McChesney's analysis of how business interests had an impact on the 1995 US Communications Act (McChesney 2008). Unlike interest theories, institutional approaches assume that institutional structure and social processes affect regulation. According to the understanding of what institutions are, regulation is either seen as shaped by polity (as the 'old' institutionalism does) or by past decisions, practices and procedures that influence current policy developments (as 'historical' institutionalism does). Moreover, institutions can also be understood as rules (e.g. property rights) that limit the range of options to rational decision-makers (as institutional economy or 'rational choice institutionalism' assumes). Sociological institutionalism understands institutions as shared 'myths' or as 'systems of rules' that are taken for granted and thus implemented in organizational structures or regulations (DiMaggio and Powell 1991: 3ff, 8–13; Hasse and Krücken 2005: 22–27). Examples of the use of institutional arguments in explaining media policy are partially Hallin and Mancini's typology, which explains media systems' structures by different kinds of institution (e.g. consensus or majoritarian government, the role of the state, rational legal authority) (Hallin and Mancini 2004: 66ff) or Puppis's analysis of press and media councils' organizational structures (Puppis 2009b).

Finally, the force-of-ideas approach explains media regulation by actors' normative and ontological beliefs, by their perceptions of policy issues, by their understandings of causal relationship or by policy paradigms (Poteete 2003: 531). There are some important studies that explain media policy at least in part by ideas. As an example, Feintuck compares rationales and objectives of media regulation in western Europe and in the US (Feintuck 1999). Another example of this approach to media policy research is Streeter's analysis of the development of commercial broadcasting in the US (Streeter 1996). Napoli's study of the foundations of the principles and processes on which the US system of electronic media regulation is based also deals with ideas. Napoli points out that the First Amendment is the most important 'foundation principle' from which all other principles of US communication policy, such as the public interest, localism or the marketplace of ideas, are derived (Napoli 2001: 22f). Likewise, some historical studies explain the development of policies partially by ideas. Examples are Briggs's comprehensive study of the history of the BBC (Briggs 1961, 1965, 1970, 1979, 1995) or Vos's analysis of US policy on networks in the 1920s (Vos 2006).

These and many other studies like those by Freedman or Streeter emphasize the importance of ideas on the policy process (Streeter 1996: xii; Freedman 2008: 4, 2010: 351f, for a literature review at full length, see Künzler 2009: 74–85). The analysis of ideas makes it possible not only to examine issues that regulation refers to but also to analyse the objectives, values and norms decision-makers were guided by when they implemented regulations. Thus, the force-of-ideas approach is an opportunity to deal with meaning associated with policy decisions (Hall 1993: 43; Weingast 1995: 461). However, this approach has been criticized, at least in the past, as being idealistic and therefore naïve, as the potential effect of ideas on media policy was considered to be low in comparison to that of interests and institutions (Campbell 1998: 377; Latzer 1997: 43). Furthermore, the approach still lacks on some theoretical and empirical foundations. The prevailing empirical approach to analysing ideas is deductive, deriving some universal ideas such as 'press freedom', 'diversity', 'marketplace of ideas' from democracy theories or constitutions (as Napoli and Feintuck do). Although these studies give some important insights into media policy, they cause problems in analysing the specific ideas of different actors, which are not universal in all democracies (Thomass 2007: 49). Even studies (such as Briggs's) that indicate specific ideas of policy actors define and conceptualize ideas poorly. This not only hinders the establishment of the relation between ideas and other media policy factors at a theoretical level, it also hinders further empirical research into policy ideas.

In order to overcome these deficiencies and to make ideas the very object of empirical research, I first define the term 'idea' and differentiate several types of idea. Secondly, I present a framework to establish the force-of-ideas approach on a theoretical level by suggesting basing it on Berger and Luckmann's social constructivist theory. Finally, I demonstrate the potential of this approach by analysing broadcasting liberalization in three small European states.

Definition and Differentiation of Ideas

Looking for definitions of 'idea' in social sciences, it becomes obvious that the term indicates different normative and cognitive concepts, which themselves are denoted in a variety of terms, such as 'causal belief', 'world view', 'regime', 'policy paradigm', 'political idea' (e.g. Goldstein 1993; Hall 1992; King 1992; Krasner 1983). Poteete states that 'ideas […] encompass everything from normative and ontological beliefs to perceptions about the disposition of other actors to understandings of causal relationships' (Poteete 2003: 531). Bleich has a similar understanding of ideas. For him 'ideational arguments draw attention to a wide range of variables, including world views, cultures, societal scripts, norms, models, and causal beliefs' (Bleich 2002: 1063). On the other hand, 'interests' are defined as actors' ambitions to gain possession of material or immaterial resources (Esser 1999: 37f, 125f).

The broad understanding of ideas is followed here too. This makes it possible to specify different types of ideas, which can be conceptualized for empirical analysis. Ideas vary in their complexity and the phenomena they bring into focus. As Campbell and Goldstein/ Keohane have stated, ideas consist either of one single idea element or of two or more related idea elements. There are two basic types of idea (Campbell 1998: 378; Goldstein and Keohane 1993: 9f, 11f): 'cognitive' and 'normative' ideas. 'Cognitive ideas' (also called 'causal beliefs') are ideas about cause–effect relationships. They imply assumptions about the reasons for a (policy) problem or about measures to achieve a (policy) goal. 'Normative ideas' (or 'principled beliefs') on the other hand contain perceptions of what a state or a situation should be. Thus, these ideas express values that are regarded as right or just.

Whereas a cognitive and a normative idea specify exactly one single cause–effect relationship or one normative presumption, more complex types of ideas combine at least two or more cognitive and/or normative ideas. 'Guiding principles' and 'problem perceptions' are ideas whose level of complexity is low, as they consist of a combination of two basic types of idea. 'Guiding principles' ('*Leitbilder*') combine a normative and a cognitive idea. Thus, guiding principles express a norm and how this norm should be achieved. An example of a guiding principle is the statement 'diversity by community radio.' The norm called for is 'diversity,' and 'community radio' is the measure how this norm should be achieved. Therefore, guiding principles refer to a goal or aspired-for state in the present or in the future (Dierkes et al. 1996; Künzler 2009: 132ff). On the other hand, 'problem perceptions' ('*Deutungsmuster*') consist of a perceived state or development that is seen as a policy problem and the normative estimate of this problem (Künzler 2009: 137f; Meuser and Sackmann 1992: 15; Wessler 1999: 79). An example of a problem perception is the statement, 'the monopoly of the public service broadcaster distorts media diversity.' The perceived state is that the public service broadcaster has a monopoly. The normative estimation of this state is negative, as it is seen as a threat of media diversity. Thus, problem perceptions denominate the underlying actual problem.

The most complex types of ideas are 'policy paradigms,' 'world views' or 'belief systems,' which consist of a combination of several cognitive and normative ideas. Policy paradigms provide 'an overarching set of ideas that specify how […] problems […] are perceived, which goals might be attained through policy and what sorts of techniques can be used to reach those goals' (Hall 1992: 91, for definitions of world views and policy paradigms see Goldstein and Keohane 1993: 8; Sabatier 1993: 132).

This conceptualization makes it possible to perceive different types of idea in the statements of the actors involved in media policy decisions. On one hand, it makes it possible to examine the issues or states that actors perceive as policy problems and how they assess these problems. On the other hand, it also facilitates an analysis of the goals and underlying norms policy that decision-makers were guided by when they introduced regulations.

Theoretical Foundation

Having conceptualized the term 'idea', the question still remains of how ideas evolve and what potential impact they have on the policy process. In order to analyse these questions empirically, it is necessary to theorize them at a theoretical level. Looking at approaches that refer the concept of ideas to a theoretical framework, two main ones can be identified: the ontological position of either idealism or social constructivism.

Idealism

Idealism conceives ideas as mental objects, such as perceptions, thoughts or aims. Material objects such as buildings, organizations, as well as historical events and immaterial objects such as arts or laws are seen as the realization of ideas. Thus, reality is shaped by ideas. The origins of idealism lay in the writings of philosophers such as Kant and Hegel, but their thoughts have also been assumed by current social scientists. As an example, Fukuyama (1992) considered the break-up of the Soviet Union as the 'end of history'. He explains this major event in history by the global diffusion of the concept of liberalism.

Studies based on idealism have been heavily criticized. Its assumptions are criticized as naïve, as it would neglect the influence of institutions, interests and power structures (O'Malley 2002: 164; Scheuch 2003: 25f; Tomaselli and Shepperson 1999: 244). In fact, this critique focuses attention on a weak point of idealism: it can neither respond to the question of why ideas are as or even more powerful than institutions and interests nor can it explain how ideas evolve. Idealism takes the existence of ideas for granted and considers them as elements that exist relatively autonomously of social developments. Actors just find ideas and realize them through their actions. This assumption is clearly expressed by Hauriou, a French scholar whose writings have been the basis of some institutional approaches in political sciences (e.g. Waschkuhn 1987: 72f, in parts Lepsius 1995): 'In reality, ideas are not brought into being, ones just comes upon them. [...] Thus, ideas already exist in the wide world' (Hauriou 1965: 39, [translation MK]).

Hence, idealism answers the question of whether ideas exist or whether they shape reality by an ontological presumption that either can be accepted or not. In the end, the impact of ideas is justified in a philosophical manner that does not permit empirical revision. Idealism therefore provides only a weak theoretical basis for the force-of-ideas approach in social science. Thus, the approach needs to be based on a theory other than idealism.

Social Constructivism

The initial point of most idea-centric policy-research approaches that are not based on idealism is the so-called interpretative paradigm. This is based on the notions of symbol interactionism, ethno-methodology and social phenomenology. It is assumed that policy-making is always based on meaning that actors prescribe to problems, the action of other actors or objects. The paradigm is divided into two main alternatives: social constructivism and the 'dramaturgical' version of the theory (Esser 2001: 80–90; Nullmeier 2001: 102–110). Whereas the dramaturgical version stresses the impact of norms, rules and rituals on policy-making (especially Goffmann), social constructivism focuses to a greater extent on the question of how norms and rules evolve and how actors create and change meaning. Therefore, social constructivism offers a good opportunity to discuss the impact of ideas and the change of ideas in policy-making processes on a theoretical level. This approach is decisively shaped by Berger and Luckmann's sociology of knowledge. Thus, an examination of their classical theory makes it possible to debate how ideas evolve. In turn, their theory is also the basis of some neo-institutionalist approaches (see e.g. Scott 2003: 136f).

In their classical work *The Social Construction of Reality*, Berger and Luckmann show that social reality and the understanding of reality is based on actors' knowledge. In Berger and Luckmann's definition, knowledge is everything that a society considers as 'knowledge' and which is taken for granted 'regardless of the ultimate validity or invalidity (by whatever criteria) of such "knowledge"' (Berger and Luckmann 1966: 3). This broad understanding of knowledge encompasses knowledge about cause–effect relations and conceptions of justice or legitimacy. Thus, referring to our general definition of ideas as normative and cognitive concepts, knowledge is a comprehensive type of ideas, which encompasses causal and normative ideas as well.

Berger and Luckmann's conceptualization of knowledge also includes an explanation of the question of how ideas evolve. By referring to the origins of interpretative sociology as developed by Alfred Schütz and Max Weber, Berger and Luckmann understand the reality of everyday life as a reality that is interpreted by people and is subjectively meaningful to them. Reality is an interpreted reality that is meaningful to each member of society. Meaning is the result of consciousness and not of transcendental nature (Berger and Luckmann 1966: 19). It evolves by a person's interaction with others or with their natural or social environment. However, the interpretation of reality is not a process that takes place completely subjectively. On the contrary, the interpretation of reality consists to a great extent of shared meaning. This commonly shared meaning allows for mutual understanding and concerted action in the first place. Berger and Luckmann signify this socially shared meaning as 'knowledge.' Therefore, reality, the understanding of reality and the production of reality are based on knowledge, or on shared meaning (Berger and Luckmann 1966: 19–23). Berger and Luckmann have developed a model of how the social construction of reality takes place. According to them, reality is constituted in three steps, which are exemplified in the following.

The *first* step is the *externalization of subjective meaning.* By acting or expressing subjective meaning to others, people project their own meaning into reality. Based on knowledge and past experiences, people externalize their interpretation of a social situation or a physical state. This initiates externalization by other people and leads to mutual interaction. The *second* step is the *objectivation of knowledge,* which is the result of habitualized actions. Frequently repeated actions become habitualized and can be reproduced with a little effort and a minimum of decision-making. If habitualized action is repeated by certain types of actors, institutions occur and set up predefined patterns of conduct. Institutions become taken for granted and become part of the objective reality. An example of an institution is a law court: it is run by specialized personnel (judges, clerks etc.) who assume specific actions (to render and pronounce a judgement). Such institutions require legitimation. The meaning of an institution needs explanation, justification and acceptance (Berger and Luckmann 1966: 61). Everyone in the society needs to know what an institution such as a law court is and what its underlying norms are (e.g. general principles of legislation). Thus, in a *third* step, the institutionalized world needs to be *internalized* by individuals. The process of internalization takes place through socialization, either by learning, by imposing sanctions on certain behaviour or by coercion. As a result of internalization, the surrounding world is assumed as an objective reality. Having internalized the cultural and social order as well as the commonly shared meaning ('knowledge') by socialization, people recognize the world as real and meaningful (Berger and Luckmann 1966: 136ff).

Even institutions become stable through the processes described; the construction of reality takes place continuously. Each action causes externalization. Socialization is an ongoing process as well, as it is necessary to sustain an existing reality. However, changes in the social structure or the development of new technologies require new knowledge and justifications and call existing knowledge into question. This can either lead to de-legitimation, to new justifications of existing institutions or to the development of new institutions and new knowledge. As actions and institutions (e.g. the state, common norms and rules) are based on different kinds of knowledge (e.g. on values, aims, perceptions), reality can only persist or be transformed by continuous processes of interaction, communication and interpretation of reality. Thus, people and scientists deal with a pre-interpreted world in which meaning is developed by active subjects (Servaes 1991: 157f).

Nevertheless, the ongoing process of constructing reality is shaped not only by knowledge. Berger and Luckmann themselves point out that some different conditions shape the social construction of knowledge and reality: cognitive abilities, individual biographically rooted idiosyncrasies, socio-structural conditions of the existing world and the way in which socialization processes take place (Berger and Luckmann 1966: 131, 140f, 163, 165f, 182).

Thus, there are not only ideas shaping reality but also structural conditions including the form of institutions and the self-interest of actors.

Even if this social–constructivist theory at first seems to be far from the subject of media policy, there are three reasons it suits as a theoretical foundation for an idea-centric approach to media policy:

(1) The theory overcomes idealistic assumptions. Instead of considering ideas as taken for granted, social constructivism perceives ideas as the product of human consciousness, people's interpretations of actions and objects. Thus, social constructivism considers ideas as the product of human action and not as transcendental objects whose origins cannot be explained.

(2) Social constructivism does not deny the impact of institutions and interest. The social construction of reality is understood as a process shaped by ideas, existing institutions, the abilities of the actors involved and by their interests. This makes it possible to discuss how these three factors rely on each other. Bhagwati (1988: 19–42) has stressed the importance of all three factors in shaping policy.

(3) Berger and Luckmann describe the construction of reality as a process that is based on prevailing processes. Therefore, their theory can be applied to research that deals with change. This is relevant for media policy research, as this policy field is highly dynamic. The introduction of new technologies especially has led to a rapid change in policies and regulation practices during recent decades (e.g. Freedman 2008: 16f).

The Transfer of Social Constructivism to Media Policy

Berger and Luckmann's model does not directly explain how ideas challenge policy-making. Although it provides a model of social action of individuals and claims to explain how the whole society is built, Berger and Luckmann did not apply their model on the level of corporate and collective actors (e.g. organizations, pressure groups). If the model is to be used to debate the potential impact of ideas on the media policy process, the theory needs to be transformed from the micro level up to the meso and macro levels.

According to definitions of media regulation in communication science, I understand media regulation as the formulation of rules by law, the enforcement of rules and imposing sanctions for the breach of rules concerning the media. Whereas media regulation is based on law, self- and co-regulation are carried out by private actors or by private actors who collaborate with the state (Baldwin and Cave 1999: 2f; Jarren et al. 2002: 16). Based on this definition, Berger and Luckmann's social constructivist theory can now be applied to media regulation.

Externalization relates to the formulation of rules concerning the media. This process usually starts if citizens' groups, lobby groups, civil society actors, politicians, the government and the media themselves formulate a perceived policy problem and register their claims publicly. If these activities lead to the formulation of a bill concerning the media, the process of interaction continues. The different policy groups express their political position and lobby in order to implement their interests in the law. Within this process of interaction, policy groups confront each other with their ideas and interests.[1] The institutional design of the state determines which policy groups are directly involved in the policy-making process and what impact they may have on this process. The relevant modifications of the bill are assumed by parliamentarians, as parliament is the authority legitimated to make the ultimate policy decisions in democracies.

If the bill passes legislation, *objectivation* takes place. A new or a modified law comes into force. On one hand, this leads to the institutionalization of new authorities or new media organizations. On the other hand, new or modified rules come into effect and thus may also change the way in which existing organizations are institutionalized. Based on a new act, new media organizations and regulation authorities come into existence or have to modify their operations. Thereby *socialization* begins. Even the term 'socialization' is normally used for processes of how individuals adapt norms and rules; it can also be used to analyse how organizations or even states assume norms and rules that guide their operations (Schimmelfennig 2003: 410f). By adopting this concept of media regulation, regulators try to enforce rules, either by coercion, by offering incentives, by bargaining or by social pressure (e.g. communication). On the other hand, media organizations may try to broaden the rules or may subvert regulation authorities by pressure and influence. This can lead to the 'capture' of the regulation authority, which means that authorities regulate in the interest of the private actors (Ogus 1994: 57f). If existing rules are not seen as appropriate anymore, the underlying law will be revised. At this moment, the process starts with externalization again.

The transfer of Berger and Luckmann's model of the social construction of reality makes it possible to identify the potential impact of ideas on the formulation and on the enforcement of media policy. In the process of externalization and socialization, actors verbalize the policy problems or conditions to which their attention is attracted by their problem perceptions. Thus, ideas help to prioritize the numerous potential concerns (Moore 1988: 72f). Ideas provide a concept of which norms and capabilities are perceived as better and are worthy of support (Legro 1997: 36f). Thus, they offer criteria for deciding what policy goals should be set and which goals are seen as required, fair or acceptable (Majone 1988: 165). Nevertheless, ideas not only shape norms and interests of each individual actor. They also provide a focal point to coordinate perceptions, interests and priorities of different actors and thus give additional motivations to the pursuit of interests (White 2002: 726). On the other hand, ideas also provide causal evidence about the effect of the means to reach a desired policy goal or interest. According to the causal evidence provided, some regulations are taken into consideration whereas others are not. However, in addition to providing assumptions about causal relation effects, ideas indicate how policy goals can be achieved in an ideologically correct way (Goldstein and Keohane 1993: 13f). Nevertheless, it is not only ideas that shape media policy. Actors also try to influence future media policy in order to gain as big a share of resources they are interested in as possible. Their ability to express their goals and to take part in policy decisions depends on the institutional design of the media system and the democracy.

The chance of a policy idea being implemented in a new act is considered to be strong if three conditions are fulfilled. An idea should be consistently and precisely expressed ('specificity'). It should clearly distinguish between appropriate and inappropriate behaviour or it should specify perceptions precisely. Moreover, an idea should be shared by powerful actors or by a coalition of various different actors ('concordance'). Last but not least, ideas that have been debated or have shaped policies for a long time ('durability') are considered to be strong (Boekle et al. 2000: 8–12; Legro 1997: 34f).

At a theoretical level, these assumptions explain that ideas might shape media policy, but they do not provide an answer to the question of when ideas influence policies. Summing up studies into this question, there are four conditions that promote the implementation of new ideas. Firstly, in a crisis caused by 'exogenous shocks' (e.g. wars, international depression), the advent of new (media) technologies or market transformations existing ideas and interests are taken into consideration. Existing policies no longer meet the needs of media companies, politicians etc., as they neither seem to be desirable nor do they seem to respond appropriately to policy issues. At such 'break points' alternative cause–effect explanation, perceptions, targets and interests come into the debate (Goldstein 1993: 13; Hall 1992: 104f). The failure of a current policy can be another condition for ideational change, which is often intertwined with crises. If various policy actors consider that an existing policy has failed, decision-makers have an incentive to search for new policy ideas and for policy change (Goldstein 1993: 13). A third possibility for why new policy ideas are implemented is a power shift within politics. Especially if the opposition comes to power, the new decision-makers may enforce their own policy ideas. In this case, the implementation of new policy ideas is rather based on the outcome of power struggle between actors with different interests and not on the persuasive power of ideas itself (White 2002: 483f). In contrast, learning can be another reason for the emergence or diffusion of new ideas. If actors confront each other with differing perceptions about cause–effect relations, norms, aims etc. in ongoing policy debates, they may begin to engage in policy issues they previously ignored and may, at least in part, start to adopt new causal and normative ideas (Finnemore and Sikkink 1998: 895, 904; Majone 1988: 177).

Empirical Evidence in Brief: A Comparative Analysis of Broadcasting Liberalization in Small States

In the final step, the empirical potential of the force-of-ideas approach is briefly demonstrated by the analysis of broadcasting liberalization in Ireland, Austria and Switzerland. These three countries share the same structural conditions, whose main characteristics are the small media market (between 4.5 and 8 million inhabitants) and a giant next-door neighbour country sharing the same language, which leads to high market shares for foreign television channels (on small states' characteristics, see Puppis 2009a). Despite these similarities, all three countries have introduced private broadcasting at different times and in a different manner.

In the following, some results of a study (Künzler 2009) that examined policy ideas of broadcasting liberalization in the three countries are presented. By focusing on the most important ideas of broadcasting liberalization and on the change of ideas, an answer can be given regarding one of the four conditions for the implementation of new ideas. These results are based on a qualitative document analysis of broadcasting laws and the underlying parliamentary debates concerning the introduction or development of private broadcasting (on the method see e.g. Silverman 2005).

Ireland

Ireland opened up its broadcasting sector to private radio at the national and regional levels and to private television at the national level in 1988, after having accepted pirate radio for over a decade (Byrne 2007: 12f; Noam 1991: 238). The analysis of the parliamentary debates about the 'Radio and Television Act' (1988) points out that politicians from the parties involved in the government wanted to introduce private broadcasting because they considered the current policy had failed. They not only criticized the fact that the public service broadcaster RTÉ had a monopoly, which is inefficient and hinders media diversity, but they also considered the toleration of pirate broadcasting to be inconvenient. Thus, the aim of introducing private broadcasting was to encourage media diversity, to strengthen the Irish broadcasting industry as a whole and to establish legal order in the broadcasting sector.

Despite the new legal basis and plans of several investors, no national private television station came into existence and the national private radio station lost income (Corcoran 2004: 46). Again, parliamentarians from the governing parties (especially Fianna Fail) and some from the opposition still considered the degree of liberalization to be insufficient. They assumed that RTÉ was hindering the entrance of a private national TV station by using its strong position and the licence fee to sell advertising time too cheaply. Thus the revised broadcasting law of 1990 aimed at encouraging the development of private broadcasting stations by cutting and limiting the advertising income of the public service broadcaster to a certain amount a year (Corcoran 2004: 40–50).

After only three years, this limit was revoked (Corcoran 2008: 170f). This policy change can only partly be explained by a power shift. Fianna Fail lost its dominance in the government and had to share its power with some opposition parties. Nevertheless, this policy shift is also the result of learning and of policy failure. In particular, politicians from parties in the government and in the opposition considered the consequences of limiting RTÉ's advertising income to be negative. Despite the new act, no private television station had come into being and the national private radio station became insolvent. Advertisers did not invest their money on the Irish private broadcasting station as had been assumed either. They rather placed their advertising on British TV channels based in Northern Ireland. As a consequence, even decision-makers from Fianna Fail changed their perception of the public service broadcaster. Whereas some Fianna Fail members of parliament still saw RTÉ's position as one of dominance, others commended its programmes and considered the previous policy measures to have failed.

In 2001 and 2003, the radio and television law was revised again. The 2001 act continued to liberalize broadcasting by facilitating private TV at the local and regional levels, by explicitly mentioning community broadcasting and by introducing digital broadcasting (Truetzschler 2009: 39). However, it was not aimed at weakening public service broadcasting. On the contrary, public service broadcasting was strengthened in 2003 by establishing the legal basis for future increases in the licence fee. A 'Sound and Vision Scheme' was immediately introduced, which permitted support for cultural and educational programmes and projects aimed at archiving programmes on private and public service broadcasters (BCI 2010). In the parliamentary debate, politicians from the governing party, Fianna Fail, and from other parties expressed their satisfaction with the public service broadcaster. They now supported the idea of preserving a strong public service broadcaster in order to encourage both media diversity and jobs in the audio-visual sector. Contrary to their position a decade previously, they agreed to encourage public service by raising the licence fee (Künzler 2009: 306–315). Based on the failure of past policies, a process of learning has taken place and has led to an ideational change among decision-makers from different parties.

Austria

Austria introduced private broadcasting for the first time in 1993, five years later than Ireland. Previously, illegal radio stations had produced their programmes at home and abroad but the government took strict action against them (Hirtner 2003: 21; Reichel et al. 2006: 159f). However, the European Court of Human Rights considered the monopoly of the public service broadcaster to be inconsistent with the European Convention on Human Rights, as it did not see any compelling reason for this monopoly (Dörr 2004: 74). Accordingly, the members of the two parties forming the government (the social democrat SPÖ and the conservative ÖVP) justified the introduction of private radio mainly by adapting the broadcasting law to international standards. They objected to the introduction of private radio and television at the national level in order to sustain a strong public service broadcaster that contributes to information and integration. Only members of the other left- and right-wing parties who were not participating in the government (especially the Greens and the far right FPÖ) supported either the introduction of community broadcasting or of private broadcasters operating at national level in order to encourage media diversity.

In 1997, the broadcasting sector was opened to private TV and private radio stations operating on satellite and cable. This development was partly a reaction to the introduction of 'advertising windows' on some German private television stations, which are aimed at the Austrian audience. In addition, the national constitutional court called for modifications to the current broadcasting law (Knoche 1997: 15; Steinmaurer 2004a: 512). The debates in the parliament show some ideational change especially within the conservative ÖVP. Some of their members of parliament began criticizing the public service broadcasters and demanded further liberalization.

Private TV and private radio stations were not authorized at the national level until 2001. This policy change mainly became possible due to a power shift in the national government. After federal elections, the ÖVP formed the government together with the former opposition far-right FPÖ, whereas the SPÖ went into opposition (Steinmaurer 2004b: 34f). This enabled these two parties to implement their policy idea of national private broadcasting.

In the following years, some further amendments to the broadcasting acts were made. These were mainly related to digital broadcasting but did not change the media sector to a great extent (even after there was another change of the government) (Steininger and Woelke 2007). Since 2004, private broadcasting has been facilitated by four funds, financed by the broadcasting licence fee, which support the production of programmes in commercial and community broadcasters (RTR 2010a; 2010b).

Switzerland

In Switzerland, the first private radio stations transmitted their programmes illegally from the 1970s onwards. The government took action against pirate radio but it allowed local private radio and TV stations on a trial basis in 1983. This was intended to gain experience with private broadcasting and to make it possible to take these experiences into account in the new broadcasting act. After a long period of deliberation, the 'Law on Radio and Television' (LRTV) was passed in 1991 (Schneider 2006). It enabled private radio and TV at the local/regional and the international levels, whereas the national level was to remain reserved for the public service broadcasters (exemptions were possible). All private broadcasting stations were obliged to fulfill certain conditions concerning information and culture. There was a consensus among politicians from left-wing, centre and right-wing parties that this kind of 'controlled competition' should both preserve strong public service broadcasting and encourage media diversity. There was also a consensus among politicians from different parties to facilitate media diversity in rural areas by introducing a 'licence-fee splitting.' Local private broadcasters in regions without a sufficient economic basis and community channels were supported with a small part of the licence fee (1%).

The LRTV was modified in 2006. One of the structural reasons for this was the collapse of two national private TV stations in 2001 as a consequence of the economic crisis, which greatly reduced advertising revenue. The revised broadcasting act intensified the liberalization of the broadcasting sector. It permitted the transmission of private broadcasting without a licence, which is only needed if a private radio or TV station aims at broadcasting on distribution channels where frequencies are still scarce (e.g. FM radio). Whereas private broadcasting stations without a licence face little regulation concerning advertising and content, licensed private broadcasters have to contribute to information and culture on the local level. They also have to comply with stricter advertising regulation (Künzler 2009: 189–198). Some of these private broadcasters are supported by licence fee, with their share of the fee having been raised to 4% (OFCOM 2007).

The enhanced liberalization is partially based on learning and on a perceived failure of the present regulation. Politicians from centre and right-wing parties had considered the previous regulation to be no longer adequate, owing to the rise of the Internet, digitization and globalization (advertising windows on German and French TV stations have become increasingly successful). In addition, the guiding principles of politicians from the centre and the right-wing parties have to some extent changed their opinions concerning 'controlled competition.' Thus learning was another reason for policy change. These politicians no longer considered it necessary to compel all private broadcasters to fulfill obligations concerning information and culture.

Conclusion

Comparative media policy research highlights the fact that similar policy decisions such as the liberalization of the broadcasting sector are implemented in different ways. In this article I have pointed out how media regulation can be explained by ideas, as this approach has been less elaborated than the two other approaches (interest and institutional approach) normally used to explain media regulation. This partial neglect of the force-of-ideas approach may stem from older research, which was founded on idealism and which often defined the term 'idea' poorly. However, a conceptualization of this term is important in order to analyse ideas in the statements of different actors empirically. Thus, based on ideational approaches developed in other social sciences, I suggest differentiating between two basic types of ideas: cognitive ideas, which consist of an assumption about cause–effect relations, and normative ideas, which contain a perception of what a state or a situation ought to be. More complex types of ideas (e.g. 'policy paradigms') combine these two basic types.

At a theoretical level, ideas do not need to be understood as objects that are just in the world and whose existence cannot be explained, as idealism does. Rather I suggest basing the force-of-ideas approach on social constructivism, as this theory makes it possible to explain how ideas evolve. Based on Berger and Luckmann, ideas evolve if a person interacts with others. Thus, ideas are the result of actors' consciousness. If we adapt Berger and Luckmann's social constructivist theory to the subject of media policy, actors express their ideas and interest in debates about future policies. Their opportunity to externalize ideas, interests and to shape policy also depends on how polity is institutionalized. The result of these debates is objectivized if a law is enacted. Subsequently, regulators seek to enforce statutory norms, whereas media companies may try to subvert regulation authorities by pressure and influence.

The empirical analysis of reasons for introducing and developing private broadcasting in three small European states pointed out that the implementation of new ideas was either based on 'exogenous shocks,' a perceived failure of current policies, power shift or on learning. As shown earlier, the introduction of national private broadcasting in Austria was mainly based on a power shift in 2001. On the other hand, public service broadcasting in Ireland was strengthened by processes of learning. Politicians from parties that objected to public service broadcasting changed their opinions and agreed to an increase in the licence fee over the years. These examples show that an ideational explanation of media policy gives additional new insights into processes of policy change. Further research should thus increasingly focus on analysing ideas empirically in the statements of actors and should integrate these explanations into interest and institutional explanations.

References

Baldwin, R. and Cave, M. (1999), *Understanding Regulation: Theory, Strategy, and Practice*, New York: Oxford University Press.

BCI – Broadcasting Commission of Ireland (2010), 'About Us – Governing Acts', http://www.bci.ie/about/governing_acts.html. Accessed 14 December 2010.

Berger, P. L. and Luckmann, T. (1966), *The Social Construction of Reality. A Treatise in the Sociology of Knowledge*, New York: Anchor.

Bhagwati, J. (1988), *Protectionism*, Cambridge and London: MIT Press.

Bleich, E. (2002), 'Integrating Ideas into Policy-Making Analysis: Frames and Race Policies in Britain and France', *Comparative Political Studies*, 35: 9, pp. 1054–1076.

Boekle, H., Rittberger, V. and Wagner, W. (2000), *Norms and Foreign Policy: Constructivist Foreign Policy Theory*, Tübinger Arbeitspapiere zur Internationalen Politik und Friedensforschung, Nr. 34a.

Briggs, A. (1961), *The Birth of Broadcasting*, London, New York and Toronto: Oxford University Press.

——— (1965), *The Golden Age of Wireless*, London, New York and Toronto: Oxford University Press.

——— (1970), *The War of Words*, London, New York and Toronto: Oxford University Press.

——— (1979), *Sound and Vision*, London, New York and Toronto: Oxford University Press.

——— (1995), *Competition*, London, New York and Toronto: Oxford University Press.

Byrne, J. (2007), 'If Community Radio Is the Answer … What Is the Question? The Birth of Community Radio in Ireland, 1975–1995', in R. Day (ed.), *Bicycle Highway. Celebrating Community Radio in Ireland*, Dublin: The Liffey, pp. 11–28.

Campbell, J. L. (1998), 'Institutional Analysis and the Role of Ideas in Political Economy', *Theory and Society*, 27: 3, pp. 377–409.

Corcoran, F. (2004), *RTÉ and the Globalisation of Irish Television*, Bristol and Portland: Intellect.

—— (2008), 'Ireland: From Cultural Nationalism to Neoliberalism', in David Ward (ed.), *Television and Public Policy. Change and Continuity in an Era of Global Liberalization*, New York and London: Lawrence Erlbaum Associates, pp. 165–181.

Dierkes, M., Hoffmann, U. and Marz, L. (1996), *Visions of Technology. Social and Institutional Factors Shaping the Development of New Technologies*, Frankfurt: Campus.

DiMaggio, P. J. and Powell, W. W. (1991), 'Introduction', in W. W. Powell and P. J. DiMaggio (eds.), *The New Institutionalism in Organizational Analysis*, Chicago and London: The University of Chicago Press, pp. 1–38.

Dörr, D. (2004), 'Die europäische Medienordnung', in Hans-Bredow-Institut (ed.), *Internationales Handbuch für Hörfunk und Fernsehen 2004/2005*, 27. Auflage, Baden-Baden: Nomos, pp. 40–77.

Esser, H. (1999), *Soziologie: Spezielle Grundlagen. Band 1: Situationslogik und Handeln*, Frankfurt and New York: Campus.

—— (2001), *Soziologie: Spezielle Grundlagen. Band 6: Sinn und Kultur*, Frankfurt and New York: Campus.

Federal Office of Communication (OFCOM) (2007), 'The Completely Revised LRTV – Key Points and New Features', http://www.bakom.admin.ch/dokumentation/gesetzgebung/00512/01031/01404/index.html?lang=en. Accessed 14 December 2010.

Feintuck, M. (1999), *Media Regulation, Public Interest and the Law*, Edinburgh: Edinburgh University Press.

Finnemore, M. and Sikkink, K. (1998), 'International Norm Dynamics and Political Change', *International Organization*, 52: 4, pp. 887–917.

Freedman, D. (2008), *The Politics of Media Policy*, Cambridge and Malden: Polity.

—— (2010), 'Media Policy Silences: The Hidden Face of Communications Decision Making', *The International Journal of Press/Politics*, 15: 3, pp. 344–361.

Fukuyama, F. (1992), *The End of History and the Last Man*, New York: Free.

Goldstein, J. (1993), *Ideas, Interests, and American Trade Policy*, Ithaca and London: Cornell University Press.

Goldstein, J. and Keohane, R. O. (1993), 'Ideas and Foreign Policy: An Analytical Framework', in J. Goldstein and R. O. Keohane (eds.), *Ideas and Foreign Policy. Beliefs, Institutions, and Political Change*, Ithaca and London: Cornell University Press, pp. 3–30.

Hall, P. A. (1992), 'The Movement from Keynesianism to Monetarism: Institutional Analysis and British Economic Policy in the 1970s', in S. Steinmo, K. Thelen and F. Longstreth (eds.), *Structuring Politics. Historical Institutionalism in Comparative Analysis*, Cambridge: Cambridge University Press, pp. 90–113.

—— (1993), 'Ideas and the Social Sciences', in J. Goldstein and R. O. Keohane (eds.), *Ideas and Foreign Policy. Beliefs, Institutions, and Political Change*, Ithaca and London: Cornell University Press, pp. 31–54.

Hallin, D. C. and Mancini, P. (2004), *Comparing Media Systems. Three Models of Media and Politics*, Cambridge: Cambridge University Press.

Hasse, R. and Krücken, G. (2005), *Neo-Institutionalismus. Mit einem Vorwort von John Meyer*, 2., vollständig überarbeitete Auflage, Bielefeld: Transcript.

Hauriou, M. (1965), 'Die Theorie der Institution und deren Gründung', in R. Schnur (ed.), *Die Theorie der Institution und zwei andere Aufsätze von Maurice Hauriou*, Berlin: Duncker & Humblot, pp. 27–66.

Hirtner, W. (2003), 'Vom PiratInnenradio zum Freien Radio. Der lange Weg zur Lizenz', *Medien Journal*, 4, pp. 20–31.

Jarren, O., Weber, R. H., Donges, P., Dörr, B., Künzler, M. and Puppis, M. (2002), *Rundfunkregulierung. Leitbilder, Modelle und Erfahrungen im Internationalen Vergleich: Eine sozial- und rechtswissenschaftliche Analyse*, Zürich: Seismo.

King, D. S. (1992), 'The Establishment of Work-Welfare Programs in the United States and Britain: Politics, Ideas, and Institutions', in S. Steinmo, K. Thelen and F. Longstreth (eds.), *Structuring Politics. Historical Institutionalism in Comparative Analysis*, Cambridge: Cambridge University Press, pp. 217–250.

Knoche, M. (1997), 'Medienpolitik als Konzentrationsförderungspolitik. Auch Österreich tappt in die Privatisierungsfalle', *Medien Journal*, 2, pp. 14–25.

Krasner, S. D. (1983), 'Structural causes and regime consequences: regimes as intervening variables', in S. D. Krasner (ed.) *International Regimes*, Ithaca and London: Cornell University Press, pp. 3–21.

Künzler, M. (2009), *Die Liberalisierung von Radio und Fernsehen. Leitbilder der Rundfunkregulierung im Ländervergleich*, Konstanz: UVK.

Latzer, M. (1997), *Mediamatik - die Konvergenz von Telekommunikation, Computer und Rundfunk*, Opladen: Westdeutscher.

Legro, J. W. (1997), 'Which Norms Matter? Revisiting the "Failure" of Internationalism', *International Organization*, 51: 1, pp. 31–63.

Lepsius, M. R. (1995), 'Institutionenanalyse und Institutionenpolitik', in B. Nedelmann (ed.), *Politische Institutionen im Wandel*, Opladen: Westdeutscher, pp. 392–403.

Majone, G. (1988), 'Policy Analysis and Public Deliberation', in R. B. Reich (ed.), *The Power of Public Ideas*, Cambridge: Ballinger, pp. 157–178.

McChesney, R. W. (2008), 'The Internet and U.S. Communication Policymaking in Historical and Critical Perspective', in R. W. McChesney (ed.), *The Political Economy of Media. Enduring Issues, Emerging Dilemmas*, New York: Monthly Review, pp. 355–381.

McQuail, D. (1992), *Media Performance. Mass Communication and the Public Interest*, London, Newbury Park and New Delhi: Sage.

Meuser, M. and Sackmann, R. (1992), 'Zur Einführung: Deutungsmusteransatz und empirische Wissenssoziologie', in M. Meuser and R. Sackmann (eds.), *Analyse Sozialer Deutungsmuster. Beiträge zur Empirischen Wissenssoziologie*, Pfaffenweiler: Centaurus, pp. 9–37.

Moore, M. H. (1988), 'What Sort of Ideas Become Public Ideas?', in R. B. Reich (ed.), *The Power of Public Ideas*, Cambridge: Ballinger, pp. 55–83.

Napoli, P. M. (2001), *Foundations of Communications Policy: Principles and Process in the Regulation of Electronic Media*, Cresskill: Hampton.

Noam, E. (1991), *Television in Europe*, New York and Oxford: Oxford University Press.

Nullmeier, F. (2001), 'Politikwissenschaft auf dem Weg zur Diskursanalyse?', in R. Keller, A. Hirseland, W. Schneider and W. Viehöver (eds.), *Handbuch Sozialwissenschaftliche Diskursanalyse. Band I: Theorien und Methoden*, Opladen: Westdeutscher, pp. 285–311.

O'Malley, T. (2002), 'Media History and Media Studies: Aspects of the Development of the Study of Media History in the UK 1945–2000', *Media History*, 8: 2, pp. 155–173.

Ogus, A. I. (1994), *Regulation. Legal Form and Economic Theory*, Oxford and New York: Oxford University Press.

Poteete, A. R. (2003), 'Ideas, Interests, and Institutions: Challenging the Property Rights Paradigm in Botswana', *Governance: An International Journal of Policy, Administration, and Institutions*, 16: 4, pp. 527–557.

Puppis, M. (2009a), 'Introduction. Media Regulation in Small States', *International Communication Gazette*, 71: 1–2, pp. 7–17.

——— (2009b), *Organisationen der Medienselbstregulierung. Europäische Presseräte im Vergleich*, Cologne: Herbert von Halem.

Reichel, W., Konvicka, M., Streit, G. and Landgraf, R. (2006), 'Anhang', in W. Reichel, M. Konvicka, G. Streit and R. Landgraf (eds.), *Privatradio in Österreich. Eine schwere Geburt*, Munich: Reinhard Fischer, pp. 159–177.

RTR – Rundfunk und Telekom Regulierungs-GmbH (2010a), *Fonds zur Förderung des nichtkommerziellen Rundfunks. Richtlinien*, Wien: RTR.

——— (2010b), *Fonds zur Förderung des privaten Rundfunks. Richtlinien*, Wien: RTR.

Sabatier, P. A. (1993), 'Advocacy-Koalitionen, Policy-Wandel und Policy-Lernen: Eine Alternative zur Phasenheuristik', in A. Héritier (ed.), *Policy-Analyse. Kritik und Neuorientierung*, Opladen: Westdeutscher, pp. 116–148.

Scheuch, E. K. (2003), *Sozialer Wandel. Band 1: Theorien des sozialen Wandels*, Wiesbaden: Westdeutscher.

Schimmelfennig, F. (2003), 'Internationale Sozialisation: Von einem "erschöpften" zu einem produktiven Forschungsprogramm?', in G. Hellmann, K. D. Wolf and M. Zürn (eds.), *Die neuen Internationalen Beziehungen. Forschungsstand und Perspektiven in Deutschland*, Baden-Baden: Nomos, pp. 401–427.

Schneider, T. (2006), 'Vom SRG-"Monopol" zum marktorientierten Rundfunk', in T. Mäusli and A. Steigmeier (eds.), *Radio und Fernsehen in der Schweiz. Geschichte der Schweizerischen Radio- und Fernsehgesellschaft SRG 1958-1983*, Baden: hier + jetzt, pp. 86–137.

Scott, R. W. (2003), *Organizations. Rational, Natural, and Open Systems*, 5th ed., Upper Saddle River: Prentice Hall.

Servaes, J. (1991), 'Into the Twilight Zone. Commentary on McQuail', in J. A. Anderson (ed.), *Communication Yearbook 14*, Newbury Park, London and New Delhi: Sage, pp. 154–162.

Silverman, D. (2005), *Doing Qualitative Research: A Practical Handbook*, 2nd ed., London, Thousand Oaks and New Delhi: Sage.

Steininger, C. and Woelke, J. (eds.) (2007) *Fernsehen in Österreich 2007*, Konstanz: UVK.

Steinmaurer, T. (2004a), 'Das Mediensystem Österreichs', in Hans-Bredow-Institut (ed.), *Internationales Handbuch für Hörfunk und Fernsehen 2004/2005*, Baden-Baden: Nomos, pp. 505–520.

——— (2004b), 'Medienangebot in Österreich', in H. Pürer, M. Rahofer and C. Reitan (eds.), *Praktischer Journalismus. Presse, Radio, Fernsehen, Online*, 5., völlig neue Auflage, Konstanz: UVK, pp. 29–39.

Streeter, T. (1996), *Selling the Air: A Critique of the Policy of Commercial Broadcasting in the United States*, Chicago and London: University Of Chicago Press.

Theis-Berglmair, A. M. (1994), 'Medienwandel – Modellwandel? Reflexionen über die gesellschaftliche Komponente der Massenkommunikation', in O. Jarren (ed.), *Medienwandel – Gesellschaftswandel? 10 Jahre dualer Rundfunk in Deutschland: Eine Bilanz*, Berlin: Vistas, pp. 35–50.

Thomass, B. (2007), 'Ausgewählte Themen des Vergleichs von Mediensystemen', in B. Thomass (ed.), *Mediensysteme im Internationalen Vergleich*, Konstanz: UVK, pp. 42–58.

Tomaselli, K. G. and Shepperson, A. (1999), 'The Poverty of Journalism: Media Studies and "Science"', *Continuum*, 13: 2, pp. 237–253.

Truetzschler, W. v. (2009), 'The Irish Media Landscape', in G. Terzis (ed.), *European Media Governance. National and Regional Dimensions*, Bristol and Chicago: Intellect, pp. 33–42.

Vos, T. P. (2006), 'Professionalism, Voluntarism, and American Broadcasting Networks: A Cultural Explanation for Broadcasting Policy', *Annual Meeting of the International Communication Association*, Dresden, 19–23 June.

Waschkuhn, A. (1987), 'Politische Institutionen und Allgemeine Institutionentheorie. Allgemeine Institutionentheorie als Rahmen für die Theorie Politischer Institutionen', in G. Göhler (ed.), *Grundfragen der Theorie politischer Institutionen*, Opladen: Westdeutscher, pp. 71–97.

Weingast, B. R. (1995), 'A Rational Choice Perspective on the Role of Ideas: Shared Belief Systems and State Sovereignty in International Cooperation', *Politics Society*, 23: 4, pp. 449–464.

Wessler, H. (1999), *Öffentlichkeit als Prozess. Deutungsstrukturen und Deutungswandel in der der Deutschen Drogenberichterstattung*, Opladen and Wiesbaden: Westdeutscher.

White, L. A. (2002), 'Ideas and the Welfare State: Explaining Child Care Policy Development in Canada and in the United States', *Comparative Political Studies*, 35: 6, pp. 713–743.

Note

1   The ideas of policy groups are advocated by individuals who act in their role as representatives of their organizations. This might cause role conflicts because a person as an individual does not necessarily support the same ideas as they do in their role as a representative of a group or an organization. As role theory has shown, such conflicts are normally minimized by recruiting employees sharing similar ideas and by the following process of socialization. Nevertheless, representatives always have a certain scope as regards how they fulfill their role.

Chapter 5

The Accountability and Legitimacy of Regulatory Agencies in the Communication Sector

Manuel Puppis & Martino Maggetti

Introduction

During the past 15 years, regulatory agencies have become key actors in the governance of different policy domains across Europe and beyond. The communication sector is no exception. Following the privatization of formerly state-owned enterprises in telecommunications and the liberalization of both telecommunications and broadcasting markets (Dyson and Humphreys 1989; Humphreys 1996; Schneider 1997; Schneider and Werle 2007), the re-regulation of the newly established competitive markets became necessary. In most countries, the responsibility for the regulation of both sectors has been delegated to the so-called independent regulatory agencies. A significant and increasing share of policy-making is thus carried out by organizations that are neither democratically elected nor directly accountable to elected politicians (Coen and Thatcher 2005; Gilardi 2008; Lodge 2004; Majone 1994, 1999; Vibert 2007).

However, previous communication policy research has only rarely dealt with these new policy-making actors. Despite some efforts (Robillard 1995), scholars have mainly focused either on liberalization and deregulation itself (Dyson and Humphreys 1989) or on best-practice models for regulation (Collins and Murroni 1996; Jarren et al. 2002; Latzer et al. 2002; Schulz and Held 2004). Furthermore, although the possible tension between delegation to independent regulatory agencies and democratic legitimacy has been widely discussed in political science studies (Lodge 2004; Scott 2000; Majone 2001; Maggetti 2010), the role of networks and communication has been disregarded so far.

In this conceptual article, we thus focus on accountability and legitimacy problems of regulatory agencies in the communication sector. The main argument put forward here is that regulatory networks and regulatory communication matter in understanding how regulators enhance their democratic accountability, which may eventually lead to legitimacy gains. On the one hand, we highlight that national regulatory agencies operate in a context of interdependence, as they are increasingly embedded in transnational networks of regulators. On the other hand, we discuss the importance of communication in times of mediatization.

In what follows, we firstly deal with definitions of regulatory agencies and touch upon the delegation of powers to as well as the independence of agencies. Secondly, we discuss their lack of democratic accountability and legitimacy. Thirdly, we focus on the contribution of regulatory networks and regulatory communication for solving this problem. Specifically, we draw on policy-diffusion theory and denationalization on the one hand and on new institutionalism in organization studies and mediatization on the other. Finally, a short conclusion emphasizes the importance and the benefits of analysing regulatory agencies.

Regulatory Agencies in a Nutshell

Regulatory Agencies in the Communication Sector

In a very general sense, an *agency* is a public-sector organization that is functionally disaggregated from the public administration and enjoys some degree of autonomy from the government, even though it cannot be fully independent (Christensen and Lægreid 2006: 12f; Maggetti 2007; Pollitt et al. 2004: 10; 2001: 274f; Talbot 2004: 5). One of the duties agencies may carry out is regulation (Christensen and Lægreid 2006: 13). Accordingly, Thatcher (2002b: 956) defines a *regulatory agency* as 'a body with its own powers and responsibilities given under public law, which is organizationally separated from ministries and is neither directly elected nor managed by elected officials.' Similarly, Jordana and Sancho (2004: 301) describe regulatory agencies as 'new specialized public bodies that guide and implement policy regulations, often combining legislative, executive and judicial functions.'

Although regulatory agencies are key actors in policy-making nowadays, they were established in Europe quite recently (Maggetti 2009). Following the liberalization and/or privatization of various economic sectors since the 1980s, regulatory agencies were created in order to regulate competition in the newly established markets (Gilardi 2008). The communication sector was no exception (Puppis 2009: 30f).

In *telecommunications*, the Postal, Telegraph and Telephone services (PTTs) were abolished, involving a separation of operational from regulatory functions. One the one hand, the former state monopolists were privatized and competition was introduced. On the other hand, independent sector-specific regulatory agencies were institutionalized in order to continue to uphold certain public-interest goals (e.g. universal service) and to prevent the incumbent from abusing its market power (Geradin and Kerf 2004: 130, 135):

> In a liberalized telecommunications environment the regulator invariably has to contend with peculiar problems posed by the inheritance from the past. The regulator does not inherit a 'level playing field' on which new firms of equal power compete freely, but a playing field on which one of the players – the old incumbent – is larger, richer and in almost all respects more powerful than the others. (Collins and Murroni 1996: 19)

The formation of independent regulatory agencies was called for by the WTO as well. Countries that committed to a liberalization of basic telecommunications services by signing the fourth protocol of the GATS also have to comply with certain regulatory principles, including a regulator that is separated from any supplier of basic telecommunications services.

In *broadcasting*, privatizations were rare and the liberalization was limited to the authorization of private (often commercial) broadcasters in most countries, resulting in so-called dual systems: 'There was limited political wish or will [...] to discard the existing public sector (broadcasting) or to harm various social and cultural interests. The sacrifice of monopoly was about as far as governments would go to create space for new competitors in the media marketplace' (Cuilenburg and McQuail 2003: 196). Although regulatory agencies have only limited powers in respect to public service broadcasters, they are usually responsible for licensing and supervising private broadcasters (Puppis 2010b: 110–114; Robillard 1995). In recent years, some countries have responded to the convergence of broadcasting and telecommunications by forming new 'single regulators' and merging hitherto separate agencies (e.g. OFCOM in the UK back in 2003).

The Delegation of Powers to Regulatory Agencies

Previous research on regulatory agencies in political science primarily dealt with the delegation of powers and the independence of agencies.

Although the rationales for regulating recently privatized and liberalized markets such as telecommunications and broadcasting are easily understandable, the decision to delegate regulatory competencies to agencies is a more complex phenomenon. The delegation of powers is often justified on *functional grounds*. Regulatory agencies are said to be more efficient than democratic institutions because of their isolation from partisan political pressures and their technical expertise (Bouckaert and Peters 2004: 39f; Jordana and Levi-Faur 2004: 12; Majone 1996a: 40f; Pollitt et al. 2004: 13; Thatcher 2002a: 105). However, what needs to be explained is not just why regulatory powers are delegated to an agent 'but why they are delegated to an independent agent' (Gilardi 2005a: 142), which is difficult for elected politicians to control. Hence it is also argued that delegating powers on the one hand allows governments to commit themselves credibly to certain regulatory measures and to make sure that their policy choices endure beyond future changes of government (Christensen and Lægreid 2006: 34; Gilardi 2004: 72ff; 2005a: 142f; 2005b: 87ff; Jordana and Levi-Faur 2004: 12; Majone 1996a: 44; Thatcher 2002a: 105). On the other hand, delegation is a means by which governments can 'shift blame' for unpopular decisions (Christensen and Lægreid 2006: 35; Thatcher 2002a: 105; 2002c: 131).

Nevertheless, cross-national and cross-sector variations in delegation suggest that functional advantages alone cannot explain the establishment of regulatory agencies (Thatcher 2002c: 136). Rather, country- and sector-specific characteristics need to be considered as well. For one thing, the establishment of regulatory agencies is argued as being part of a *path-dependent process*, as state traditions and structures strongly mediate functional pressures (Christensen and Lægreid 2006: 36; Gilardi 2004: 79ff). For another, *institutional isomorphism* within and between countries needs to be considered as well (Gilardi 2004: 75–79; Levi-Faur 2005: 26; Puppis 2009; Thatcher 2002c: 136f). Gilardi (2005b) documented how the creation of regulatory agencies in western Europe followed a coherent syndrome of diffusion: governments made decisions interdependently, according to an emulation process, where the symbolic properties of regulatory agencies appear to be more important than the functions they perform. More specifically, regulatory agencies became 'taken for granted' as the 'right' solution for implementing the new regulatory order. Agencies were established because they represent a socially valued organizational model that may increase the legitimacy of regulatory reforms in the view of policy-makers.

The Formal and Informal Independence of Regulatory Agencies

Apart from delegation, research in political science has mainly focused on the question of how independent regulatory agencies are. After all, independence from elected politicians and organized interests is the main characteristic of regulatory governance by agencies.

The concept of organizational independence was originally adopted to portray the institutional status of central banks (Rogoff 1985). In its most comprehensive version, the measure of central bank independence comprises two elements (Alesina and Summers 1993): political independence, defined as the ability to select policy objectives without influence from the government, and economic independence, that is, the ability to use instruments of monetary policy without restrictions. The seminal work by Gilardi (2002; 2008) drew inspiration from this approach to assess the *formal independence* of regulatory agencies, with reference to a series of prescriptions enshrined in the agencies' constitutions, which are supposed to guarantee independence from elected politicians. In his empirical research, he found that economic regulators, and especially those regulating utilities, are on average significantly more independent than agencies in charge of social regulation, such as food safety, pharmaceuticals and environment. Furthermore, regulators tend to be more independent in countries with fewer veto players and where political uncertainty is high (i.e. frequent changes of government). These results show that credibility, political uncertainty and veto players are important factors for the formal independence of regulators.

The concept of *de facto independence* extends the study of regulatory independence to its informal aspects. It is used to connote the extent of regulators' effective autonomy. In this sense, independence comprises the self-determination of agencies' preferences and their ability to execute the autonomous day-to-day activity of regulation (Maggetti 2007). Furthermore, the level of agencies' de facto independence should be conceived not only with reference to elected politicians but also with regard to the representatives of the sectors targeted by regulation, which constitute the 'second force' in regulation (Gilardi and Maggetti 2010; Thatcher 2005). Maggetti (2007) demonstrates that formal independence is neither a necessary nor a single sufficient condition to explain the variations in regulatory agencies' de facto independence from political decision-makers and regulatees. Instead, factors such as their life cycle, their inclusion in (European) networks of regulators and the presence of veto players must be taken into account. Additionally, it appears that regulatory agencies are also the most important actors in policy-making related to their area of competence. Exploratory evidence suggests that de facto independent regulatory agencies are particularly influential in policy-making. In fact, beyond their regulatory competencies, they frequently initiate, prepare and amend new pieces of legislation, especially where the legislature is weakly professionalized and lacks resources and expertise (Maggetti 2009).

Accountability and Legitimacy of Regulatory Agencies

Regulatory independence entails a specific shortfall that deserves special attention. In fact, the 'most persistent and fundamental criticisms of statutory regulation by independent agencies have been concerned [...] with the normative issues of public accountability and democratic legitimacy' (Majone 1996b: 284). The delegation of considerable public authority to independent regulatory agencies involves a reallocation of political power from democratic institutions to non-elected actors that are neither directly accountable to voters nor to elected officials (Majone 1996b: 285; 1999; Scott 2000). Although governments can transfer their powers to agencies, they cannot transfer their democratic legitimacy, which, in turn, leads to a net loss of legitimacy of regulatory governance (Majone 2005). The democratic deficit of the regulatory state is therefore immanent by design: regulatory agencies simply cannot rely on the *input legitimacy* ultimately generated by democratic elections.

Instead, regulatory agencies could try to rely on output (or substantial) legitimacy (Majone 1996b; Scharpf 1999). *Output legitimacy* refers to agencies' problem-solving capacity in terms of effectiveness and efficiency. The question of agencies' performance exceeds the scope of this article, but it is worth noting that empirical research has led to mixed and inconclusive results and that the legitimization strategies based on output legitimacy suffer from serious conceptual weakness (Maggetti 2010). The rest of this section is therefore devoted to the discussion of a third type of legitimacy, which stems from the procedural fairness of the regulatory process itself. The argument is that perceptions of procedural fairness will enhance acceptance of agencies' decisions, regardless of their content (Papadopoulos 2003). With respect to independent regulators, this *throughput legitimacy* may derive from the belief that they have neither been captured by particular interests nor are they completely out of control, but they are being held accountable for their decisions.

The concept of *accountability* refers to the need to control and restrain the exercise of political power and is often considered a necessary but insufficient component of legitimacy (Baldwin et al. 1998; Flinders and Buller 2006; Maggetti 2010). Accountability means that an actor in a position of responsibility in relation to the interests of another actor is required to give an account of the conduct of his duties while the second actor can either reward or sanction the former (Castiglione 2006). Bovens (2007: 450) emphasizes that accountability is 'a relationship between an actor and a forum, in which the actor has an obligation to explain and to justify his or her conduct, the forum can pose questions and pass judgment, and the actor may face consequences.'

The problem is that, as anticipated, agencies display specific constitutional features that challenge the traditional conception of political accountability. Most importantly, their formal independence from democratic institutions entails an inherently limited responsiveness to political decision-makers, which in turn implies a potential trade-off between agency independence and traditional forms of top-down and bottom-up accountability (Maggetti 2010). This trade-off should not be considered inevitable, as independence can to some extent be compatible with ex-post instruments that endeavour to promote accountability, such as ministerial oversight, parliamentary reporting, judicial review and openness to the public (Quintyn et al. 2007). However, given that the fragmentation and dispersion of political authority in the regulatory state is blurring – at least discursively – the traditional accountability structures and producing a situation of complex interdependence between the political decision-makers, the independent regulators and the private actors, then in practice the balance between autonomy and control seems very difficult to find (Scott 2000). This state of affairs might imply serious legitimacy concerns as well – in the sense of social acceptance of the regulatory order.

Consequently, we argue that agencies should rely on alternative and complementary accountability strategies, involving new accountability fora: the first is the participation in transnational networks, where agencies might become mutually accountable; the second is regulatory communication, involving openness, transparency and justification to the public.

Enhancing the Accountability and Legitimacy of Regulatory Agencies

Given the significance of these new political actors for the regulation of communication and the above-mentioned tensions between delegation and accountability, we aim at investigating the role of regulatory networks and regulatory communication in enhancing democratic accountability and legitimacy. In the following, the use of peer pressure and best practices within regulatory networks and regulatory communication will be dealt with.

Peer Pressure and Best Practices in Regulatory Networks

Nowadays, regulators in many sectors are members of regulatory networks. The creation of such networks is part of a denationalization process, which involves the transformation of the Westphalian order based on state sovereignty towards a multi-layer system where political power is increasingly spread across levels of governance, new patterns of decision-making emerge and new political actors are involved increasing the interdependence of policy-making.

The literature on multi-level governance points to the upward, downward and sideways reallocation of authority (Bache and Flinders 2005; Hooghe and Marks 2001; Peters and Pierre 2004). The shift of policy-making capacity towards regulatory networks corresponds to the third category of this typology, which concerns the development of horizontal, transnational, unelected bodies with considerable political and regulatory power (Slaughter 2004). For instance, domestic telecommunications and broadcasting regulators participate in networks such as the Independent Regulators Group and Body of European Regulators for Electronic Communications (IRG/BEREC) and the European Platform of Regulatory Authorities (EPRA). The IRG/BEREC is a hybrid network. It brings together bottom-up and top-down groups of national telecommunications regulators, which largely overlap. Bottom-up groups, such as IRG, are voluntary associations of national regulatory authorities with the aim of facilitating consultation, coordination, cooperation, information exchange and assistance among regulators. Top-down groups, such as BEREC (which recently replaced the European Regulators Group), were established through European Directives and Commission decisions in order to function as advisory bodies and foster harmonization of national regulations thanks to the development and enactment of 'soft law', such as standards, guidelines and recommendations. The EPRA is a weakly institutionalized network providing a discussion platform for broadcasting regulators. It operates externally and somewhat in parallel with European institutions, basically functioning as an open forum for information exchange and informal discussions among regulatory authorities in Europe and beyond.

Agencies within networks may develop common standards and take collective action, to be implemented at the domestic level. The IRG/BEREC has adopted several agreements, such as the 2003 implementation requirements for principles of mobile-call termination, concerning a maximum tariff to be charged by all the mobile-phone operators in member countries. What is more, agencies develop common positions in the form of analytical collections of 'remedies' adapted to each market situation, which enables national regulators to apply the same solutions to similar problems. The goal of the EPRA is less to harmonize rules than to offer a collective arena for sharing experiences and circulating information. A number of workshops with representatives of agencies and external experts are regularly organized at network level, dealing with diverse topics such as the protection of minors in public and private broadcasting and the concentration of the audio-visual market in relation with the need to preserve and enhance political pluralism in news coverage.

The crucial question is whether the embeddedness in networks may contribute to legitimacy. Although there is some reason to suspect that the specialist interaction with unelected peers in networks may de-politicize policy options and thus aggravate the problem of lacking input legitimacy (Michalis 2007: 213), networks potentially add to the promotion of accountability and, eventually, throughput legitimacy.

On the one hand, the emergence and ongoing consolidation of transnational networks of regulators could provide, 'as a more or less unintended by-product' (Majone 2000), incentives and means to agencies for the development of a system of mutual controls, producing a situation where 'no one controls the agency yet the agency is under control,' ideally making the agencies horizontally accountable (Moe 1985). In other words, networks could offer the leeway to secure accountability through reciprocal monitoring, by the means of a shift from democratic responsiveness to peer accountability. The extent to which this new form of procedural accountability can really enhance the legitimacy of the regulatory state in the eyes of stakeholders and citizens at large is still an open question.

On the other hand, their embeddedness in networks may provide regulators with additional dynamism, resources and expertise, and favour a process of policy diffusion, which is expected to follow rational and problem-solving orientations, eventually producing 'better' regulatory outputs. In particular, one could expect regulatory networks to promote the spread of 'best practices' among agencies through a mechanism of organizational learning, with actors updating their prior beliefs according to relevant information derived from the experience of other actors (Braun and Gilardi 2006). It is worth noting, again, that the effective development of this process should not be taken for granted nor is it directly observable, and it is likely to occur only under certain conditions, which remain to be empirically investigated (Maggetti and Gilardi 2010).

In sum, one should consider that these institutional arrangements could reinforce agencies' accountability and contribute to the social construction of their legitimacy (Black 2008). What is more, the system of reciprocal control could foster mutual adjustment in order to achieve both factual independence and credible/efficient regulation, reconciling throughput- and output-oriented legitimization strategies (Maggetti 2010). However, given that citizens provide the only actual source of legitimacy, another possible necessary condition for legitimizing agencies in the absence of democratic responsiveness is the transparency and openness of regulatory institutions, which are crucial requirements for the public scrutiny of regulatory governance. The next section will thus deal with regulatory communication.

Regulatory Communication

Not only the diffusion of best practices in regulatory networks but communication may indeed enhance the legitimacy of regulatory agencies.

Nowadays, *political communication* is an integral part of politics, as modern politics is mediated in the sense that the mass media mediate between the citizenry and political institutions (Hjarvard 2008: 114; Strömbäck 2008: 230; Strömbäck and Esser 2009: 207f):

> Communication, including mass mediated communication, is a necessary prerequisite for the functioning of any political system. Inputs to the political system – the demands of citizens as well as their expressions of system support – must be articulated by communication, channeled into the political arena by mass media, and converted into system output. In a similar way, system output – political decisions and actions – has to be communicated to the public, and in modern societies the mass media are essential for this function. (Mazzoleni and Schulz 1999: 250)

Despite the facts that regulatory agencies have become key political actors following the liberalization of markets in the 1980s and that political communication is an integral part of politics, regulatory communication marks a largely unexplored subject. It has been neglected to date by both political communication scholars and communication policy scholars. Neither have the former been particularly interested in regulators, nor have the latter cared much about communication. Few exceptions with a rather narrow focus aside (Coglianese and Howard 1998; Deacon and Monk 2001; Yeung 2009), research focusing on the regulators' communication is virtually nonexistent, least of all in the communication sector. Given the importance of regulatory agencies in policy-making, this seems rather surprising.

When looking at regulatory communication, it is important to recall that *regulatory agencies are organizations* (Black 2008; Morgan and Soin 1999; Puppis 2009). As Scott (1985: 304) put it, only then we are able 'to fully understand regulatory processes, their determinants and consequences.' *New institutionalism* in organization studies seems particularly well suited to analysing the legitimacy of regulatory organizations. In contrast to normative approaches in political theory, new institutionalism emphasizes the socially constructed nature of legitimacy. Legitimacy is rooted in the acceptance of an organization by others (Black 2008: 144). In other words, it 'is a generalized perception or assumption that the actions of an entity are desirable, proper, or appropriate within some socially constructed system of norms, values, beliefs, and definitions' (Suchman 1995: 574). New institutionalism specifically addresses this interdependence between organizations and their respective environments (Scott 2003). It stresses that organizations conform to their institutional environments in order to gain legitimacy (Baldwin and Cave 1999; Hall and Taylor 1996; Meyer and Rowan 1991; Scott 2001; Suchman 1995). Organizations receive legitimacy to the extent that their structures and practices fit 'rationalized myths' concerning the allegedly appropriate way to organize (Meyer and Rowan 1991; Scott 2003). This is especially important for regulatory organizations. On the one hand, regulators not only require others to accept them but to change their own behaviour: 'it is not enough that they are "generally accepted," they need to be actively supported' (Black 2008: 154). On the other hand, they produce outputs that are difficult to appraise. As a consequence, the structures and practices of regulatory organizations are mainly shaped by institutional environments in order to obtain the legitimacy they require for survival (Edelman and Suchman 1997; Meyer and Zucker 1989; Puppis 2009, 2010a).

Yet, what are institutions? Barley and Tolbert (1997: 96) define them as 'shared rules and typifications that identify categories of social actors and their appropriate activities or relationships.' According to Scott (2001), institutions are made up of a cultural–cognitive, a normative and a regulative pillar.

- The *cultural–cognitive pillar* of institutions refers to the way taken-for-granted assumptions and collectively shared understandings influence organizational structures and practices. Because of the shared nature of these common beliefs, alternatives are simply inconceivable.

- The *normative pillar* of institutions stresses the importance of values and norms. Certain structures and practices are implemented because of moral obligations: organizations try to conform to external expectations.
- The *regulative pillar* of institutions draws our attention to the coercive nature of institutional pressures. Structures and practices are implemented because non-conformity results in sanctions.

Suchman (1995) argues that, corresponding to these pillars, legitimacy may be cognitively, morally or pragmatically based.

Although the role of agency was first neglected in favour of a deterministic quality of institutions, more recently the argument has been put forward that organizations do not simply conform to institutional environments (Goodrick and Salancik 1996; Goodstein 1994; Scott and Davis 2007). Thus, new institutionalism draws our attention not only to the influence of institutional environments on organizational structures and practices but also to the way organizations *strategically respond* to these environments. The theory can incorporate 'both the ways in which legitimacy acts like a manipulable resource and the ways in which it acts like a taken-for-granted belief system' (Suchman 1995: 578). In her seminal paper, Oliver (1991) suggests distinguishing five strategic responses of organizations: acquiescence, compromise, avoidance, defiance and manipulation (see Table 1).

This means that regulatory organizations 'may attempt to create and manipulate others' perceptions of their legitimacy.' However, their scope for strategic action is not only bounded by their institutional environments but also limited to the normative and the regulative

Table 1: Strategic Responses to Institutional Requirements.

Strategies	Tactics	Examples
Acquiescence	Habit	Following invisible taken-for-granted rules
	Imitate	Imitating role models
	Comply	Voluntary compliance
Compromise	Balance	Balancing expectations of multiple constituents
	Pacify	Placating and accommodating institutional elements
	Bargain	Negotiating with institutional stakeholders
Avoidance	Conceal	Disguising non-conformity
	Buffer	Loosening institutional attachments
	Escape	Changing goals, activities or domains
Defiance	Dismiss	Ignoring norms
	Challenge	Contesting rules
	Attack	Attacking the sources of institutional pressure
Manipulation	Co-opt	Co-opting influential constituents
	Influence	Shaping values
	Control	Dominating institutional constituents

Source: based on Oliver (1991: 152).

pillars. Although a strategic management of cognitive legitimacy is beyond any organization's capabilities, regulators are able to manage their pragmatic and normative legitimacy (Black 2008: 147; Puppis 2009: 127).

Be that as it may, communication plays an important role in responding to institutional environments. As Black (2008: 149) elaborates, accountability relationships are a critical element in the construction and contestation of legitimacy claims. And accountability is closely connected to communication: 'In order to recognize just what "rendering account" can mean for an organization, we need […] an appreciation of the communicative structures in which accountability occurs' (Black 2008: 151). Legitimacy is thus essentially constructed by communication. Regulatory communication is at the same time influenced by institutional environments and a strategic device used to manipulate perceptions of a regulator's activities and performance.

Previous political and organizational communication research focusing on the communication by (political) organizations offers valuable contributions to such an organizational approach to regulatory communication. Lammers and Barbour (2006) discuss how institutions affect, and how they are affected by, organizational communication. And although political communication scholars for a long time have primarily dealt with questions of news content (mostly in the context of election campaigns), more recently they began to conceptualize political actors such as governments or parties as organizations. Donges (2008), for instance, investigated the influence of institutions on the communication structures and practices of political parties.[1] In this view, the media are part of the institutional environments of political organizations and thus affect their communication. Conceiving the media as institutions allows for conceptualizing the so-called *mediatization* of political communication as an interplay between political organizations and their institutional environments (Donges 2008; Hjarvard 2008; Schrott 2009).

Mediatization is said to go beyond mere mediation of politics (Hjarvard 2004: 47; Mazzoleni and Schulz 1999: 250). It is seen as a profound change that gives birth to a 'third age of political communication' (Blumler and Kavanagh 1999: 209), and refers to the impact of a media logic (as opposed to a political logic) on political communication (Altheide and Snow 1988: 195; Couldry 2008: 376; Hjarvard 2008: 113; Mazzoleni 2008: 3047; Strömbäck 2008: 233; Strömbäck and Esser 2009: 212f).[2] Mediation, then, is a prerequisite for mediatization. Moreover, the media have to attain autonomy as social institutions that operate according to their own logic (Asp and Esaiasson 1996: 81; Hjarvard 2008: 113; Lundby 2009: 8; Strömbäck 2008: 236f). The argument is that political actors adapt and adopt the logic of the media. In the first phase, because of the independence of the media, political actors have to adapt to its logic. However, the media logic is still perceived to be external to the political system. In the second phase, they internalize or adopt the media logic (Strömbäck 2008: 238ff).[3] This argument can be linked to the earlier discussion of different institutional pillars and the possibilities of organizations to respond strategically.

To sum up, it can be argued that institutional environments, including the media, affect the communication structure, practices and content of regulatory organizations through regulative pressures, normative expectations and taken-for-granted assumptions. At the same time, regulators are not determined by their institutional environments. Hence, their communication structures, practices and content may also be a strategic attempt to enhance legitimacy.

Conclusion

Regulatory agencies have become key actors in policy-making in the communication sector. In this conceptual article, we set out to discuss the role of networks and communication in enhancing the accountability and legitimacy of these regulators. Specifically, we first dealt with the question of whether the deployment of peer pressure and best practices within regulatory networks could reinforce the accountability of regulatory agencies. Secondly, we focused on the construction of legitimacy by communication, posing the questions of how institutional pressures such as mediatization influence regulatory communication and to what extent communication is a strategic device used to enhance legitimacy.

By drawing on policy-diffusion theory and denationalization on the one hand and on new institutionalism in organization studies and mediatization on the other, this article adds to previous research in several respects. Regarding political science, it offers valuable insights into the ways democratic accountability and legitimacy of regulators are created by the embeddedness into networks and communication. Regarding communication science, the article contributes to our knowledge of how key actors of media governance work and extends political communication research beyond traditional policy-making actors.

By presenting a theoretical approach on the role of networks and communication in enhancing the legitimacy of regulators in telecommunications and broadcasting, this paper takes a first step towards a better understanding of these powerful organizations.

Acknowledgements

This article is based on a research project funded by the Swiss National Science Foundation (SNF) in the framework of the 'National Center of Competence in Research (NCCR): Challenges to Democracy in the 21st Century' (NCCR Democracy).

References

Alesina, A. and Summers, L. (1993), 'Central Bank Independence and Macroeconomic Performance: Some Comparative Evidence', *Journal of Money, Credit and Banking*, 25: 2, pp. 151–162.
Altheide, D. L. and Snow, R. P. (1988), 'Toward a Theory of Mediation', in J. A. Anderson (ed.), *Communication Yearbook 11*, Newbury Park, Beverly Hills, London and New Delhi: Sage, pp. 194–223.

Asp, K. and Esaiasson, P. (1996), 'The Modernization of Swedish Campaigns: Individualization, Professionalization, and Medialization', in D. L. Swanson and P. Mancini (eds.), *Politics, Media, and Modern Democracy. An International Study of Innovations in Electoral Campaigning and Their Consequences*, Westport and London: Praeger, pp. 73–90.

Bache, I. and Flinders, M. (2005), *Multi-Level Governance*, Oxford and New York: Oxford University Press.

Baldwin, R. and Cave, M. (1999), *Understanding Regulation. Theory, Strategy, and Practice*, Oxford and New York: Oxford University Press.

Baldwin, R., Scott, C. and Hood, C. (1998), *A Reader on Regulation*, Oxford and New York: Oxford University Press.

Barley, S. R. and Tolbert, P. S. (1997), 'Institutionalization and Structuration: Studying the Links between Action and Institution', *Organization Studies*, 18: 1, pp. 93–117.

Black, J. (2008), 'Constructing and Contesting Legitimacy and Accountability in Polycentric Regulatory Regimes', *Regulation & Governance*, 2: 2, pp. 137–164.

Blumler, J. G. and Kavanagh, D. (1999), 'The Third Age of Political Communication: Influences and Features', *Political Communication*, 16: 3, pp. 209–230.

Bouckaert, G. and Peters, G. B. (2004), 'What Is Available and What Is Missing in the Study of Quangos?', in C. Pollitt and C. Talbot (eds.), *Unbundled Government. A Critical Analysis of the Global Trend to Agencies, Quangos and Contractualisation*, London and New York: Routledge, pp. 22–49.

Bovens, M. (2007), 'Analysing and Assessing Accountability: A Conceptual Framework', *European Law Journal*, 13: 4, pp. 447–468.

Braun, D. and Gilardi, F. (2006), 'Taking "Galton's Problem" Seriously: Towards a Theory of Policy Diffusion', *Journal of Theoretical Politics*, 18: 3, pp. 298–322.

Castiglione, D. (2006), 'Accountability', in M. Bevir (ed.), *Encyclopedia of Governance*, London: Sage, pp. 1–7.

Christensen, T. and Lægreid, P. (2006), 'Agencification and Regulatory Reforms', in T. Christensen and P. Lægreid (eds.), *Autonomy and Regulation. Coping with Agencies in the Modern State*, Cheltenham and Northampton: Edward Elgar, pp. 8–49.

Coen, D. and Thatcher, M. (2005), 'The New Governance of Markets and Non-Majoritarian Regulators', *Governance*, 18: 3, pp. 329–346.

Coglianese, C. and Howard, M. (1998), 'Getting the Message Out: Regulatory Policy and the Press', *The Harvard International Journal of Press/Politics*, 3: 3, pp. 39–55.

Collins, R. and Murroni, C. (1996), *New Media, New Policies. Media and Communications Strategies for the Future*, Cambridge: Polity Press.

Cook, T. E. (2006), 'The News Media as a Political Institution: Looking Backward and Looking Forward', *Political Communication*, 23: 2, pp. 159–171.

Couldry, N. (2008), 'Mediatization or Mediation? Alternative Understandings of the Emergent Space of Digital Storytelling', *New Media & Society*, 10: 3, pp. 373–391.

Deacon, D. and Monk, W. (2001), 'Quangos and the "Communications Dependent Society"', *European Journal of Communication*, 16: 1, pp. 25–49.

Donges, P. (2008), *Medialisierung Politischer Organisationen. Parteien in der Mediengesellschaft*, Wiesbaden: VS.

Dyson, K. and Humphreys, P. (1989), 'Deregulating Broadcasting. The West European Experience', *European Journal of Political Research*, 17: 2, pp. 137–154.

Edelman, L. B. and Suchman, M. C. (1997), 'The Legal Environments of Organizations', *Annual Review of Sociology*, 23, pp. 479–515.

Flinders, M. and Buller, J. (2006), 'Depoliticization, Democracy and Arena Shifting', in T. Christensen and P. Lægreid (eds.), *Autonomy and Regulation. Coping with Agencies in the Modern State*, Cheltenham and Northampton: Edward Elgar, pp. 53–80.

Geradin, D. and Kerf, M. (2004), 'Levelling the Playing Field: Is the WTO Adequately Equipped to Prevent Anti-Competitive Practices in Telecommunications?', in D. Geradin and D. Luff (eds.), *The WTO and Global Convergence in Telecommunications and Audio-Visual Services*, Cambridge: Cambridge University Press, pp. 130–162.

Gilardi, F. (2002), 'Policy Credibility and Delegation to Independent Regulatory Agencies: A Comparative Empirical Analysis', *Journal of European Public Policy*, 9: 6, pp. 873–893.

——— (2004), 'Institutional Change in Regulatory Policies: Regulation Through Independent Agencies and the Three New Institutionalisms', in J. Jordana and D. Levi-Faur (eds.), *The Politics of Regulation: Institutions and Regulatory Reform in the Age of Governance*, Cheltenham and Northampton: Edward Elgar, pp. 67–89.

——— (2005a), 'The Formal Independence of Regulators: A Comparison of 17 Countries and 7 Sectors', *Swiss Political Science Review*, 11: 4, pp. 139–167.

——— (2005b), 'The Institutional Foundations of Regulatory Capitalism: The Diffusion of Independent Regulatory Agencies in Western Europe', *The Annals of the American Academy of Political and Social Science*, 598, pp. 84–101.

——— (2008), *Delegation in the Regulatory State: Independent Regulatory Agencies in Western Europe*, Cheltenham: Edward Elgar.

Gilardi, F. and Maggetti, M. (2010), 'The Independence of Regulatory Authorities', in D. Levi-Faur (ed.), *Handbook of Regulation*, Cheltenham: Edward Elgar.

Goodrick, E. and Salancik, G. R. (1996), 'Organizational Discretion in Responding to Institutional Practices: Hospitals and Cesarean Births', *Administrative Science Quarterly*, 41: 1, pp. 1–28.

Goodstein, J. D. (1994), 'Institutional Pressures and Strategic Responsiveness: Employer Involvement in Work–Family Issues', *The Academy of Management Journal*, 37: 2, pp. 350–382.

Hall, P. A. and Taylor, R. C. R. (1996), 'Political Science and the Three New Institutionalisms', *Political Studies*, 44: 5, pp. 936–957.

Hjarvard, S. (2004), 'From Bricks to Bytes: The Mediatization of a Global Toy Industry', in I. Bondebjerg and P. Golding (eds.), *European Culture and the Media*, Bristol: Intellect, pp. 43–63.

——— (2008), 'The Mediatization of Society. A Theory of the Media as Agents of Social and Cultural Change', *Nordicom Review*, 29: 2, pp. 105–134.

Hooghe, L. and Marks, G. (2001), *Multi-Level Governance and European Integration*, Lanham: Rowman & Littlefield.

Humphreys, P. (1996), *Mass Media and Media Policy in Western Europe*, Manchester and New York: Manchester University Press.

Jarren, O., Weber, R. H., Donges, P., Dörr, B., Künzler, M. and Puppis, M. (2002), *Rundfunkregulierung. Leitbilder, Modelle und Erfahrungen im internationalen Vergleich. Eine sozial- und rechtswissenschaftliche Analyse*, Zürich: Seismo.

Jordana, J. and Levi-Faur, D. (2004), 'The Politics of Regulation in the Age of Governance', in J. Jordana and D. Levi-Faur (eds.), *The Politics of Regulation: Institutions and Regulatory Reform in the Age of Governance*, Cheltenham and Northampton: Edward Elgar, pp. 1–28.

Jordana, J. and Sancho, D. (2004), 'Regulatory Designs, Institutional Constellations and the Study of the Regulatory State', in J. Jordana and D. Levi-Faur (eds.), *The Politics of Regulation: Institutions and Regulatory Reform in the Age of Governance*, Cheltenham and Northampton: Edward Elgar, pp. 296–319.

Lammers, J. C. and Barbour, J. B. (2006), 'An Institutional Theory of Organizational Communication', *Communication Theory*, 16: 3, pp. 356–377.

Latzer, M., Just, N., Saurwein, F. and Slominski, P. (2002), *Selbst- und Ko-Regulierung im Mediamatiksektor. Alternative Regulierungsformen zwischen Staat und Markt*, Wiesbaden: Westdeutscher Verlag.

Levi-Faur, D. (2005), 'The Global Diffusion of Regulatory Capitalism', *The Annals of the American Academy of Political and Social Science*. 598, pp. 12–32.

Lodge, M. (2004), 'Accountability and Transparency in Regulation: Critiques, Doctrines and Instruments', in J. Jordana and D. Levi-Faur (eds.), *The Politics of Regulation: Institutions and Regulatory Reform in the Age of Governance*, Cheltenham and Northampton: Edward Elgar, pp. 124–144.

Lundby, K. (2009), 'Introduction: "Mediatization" as Key', in K. Lundby (ed.), *Mediatization. Concept, Changes, Consequences*, New York: Peter Lang, pp. 1–18.

Maggetti, M. (2007), 'De Facto Independence After Delegation: A Fuzzy-Set Analysis', *Regulation & Governance*, 1: 4, pp. 271–294.

_____ (2009), 'The Role of Independent Regulatory Agencies in Policy-Making: A Comparative Analysis', *Journal of European Public Policy*, 16: 3, pp. 445–465.

_____ (2010), 'Legitimacy and Accountability of Independent Regulatory Agencies: A Critical Review', *Living Reviews in Democracy*, 2, pp. 1–9.

Maggetti, M. and Gilardi, F. (2010), 'Establishing Regulatory Networks and the Diffusion of Best Practices', *Network Industries Quarterly*, 12: 2, pp. 10–13.

Majone, G. (1994), 'Independence Versus Accountability? Non-Majoritarian Institutions and Democratic Government in Europe', in J. J. Hesse and T. A. J. Thoonen (eds.), *The European Yearbook of Comparative Government and Public Administration*, Baden-Baden: Nomos, pp. 117–140.

_____ (1996a), 'Theories of Regulation', in G. Majone (ed.), *Regulating Europe*, London and New York: Routledge, pp. 28–46.

_____ (1996b), 'Regulatory Legitimacy', in G. Majone (ed.), *Regulating Europe*, London and New York: Routledge, pp. 284–301.

_____ (1999), 'The Regulatory State and Its Legitimacy Problems', *West European Politics*, 22: 1, pp. 1–24.

_____ (2000), 'The Credibility Crisis of Community Regulation', *Journal of Common Market Studies*, 38: 1, pp. 273–302.

_____ (2001), 'Regulatory Legitimacy in the United States and the European Union', in K. Nicolaidis and R. Howse (eds.), *The Federal Vision. Legitimacy and Levels of Governance in the United States and the European Union*, Oxford: Oxford University Press, pp. 252–274.

_____ (2005), 'Delegation of Powers and the Fiduciary Principle', *CONNEX Workshop*, Paris, France, 11 May.

Mazzoleni, G. (2008), 'Mediatization of Politics', in W. Donsbach (ed.), *The International Encyclopedia of Communication*, Malden and Oxford: Blackwell, pp. 3047–3051.

Mazzoleni, G. and Schulz, W. (1999), '"Mediatization" of Politics: A Challenge for Democracy?', *Political Communication*, 16: 3, pp. 247–261.

Meyer, J. W. and Rowan, B. (1991), 'Institutionalized Organizations: Formal Structure as Myth and Ceremony', in W. W. Powell and P. J. DiMaggio (eds.), *The New Institutionalism in Organizational Analysis*, Chicago and London: University of Chicago Press, pp. 41–62.

Meyer, M. W. and Zucker, L. G. (1989), *Permanently Failing Organizations*, Newbury Park, London and New Delhi: Sage.

Michalis, M. (2007), *Governing European Communications. From Unification to Coordination*, Lanham: Lexington Books.

Moe, T. M. (1985), 'Control and Feedback in Economic Regulation: The Case of the NLRB', *American Political Science Review*, 79: 4, pp. 1094–116.

Morgan, G. and Soin, K. (1999), 'Regulatory Compliance', in G. Morgan and L. Engwall (eds.), *Regulation and Organizations. International Perspectives*, London and New York: Routledge, pp. 166–190.

Oliver, C. (1991), 'Strategic Responses to Institutional Processes', *The Academy of Management Review*, 16: 1, pp. 145–179.

Papadopoulos, Y. (2003), 'Cooperative Forms of Governance: Problems of Democratic Accountability in Complex Environments', *European Journal of Political Research*, 42: 4, pp. 473–501.

Peters, B. G. and Pierre, J. (2004), *Politicization of the Civil Service in Comparative Perspective: The Quest for Control*, London: Routledge.

Pollitt, C., Bathgate, K., Caulfield, J., Smullen, A. and Talbot, C. (2001), 'Agency Fever? Analysis of an International Policy Fashion', *Journal of Comparative Policy Analysis: Research and Practice*, 3: 3, pp. 271–290.

Pollitt, C., Talbot, C., Caulfield, J. and Smullen, A. (2004), *Agencies. How Governments do Things Through Semi-Autonomous Organizations*, Basingstoke and New York: Palgrave Macmillan.

Puppis, M. (2009), *Organisationen der Medienselbstregulierung. Europäische Presseräte im Vergleich*, Köln: Halem.

_____ (2010a), 'Media Governance: A New Concept for the Analysis of Media Policy and Regulation', *Communication, Culture & Critique*, 3: 2, pp. 134–149.

_____ (2010b), *Einführung in die Medienpolitik*, 2nd edition, Konstanz: UVK.

Quintyn, M., Ramirez, S. L. and Taylor, M. (2007), 'The Fear of Freedom. Politicians and the Independence and Accountability of Financial Supervisors', in D. Masciandaro and M. Quintyn (eds.), *Designing Financial Supervision Institutions: Independence, Accountability and Governance*, Cheltenham: Edward Elgar, pp. 63–116.

Robillard, S. (1995), *Television in Europe: Regulatory Bodies. Status, Function and Powers in 35 European Countries*, London: John Libbey.

Rogoff, K. (1985), 'The Optimal Degree of Commitment to an Intermediate Monetary Target', *Quarterly Journal of Economics*, 100: 4, pp. 1169–1189.

Ryfe, D. M. (2006), 'Guest Editor's Introduction: New Institutionalism and the News', *Political Communication*, 23: 2, pp. 135–144.

Scharpf, F. (1999), *Governing in Europe: Effective and Democratic?*, Oxford: Oxford University Press.

Schneider, V. (1997), 'Privatisierung und Regulierung in der Telekommunikation aus politikwissenschaftlicher Perspektive', in K. König and A. Benz (eds.), *Privatisierung und staatliche Regulierung. Bahn, Post und Telekommunikation, Rundfunk*, Baden-Baden: Nomos, pp. 248–261.

Schneider, V. and Werle, R. (2007), 'Telecommunications Policy', in P. Graziano and M. Vink (eds.), *Europeanization: New Research Agendas*, Basingstoke: Palgrave Macmillan, pp. 266–280.

Schrott, A. (2009), 'Dimensions: Catch-All Label or Technical Term', in K. Lundby (ed.), *Mediatization. Concept, Changes, Consequences*, New York: Peter Lang, pp. 41–61.

Schulz, W. and Held, T. (2004), *Regulated Self-Regulation as a Form of Modern Government. An Analysis of Case Studies from Media and Telecommunications Law*, Eastleigh: John Libbey.

Scott, C. (2000), 'Accountability in the Regulatory State', *Journal of Law and Society*, 27: 1, pp. 38–60.

Scott, W. R. (1985), 'Comment [on: Caplow, Theodore: Conflicting Regulations. Six Small Studies and an Interpretation]', in R. G. Noll (ed.), *Regulatory Policy and the Social Sciences*, Berkley, Los Angeles and London: University of California Press, pp. 304–311.

———— (2001), *Institutions and Organizations*, 2nd edition, Thousand Oaks, London and New Delhi: Sage.

———— (2003), *Organizations. Rational, Natural, and Open Systems*, 5th edition, Upper Saddle River: Prentice Hall.

Scott, W. R. and Davis, G. F. (2007), *Organizations and Organizing. Rational, Natural, and Open System Perspectives*, Upper Saddle River: Pearson Prentice Hall.

Slaughter, A. (2004), *A New World Order*, Princeton: Princeton University Press.

Sparrow, B. H. (2006), 'A Research Agenda for an Institutional Media', *Political Communication*, 23: 2, pp. 145–157.

Strömbäck, J. (2008), 'Four Phases of Mediatization: An Analysis of the Mediatization of Politics', *The International Journal of Press/Politics*, 13: 3, pp. 228–246.

Strömbäck, J. and Esser, F. (2009), 'Shaping Politics: Mediatization and Media Interventionism', in K. Lundby (ed.), *Mediatization. Concept, Changes, Consequences*, New York: Peter Lang, pp. 205–223.

Suchman, M. C. (1995), 'Managing Legitimacy: Strategic and Institutional Approaches', *The Academy of Management Review*, 20: 3, pp. 571–610.

Talbot, C. (2004), 'The Agency Idea. Sometimes Old, Sometimes New, Sometimes Borrowed, Sometimes Untrue', in C. Pollitt and C. Talbot (eds.), *Unbundled Government. A Critical Analysis of the Global Trend to Agencies, Quangos and Contractualisation*, London and New York: Routledge, pp. 3–21.

Thatcher, M. (2002a), 'Analysing Independent Regulatory Agencies in Western Europe: Functional Pressures Mediated by Context', *Swiss Political Science Review*, 8: 1, pp. 103–110.

_____ (2002b), 'Regulation after Delegation: Independent Regulatory Agencies in Europe', *Journal of European Public Policy*, 9: 6, pp. 954–972.

_____ (2002c), 'Delegation to Independent Regulatory Agencies: Pressures, Functions and Contextual Mediation', *West European Politics*, 25: 1, pp. 125–147.

_____ (2005), 'The Third Force? Independent Regulatory Agencies and Elected Politicians in Europe', *Governance*, 18: 3, pp. 347–373.

Van Cuilenburg, J. and McQuail, D. (2003), 'Media Policy Paradigm Shifts. Towards a New Communications Policy Paradigm', *European Journal of Communication*, 18: 2, pp. 181–207.

Vibert, F. (2007), *The Rise of the Unelected*, Cambridge: Cambridge University Press.

Yeung, K. (2009), 'Presentational Management and the Pursuit of Regulatory Legitimacy: A Comparative Study of Competition and Consumer Agencies in the United Kingdom and Australia', *Public Administration*, 87: 2, pp. 274–294.

Notes

1   It is more common in political communication research to focus on news organizations and how their institutional environments, by way of taken-for-granted organizational routines and practices of journalism, lead to homogenous news content (Cook 2006; Ryfe 2006; Sparrow 2006).

2   Very often, it is suggested that mediatization has problematic consequences for democratic processes (e.g. Mazzoleni and Schulz 1999: 249). However, any definition of mediatization should be non-normative (Hjarvard 2008: 114; Strömbäck 2008: 230). It is an empirical question whether mediatization indeed takes place and what its effects are.

3   In this regard, it is also possible to distinguish between direct and indirect mediatization. On the one hand, political communication is transferred from non-mediated settings to media environments. On the other hand, the media logic also influences non-mediated forms of political communication (Hjarvard 2004: 49; 2008: 114f).

Chapter 6

Change and Divergence in Regulatory Regimes:
A Comparative Study of Product Placement Regulation

Avshalom Ginosar

Introduction

Product placement – the purposeful incorporation of commercial content into non-commercial settings – has a long history. It was first widely used in the movie industry in the early twentieth century and then also in commercial advertisements in the early days of American television (Newell et al. 2006; Russell and Belch 2005). Despite these early origins, product placement remained a marginal source of advertising revenue until the late 1980s. Compulsory license fees (in the case of publicly owned channels) and spot advertising (in the case of commercial television) were and still are the major sources of funding for broadcasters. Four major changes in the technological and business environments led to a search for alternative sources of revenue for commercial broadcasting. First, the digital revolution enables viewers to access hundreds of television channels. This in turn makes it much more difficult and less useful to address the various television audiences with the same spot advertisements (Russell and Belch 2005; Tiwsakul et al. 2005). Secondly, new recording machines that enable viewers to skip advertisements make spot advertising less effective (Schejter 2007; Wenner 2004). Thirdly, the Internet has introduced competition from a new medium, which is attracting advertisers' attention and a growing share of their budgets. Fourthly, product placement may prove to be easier and cheaper to produce than spot advertisements (Avery and Ferraro 2000). For these reasons advertisers and broadcasters have gradually increased their use of product placement.[1]

This growing market has prompted regulators worldwide to pay much more attention to product placement. Three concerns in particular have been raised in the discussion on the governance of product placement: undue influence on viewers, the integrity of journalistic values and creative independence. The first concern is that audiences cannot always adequately distinguish between commercial content and editorial content. Thus, Balasubramanian (1994: 29f) refers to product placement as a 'hybrid message,' and Avery and Ferraro (2000: 217f) claim that it poses 'a question of deception.' Schejter (2006: 4) asserts that it is 'a message chosen by advertisers in a context designed to mislead audience about their control over the content.' This raises the question of whether the viewers should always have the right to know when and by whom they are being influenced (Avery and Ferraro 2000; Balasubramanian 1994). This is clearly associated with two sensitive issues: first, because a product placement is not clearly identified as an advertisement and in many cases the product or service is associated with television and movie stars, children are especially vulnerable to manipulation (Stinger 2006). Secondly, product placement might involve contentious products such as tobacco, alcohol and high-fat food. Public concerns have also been raised with respect to editorial, journalistic and creative independence (Baerns 2003; Wenner 2004). As a product is embedded within the programme's script, advertisers may want to adapt the script as much as possible to their commercial interests and are willing to pay for it. This is a temptation for producers who would like to reduce their costs. In this way, the advertiser can gain significant influence over a programme's content, which would reduce the responsibility and the independence of the creators.

Policy-makers and regulators worldwide have responded differently to the challenges listed earlier. Some perceive product placement as just another legitimate source of revenue, others see it as synonymous with surreptitious advertising and thus prohibit it altogether. Others again distinguish between product placement that amounts to surreptitious advertising (which should be prohibited) and product placement that is identifiable as such by the audience (which should be permitted).

This study examines the policy processes that in 2007 led to the creation of three product placement regimes in the European Union,[2] Canada and Israel. Whereas the new regimes in the EU and Israel can be characterized as restrictive and socially oriented, the Canadian regime is oriented towards commercial interests and has permissive guidelines and regulations. Three main questions are raised:

(1) What forces and actors have shaped the product placement regimes in each of the three cases?
(2) What are the similarities and differences between the three product placement regimes?
(3) Why do the EU and Israel, which have similar regimes, differ from the Canadian regime?

Following the analysis and the comparison among the three new regimes, two explanatory approaches are suggested for understanding and explaining the similarities and differences among them: the actor-centred approach and the new institutionalism.

Product Placement Regulations

Before 2007, product placement was governed in the European Union, Israel and Canada by general provisions of the advertising regimes. The EU's old advertising regime was part of the Television Without Frontiers (TVWF) directive published in 1989 (Council Directive 89/552/EEC) and was amended in June 1997 by the EC Directive 97/36/EC. In Canada it is necessary to refer both to state regulation and voluntary industry regulation.[3] The Canadian Radio, Television and Telecommunication Commission (CRTC) is the state regulator that implements the 1987 Television Broadcasting Regulations; the two relevant self-regulatory authorities are Advertising Standards Canada (ASC) and the Canadian Association of Broadcasters (CAB), both with codes addressing certain aspects of advertising. In Israel the advertising regime is reflected in two different systems of legislation:

(1) The 1982 Communication Law (Telecommunication and Broadcasting) ('The Bezeq Law'), which governs the cable and satellite channels and is administered by the Council for Cables and Satellite.
(2) The Second Authority for Radio and Television Law of 1990, which governs the commercial channels and is administered by the Second Authority for Radio and Television.

Both of these authorities have published detailed rules to implement the above laws.

Product placement is not explicitly mentioned in the documents mentioned earlier. However, three principles that are major parts of EU and Israeli regulations can be indirectly associated with product placement:

(1) The obligation to identify any commercial message;
(2) The obligation to separate any advertising from any other content; and
(3) Total prohibition of surreptitious advertising.

These principles completely contradict the very essence of product placement: embedding commercial messages within programme content without identifying it as such, and/or separating it from the editorial content. This is not the case in the old Canadian regime, where the three principles are not explicit components of the statutory advertising regulation and are only partially and indirectly referred to within the self-regulation codes.

The references to product placement within the old advertising regimes are the baselines of the new product placement regimes that emerged during 2007 in each of the three constituencies. In each case, the new regimes are the outcomes of long and detailed policy processes.[4] The new product placement regimes are reflected in the regulators' formal documents in each case: in Europe, the Audio-Visual Media Service Directive (AVMSD; Directive 2007/65/EC published on 11 December 2007 and codified in March 2010 as Directive 2010/13/EU); in Canada: in 'Determinations Regarding Certain Aspects of the Regulatory Framework for Over-the-Air Television' (Broadcasting Public Notice CRTC 2007-53), published on 17 May 2007; in Israel two documents are relevant: Resolution No. 1-27-2005 of the Council for Cables and Satellite, 12 December 2005, and the Kasher Committee report, which was submitted in January 2007 and approved by the Second Authority for Radio and Television on 25 February 2007.[5]

Although the new European regime explicitly prohibits the use of product placement (Article 11(2) Directive 2010/13/EU), it allows it under several restrictive conditions. Firstly, product placement is permitted only in certain programmes (Article 11(3) Directive

2010/13/EU). Secondly, there are certain limitations even in programmes in which product placement is permitted (Article 11(3) Directive 2010/13/EU):

- Product placement shall not influence the responsibility and editorial independence of the broadcaster;
- Product placement shall not directly encourage the purchase or rent of goods or services;
- Product placement shall not give undue prominence to the product; and
- Viewers shall be clearly informed of the existence of product placement by announcements at the start and the end of the programme.

Thirdly, product placement for certain harmful products is prohibited (Article 11(4) Directive 2010/13/EU). It can be argued that the new European product placement regime is more liberal than the old one, yet it is still very restrictive. Furthermore, the new directive enables EU member states to continue the old policy of total prohibition of product placement. Alternatively, it allows stricter rules in any decision to permit the practice (Article 4(1) Directive 2010/13/EU). This means that the long list of restrictions included in the AVMSD are merely minimum standards.[6]

Unlike in Europe, the new Canadian regulations do not directly address product placement and its social and cultural implications. The only reference to the practice in the new CRTC policy document is to the effect that product placement (like other non-traditional forms of advertising) is not considered when calculating the total permitted advertising time that can be broadcast (Article 43 Broadcasting Public Notice CRTC 2007-53). For Canadian broadcasters, product placement becomes an additional source of revenue without any restrictions. It is worth noting that the de-regulation of non-traditional advertising, including product placement, is just a part of a new advertising policy that gradually eliminates any limitation on the amount of advertising permitted. In addition, there has been no revision of the ASC code (the industry self-regulation code) following the policy process handled by the CRTC.

The new Israeli product placement regime[7] does not entirely prohibit the use of the practice although it sets a long line of restrictions. These can be classified into seven main categories: restrictions on programmes; the duty of identification; limitation on the financing of a programme through product placements; the duty to preserve editorial independence; restrictions on the length and the number of occasions in which a product or a service would be presented; the obligation to broadcast informative/explanatory messages before the first placement; restrictions on certain programmes and products. Both Israeli regimes can be characterized as restrictive, but neither is implemented. As for the Council for Cables and Satellite, the new regulations were approved only for a six-month trial period, which ended on 30 June 2006, and since then they have not been re-approved. Currently the council implements the traditional approach towards product placement, meaning a prohibitive policy.[8] As to the Second Authority, the new regime has not been implemented yet because the regulator made implementation conditional on new parliamentary legislation that would enable the authority to seriously fine broadcasters for violation of the new regulation. Bureaucratic and political reasons mean that such legislation has not yet been completed. Currently the policy is in accordance with the Rules for Ethics in Advertising (1994), which implicitly prohibit the use of product placement.[9]

In the next sections, two explanatory approaches – the actor-centred approach and the new institutionalism – are employed in order to provide a convincing explanation for the similarities and differences among the regimes.

The Actor-Centred Explanation: Sectors and Positions

The actor-centred approach suggests that actors' interests are the dominant factor within a policy process and its outcomes, and might provide a sufficient explanation for the similarities and differences among regimes. Each of these actors has a different agenda they wish to impose on all the others, and each has a different competence and political ability. The outcome of a policy process reflects the balance that was achieved among the various groups according to each group's (or coalitions of groups) ability to meet its interests (Peltzman 1976; Posner 1974; Stigler 1971).

Based on the approach given earlier, the first hypothesis regarding similarities and differences among the three regimes is:

> The relatively conservative restrictive regimes in the EU and Israel reflect the strength of actors who expressed *public interests* and defended them, while the relatively liberal–permissive regime in Canada reflects the strength of business actors who succeeded in protecting their *self-interest* (mainly financial interests).

In each of the three policy processes the positions the actors submitted were analysed with respect to their sector affiliation in order to validate or falsify this hypothesis. The positions were classified according to two categories: liberal versus conservative;[10] the sector classification was into eight categories: citizen/experts, state actors, non-governmental organizations (NGOs), public broadcasters, private broadcasters and producers, advertising companies and associations, trade unions and associations, and other business (including other media organizations).

A total of 177 position papers were submitted to the EU Commission's public consultation in 2005, of which 154 were analysed.[11] Of these, 78 papers (51%) included positions on product placement. In the Canadian case, 110 position papers were submitted to the CRTC's public hearing in 2006, but only 24 of them (22%) included actors' positions on product placement. In Israel, the Kasher Committee (nominated by the Second Authority for Radio and Television) heard 39 positions, of which 27 were analysed.[12] Six positions of committee members (out of eight), who represented various interest groups and expressed their positions during the committee's sessions, were added to the analysis,[13] bringing the total number of actors' positions analysed to 33.

The initial analysis regarding actors' positions on product placement (presented in Table 1) reveals that:

- In Europe and in Israel the vast majority of actors supported the conservative–restrictive position (allowing the use of product placement only under certain conditions or prohibiting it altogether).
- In Canada most of the actors favoured the liberal–permissive approach (excluding product placement and other non-traditional advertising from the calculation of the total amount of advertising permitted or eliminating all limitations on the amount of advertising).

It is quite outstanding that the dominant position in each of the three cases gained overwhelming support (94% in Europe, 88% in Israel, and 87% in Canada) from the participants, which implies that there is a 'constituency position' towards product placement.

The positions associated with the actors' categories are more significant (see Table 2). In Europe, only a third of private broadcasters and producers (who are the direct beneficiaries of product placement) and only one in eight (12%) trade unions and associations supported the liberal approach. But the majority within these two groups and all the other groups of actors (including actors from the advertising industry) supported the more restrictive approach. This picture is identical in Israel: only one actor in five (20%) from the advertising industry and only two in six (33%) trade union actors supported the liberal position. All the other groups (excluding one state actor) supported the more conservative approach. A mirror image was found in Canada: only one NGO (of two) and only two trade union organizations (of five) supported the restrictive position. All the other actors, even a state actor and a public broadcaster, supported the liberal position.

In summary, actors' positions in the three cases differ across constituencies rather than across interest groups and converge in each constituency, regardless of actors' sectors. These findings falsify the hypothesis presented earlier: the supposed dominance of a certain coalition of actors (public/civil or business) in each jurisdiction does not explain the outcome

Table 1: Actors' Positions on Product Placement.

	N	Liberal Position	Conservative Position
Europe	78	6%	94%
Israel	33	12%	88%
Canada	24	87%	13%

Source: Positions papers submitted to the European Commission's public consultation in 2005, to the Canadian Public hearing of 2006 and protocols of the Kasher Committee.

Table 2: Positions by Actors' Categories.

Actors' sector	N	Europe Liberal position	Conservative position	N	Israel Liberal position	Conservative position	N	Canada Liberal position	Conservative position
Citizen/ Experts	–	–	–	5	–	100%	1	100%	–
State	11	–	100%	8	12%	88%	1	100%	–
NGO	13	–	100%	1	–	100%	2	50%	50%
Public Broadcasters	6	–	100%	2	–	100%	1	100%	–
Private Broadcasters & Producers	14	29%	71%	6	–	100%	11	100%	–
Advertising Firms & Associations	7	–	100%	5	20%	80%	1	100%	–
Trade Unions & Associations	8	12%	88%	6	33%	67%	5	60%	40%
Other Business	19	–	100%	–	–	–	2	100%	–
Total	78	6%	94%	33	12%	88%	24	87%	13%

Source: Position papers submitted to European Commission's public consultation in 2005 and to the Canadian public hearing of 2006 and the Kasher Committee's protocols.

of the policy process. It can therefore be argued that an actor-centred approach can explain neither the variations in the preferences of business actors across the three constituencies nor the convergence among the actors within each constituency during the policy process.

The Institutional Explanation: Framing the Issue

While referring to institutional factors as possible explanations for the findings given earlier, it might be useful to address the framing process of the issue in each case. Framing, as Rein and Schön argue, 'leads to different views of the world and creates multiple social realities' (1991: 264). Framing means 'to select some aspects of perceived reality and make them more salient' (Entman, 1993: 55). Kohler-Koch (2000) adds that framing is a process of discrimination among competing frames. To frame problems in particular ways (meaning, choosing a certain frame) restricts policy choices and makes a particular policy outcome more likely (Mazey and Richardson 1997).

In this case study, facing the new reality of product placement, the relevant actors – public and industrial – were forced to pay attention to the practice. Yet, they could do it in different ways, employing different frames of the issue. Based on this idea, the second hypothesis for the similarities and differences among the regimes is:

> The relatively conservative–restrictive regimes in the EU and Israel reflect the fact that product placement was framed as *a problem* against which viewers and creators have to be protected, while the relatively liberal–permissive regime in Canada reflects the fact that product placement was framed as *a solution* for the broadcasting industry's need for new source of revenue.

The framing of the issue in each case is reflected in the regulators' policy documents, which are significant milestones throughout the policy processes. The analysis therefore aims to expose the frame of the issue as it is expressed in each of these documents.

The framing process in the EU is reflected mainly within two documents. The first is the working paper of Focus Group No. 2, which the EU Commission established in 2004 following a public consultation in 2003. This group dealt with the 'Level of detail in regulation of television advertising.' The second document is Issue Paper No. 4, 'Commercial Communications.' This was one of the six papers that the Commission published following the focus groups' work and before the September 2005 Liverpool conference 'Between Culture and Commerce.' These two documents are most relevant because they openly reveal the commission's policy preferences regarding the issue. They set the background for the 2005 public consultation and for the commission's proposal for the revision of the TVWF directive (Commission of the European Communities 2005).

The focus group's paper, 'Protection of Viewers and Rights Holders' (in provision 3.1), addresses the principle of 'being able to recognize and distinguish advertising from editorial content' in order 'to make sure that viewers do not confuse commercial and editorial content.' Without mentioning product placement explicitly, relying on the 2003 public consultation, the paper states that the principle (of identifying and separating commercial messages) 'remains valid.' In a clearer reference to product placement, but still refraining from mentioning the practice as such, the paper addresses the prohibition of surreptitious advertising. The question introduced in this respect is: 'Should this provision [of the TVWF directive] be maintained or clarified in the light of the principle of the recognizability and separation of advertising?' In other words, advertisements that are not identified as such and are not separated, as well as surreptitious advertisements, are referred to as regulatory problems. Unlike the focus group's paper, the issue paper refers directly and explicitly to product placement in two ways: its definition as 'commercial communication' and its direct linkage to the principles of identification and separation. It suggests a new definition of 'audio-visual commercial communication' that consists of all kinds of advertising, including product placement. In addition, all kinds of advertising will be subject to the same rules, including the identification principle (pp. 2ff). In other words, in this paper, product placement is addressed as a reality that has to be taken into consideration, but the main (in fact, the only) concern is how to protect the audience from its surreptitious use.

In Israel as in Europe, product placement was framed as a problem. There are two types of relevant documents investigating the framing processes:

(1) Two internal reports: the 'Shemesh report', which was submitted to the Council for Cables and Satellite, and the 'Elefent-Lefler report', submitted to the Second Authority for Radio and Television;

(2) The formal resolution by each regulator through which the policy process was initiated.

The Shemesh report addresses product placement in television programmes as a fact of life and as a necessity for the broadcasting industry. The report states (p. 37) that product placement has a benefit not just for the industry but for the public as well, by enabling financial support for local production. However, the report's main recommendations address the need to protect both the viewers and the creative/artistic contents. It suggests a long line of restrictions on applying product placement in order to meet protection needs (pp. 37ff). In the same vein, the Elefent-Lefler report introduces product placement as a regulatory problem but it does it in a more specific approach. The emphasis is on identifying product placement with prohibited, surreptitious advertising, while referring to the need to protect both audience and creators from this kind of advertising (p. 4). In its resolution (4 September 2005), the authority nominated a public committee to address, investigate and submit recommendations regarding product placement regulations. Less than a year earlier, the same committee (with a minor change of its members) had submitted recommendations regarding advertising ethics. The authority's choice to nominate the ethics committee to advise on product placement regulations strengthens the observation that the authority considers product placement as a problem that has to be considered according to some ethical considerations. And indeed, one of the first steps of the public committee (the Kasher Committee) was to introduce a list of 'relevant considerations' regarding product placement regulations (provision 4 of the committee report). Only one of the 12 considerations suggested in that list addresses the economic aspect of product placement. All the others refer to various rights of the viewers and to their expectations of television programmes. It seems that the Kasher Committee draws clear borders in its investigation of the issue of product placement: although the practice is considered to be a reality and a necessity for the well-being of the industry, the social, cultural and ethical implications are regarded as fundamental elements of the discussion. These borders are even more explicit and sharp in the other Israeli regulator's policy process. In its resolution (7 July 2004), the Council for Cables and Satellite published a call for positions in which the stakeholders were asked to address certain questions about product placement regulations. These questions clearly reveal the council's framing of the issue: product placement is a reality but it has to be restricted in various ways because of its negative socio-cultural implications – meaning product placement is a problem that has to be solved. These are the council's main questions: whether and how to inform the viewers of the presence of product placement, whether the regulator should restrict product placement with regard to certain programmes and/or certain audiences (such as children), whether the amount of product placement should be restricted, etc.

Unlike the EU and the Israeli cases, the Canadian regulator (CRTC) framed the issue of product placement as one solution to the financial needs of the broadcasting industry. In its notice of the 2006 public hearing (which started the policy process in Canada), the CRTC introduced four objectives, two of which are related to the ability of broadcasters to broadcast 'high quality Canadian programming' (Broadcasting Notice of Public Hearing CRTC 2006-5, provision 23).[14] Objective B introduces a direct linkage between the obligation to broadcast Canadian programmes and the need to enhance the economic strength of Canadian broadcasters. The CRTC then asks whether it should 'consider restricting its limitation of twelve advertising minutes per hour to traditional commercial messages inserted as breaks in the program schedule' (provision 39 (a)). The CRTC explains that, according to its regulations (from 1987), non-traditional advertising, including product placement, should be included within the 12-minute limitation, but that 'both advertisers and broadcasters have raised concerns about the continuing effectiveness of traditional advertising messages' (provision 33). In short, when addressing the stakeholders, the Canadian regulator frames the issue by referring to product placement as a source of revenue in order to enable the industry to broadcast 'high-quality Canadian programming.' There is no reference at all, within this notice, to other social considerations. Product placement is thus seen as a solution (a source of revenue) and not as a problem, as it was in the EU and Israel.

The framing of product placement by the regulator in each constituency sets the boundaries of the discussion: product placement as a problem (EU and Israel) and as a solution (Canada). Most of the stakeholders' positions were within these boundaries, as is presented in the next section.

The Discourses: Following the Framing[15]

It is understandable that Canadian broadcasting organizations in the over-the-air (OTA) industry, such as CanWest MediaWorks, CTV and Corus Entertainment, have cited the need for new sources of revenue as the main argument for liberalizing advertising regulation, including exempting non-traditional advertising (including product placement) from the 12-minute limit. For example, here is the highlight of CanWest MediaWorks:

> While advertising regulation in Canada has evolved, it has not evolved nearly enough in the sector that relies on it most. [...] At this time, we recommend the following changes to the Regulations respecting advertising: the elimination of any restrictions regarding non-traditional advertising, including, but not limited to, brand integration and/or product placement within a program, virtual advertising, and all forms of sponsorship.

The same position was expressed even by competitors of the OTA television industry, such as cable companies and associations: Bell Canada, Shaw Communications, Telco TV and Quebecor Media. Even independent broadcasters, such as Independent Specialties, Astral Media, Independent Small Market TV Broadcasters, and Alliance Atlantis Communications expressed the same view. Bell Canada is a good example of these actors' views:

> Bell urges the Commission to consider relaxing its definition of advertising to exclude non-traditional ads, such as product mentions and placements, from the ambit of the twelve-minute limit. This would simplify the Commission's task of policing the cap on minutes per hour and provide greater flexibility and revenue to broadcasters.

Not surprisingly, the advertising industry, represented by the Association of Canadian Advertisers, shared the same view of the broadcasting industry:

> Given the importance of advertising revenues to the system, we urge the Commission to refrain from any attempt to re-classify this non-traditional program-integrated type of advertising as part of the twelve-minute per hour limitation.

Unlike these two industries, the positions of unions and creators' organizations were not in such harmony. Whereas the Director Guild of Canada, the English Language Arts Network and the Coalition of the Canadian Audio-Visual Unions (CCAU) cited the revenue argument in support of exempting non-traditional advertising from the time limitation, in the name of the public interest the Canadian Conference of Arts strongly objected to any relaxation of advertising restrictions:

> Is it in the best interests of Canadian audiences for no limits at all to be placed on non-traditional advertising? We would argue it is not. Given the apparent unpopularity of existing levels of advertising, would new advertising not simply further repel existing audiences for privately-owned, over-the-air broadcasters programming?

In contrast, even a state actor, the Ontario Ministry of Culture, supported the industry position of relaxing the restrictions on advertising. The Friends of Canadian Broadcasting (an NGO) shared this position:

> Friends notes an enormous inequity in the fact that US prime time shows with significant product placement air in Canada without consequence while smaller specialty Canadian programs […] are subject to frame-by-frame scrutiny by the Commission.

Another NGO, Our Public Airways, limited its objection to deregulating product placement to the public channels.

In summary, most Canadian actors, regardless of their types and sectors, supported the liberal regime for product placement and based this position mainly on the need to enhance the financial position of the broadcasting industry.

To return to the European case, it should come as no surprise that consumer organizations and other public organizations do not approve the use of product placement (the European consumers' organization, BEUC, and the two British public organizations, Mediawatch and the Campaign for Press and Broadcasting Freedom, CPBF), or approved of it only under severe restrictions (the European Alliance of Listeners and Viewers Association [Euralva] and the Voice of Listeners & Viewers). The European consumers' organization represents the first group well:

> Product placement and many other new forms of 'integrated' marketing are in clear breach of the industry's own code and represent an erosion of editorial independence. [...] the requirements which have existed until now of identifying advertising and at the same time separating it from editorial content are the most elementary principles of media policy. They must in no event be jettisoned.

The European Alliance of Listeners and Viewers Association represents the second group of actors, which presents the restrictive position:

> We therefore welcome the Commission's proposal to authorise communications involving product placement, accompanied by the obligation to provide clear identification of its commercial nature. [...] Moreover, there is a strong argument that there should permanently be a logo on the screen indicating the commercial nature of the programme.

In the same way it is understandable that a public broadcaster such as the BBC or a professional organization such as the European Federation of Journalists (EFJ) should express negative positions on product placement. The BBC position, which is the most conservative view on product placement, states:

> Allowing product placement, even under limited and clearly defined circumstances, would entail a major change in the economic and editorial conditions content providers operate in. [...] Product placement could lead to a drop in editorial standards and subsequently public confidence in the integrity of European programming.

Similar extreme positions against product placement, based on the need to protect viewers and/or creators, were presented by state actors such as the Lithuanian Ministry of Culture, the Ministry of Tourism & Culture of Malta, and the UK government (which later, in 2009, changed its position). These actors recommended a complete ban on product placement. The same argument – to protect viewers and/or creators – was central to the positions of many other participants who supported allowing the use of product placement with certain limitations. Most of these cited the identification principle as the major necessary restriction on the practice. They even included industrial actors from both the broadcasting and the advertising industries: the Association of Commercial Television in Europe (ACT), the European Broadcasting Union (BDU), the European Association of Communication Agencies (EACA), the European Group of Television Advertising (EGTA), Fox International Channels, the Voice of British Advertisers, the RTL Group, Versatel Deutschland, the World Federation of Advertisers (WFA), etc. The International Advertising Association stated:

> Product placement is clearly to be accepted as a legitimate means of commercial communication. On the other hand, it is not to be used to bypass the current rules on restricted products or programmes and it must comply with the existing framework. Identification at the beginning of the programme is an acceptable solution.

Finally, it is worth introducing the position of a private broadcaster, the RTL Group, which in spite of its direct benefit from product placement supported the restrictive regime rather than the permissive one:

> RTL Group would take the view that in order to stop European programmes from being discriminated against, e.g. US content, product placement should be allowed to operate within a regulated environment. If product placement is to be authorised, it should comply with the principle of identification.

This last example is a good summary of most of the European actors' positions: on the one hand, most of them supported allowing product placement but on the other hand they were in favour of limiting it in various ways. The actors' main argument addressed the need to protect viewers and creators from product placement implications.

Most of the Israeli participants in the policy process, including actors from the broadcasting and advertising industries, were in favour of the restrictive regime. Keshet, the most successful private broadcaster in Israel, represents this common position:

> We want to have advertising beyond the traditional advertisements, in a formal (regulated) way, and we are ready to commit in any possible way that there will be no interference in the programs' contents […] we support product placement in entertainment programs (every program which is not news, documentary or investigating program), with an appropriate exposure to the fact that there is commercial message in the program.

The advertising industry shared the same position and argumentation. One of its representatives pointed to a different argumentation for allowing product placement (although under restrictions):

> Product placement enables financing programs […] if there is more money through the promoter, the program will be better.

Very similar positions and argumentations were presented by representatives of the scriptwriters' association, the producers' association and the cinema and television workers' union. The union representative suggested rephrasing the concept of 'commercial content' (the Israeli common name for product placement) and calling it 'surreptitious advertising.' Yet he supported the restrictive regime:

> We are in favor of surreptitious advertising, but only under certain conditions: that the placement will add to the original production budget and will not be a part of this budget, an appropriate transparency, and a total disengagement between the advertiser and the producer and the creator.

Some public actors, such as the two regulatory authorities – the Council for Cables and Satellite and the Second Authority for Radio and Television – presented the same position and supported the restrictive regime for product placement. But a state actor – the Department of Industry, Commerce and Tourism – and a non-governmental organization, the Israeli Council for Consumerism, expressed an entirely different position: the prohibition of product placement because of the damage to the viewers as media consumers and to the freedom of the creators. In its written submission to the Kasher Committee the Israeli Council for Consumerism argued:

> Even if the viewer is aware of the fact that commercial messages are embedded within the program, it would be difficult for him/her to distinguish between these messages and other content, and therefore the viewer will not be able to have a critical attitude towards the commercial messages.

Two independent actors (from academia) believed product placement should be prohibited. They argued that product placement is a 'deceptive practice' that the viewers must be protected from.

Discussion and Conclusion

It can be argued that there is an affinity between the framing of the issue by the regulator in each constituency and the actors' positions on product placement. An interesting question is to what extent the discourse in each of the three policy processes is a new one, reflecting a turning point in media and advertising policy, rather than another new layer in a well-rooted policy tradition in each case. The seeds of the current discourses can be found within the original European TVWF directive of 1989, the 1994 Israeli Law of the Second Authority for Radio and Television, and the regulations in Canada's 1987 Broadcasting Act. The discourse regarding advertising policy has not changed throughout these three policy processes: the general direction was towards greater liberalization and deregulation of the advertising market, but the emphases in the EU and Israel were on protecting the audience against liberalization's social and cultural implications whereas in Canada the emphasis was on ways of strengthening the broadcasting industry. The last phase of these processes, regarding regulating (or deregulating) product placement, is congruent with the policy path in each case.

Two significant questions are raised in order to understand the similarities and differences among the regulatory regimes: First, why a certain policy path is chosen by the regulator rather than others paths? Second, in what way does the regulator lead the other actors through the chosen policy path?

As to the first question, it is reasonable to suggest that the policy path in each constituency was chosen according to what March and Olsen (1984, 1989) referred to as the 'logic of appropriateness' and Hall and Taylor (1996) addressed as 'frame of meaning.' In Europe and Israel the logic of appropriateness, which created a frame of meaning for participants in the policy process, was the acceptance of product placement while protecting the viewers and the creators in various ways. In Canada, the logic of appropriateness was in line with allowing product placement without any restrictions, in order to provide the broadcasting industry with an additional and almost unlimited source of new revenue. In the three cases, the vast majority of the actors shared these logics of appropriateness regardless of their immediate self-interest. In each case, the convergence of actors' positions around a certain logic of appropriateness suited the historical policy path in each constituency. Protecting the viewers and creators has been a major factor in the European and Israeli advertising regulations not only during the current process but in previous years too. In the same way, strengthening the broadcasting industry in order to enable the broadcasters to provide 'high quality Canadian programmes' was a major element of the Canadian advertising regulations long before the current policy process. One possible explanation for the European approach might be the idea of the 'European social model.' This term is commonly used with regard to social and welfare policy in Europe and not with reference to market reforms. It stresses the fact that social considerations are central to political decisions within these fields and that these considerations moderate and act as a shield against the negative impact of globalization processes in Europe (Graziano 2003; Hennis 2001). Borrowing this term for the purpose of this study may imply that EU institutions employ the standards of the European social model while referring to practices such as product placement. The policy path in Canada has been characterized for decades by Canadian government efforts to assist private interest in broadcasting. These can be identified since the appearance of private broadcasting in Canada in the 1930s and have been even more apparent since cable channels appeared in the 1960s. Throughout this long period, until the current digital era, the threat of Americanization has dogged the Canadian broadcasting industry and has been one of the central incentives for assisting the Canadian broadcasting market (Sarikakis 2007; Young 2003).

The second question presented earlier was: in what way does the regulator lead the other actors through the chosen policy path? Vogel (1996: 19) indicated that the various interests are 'mediated by state institutions'. This mediation, according to March and Olsen (1989: 160f), is done by providing the different actors 'logic of appropriateness' or by suggesting 'frames of meanings' (Hall and Taylor 1995: 14). It is reasonable to assume that if there are different logics of appropriateness and a different frame of meaning between two constituencies then these differences would drive them to different policy paths. This study suggests that framing the issue in a certain way was the process through which the regulator pushed the other stakeholders along a particular policy path. In the three constituencies, stakeholders considered product placement as a given reality within the broadcasting and advertising markets. Yet this reality could be seen in various ways: it might be a problem for the viewers and creators on one hand (EU and Israel), but it could be seen as a solution for the industry's financial needs on the other (Canada). These are two different points of view with respect to the same reality; choosing one point of view is the core of the framing process (Mazey and Richardson 1997; Rein and Schön 1991). These different framings of the issue were followed by different common positions of the actors in each constituency, which represent the policy discourse. Discourse, as argued by Schmidt and Radaelli (2004: 197), needs to be understood 'within an institutional context'. Framing of the issue in one way rather than the other and the appearance of a particular policy discourse create the 'institutional context' that characterizes the policy process and its outcomes.

In sum, the findings indicate that there is a linkage among the historical advertising policies, the framing of the current policy issue (product placement) and the new regulatory policies regarding this issue. This study therefore suggests that institutional analysis of policy processes (and path dependency as a main factor within such analysis) provides a fruitful explanation for the shaping of new regulations and for the understanding of similarities and differences among regulatory regimes.

References

Avery, R. J. and Ferraro, R. (2000), 'Verisimilitude or Advertising? Brand Appearances on Prime-Time Television', *Journal of Consumer Affairs*, 34: 2, pp. 217–245.

Baerns, B. (2003), 'Separating Advertising from Programme Content: The Principle and Its Relevance in Communications Practice', *Journal of Communication Management*, 8: 1, pp. 101–112.

Balasubramanian, S. K (1994), 'Beyond Advertising and Publicity: Hybrid Messages and Public Policy Issues', *Journal of Advertising*, 23: 4, pp. 29–46.

Canada (1987), 'Television Broadcasting Regulations. SOR/87-49', http://laws.justice.gc.ca/PDF/Regulation/S/SOR-87-49.pdf. Accessed 15 November 2010.

Commission of the European Communities (2005), 'Proposal for a Directive of the European Parliament and of the Council Amending Council Directive 89/552/EEC on the Coordination of Certain Provisions Laid Down by Law, Regulation or Administrative Action in Member States Concerning the Pursuit of Television Broadcasting Activities. COM (2005) 646 final', http://eur-lex.europa.eu/LexUriServ/site/en/com/2005/com2005_0646en01.pdf. Accessed 15 November 2010.

CRTC (2006), *Broadcasting Notice of Public Hearing CRTC 2006-5*, http://www.crtc.gc.ca/eng /archive/2006/n2006-5.htm. Accessed 15 November 2010.

—— (2007), *Broadcasting Public Notice CRTC 2007-53. Determinations Regarding Certain Aspects of the Regulatory Framework for Over-the-Air Television*, http://www.crtc.gc.ca/eng /archive/2007/pb2007-53.htm. Accessed 15 November 2010.

Entman, R. M. (1993), 'Framing: Towards a Clarification of a Fractured Paradigm', *Journal of Communication*, 43: 4, pp. 51–58.

European Union (2010), 'Directive 2010/13/EU of the European Parliament and of the Council of 10 March 2010 on the Coordination of Certain Provisions Laid Down by Law, Regulation or Administrative Action in Member States Concerning the Provision of Audiovisual Media Services (Audiovisual Media Services Directive) (codified version)', http://eur-lex.europa.eu /LexUriServ/LexUriServ.do?uri=OJ:L:2010:095:0001:0024:EN:PDF. Accessed 15 November 2010.

Ginosar, A. and Levi-Faur, D. (2010), 'Regulating Product Placement in the European Union and Canada: Explaining Regime Change and Diversity', *Journal of Comparative Policy Analysis*, 12: 5, pp. 467–490.

Graziano, P. (2003), 'Europeanization or Globalization? A Framework for Empirical Research', *Global Social Policy*, 3: 2, pp. 173–194.

Hall, P. A. and Taylor, R. C. R. (1996), 'Political Science and the Three New Institutionalisms', *Political Studies*, 44: 4, pp. 936–957.

Hennis, M. (2001), 'Europeanization and Globalization: The Missing Link', *Journal of Common Market Studies*, 39: 5, pp. 829–850.

Kohler-Koch, B. (2000), 'Framing the Bottleneck of Constructing Legitimate Institutions', *Journal of European Public Policy*, 7: 4, pp. 513–531.

March, J. G. and Olsen, J. P. (1984), 'The New Institutionalism: Organizational Factors in Political Life', *American Political Science Review*, 78: 3, pp. 734–749.

—— (1989), *Rediscovering Institutions: The Organizational Basis of Politics*, New York: Collier Macmillan.

Mazey, S. and Richardson, J. (1997), 'Policy Framing: Interest Groups and the Lead up to 1996 Inter-governmental Conference', *West European Politics*, 20: 3, pp. 111–134.

Newell, J., Salmon, C. T. and Chang, S. (2006), 'The Hidden History of Product Placement', *Journal of Broadcasting & Electronic Media*, 50: 4, pp. 575–594.

Posner, R. A. (1974), 'Theories of Economic Regulation', *The Bell Journal of Economics and Management Science*, 5: 2, pp. 335–358.

Peltzman, S. (1976), 'Toward a More General Theory of Regulation', *Journal of Law and Economics*, 19: 2, pp. 211–240.

Rein, M. and Schön, D. A. (1991), 'Frame-Reflective Policy Discourse', in P. Wagner (ed.), *Social Services and Modern States: National Experiences and Theoretical Crossroads*, Cambridge: Cambridge University Press, pp. 262–289.

Russell, C. A. and Belch, M. (2005), 'A Managerial Investigation into the Product Placement Industry', *Journal of Advertising Research*, 45: 1, pp. 73–92.

Sarikakis, K. (2007), 'Mediating Social Cohesion: Media and Cultural Politics in the European Union and Canada in Context', *European Studies*, 24, pp. 65–90.

Schejter, A. M. (2006), 'Art Thou For Us, or For Our Adversaries? Communicative Action and the Regulation of Product Placement: A Comparative Study and a Tool for Analysis', *Tulane Journal of International and Comparative Law*, 15: 1, pp. 89–119.

—— (2007), 'Jacob's Voice, Esau's Hands: Transparency as a First Amendment Right in an Age of Deceit and Impersonation', *Hofstra Law Review*, 35: 3, pp. 1489–1518.

Schmidt, V. A. and Radaelli, C. M. (2004), 'Policy Change and Discourse in Europe: Conceptual and Methodological Issues', *West European Politics*, 27: 2, pp. 183–210.

Stigler, G. J. (1971), 'The Theory of Economic Regulation', *The Bell Journal of Economics and Management Science*, 2: 1, pp. 3–21.

Stinger, K. (2006), 'Product Placements Creep into Children's Entertainment', http://www.commercialfreechildhood.org/news/productplacementcreep.htm. Accessed 9 November 2010.

Tiwsakul, R., Hackley, C. and Szmigin, I. (2005), 'Explicit, Non-Integrated Product Placement in British Television Programmes', *International Journal of Advertising*, 24: 1, pp. 95–111.

Vogel, S. K. (1996), *Freer Markets, More Rules: Regulatory Reform in Advanced Industrial Countries*, Ithaca: Cornell University Press.

Wenner, L. A. (2004), 'On the Ethics of Product Placement in Media Entertainment', *Journal of Promotion Management*, 10: 1/2, pp. 101–132.

Young, D. (2003), 'Discourses on Communication Technologies in Canadian and European Broadcasting Policy Debates', *European Journal of Communication*, 18: 2, pp. 209–240.

Notes

1 See for examples: http://www.pqmwdia.com/about-press-20080212-bemf.html (14.8.08) and: http://www.reuters.com/article/pressRelease/idUS82123+05-May-2008+PRN20080505 (14.8.08)

2 In this research, only the European supranational level is analysed and compared to the other two cases.

3 At the EU level, unlike the member-state level, there is no self-regulation organization with its own code and/or compulsory authority. The European Advertising Standards Alliance (EASA) promotes the establishment of self-regulation bodies in the EU member states and adjudicates between them when there are cross-border complaints. In Canada, media content is subject to the industry self-regulation as well. In Israel, there is a partial co-regulation mechanism.

4 For a detailed description and analysis of the EU and the Canadian policy processes, see Ginosar and Levi-Faur (2010). The Israeli policy process was different because it was entirely dedicated to the issue of product placement whereas in the other two processes product placement was only one of many other regulatory issues.

5 The council resolution (in Hebrew) is available at: http://www.moc.gov.il/sip_storage/FILES/9/839.pdf

The Kasher Committee report (in Hebrew) is available at: http://www.rashut2.org.il/editor/UpLoadLow/חודה%20אלמה.pdf.

6 Member states had to adapt their local legislation and regulation to the AVMSD provisions by 19 December 2009. More than a half of the states had not completed the legislative process by then.

7 As the two Israeli regulators separately shaped product placement regulations, there are two separate regimes. Still, the main characteristics of these regimes are very similar and therefore it is addressed here as one unified regime.

8 An e-mail correspondence with Ms Merav Shtrosberg-Alkbetz, manager of the consumer-protection department of the Council for Satellite and Cables, received on 3 June 2009.

9 An e-mail message from Mr Asi Kurtz, assistant to the authority's spokesman, received on 17 November 2008.

10 Because of the different baseline between the EU and Israel on one hand and Canada on the other, the working definitions for 'liberal' and 'conservative' are different: in the EU and Israel, 'liberal' position represents the permissive regime of product placement whereas 'conservative' position stands for either the prohibitive or the restrictive regime. In Canada, the 'liberal' position is the exclusion of product placement from the allowed amount of advertising and the 'conservative' position is the inclusion of product placement within the calculation of the allowed amount of advertising.

11 For various reasons the remaining 23 position papers were not accessible.

12 The remaining 13 positions were not specifically identified within the committee's published protocols. Some of these are of actors whose organizations were represented by other representatives during the committee sessions.

13 One committee member (the chair of the screenwriters' association) had presented his position as a witness before his nomination to the committee and the chair of the committee did not explicitly express his position during the discussions.

14 The other two objectives were about digital/HD television and about the economic status of small-market television stations.

15 All the quotations in this section are from the original policy documents submitted by the relevant actors. In the case of the EU these documents are available at: http://ec.europa.eu /avpolicy/reg/history/consult/consultation_2005/contributions/index_en.htm. In the case of Canada the documents are available at: http://support.crtc.gc.ca/applicant/applicant. aspx?pn_ph_no=2006-5&lang=E. As to the Israeli case, the quotations are from the oral testimonies of the relevant actors heard by the Kasher Committee (these testimonies are included within the unpublished committee's protocols).

Chapter 7

Technologies as Institutions: Rethinking the Role of Technology in Media Governance Constellations

Christian Katzenbach

Introduction

In recent years, the focus of communication policy research has shifted away from the state as the central actor and legislation as the main instrument towards more heterogeneous regulatory structures. Media governance as an analytical perspective draws attention to the emergence, consolidation and transformation of structures and processes that facilitate and constrain as well as coordinate the range of behaviour of actors in a specific field. This perspective not only implies a renewed interest in heterogeneous sets of actors (including the state but going far beyond it) but it also means dealing with different forms of establishing order and with patterns to cope with interdependence between actors: networks, markets and communities, knowledge, *leitbilder* and social norms supplement statutory regulation in coordinating the behaviour of actors in a certain field.

But current research on communication policy and regulation seems to have its blind spot: the information and communication technologies that media communication relies upon. Whereas various forms of institutions (in a wider sense) such as common beliefs or social and professional norms have been investigated, technology has been widely neglected in this context. This article argues that communication policy research needs to reconsider closely what Robin Mansell and Roger Silverstone (1996) termed the 'politics of information and communication technologies.' Basically, the political momentum of media technologies can be conceived from two perspectives: First, there is a politics in technology itself in the sense that its very design facilitates, controls and constrains social behaviour and influences sectoral change. Second, the development of new technologies and their reconfiguration do not follow any technological logic but is itself politically and socially contested.

This article aims at laying the foundations to conceptualize the currently neglected role of technology in media governance constellations beyond technological determinism. The first building block in this undertaking is the development of an institutional view of media governance that enriches the currently discussed media governance concepts (Donges 2007a; Puppis 2010) by stressing the normative and cultural dimensions of institutions. The second building block brings in media technology by discussing current accounts of media technologies in media and communication studies and identifying key findings from the sociological and technology studies. The article concludes with an outline of an institutional view of technology in media governance and a discussion of its implications.

Governance and Institutions in Communication Policy Research

Focus on Actors in Communication Policy Research

Changing societal, economic and technological contexts have led communication scholars in recent years to assert and promote a shift in media and communication regulation (Just and Latzer 2005; Latzer et al. 2003; Van Cuilenburg and McQuail 2003). Varieties of industry co- and self-regulation as well as forms of citizen participation have come into focus of research, implying a more inclusive perspective on media regulation. Just and Latzer (2005), for example, identify a general shift from vertical to horizontal regulation in the media sector, increasingly involving private actors across a wide range of communication policy issues; independent regulatory agencies have taken over operative tasks of regulation from public administration in most OECD states (Latzer 2009; OECD 2005; Thatcher 2002). Also, traditional self-regulatory institutions such as press councils have been rediscovered by research (Puppis 2009). In addition, a whole strand of research investigates public participation in regulation processes.

This shift in regulatory structures – and in its analysis – also implies a shift in the role of the state. In communication policy research, as in other disciplines, research has asserted the decline of the 'golden age of the nation state': the state and legislation having lost in importance in favour of more heterogeneous regulatory constellations in which the state sets rules but does not necessarily itself regulate, supervise and sanction the behaviour of actors.

Given this context, it is no surprise that communication scholars – rather slowly, but obviously effectively – have received and adapted the notion of *governance* as a central concept or 'umbrella term' for their research (d'Haenens et al. 2007; Donges 2007b for an overview). The question of whether governance as a concept or approach provides an analytical surplus and is of practical relevance has been discussed widely and wildly (Benz 2003; Mayntz 2005; Schuppert 2008) – and has probably more promoted than hindered its career. 'Governance' is used to describe many kinds of regulative structure that seem to go beyond the state as a central actor and conventional legislation as the main instrument: self- and co-regulation, organizational means of ensuring the media's accountability, the role of professional ethics and much more.

Although used so frequently and in many different contexts, it often remains vague what governance as a concept in communication policy actually means, what its analytical surplus is. Primarily, it has been used effectively and convincingly to put the depicted developments towards self- and co-regulation in a more general frame that is conceivable across different policy fields. Due to the increasing complexities, dynamics and diversity of contemporary societies and their communication structures, the efficacy of statutory regulation is seen as limited; therefore, private actors are included in regulative structures (Just and Latzer 2005; Kooiman 2003; Latzer et al. 2003;). Additionally, it is frequently used to analyse the relations between policy processes in supranational institutions such as the European Union (EU), international institutions such as the International Telecommunication Union (ITU) or the

World Trade Organization (WTO) and national legislation (Ó Siochrú and Girard 2002). In this perspective, with a strong focus on the pluralization of actors involved in media and communication regulation, media governance is understood as a *horizontal* and *vertical* extension of government (Puppis 2007).[1]

But this application of the governance approach to actor constellations does not tap its full potential. Whereas the widened spectrum of actors has been investigated considerably in communication policy research, the heterogeneous forms and mechanisms of rule-making and coordination have not yet attracted comparable attention. Werner Meier, Josef Trappel and Irene Perrin discuss market mechanisms and their role in media concentration (Meier and Perrin 2007; Meier and Trappel 2007), Barbara Thomass (2007) works with the concept of media ethics and its status as a governance resource. But generally, governance research in the field of media and communication has not yet dealt much with transforming forms and mechanisms of regulation in the 'governance mix.' One of these currently neglected forms (and objects) of regulation and coordination is, as argued in this article, media technology itself, the infrastructure and framework of media communication.

In sum, the gradual, but emblematic shift from regulation to governance as concept of reference has been received and adapted by communication scholars. They have used the governance approach primarily in continuing research on self- and co-regulation. But there is more in the governance concept than just a variety of actors. Manuel Puppis (2010) noted generally that the immense upturn of governance as *the* term for regulative structures has not been accompanied by a thorough discussion of the theoretical underpinnings of the concept and its implications for communication policy research. This holds especially true for the various forms of establishing order and of coordinating the behaviour of actors. Hence, communication policy research needs to re-read the governance literature of other disciplines to get a general idea of the varieties of regulation and coordination and to identify relevant mechanisms for the media sector.

Varieties of Regulation and Coordination in Governance Research

Governance both as an analytical concept and practical approach has attracted a lot of attention and importance in various disciplines in recent years (Bang 2003; Kooiman 2003; Schuppert and Zürn 2008; van Kersbergen and van Waarden 2004). Manuel Puppis (2010) has undertaken the effort of reviewing the general governance literature in order to synthesize its findings for a theoretically founded concept of governance for communication policy research. On this basis, this article can restrict itself to aspects that are central to the arguments put forward here.

In line with Puppis and recent governance literature in other fields (Blumenthal 2005; Schuppert 2008), governance is understood here as a rather broad concept that not only covers allegedly new forms and mechanisms of regulation that are characterized by non-hierarchical structures and the inclusion of non-governmental actors but also the regulatory structure in its entirety. It is thus not used as a normative notion but as an analytical concept that draws attention to the emergence, consolidation and transformation of structures and processes that facilitate and constrain as well as coordinate the range of behaviour of actors in a specific field.

What then is the analytical surplus of the governance notion as a concept – especially in the context of this article, which is attempting to rethink the role of technology in media regulation? Puppis (2010: 139) stresses the opportunity of the governance approach to take up an integrated view on rules: 'It is a new way of describing, explaining, and criticizing the entirety of forms of rules that aim to organize media systems.' He puts forward the convincing argument that the structure and dynamics of a media system and its actors are not only shaped by collective rules that are obligatory for every actor but also by internal, organizational rules such as editorial guidelines, codes of conduct or other control mechanisms implemented by single actors or a group of actors themselves.

As convincing as it is, this concept seems to miss an important aspect that has been highlighted across the body of literature on governance: it is not only explicit, formulated rules that regulate and coordinate the behaviour of actors in a field but also common beliefs, mutual expectations and cognitive frameworks. The sociological literature – upon which Puppis draws with good reason – puts patterns of coping with interdependencies between actors at the core of the governance concept, referring both to structures as well as processes (Lange and Schimank 2004). Schuppert (2008) similarly argues that it is rather structures of coordination than structures of regulation that we should investigate, because these best capture the research frame: social behaviour, interaction and institutional frameworks and affordances (Benz et al. 2007). These structures of coordination are not only constituted, to put it in W. Richard Scott's terms, by the 'regulative pillar' but also by a 'normative' and a 'cognitive pillar' (Scott 1995: 35). Norms, values, shared meanings and symbolic systems are seen as central elements that provide orientation and guidance.[2] 'Norms and values become appropriated and internalized by individuals, groups or organizations, which motivates them to respect and defend the status quo even in the absence of controls or sanctions' (Djelic and Quack 2003: 19). If shared meanings and common beliefs emerge and stabilize (by undermining and displacing competing dispositifs) they provide frames for situations and policy issues and propose certain patterns of behaviour and decisions more than others. This implies that discursive struggles can translate into regulative struggles and vice versa (Göhler et al. 2009). For example, Janice Denegri-Knott (2004) has analysed changes in discourse over the labelling of music file-sharing in the context of copyright and how 'power machinates in establishing the parameters between acceptable and unacceptable behaviours.' Also Matthias Künzler's study on the role of ideas and normative principles in the liberalization and privatization of European broadcasting markets illustrates the coordinative force of cognitive and discursive elements (Künzler 2009).

A similar effect can be conceived in specific practices of standardization and quantification that help policy issues emerge (and disappear) and frame them in certain ways. This 'governing by numbers' has been investigated in case studies of the European Commission and OECD programmes (Salais 2006), on Anglo-American accounting (Miller 2001) and educational reforms (Grek 2009; Heintz 2008). These accounts show that – together with normative and cultural elements – 'calculation practices' (Miller) are a means to 'load' regulative structures and policies with legitimacy. In this way, normative, cultural and symbolic elements play an important role in regulatory structures that come into focus with a sociologically informed governance perspective.

An Institutional View of Communication Regulation

Patrick Donges (2007a) and Manuel Puppis (2010) have already convincingly linked institutional theories and governance research. But as a consequence of the concepts depicted and the findings of the sociological governance literature, it seems more convincing to put the rather general notion of institutions at the core of the governance perspective than the more precise but also more limited concept of rules used by Donges and Puppis. It is the very point of the governance perspective to understand the processes of establishing (and questioning) order and coordination in a wide sense. Consequently, making rules the core concept of governance would overlook a whole range of questions in this perspective.

A focus on institutions, in contrast, allows for a broader and more complete picture. Institutions can be understood generally as 'symbolic and behavioural systems containing representational, constitutive and normative rules together with regulatory mechanisms that define a common meaning system and give rise to distinctive actors and action routines' (Scott and Meyer 1994: 68). Whereas economists and political scientists focus more on formal and structural institutions, it is important to note that institutions also have an informal dimension. Djelic and Quack (2003: 17f) understand institutions in this sense as 'consisting of both structures and formal systems on the one hand and normative and cognitive frames on the other that altogether provide stability and meaning to social behaviour.' According to Berger and Luckman (1966), shared meanings, common beliefs and social rules emerge out of day-to-day interactions in their specific cultural–institutional embeddedness. The process of institutionalization then is a process in which local interactions stabilize and become taken for granted (Jepperson 1991; Meyer et al. 1987). Berger and Kellner (1981: 31) therefore conceive institutions as 'sedimentations of meanings or, to vary the image, a crystallization of meanings in objective form.'

Two aspects of the institutional view are especially important in discussing media regulation in a governance perspective: firstly, institutions can be seen as an analytical hinge in this context. As they have both a regulatory – constraining and facilitating – impact on the behaviour of actors, as well as are emergent from the behaviour of actors and are the object of social and political negotiations in specific situations, they are both the outcome as well as the instruments of regulation (Donges 2007a: 328). This duality is what makes institutions a helpful core concept of governance research in general and for a discussion of the role of technology in governance constellations in particular.

Secondly, an institutional perspective makes it possible to describe and analyse the dynamics of regulatory change by investigating the emergence and consolidation of certain institutions and the questioning and erosion of others.[3] Institutional theorists usually describe the process of institutionalization as a process in three stages (Berger and Luckmann 1966; Tolbert and Zucker 1996): First, regular local interactions and cognitive patterns for specific problems become habitualized. At the second stage, which has been termed 'objectification,' these 'solutions' and cognitive frames become generalized beyond their local context in which they developed; a consensus on their legitimacy is established within a certain range of actors (or not). The third stage has been called 'sedimentation' by Tolbert and Zucker (1996): here, patterns become fully institutionalized in the sense that they are internalized, not questioned, and in some cases materialized into formal or structural institutions. 'It is during this last stage that institutions can potentially acquire the "quality of exteriority", that is, become taken for granted and develop a reality of their own' (Djelic and Quack 2003: 22).

As instrumental as this phase model is, it is extremely import to note that actual, empirical processes are not as linear, solid and uni-directional as the model may suggest. Institutions may change, institutions may dissolve (Berger and Luckmann 1966; Quack 2005). Institutional structures – formal and informal – are questioned especially when new actors appear or the context changes. Then the taken-for-grantedness of the patterns can dissolve and its value and legitimacy can be challenged. Marie-Laure Djelic and Sigrid Quack argue that the stability, robustness and self-reproducing character of institutions depend on the interplay of regulative pressures and systems of control with normative and cognitive frames. Institutional change occurs 'where and when internal challenges and spaces of opportunity combine with and are being reinforced by external triggers and alternatives' (Djelic and Quack 2003: 23). Thus, to understand the dynamics of an institutional setting means essentially to understand the 'internal' interplay of its compounds – regulative, normative, cultural – and the supposedly 'external' changing contexts.

These aspects of an institutional perspective on regulation – the duality of institutions and its dynamics – provide helpful means for describing and analysing continuities, dynamics and shifts in media regulation; at the same time one must carefully note that the social world not only consists of regularities, shared understandings and, in general, stability, but it is also full of uncertainty, contingency and dispute (Wagner 1994). As a consequence, institutions must not be conceptualized as stable entities but rather as fluid condensations in time that dissolve or transform sooner or later.

Foundations of an Institutional View on Technology in Media Governance

Having outlined an institutional view on regulation, how can these 'building blocks' now be instrumental in analysing the role of technology in media governance constellations? This article argues that technologies can hold the status of institutions in media communication in the sense that they embody the duality of institutions both:

(1) As a result of an institutionalization process: certain patterns of conduct and interpretation crystallize into material objects, technological devices or services – which then again are subject to negotiations and varieties of usages, starting another process of (de-)institutionalization; as well as

(2) Part of an institutional setting that facilitates, coordinates and constrains the communicative behaviour of actors (be it users, politicians, media developers or media companies).

In order to develop such a conceptual frame and connect it to the existing strands of research, I briefly outline current accounts of technology in communication research, and then sketch out core concepts of science and technology studies.

Accounts of Technology in Communication Research and Policy

Social communication is increasingly realized through media technology. Under the umbrella of notions such as 'mediatization' and 'network society' communication scholars discuss the supposedly increasing presence and importance of media (technology) for societies at large, politics, private and professional organizations, groups and networks and social interactions in everyday life (Castells 1996; Hjarvard 2008; Hepp et al. 2008; Krotz 2007; Lundby 2009). A central finding is that media technologies permeate our life worlds; media is (generally) used routinely and fully habitualized. Features and configurations of the specific technologies therefore play a crucial role: they structure and frame social communication (Höflich 2003; Krotz 2007). On the one hand, this view appears implicitly to be common sense in communication research. On the other hand, theoretical accounts of the relationship between technology and social communication are heavily dominated by constructivist approaches that emphasize the varieties of social shaping, appropriation and domestication – in short, the construction of media technology.

This constructivist perspective stresses that technology in use does not blindly follow any inherent logic but is always appropriated, reinterpreted and domesticated by its users. Social values, financial as well as 'moral economies', political and family hierarchies, the material aspects of the household, they all essentially shape the use and the meanings of technological devices and services (for example Berker et al. 2006; Röser 2007a; Silverstone and Hirsch 1992). The other facet of this social-construction-of-technology approach focuses on an earlier – and simultaneously later – stage: the development and governance of technologies. Drawing on sociological literature, scholars have investigated processes and key determinants in the development of (media) technology. Here, coordination and negotiation between different sets of actors in standardization processes, the impact of *leitbilder*[4] on technological development and its regulation, and – more generally – the social and moral values inscribed in technology come into focus of research (Bröchler 2008; Schmidt and Werle 1998).

Whereas this perspective, which stresses the impact of social processes and structures on technology, has produced a considerable amount of research, though receiving not so much attention from communication policy scholars lately, the opposite perspective, which conceives technology less as an object of social shaping or regulation than as a means of regulation and as a formative element of media structures that causes change, has not been investigated in a similar manner. However, at the fringes of communication policy research there are stances that start from the assumption that the specific design of technology facilitates and constrains certain ways of regulation and of using this device or service. Such an approach is always in danger of falling into the trap of technological determinism, but it does provide starting points for tackling the role of technology in governance constellations.

Such a position was prominently stated in the debate around the regulation of the Internet in the mid-1990s. The architecture of the Internet was conceived as being immune to statutory regulation: 'Indeed, the very design of the Internet seemed technologically proof against attempts to put the genie back in the bottle. [...] [It] treats censorship like damage and routes around it' (Walker 2003: 25). Rather, legal scholars argued that the architecture of the net and the software code itself must be seen as elements that facilitate, set the norm for or constrain social behaviour: 'Law and government regulation are [...] not the only source of rule-making. Technological capabilities and system design choices impose rules on participants [...] the set of rules for information flows imposed by technology and communication networks form a "lex informatica"' (Reidenberg 1998). For this idea, Lessig (1999) has coined the catch phrase 'code is law': software code or – more generally – technical architectures are seen as one of four constraints regulating social behaviour (alongside law, the market and norms).

Lessig also hinted at interdependencies among the constraining forces, but his model remains sociologically under complex: e.g. it does not deal with the emergence of norms at all nor the interdependencies with software; the market is depicted as rather working under perfect conditions. These accounts need to be reconditioned on the grounds of a thorough institutional view of regulation as sketched out in this article.

These accounts – those focusing on standardization as well as those on code-is-law – touch core issues of communication policy research but actually stem from different disciplines (sociology and law). We can therefore state that technology does not play a prominent part in media governance research; and when it is present, its status and its interdependencies are not in the focus of interest.[5] The general literature in communication research is divided: in numerous accounts of changes in media communication in general, journalism, public relations and media usage in particular, new media technologies and infrastructure are seen – rather implicitly – as key external (!) factors challenging existing structures and causing change and the adaptation of actors to a changed context. But in the theoretical discourse on the relationship between technology and social communication a position that explicitly states definite influences of technology is obviously marginalized in communication research. An association with technological determinism is probably one of the few labels that a communication scholar should avoid at all costs.

Learning from Science and Technology Studies

In order to develop an outline of the role of technology in media governance constellations beyond determinism, it is useful to review the literature in the sociological science and technology studies. There, the mutual interdependencies among technology, individual action and social and political structures are the core issues of interest. This field has long been divided by a gap between technology-centric and culturalist perspectives (Passoth 2008), but nevertheless provides us with helpful starting points that take into account both sides of the coin.

Approaches that focus on the development and use of technologies stress the institutional and cultural impacts on technology and its use. In addition to the studies on standardization and the regulation of technological development mentioned earlier, scholars discuss the effects of national or sectoral institutional structures on technological innovations (Carlsson et al. 2002; Freeman 1987; Porter 1990), investigate the causes of different trajectories of a certain technology in different countries (Hughes 1983) or the role of actor relationships and coalitions in the development and diffusion of new technologies (Castilla et al. 2000; Giesecke 2001; Weyer et al. 1997). But it is not only institutional macro- and meso-settings in this narrow sense of formal structures and rules that shape the development and use of technologies, but also normative and cultural elements. In a stimulating study comparing the diffusion of clocks and computers as decentralized means of synchronization, Harmeet Sawhney (2004), for example, shows that technological artefacts do not necessarily foster change. The decentralization of artefacts – from turret clocks to wrist watches, from mainframes to personal computers, laptops and mobile devices – did not lead to greater individual autonomy but rather to more compliance to general 'system rules':

> While the reduction in size and cost of a technology facilitates mass adoption and thereby creates a sense of empowerment, the interconnection process reties the discrete devices together to create a new apparatus for exerting control. [...] In the case of the clock [...] it was the culture of punctuality that drove individuals to synchronize their watches. Similarly, in the case of computers [...] it is the culture of flexibility and teamwork that holds networked organizations together. (Sawhney 2004: 371)

In sum, these findings show that technology is neither an artefact outside of politics and society that follows its own teleological path nor simply a steerable object of statutory regulation; technology is subject to complex negotiations and politics. It is essentially formed by formal institutions and normative and cultural factors, constituting an essential and shapeable part of its institutional environment.

Another strand of research focuses on impacts in the opposite direction: structural and individual impacts of emerging and existing technologies on users and social structures. The core assumption here is that the very design of technology facilitates, controls and constrains social behaviour and influences sectoral change (Bijker and Law 1992; Dolata 2009; Winner

1980). Technology is conceived as an integral part of society and social relations; with Latour (1991), this view states that 'technology is society made durable.' Sleeping policemen, bridges, automatic door closers or heavy hotel keys are the classic examples in this 'sociology of things' that illustrate how artefacts have a strong impact on how we move, talk and interact. In this sense, technology is an institutionalized form of social action or structure that itself has a reflex effect on social interactions and structures.[6]

In short, theories and findings of the sociology of science and technology show that technologies have their politics, both as shapeable elements, developed, used and regulated within existing institutions, norms, cultures and established modes of interaction, as well as simultaneously being essential elements of the institutional environment that themselves facilitate and constrain the range of behaviour (and preferences) of actors.

Sociologists have tried to conceptualize these interplays and mutual relations of impacts with slightly varying concepts such as the 'co-evolution' of technology and institutions or – referring to Giddens' (1984) structuration theory – the 'duality' of technology and society. From a macro-perspective, scholars have investigated the 'co-evolution' of social structures and technologies in which periods of technological changes and path creations on the one hand and of institutional and societal (re-) framing on the other hand alternate and overlap (for an overview Dolata 2009; Geels 2004; Nelson 1994). In some cases, a technological leapfrog may lead to 'periods of mismatch' in which 'the established social and institutional framework no longer corresponds to the potential of a new techno-economic paradigm' (Dosi et al. 1988: 11). Along these lines, with several refinements, Ulrich Dolata and Raymund Werle have recently argued convincingly for the need to 'bring technology back in' and to look more into the details of structural impacts of technology (Dolata 2009; Dolata and Werle 2007). On a micro-meso-level, Schulz-Schaeffer (2000) describes these interrelations stimulatingly as an interplay of resources and routines. In this concept, the social potency and embeddedness of a technology relies on the duality of two structural aspects: the emergence and institutionalization of reliable sets of events that – as a technology – can be used as resources for actions, and the establishment of routines in the use of such events.

Outline for an Institutional View of Technology in Media Governance

On these grounds, a description and an analysis of technologies as institutions for communication policy research can be put forward. This article has argued that it is not only explicit, formulated rules and organizational structures that regulate and coordinate the behaviour of actors in the media sector but also normative and cultural elements: e.g. common beliefs, mutual expectations and cognitive frames. As media communication heavily relies on media technologies, these technologies themselves gain the status of an institution in the media environment. One side of the coin is that they are very concrete examples of what Berger has called 'sedimentation of meanings': both in the process of development as well as in the diffusion and adaptation of media technologies, regulative, normative and cultural elements come into play and to varying degrees form technologies to fit existing institutions, the interests of actors in a field and user expectations (for an overview Berker et al. 2006; Röser 2007a).[7] In this view, media technologies embody one result of an institutionalization process: certain regulative structures, values and patterns of conduct and interpretation crystallize into material objects, technological devices or services – which then again are subject to negotiations and varieties of usages starting another process of (de-) institutionalization.[8] This recursive process leads to the other side of the technologies-as-institutions coin: media technologies frame media communication through the infrastructure they provide and the negotiated or established uses attached to it. In this sense, they are 'taken-for-granted,' a more-or-less invisible and untested background and frame for social structures and our daily courses of action.[9]

Hence, media technologies can be seen as crystallized institutions that typify the general duality of institutions: they have both a regulatory – constraining and facilitating – impact on the communicative behaviour of actors as well as emerging from the actors' behaviour, an object of social and political negotiation in specific situations. Or, to put it closer to regulation theory, they are both the outcome as well as the instruments of regulation.

Another essential aspect to be considered is the dynamics of the processes of institutionalization and de-institutionalization. On the one hand, technological decisions, or closures, do imply future constraints: reversing them back will in most cases be utterly complex and expensive, or just impossible, as research on path-dependency has shown. On the other hand, institutional structures – formal and informal – are questioned especially when new actors appear or the context changes. These 'external triggers' can often be embodied through, or at least related to, new or changing technologies. For example, the Internet as an infrastructure and related services and devices have provided low-cost, decentralized means of communication, distribution and exchange to the end-user with very few points and possibilities of control, and thereby they have changed the context of the music sector considerably (Dolata 2008). So, especially in media and communication, where the users can also adapt, reconfigure and recombine the devices and services they use, institutional settings must not be conceptualized as stable entities but as a process in which rather fluid condensations crystallize at one point in time but also sooner or later dissolve or transform again.

Implications for Communication Policy Research

How can such a conceptualization of technology promote communication policy research? It points at three important aspects of the relation between media regulation and technology:

(1) It stresses the importance of communication policy research addressing in depth the development and regulation of new and emerging technologies. Once established, information and communication technologies and their specific design set the frame both for media communication as well as further communication policy and technology

development. They become part of the institutional environment and the established 'rules of the game' (Scott 1994: 207), which sets the frame for further design and policy decisions (path dependency). Donges (2007a: 327) reminds us that it is essential to consider a time lag in the emergence of institutional settings. 'The critical agenda for institutional analysis should be to show how choices made at one point in time create institutions that generate recognizable patterns of constraints and opportunities at a later point' (Powell 1991: 188). This is especially true for hard-wired institutions such as technological systems, devices and services. In this sense, 'technology matters in politics because it explicitly and deliberately is "politics by other means"' (Bijker 2006: 684), a form of indirect regulation.

(2) On the micro-level, established information and communication technologies set the frame for individual action. Domestication research has shown us many examples of how technology is being used in an 'oppositional' or 'counter-hegemonic' way. Nevertheless, technology in use facilitates, controls and constrains individual action by allocating resources that communicative routines can draw upon. Together with norms, laws, economic considerations and social elements it forms the institutional structure that communication is embedded in.

(3) Simultaneously, these practices on the micro- and – as they usually develop within communities – meso-levels have a feedback effect on the development and regulation of technology. This is especially true in highly modular and readjustable fields such as online services, where the disputable concept of 'web 2.0' is interlinked with the notion of 'perpetual beta': that the development of online services is never really finished but is always being readjusted according to the practices of its users and the interests of its owners. As a consequence, describing the role of technology in media governance constellations not only tells a story of growing stabilization and shared understandings but also one of constant (re-) negotiations and de- and re-destabilization.

Conclusion

This article has argued that it is necessary to rethink the role of technology in media governance constellations. As media technologies permeate our life worlds, their features and configurations play a crucial role: they structure and frame social communication. It has been shown that the two-sided political momentum of media technologies can be analysed as a condensation of the duality of institutions: they have both a regulatory – constraining and facilitating – impact on the behaviour of actors as well as are emerging from actors' behaviour. They are both the outcome as well as the instruments of regulation.

For current policy debates on net neutrality, copyright and access blocking this institutional view on technology and media governance will prove instrumental by taking technology into account both as an object and as an institutionalized factor of media governance. Additionally, the article provides a theoretical contribution to the interdisciplinary governance perspective by developing foundations to analyse the role of technology in governance constellations generally – maybe yielding one of the 'missing masses' (Latour 1992; 2007) in the governance discourse.

Acknowledgements

The author would like to thank Jeanette Hofmann, Jan Schmidt and Leyla Dogruel for their extremely helpful comments on early (and very late) drafts of this article.

References

Bang, H. P. (ed.) (2003), *Governance as Social and Political Communication*, Manchester: Manchester University Press.

Bechtold, S. (2002), *Vom Urheber- zum Informationsrecht : Implikationen des Digital Rights Management*, München: Beck.

_____ (2003), 'The Present and Future of Digital Rights Management – Musings on Emerging Legal Problems', in E. Becker, W. Buhse, D. Günnewig and N. Rump (eds.), *Digital Rights Management – Technological, Economic, Legal and Political Aspects*, Berlin: Springer, pp. 597–654.

Bendrath, R. (2009), 'Global Technology Trends and National Regulation: Explaining Variation in the Governance of Deep Packet Inspection', in ISA (International Studies Association), *International Studies Annual Convention*, New York City, USA, 15–18 February, ISA: Tucson.

Benz, A. (2003), *Governance - Regieren in komplexen Regelsystemen*, Opladen: Leske + Budrich.

Benz, A., Lütz, S., Schimank, U. and Simonis, G. (eds) (2007) *Handbuch Governance: Theoretische Grundlagen und empirische Anwendungsfelder*, Wiesbaden: VS.

Berger, P. L. and Kellner, H. (1981), *Sociology Reinterpreted: An Essay on Method and Vocation*, New York: Anchor/Doubleday.

Berger, P. L. and Luckmann, T. (1966), *The Social Construction of Reality : A Treatise in the Sociology of Knowledge*, Garden City: Doubleday & Comp.

Berker, T., Hartmann, M., Punie, Y. and Ward, K. (2006), *Domestication of Media and Technology*, Maidenhead: Open University Press.

Bijker, W. E. (2006), 'Why and How Technology Matters', in R.E. Goodin and C. Tilly (eds.), *Handbook of Contextual Political Analysis* Oxford: Oxford University Press, pp. 681–706.

Bijker, W. E. and Law, J. (eds.) (1992) *Shaping Technology/Building Society: Studies in Sociotechnical Change*, Cambridge: MIT Press.

Blumenthal, J. v. (2005), 'Governance – eine kritische Zwischenbilanz'. *Zeitschrift für Politikwissenschaft*, 15: 4, pp. 1149–1180.

Botzem, S., Hofmann, J., Quack, S., Schuppert, G. F. and Straßheim, H. (eds) (2009), *Governance als Prozess – Koordinationsformen im Wandel*, Baden-Baden: Nomos.

Bröchler, S. (2008), 'Governance im Lichte der sozialwissenschaftlichen Technikforschung', in S. Bröchler and H.-J. Lauth (eds.), *Politikwissenschaftliche Perspektiven*, Wiesbaden: VS, pp. 45–56.

Carlsson, B., Jacobsson, S., Holmen, M. and Rickne, A. (2002), 'Innovation Systems: Analytical and Methodological Issues', *Research Policy*, 31: 2, pp. 233–245.

Castells, M. (1996), *The Rise of the Network Society*, Cambridge, Oxford: Blackwell.

Castilla, E. J., Hwang, H., Granovetter, E. and Granovetter, M. (2000), 'Social Networks in Silicon Valley', in C.-M. Lee (ed.), *The Silicon Valley Edge: A Habitat for Innovation and Entrepreneurship*, Stanford: Stanford University Press, pp. 218–247.

d'Haenens, L., Donges, P., Puppis, M., Meier, W. A., Perrin, I., Latzer, M., Künzler, M. and Held, T. (2007), 'Commentary and Debate: Special Section "Media Governance: New Ways to Regulate the Media"', *Communications*, 32: 3, pp. 323–362.

Denegri-Knott, J. (2004), 'Sinking the Online "Music Pirates": Foucault, Power and Deviance on the Web', *Journal of Computer-Mediated Communication*, 9: 4.

Dierkes, M., Hoffmann, U. and Marz, L. (1996), *Visions of Technology: Social and Institutional Factors Shaping the Development of New Technologies*, Frankfurt: Campus.

Djelic, M.-L. and Quack, S. (2003), 'Theoretical Building Blocks for a Research Agenda Linking Globalization and Institutions', in S. Quack (ed.), *Globalization and Institutions: Redefining the Rules of the Economic Game*, Cheltenham: Edward Elgar, pp. 15–34.

Dolata, U. (2008), 'Das Internet und die Transformation der Musikindustrie. Rekonstruktion und Erklärung eines unkontrollierten sektoralen Wandels', *Berliner Journal für Soziologie*, 18: 3, pp. 344–369.

———— (2009), 'Technological Innovations and Sectoral Change: Transformative Capacity, Adaptability, Patterns of Change: An Analytical Framework', *Research Policy*, 38: 6, pp. 1066–1076.

Dolata, U. and Werle, R. (2007), *Gesellschaft und die Macht der Technik: Sozioökonomischer und Institutioneller Wandel durch Technisierung* Frankfurt: Campus.

Donges, P. (2007a), 'The New Institutionalism as a Theoretical Foundation of Media Governance', *Communications*, 32: 3, pp. 325–330.

———— (ed.) (2007b), *Von der Medienpolitik zur Media Governance?*, Köln: Halem.

Dosi, G., Freeman, C., Nelson, R., Silverberg, G. and Soete, L. (eds.) (1988), *Technical Change and Economic Theory*, London and New York: Pinter.

Freeman, C. (1987), *Technology, Policy, and Economic Performance: Lessons from Japan*, London and New York: Pinter.

Geels, F. W. (2004), 'From Sectoral Systems of Innovation to Socio-Technical Systems: Insights about Dynamics and Change from Sociology and Institutional Theory', *Research Policy*, 33: 6–7, pp. 897–920.

Giddens, A. (1984), *The Constitution of Society: Outline of the Theory of Structuration*, Cambridge: Polity Press.

Giesecke, S. (2001), *Von der Forschung zum Markt Innovationsstrategien und Forschungspolitik in der Biologietechnologie*, Berlin: Edition Sigma.

Göhler, G., Höppner, U. and De La Rosa, S. (eds.) (2009) *Weiche Steuerung: Studien zur Steuerung durch Diskursive Praktiken, Argumente und Symbole*, Baden-Baden: Nomos.

Graham, S. and Mowery, D. C. (2003), 'Intellectual Property in the US Software Industry', in W. M. Cohen and S. A. Merril (eds.), *Patents in the Knowledge Based Economy*, Washington: The National Academic Press, pp. 219–258.

Grek, S. (2009), 'Governing by Numbers: the PISA "effect" in Europe', *Journal of Education Policy*, 24: 1, pp. 23–37.

Hargittai, E. (2000), 'Radio's Lessons for the Internet', *Communications of the ACM*, 43: 1, pp. 50–56.

Heintz, B. (2008), 'Governance by Numbers. Zum Zusammenhang von Quantifizierung und Globalisierung in der Hochschulpolitik', in G. F. Schuppert and A. Voßkuhle (eds.), *Governance von und durch Wissen*, Baden-Baden: Nomos, pp. 110–128.

Hepp, A., Krotz, F., Moores, S. and Winter, C. (eds.) (2008) *Connectivity, Networks and Flows: Conceptualizing Contemporary Communications*, Cresskill: Hampton.

Hjarvard, S. (2008), 'The Mediatization of Society', *Nordicom Review*, 29: 2, pp. 105–134.

Höflich, J. R. (2003), *Mensch, Computer und Kommunikation: Theoretische Verortungen und Empirische Befunde*, Frankfurt: Lang.

Hughes, T. P. (1983), *Networks of Power: Electrification in Western Society, 1880–1930*, Baltimore: Johns Hopkins University Press.

Hynes, D. and Rommes, E. (2006), '"Fitting the Internet into Our Lives": IT Courses for Disadvanted Users', in T. Berker, M. Hartmann, Y. Punie and K. Ward (eds.), *Domestication of Media and Technology*, Maidenhead: Open University Press, pp. 123–144.

Jepperson, R. L. (1991), 'Institutions, Institutional Effects, and Institutionalism', in P. Powell and P. DiMaggio (eds.), *The New Institutionalism in Organizational Analysis*, Chicago: University of Chicago Press, pp. 143–163.

Just, N. and Latzer, M. (2005), 'Self- and Co-Regulation in the Mediamatics Sector: European Community (EC) Strategies and Contributions towards a Transformed Statehood', *Knowledge, Technology & Policy*, 17: 2, pp. 38–62.

Kooiman, J. (2003), *Governing as Governance*, London: Sage.

Krotz, F. (2007), *Mediatisierung: Fallstudien zum Wandel von Kommunikation*, Wiesbaden: VS.

Künzler, M. (2009), *Die Liberalisierung von Radio und Fernsehen: Leitbilder der Rundfunkregulierung im Ländervergleich*, Konstanz: UVK.

Lange, S. and Schimank, U. (2004), 'Governance und Gesellschaftliche Integration', in S. Lange and U. Schimank (eds.), *Governance und Gesellschaftliche Integration*, Wiesbaden: VS, pp. 9–44.

Latour, B. (1991), 'Technology Is Society Made Durable', in J. Law (ed.), *A Sociology of Monsters*, London: Routledge, pp. 103–131.

———— (1992), 'Where Are the Missing Masses? The Sociology of a Few Mundane Artifacts', in W.E. Bijker and J. Law (eds.), *Shaping Technology/Building Society: Studies in Sociotechnical Change*, Cambridge: MIT Press, pp. 225–258.

———— (2007), *Reassembling the Social: An Introduction to Actor-Network-Theory*, Oxford: Oxford University Press.

Latzer, M. (2009), 'Convergence Revisited', *Convergence: The International Journal of Research into New Media Technologies*, 15: 4, pp. 411–426.

Latzer, M., Just, N., Saurwein, F. and Slominski, P. (2003), 'Regulation Remixed: Institutional Change Through Self and Co-Regulation in the Mediamatics Sector', *Communications and Strategies*, 50: 2, pp. 127–157.

Lessig, L. (1999), *Code and Other Laws of Cyberspace*, New York: Basic.

————— (2001), *The Future of Ideas: The Fate of the Commons in a Connected World*, New York: Random House.

Lundby, K. (2009), *Mediatization: Concept, Changes, Consequences*, New York: Lang.

Mansell, R. and Silverstone, R. (eds.) (1996), *Communication by Design: The Politics of Information and Communication Technologies*, Oxford: Oxford Univiversity Press.

Mayntz, R. (2005), 'Governance Theory als fortentwickelte Steuerungstheorie?', in G. F. Schuppert (ed.), *Governanceforschung. Vergewisserung über Stand und Entwicklungslinien*, Baden-Baden: Nomos, pp. 11–20.

Meier, W. A. and Perrin, I. (2007), 'Media Concentration and Media Governance', *Communications*, 32: 3, pp. 336–343.

Meier, W. A. and Trappel, J. (2007), 'Medienkonzentration und Media Governance', in P. Donges (ed.), *Von der Medienpolitik zur Media Governance?*, Köln: Halem, pp. 197–215.

Meister, M., Schulz-Schaeffer, I., Böschen, S., Gläser, J. and Strübing, J. (eds.) (2006), *What Comes after Constructivism in Science and Technology Studies?*, Special Issue of Science, Technology and Innovation Studies.

Meyer, J. W., Thomas, G. M. and Bolli, J. (1987), 'Ontology and Rationalization in the Western Cultural Account', in G. M. Thomas, J. W. Meyer, F. O. Ramirez and J. Bolli (eds.), *Institutional Structure: Constituting State, Society, and the Individual*, Newbury Park: Sage, pp. 12–37.

Miller, P. (2001), 'Governing by Numbers: Why Calculative Practices Matter', *Social Research*, 68: 2, pp. 379–396.

Nelson, R. R. (1994), 'The Co-Evolution of Technologies and Institutions', in R. W. England (ed.), *Evolutionary Concepts in Contemporary Economics*, Ann Arbor: University of Michigan Press, pp. 139–156.

Ó Siochrú, S. and Girard, B. (2002), *Global Media Governance*, Lanham and Oxford: Rowman & Littlefield.

OECD. (2005), *Telecommunication Regulatory Institutional Structures and Responsibilities: Report to the Working Party on Telecommunication and Information Services Policies*, Paris: OECD.

Passoth, J-H. (2008), *Technik und Gesellschaft: Sozialwissenschaftliche Techniktheorien und die Transformationen der Moderne*, Wiesbaden: VS.

Porter, M. E. (1990), *The Competitive Advantage of Nations*, New York: Free.

Powell, W. W. (1991), 'Expanding the Scope of Institutional Analysis', in P. DiMaggio and W. W. Powell (eds.), *The New Institutionalism in Organizational Analysis*, Chicago and London: University of Chicago Press, pp. 183–203.

Puppis, M. (2007), 'Media Governance as a Horizontal Extension of Media Regulation: The Importance of Self- and Co-Regulation', *Communications*, 32: 3, pp. 330–336.

————— (2009), *Organisationen der Medienselbstregulierung: Europäische Presseräte im Vergleich*, Köln: Halem.

————— (2010), 'Media Governance: A New Concept for the Analysis of Media Policy and Regulation', *Communication, Culture & Critique*, 3: 2, pp. 134–149.

Quack, S. (2005), 'Zum Werden und Vergehen von Institutionen – Vorschläge für eine dynamische Governanceanalyse', in G. F. Schuppert (ed.), *Governanceforschung. Vergewisserung über Stand und Entwicklungslinien*, Baden-Baden: Nomos, pp. 346–370.

Reidenberg, J. R. (1998), 'Lex Informatica: The Formation of Information Policy Rules Through Technology', *Texas Law Review*, 76: 3, pp. 553–584.

Röser, J. (ed.) (2007a) *MedienAlltag : Domestizierungsprozesse alter und neuer Medien*, Wiesbaden: VS.

———— (2007b), 'Wenn das Internet das Zuhause erobert: Dimensionen der Veränderung aus ethnografischer Perspektive', in J. Röser (ed.), *MedienAlltag: Domestizierungsprozesse alter und neuer Medien*, Wiesbaden: VS, pp. 157–171.

Salais, R. (2006), 'On the Correct (or Incorrect) Use of Indicators in Public Action', *Comparative Labor Law & Policy Journal*, 27: 2, pp. 101–120.

Sawhney, H. (2004), 'The Slide Towards Decentralization: Clock and Computer', *Media, Culture & Society*, 26: 3, p. 359.

Schmidt, J. (2007), 'Blogging Practices: An Analytical Framework', *Journal of Computer-Mediated Communication*, 12: 4, pp. 1409–1427.

———— (2009), *Das neue Netz: Merkmale, Praktiken und Folgen des Web 2.0*, Konstanz: UVK.

Schmidt, S. K. and Werle, R. (1998), *Coordinating Technology: Studies in the International Standardization of Telecommunications*, Cambridge: MIT Press.

Schulz-Schaeffer, I. (2000), *Sozialtheorie der Technik*, Frankfurt: Campus.

Schuppert, G. F. (2008), 'Governance: Auf der Suche nach Konturen eines "anerkannt uneindeutigen Begriffs"', in G. F. Schuppert and M. Zürn (eds.), *Governance in einer sich wandelnden Welt*, Wiesbaden: VS, pp. 13–40.

Schuppert, G. F. and Zürn, M. (eds.) (2008) *Governance in einer sich Wandelnden Welt*, Wiesbaden: VS.

Scott, W. R. (1994), 'Conceptualizing Organizational Fields: Linking Organizations and Societal Systems', in H. U. Derlien, U. Gerhard and F. Scharpf (eds.), *Systemrationalität und Partialinteresse*, Baden-Baden: Nomos, pp. 203–221.

———— (1995), *Institutions and Organizations*, Thousand Oaks: Sage.

Scott, W. R. and Meyer, J. W. (1994), *Institutional Environments and Organizations: Structural Complexity and Individualism*, Thousand Oaks: Sage.

Silverstone, R. and Hirsch, E. (eds.) (1992), *Consuming Technologies: Media and Information in Domestic Spaces*, London and New York: Routledge.

Thatcher, M. (2002), 'Regulation after Delegation: Independent Regulatory Agencies in Europe', *Journal of European Public Policy*, 9: 6, pp. 954–972.

Thomass, B. (2007), 'Medicnethik als Governanceproblem', in P. Donges (ed.), *Von der Medienpolitik zur Media Governance?*, Köln: Halem, pp. 233–249.

Tolbert, P. S. and Zucker, L. G. (1996), 'The Institutionalization of Institutional Theory', in S. R. Clegg, C. Hardy and W. R. Nord (eds.), *Handbook of Organization Studies*, London: Sage, pp. 175–190.

Van Cuilenburg, J. and McQuail, D. (2003), 'Media Policy Paradigm Shifts: Towards a New Communications Policy Paradigm', *European Journal of Communication*, 18: 2, pp. 181–206.

Van Kersbergen, K. and van Waarden, F. (2004), '"Governance" as a Bridge Between Disciplines. Cross-Disciplinary Inspiration Regarding Shifts in Governance and Problems of Governability, Accountability, and Legitimacy', *European Journal of Political Research*, 43, pp. 143–171.

Wagner, P. (1994), 'Dispute, Uncertainty and Institution in Recent French Debates', *Journal of Political Philosophy*, 2: 3, pp. 270–289.

Walker, J. (2003), 'The Digital Imprimatur: How Big Brother and Big Media Can Put the Internet Genie back in the Bottle', *Knowledge, Technology and Policy*, 16: 3, pp. 24–77.

Weyer, J., Kirchner, U. and Riedl, L. (1997), *Technik, die Gesellschaft schafft – Soziale Netzwerke als Ort der Technikgenese*, Berlin: Edition Sigma.

Winner, L. (1980), 'Do Artifacts Have Politics?', *Daedulus*, 109: 1, pp. 121–136.

Zittrain, J. L. (2008), *The Future of the Internet: And How to Stop It*, New Haven: Yale University Press.

Notes

1   Horizontal extension refers to the inclusion of private actors through co-regulation or self-regulation; the growing influence of international institutions can be described as a vertical extension of the traditional mode of rule-making through the nation state. If both processes are intertwined, regulatory responsibilities are transnationalized.

2   Scott (1995: 44) explains the difference between the normative and the cognitive pillars as a difference between normative expectations and social identities: 'Whereas the emphasis by normative theorists is on the power of roles – normative expectations guiding behaviour – the cognitive framework stresses the importance of social identities: our conceptions of who we are and what ways of action make sense for us in a given situation. And rather than focusing on the constraining force of norms, cognitive theorists point to the importance of scripts: guidelines for sense making and choosing meaningful actions.'

3   Botzem et al. (2009) identify the analytical surplus of the governance perspective in its potential for describing and analysing regulatory structures and especially its dynamics under a process perspective.

4   *Leitbilder* are a core concept of science and technology studies – especially with German scholars – to deal with the cognitive elements, the shared (or divergent) understandings and visions attached to a technological innovation by the actors involved (Dierkes et al. 1996).

5   See also for political science: In his pledge for 'technology-aware policy research' Bendrath (2009: 7f) states that 'political scientists do not seem to be very good at taking the specific technological properties of a techno-centric policy field (such as Internet governance) into account.'

6   Since the 1980s, this focus on the impact of technology on social life has been under the suspicion of clinging to technological determinism and has consequently been marginalized in sociological accounts of science and technology strongly dominated by a constructivistic paradigm (Meister et al. 2006).

7   See for example Eszter Hargittai's piece on early radio regulation and its analogies to Internet regulation (Hargittai 2000); Lawrence Lessig (1999, 2001) and Jonathan Zittrain (2008) for a

thorough analysis of the mutual causations in the technological development of the Internet and its regulation; for 'fitting the Internet into our lives' on the user-side Deirdre Hynes and Els Rommes (2006) and Röser (2007b).

8   A telling case for this is the regulation of copyrighted work, which has in recent years been closely accompanied not only by debates about its goals, necessities and legitimacy but also by technological measures and an immense upturn of contract law. Stefan Bechtold stressed very early on that these developments in different regulatory mechanisms lead to a privatization of copyright (Bechtold 2002; 2003). Stuart Graham and David Mowery (Graham and Mowery 2003) describe the relation between innovation in the software industry and legal reforms in patent and copyright law as a co-evolution in which 'mutual causation and influence' take place.

9   See for example the interactionist approach of Joachim Höflich (2003), who argues on the grounds of Goffman's frame theory that there are certain 'computer frames' that consist of specific use cases ascribed to a device or service and frame the interactions of users. Jan Schmidt (2007, 2009) has adapted and enhanced this to a convincing frame for the analysis of social-media practices.

Chapter 8

Veto Players and the Regulation of Media Pluralism:
A New Paradigm for Media Policy Research?

Ulrike Klinger

Introduction

A number of media reforms and their overtly friendly regulations towards the interest of powerful media conglomerates have nurtured the idea that no media policy can be made that goes against the interests of the media industry (such as Legge Gasparri 2004 in Italy or Ley Televisa 2006 in Mexico). In the wake of an ever growing media concentration and the medialization of politics, several scholars are sceptical when it comes to the bargaining potential of governments and parliamentarians vis à vis the organized interests of commercial media outlets. Can media companies indeed 'write their own communication laws,' as Bagdikian (2000) has claimed? This article deals with the widely assumed intervention of media organizations in policy-making processes aimed at regulating their core interests, such as introducing or lowering ownership limits, cross-media merger prohibition or content regulation. In political communication literature, it has been argued that market dominance of media organizations translates into bargaining power in political processes (among others, Baker 2007; Compaine and Gomery 2000; McQuail 1997). Some authors even fear the ultimate rise of 'mediocracies' and suggest that media policy could not be implemented against the private interest of powerful media outlets and owners. Here I propose confronting this notion with veto player theory (VPT), a relatively new frame of policy analysis. This approach was introduced by George Tsebelis (2000/2002) and is (so far) most prominently used by political scientists (Andrews and Montinola 2004; Ganghof 2003; Merkel 2003; Natali and Rhodes 2004; and others).

From a scholarly perspective, the question of how policy output is produced, what happens to proposals, interests and participation once those elements have been digested in the processes of policy-making, compromising and forming majorities for a reform project, is not new. Systemic, structural and actor-centred approaches have been employed to study the complex interactions that translate norms, ideas and reform pressure into generally binding laws and regulations, promulgating policy cycles, input/output schemata and analysing actor configurations. Veto player theory assumes that not all actors in policy-making processes are created equal, but that a certain number of institutional and partisan actors *have to agree* to a proposed change in order to alter the legislative status quo. It claims that if we know the political actors who have to agree to a certain reform, and if we can identify their policy preferences then we can predict the policy outcome. In this article, I aim to introduce veto player theory to media policy analysis, arguing that it may serve a fruitful purpose in distinguishing the relevant from otherwise important actors and shed a more realistic light on the media industry's potential impact on policy-making.

Media policy posits a very special policy field and is negotiated within a variety of arenas, from cultural policy to competition regulation or copyright law. Usually, media policy evokes little to no mass public mobilization and is negotiated among political elites. With the advent of governance concepts, stakeholders and media actors have increasingly been included in the analysis of policy-making process. Media owners, journalists and media activists regularly serve as experts and engage in self- and co-regulating mechanisms (Puppis 2007). Formal paths to influence policy outcomes have supplemented the wide array of informal ways that media actors have taken to place their interests on the political agenda and lobby to avoid, circumvent or establish certain regulations. In this game, media actors have strong incentives to influence media policy-making, as many of their interests inevitably rival those of political actors: if legislators promote media pluralism they eventually increase economic competition; if they lower the thresholds of media concentration, the business interest of economic expansion will be blocked. Especially in the field of regulating media pluralism and diversity of ownership, particular private actors have strong incentives to exert influence. But how can actors without any factual voting or veto power and with no right to legislative initiative influence the political agenda and the formation of majorities? Who can influence whom and with what strategies?

To assume that media actors, even large media conglomerates, can simply make their own laws underestimates the complexity of policy-making. It also incautiously equates the very different concepts of political power and media power. Neither do majorities randomly appear or disappear, and earlier theorists on policy-making have attempted to explain why and how legislators, stakeholders and civil society form coalitions to see reform projects through the legislative process. With his advocacy-coalition framework Paul A. Sabatier, for instance, has shown 'that the most useful aggregate unit of analysis is not any specific governmental institution but rather a policy subsystem, i.e. those actors from a variety of public and private organizations who are actively concerned with a policy problem' (Sabatier 1988: 131). He argued that people get involved in politics, because they seek to translate their norms and beliefs into public policy. Actors who share normative and causal beliefs as well as problem perceptions and who show a tangible coordinated activity are thought of as advocacy coalitions, attempting to initiate and to influence reform processes. Sabatier, and also governance concepts that include non-elected actors in the analysis of the legislative processes, enlarge the scope of participating actors. Tsebelis' VPT, however, attempts to distinguish important from decisive actors and to focus on the actors who have the necessary constitutional power and majorities actually to set the agenda and make policy decisions. In the following argumentation I will briefly outline Tsebelis' concept, propose a further sub-division of his typology of veto players, suggest substantiating the somewhat unclear figure of 'indirect' veto players and address some major shortfalls of VPT.

Assumptions of Veto Player Theory

Veto players are defined as actors whose consent is indispensable to change the legislative status quo – either because of constitutional provisions or partisan majority patterns.[1] In this regard, an actor does not become a veto player whenever they use their veto to block a reform but due to the *potential* to do that. Tsebelis distinguished two types of veto players: institutional and partisan. Institutional veto players are determined by the basal settings of a polity. The constitutional structure of any political system lays out whether parliaments are divided into two chambers or united in only one chamber, which competences are given to the head of state and whether this includes strong or weak veto power, or which institutions are required to ratify or review certain policy changes.[2] A one-chamber parliament and a president without veto power would count only as one institutional veto player, whereas two-chamber parliaments in presidential systems combine to two collective and one individual institutional veto players. Varying constitutional designs of political systems, which scholars have clustered in classic dichotomies such as parliamentary versus presidential, consociational versus majoritarian, direct versus representative democracy, thus translate into different veto player configurations. The intermediate step of identifying veto players in political systems can help to overcome frequent problems of comparative research, because it enables us to compare policy-making processes in very different political systems and to avoid intervening system variables. As the institutional structure of polities tends to remain stable, VPT centres on the partisan actors within these institutions. Partisan veto players are determined by majority patterns in the legislative bodies and are the political parties that can form a majority. In governmental coalitions sometimes not all the votes of smaller partners are needed to manufacture consent on an issue – however, all coalition members can be counted as veto players if small parties are relevant to the stability and the survival of government coalitions (Merkel 2003; Tsebelis 2002).

After identifying the veto players, the second step is to evaluate their political preferences in relation to the current state of regulation (status quo). Tsebelis argues that reform or policy change is the more likely when the number of veto players is low, their internal cohesion is strong and their policy preferences are largely congruent. He refers to the cross-section of policy preferences among veto players as the 'winset': The more policy objectives they share or the closer their ideological positions are, the larger the winset.

> Policy outcomes are the result of two factors: the preferences of the actors involved and the prevailing institutions. Given that the identity of players and their preferences are variable, while institutions are more stable, policy outcomes will vary depending on who controls political power as well as where the status quo is. (Tsebelis 2002: 17)

To identify veto players we thus (1) take into account the relevant institutional actors, then (2) count the number of parties necessary to form a majority and (3) review the number of partisan veto players with regard to absorption: if a veto player's preferences are already part of the preferences of another veto player, it is not counted.[3]

Example: Italian Veto Players and Majority Patterns 1996–2008:

Both Italian parliamentary chambers have to agree on a reform bill. For a policy change, the governing parties need to form minimal winning coalitions in both chambers. The number of partisan veto players within the governing coalition shows that Silvio Berlusconi's coalitions (2001–2006; 2008–2013[4]) tend to be built with significantly fewer veto players than governments of the centre-left. Considering the strong internal cohesion of Berlusconi's business-firm party Forza Italia or Popolo della Libertà and the dependence of his coalition partners, two of Tsebelis' three factors underline why he is so effective in policy-making and succeeded in passing the Gasparri Law (2004) in the face of fierce opposition and a (weak suspensive) presidential veto. Romano Prodi's centre-left coalition (2006–2008) in contrast included 12 partisan veto players. The ideological distance between these small and fragmented left parties was vast and the internal cohesion weak. VPT clearly shows that it was not the lack of a centre-left senate majority that doomed it to failure in 2008 (and ended communication minister Paolo Gentiloni's media reform project) but its specific veto player configuration, which made any policy change, and therefore effective government, unfeasible (see Table 1).

Tsebelis and other scholars have used this concept for large-N comparative studies: the number of veto players at a given time and their position on a left/right ideology scale in relation to the legislative status quo were used to measure the probability of policy change.

Table 1: Distribution of Government Coalition Mandates in the Italian Parliament and Number of Partisan Veto Players.

Legislative Period	Government Coalition	Mandates *Camera dei Deputati* (majority: 316)	Mandates *Senato* (majority: 159)	Partisan VP	Type of Veto Players (VP)
XIII (1996–2001)	Centre-Left	323	169	5	Reform-Making VP
XIV (2001–2006)	Centre-Right (Berlusconi II)	368	176	3	Reform-Making VP
XV (2006–2008)	Centre-Left (Prodi)	347	158	12	Reform-Blocking VP
XVI (2008–2013)	Centre-Right (Berlusconi III)	344	174	3	Reform-Making VP

Wolfgang Merkel, who tested VPT in three case studies on German social and tax reforms, argued convincingly that VPT provides a 'frugal, but elegant' frame, but he considered it to be particularly fruitful in medium-sized and small case study analyses. A large number of cases and a reduction to mere veto-player counting would not do justice to Tsebelis' triad of number, ideological distance and internal cohesion (Merkel 2003). Furthermore, comparative case studies of a small sample allow a more detailed analysis of policy preferences and also an assessment of influential non-veto players and their impact on the veto players' preferences, which is embedded into the context of a reform project.

Reform-Making, Reform-Blocking and Indirect Veto Players: Enlarging the Scene

As Tsebelis sought to make VPT fit for quantitative large-N comparative studies, he focused on institutional and partisan veto players. His approach aims to explain why reforms sometimes pass or fail and which factors determine the possibility of policy change. VPT is silent on the questions of when and why veto players cooperate and reach agreements not to use their veto. The role of indirect veto players or pivotal players such as labour unions, interest groups, non-governmental organizations, lobbyists, the church, courts, grassroots movements and activists or media organizations also remains unclear and under-operationalized. Because the extent of veto power varies among veto players, further sub-types of reform-making and reform-blocking veto players as well as key players should be distinguished.

Tsebelis' differentiation of institutional and partisan veto players is conclusive and reflects the logic of democratic decision-making. It is also plausible and essential to assess the internal cohesion of political parties, because – depending on political cultures and institutional traditions – parties do not always operate as homogeneous actors. Yet, VPT is blind to the varying extent of veto power. Depending on majority patterns and voting modes within the legislative institutions, veto players may set the agenda, block and create reform initiatives – or just veto a policy change. With reference to David Easton's (1965) input/output scheme of policy-making, the differentiated sub-types of veto players and their relations can be visualized as in Figure 1.

Some parties or coalitions may not have enough votes to effectively set the political agenda, formulate and pass reform projects, but they may still be able to block initiatives from other parties or coalitions. This situation can often be found in 'divided government' situations or multi-party systems without government majorities in parliament. Such actors can be referred to as *reform-blocking veto players*. In this situation, small parties who intrinsically hold no veto power can become politically significant *key players* with the mere purpose of ensuring a majority for a certain reform project. Key players only exist in concert with *reform-blocking veto players* and the intention of forming a minimal winning coalition. Only with the help of key players can *reform-blocking veto players* become *reform-making veto players*. Key players are not veto players, because they are (technically) substitutable and can neither block nor bring about policy change by themselves. Another type that is underdeveloped in Tsebelis'

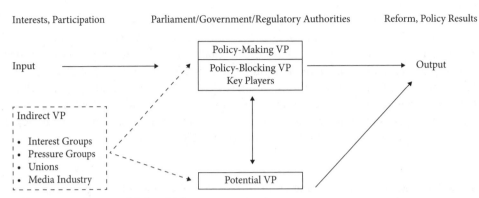

Figure 1: Veto Players and Policy-Making.
(Author's illustration)

concept are *potential veto players*. Depending on the institutional structure of a political system, these actors can hold significant veto power. Potential veto players are not a direct part of the legislative process but have to be activated to join the game: constitutional courts or qualified majorities in referendums. On the input side of policy-making processes, one can find *indirect veto players*. Non-elected actors intending to influence policy-making, such as interest groups – or powerful media organizations – can become indirect veto players if they succeed in capturing at least one of the veto players and convincing them to act on their behalf.

Media Companies as Indirect Veto Players

Although media companies are neither institutional veto players nor legitimated through elections, media-owner oriented reform projects and deregulation have nurtured the debate on their political influence. At this point, the argument leaves aside the role of media actors and media companies in the process of political intermediation (*Politikdarstellung*) but looks at their role in policy-making processes. It is important to distinguish these two roles of media actors in order not to exaggerate their undeniable interpretative power in political intermediation and to confuse it with political influence at the input side of policy-making. The central question is: Can media power supply sufficient political influence to media owners to become indirect veto players and exert significant influence on media policy-making?

For all interest groups in media politics the means of political influence is direct lobbying.[5] Media companies can thus become direct veto players if they can convince at least one veto player to become an agent for their particular interest – to put it on the legislative agenda, support it and build a minimum winning coalition. To do this, media companies, similar to interest groups, labour unions or environmental activists, have to persuade veto players of an (at least partial) congruence between their policy preferences. Media companies must succeed in effectively winning over and instrumentalizing at least one veto player. How and

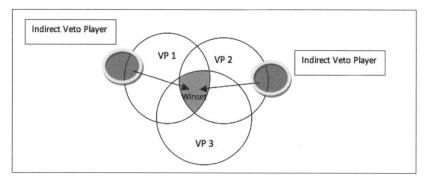

Figure 2: Indirect Veto Players and Veto Players' Preferences.
(Author's illustration, based on Tsebelis 2002)

if this can be achieved depends on the levels of corporatism and clientelism prevalent in a given political system, on the networking of political and particular actors as well as on the timing and sequencing of attempts at influence, as there are more and less opportune moments and constellations for any reform initiative. Within this configuration, particular actors emerge with a variety of strategies to become indirect veto players and to incorporate their policy preferences into the preference setting of a veto player (see Figure 2).

Here the similarities between media companies and other particular actors seeking political impact come to an end, because media companies in modern mass democracies have exclusive bargaining chips: direct access to the public and the opportunity to influence political timing through setting the media agenda. Furthermore, medialization processes have strengthened the bargaining potential of media companies, as they function as gatekeepers during electoral processes and have become central figures with regard to vote-seeking interests of political parties. The significance of the mass media for political intermediation (that is, the varying channels and modes through which people receive information about politics and policy outcome; see Gunther et al. 2007) has increased at the expense of political parties and other intermediary actors (Katz and Mair 2002). The popular postulate that Western democracies were on their way from party democracies to media democracies or 'mediocracies' illustrates the widespread idea among scholars that media companies have extended their influence from policy-explaining to policy-making. According to its proponents, parties and candidates are increasingly dependent on support from media actors. The argument goes that because it was not possible to win an election in the face of media opposition (Brettschneider 2002), no professional career in politics was possible and no law could be passed without media acceptance (Schäfer 1999). Werner A. Meier (2004: 5) pointed out:

(T)he negotiation and formation of media policy increasingly follows the interests of dominant media companies and less the necessities of the public or a democratic society.

[…] By exerting concerted influence on media policy, representatives of industry have repeatedly succeeded in influencing policies oriented at the structural framework as well as state interventions in the media sector. No government can enact media policy against the media but only in accord with them.[6]

Some authors, such as Thomas Meyer (2002), go as far as understanding the legislative action of politically legitimized veto players as mere 'acts of testing' (*Testhandeln*), where the media's reaction (not the public's) leads to policy modifications. In this view, the media are seen as veto players with a stranglehold over political actors:

> Only in rare and exceptional cases would it be advisable for a top political actor dependent on majority support to defy current media responses and hope that future electoral majorities will rally behind his program. In a media democracy these rare instances must be calculated carefully in advance because of the risks involved. In this sense most crucial political proposals take shape as bargaining processes carried on under the klieg lights of media reactions. Their tendency is to shift from being exogenous to endogenous events within the media. (Meyer 2002: 95)

This suggests that political actors anticipate the media's reaction and operate affirmatively in the interests and preferences of media owners. However, this argument does not find general acceptance among scholars. There have been convincing calls for caution against overemphasizing a 'ubiquitously notorious medialization' (*ubiquitär notorische Medialisierung*; Alemann and Marschall 2002: 8) and underestimating the role of political parties. It is certainly true that a 'party state in crisis' (Puhle 2002) cannot be equated with a 'media democracy,' in which the mass media takes over the functions and competences of parties and renders the latter dispensable. VPT puts the analytical focus of policy studies back onto political parties and allows for a thorough assessment of influence from partial actors and their attempts to become indirect veto players.

Benefits and Shortfalls of Veto Player Theory

The most important contribution of VPT to policy analysis is in making comparisons between different political systems easier. It can be employed to analyse and compare all political systems, regardless of their institutional design: one can compare policy-making in two-party presidential democracies with bicameral parliaments (United States) and unicameral multi-party parliamentary systems (Germany). (The one limit is that one can only apply it to democracies, as there is no veto politics in one-party or authoritarian systems.) This is particularly useful in transatlantic comparative studies or research into European cases, where we find dissimilar legislative structures and the explanatory reach of results is challenged by the variety of system variables that may affect the behaviour of actors and the outcome of political processes. Scholars cannot only track policy-making to understand how and why certain laws and regulations were passed or not but also evaluate and make informed predictions on the probability of policy change – which is especially interesting to political scientists and connects to the concepts of *government responsiveness* and *reform capability*. Whereas responsiveness, i.e. the perception that a government can deliver outcomes demanded by its citizens, is a central factor of generating system legitimacy, reform capability is used as a variable for assessing the quality of a given democracy and informs about whether a government is able to adapt legal frameworks to new conditions and react to reform pressure.[7]

Another substantial benefit of VPT is that it enables us to see who influences agenda setting and the political outcome – and who does not. Any reform in any policy field will find powerful opponents, whether they are nuclear-power-plant owners, the tobacco or the defence industries, pensioners or farmers. Media owners for their part not only have strong incentives to influence media policy but also convincing means of doing so: as they can control access to the mediated public sphere and the qualitative appearance of political actors in this arena, they are crucial partners and gate-keepers for parties and political elites. The discretion of most media policy-making processes and the limited public attention to this policy field (beyond political, cultural and media elites) further enhance the bargaining power of media corporate interests. However, the enormous media power that political communication scholars attribute to media organizations should not mislead them into wrongly locating the core of political power and decision-making. In his theory on communicative power, Manuel Castells (2009) underlined that although power is multi-dimensional and constructed around networks political actors and the state still define the basic rules of the game:

> The network of power constructed around the state and the political system does play a fundamental role in the overall networking of power. This is […] because the stable operation of the system, and the reproduction of power relationships in every network, ultimately depend on the coordinating and regulatory functions of the state and political system […]. So while communication networks process the construction of meaning on which power relies, the state constitutes the default network for the proper functioning of all other power networks. (Castells 2009: 427)

To focus on veto players, and therefore on the relevant actors of decision-making, can be helpful to break down and operationalize the role of 'the state', 'media power' and 'the government' into tangible research designs.

However, there are also some important weaknesses to be confronted when using this theoretical approach. As it is built on knowing the VPs policy preferences, the concept connects to rational-choice theories and all the problems involved in these assumptions (e.g. Green and Shapiro 1996). Leaving aside the problem that complete information is necessary for rational decisions, experiments have shown that people and political actors do not always choose the option that objectively maximizes their benefits. Institutional and partisan veto players are predominantly collective actors, their choices are the outcomes of internal negotiations and may differ significantly from any decisions an individual may have made. VPT is also silent on 'irrational' compromising among veto players and cannot explain when and why political actors cooperate across political lines, as in Italy's notorious *trasformismo*.

The focus on policy preferences of partisan veto players causes another blind spot. In this perspective, parties aim primarily at implementing their political goals and ideologies. But, parties also follow vote-seeking and office-seeking interests (Wolinetz 2002). This implies that a party may abandon or postpone a policy project in exchange for (expected) votes or support from another coalition partner who offers access to government office. This of course depends on the saliency of a policy content to the parties' general policy positions (a Green party may not support extended operation time of nuclear power plants in exchange for government office, but may adopt policy positions that are closer to the senior coalition partner). In short, partisan veto players follow diverse (and sometimes rival) interests and prioritize them. In the course of a legislative period and with regard to the electoral calendar, parties tend to put different emphasis on different interests at different times: unpopular reforms are not likely to be attempted before elections, even though they may fit well into the veto player's winset. Small parties may modify their policy preferences in order to become junior partner in a government coalition. Party positions may change from hardline (during electoral campaigns) to progressive or more lenient in certain policy fields (when in office) or even reverse – a phenomenon that became prominent with the *Nixon goes to China* paradigm (Cukierman and Tommasi 1998). Tsebelis is certainly right to underline the fact that veto players' incentives are crucial, but their vote- and office-seeking interests should be taken into account when analysing what exactly their incentives are. This, again, suggests that medium-sized and small case studies may be more fruitful for testing VPT than large-N samples.

Given that parties prioritize divergent interests, the factor of *timing* becomes important while studying why and how a reform process produces a certain output. Timing relates to the idea that interests and preferences of partisan veto players are not stable throughout legislative periods. Therefore, the size of the winset of shared preferences between veto players is in constant flux, although their ideological preferences may remain stable. This is also important for the question of when and how particular actors, such as media companies, may exert influence on veto players and become indirect veto players. Before electoral campaigns, parties and their elites are more vulnerable to lobbying, especially when they rely on financial support from private donors and media presence depends on their financial resources.[8] The *sequencing* of reforms is related to timing: to understand the positions of veto players vis à vis the status quo, previous reforms or reform attempts should be considered. Only on rare occasions do legislators decide on completely new issues; usually there is a 'reform history,' i.e. trajectories that can influence the preferences of veto players.

Conclusions: The Limits of Media Power in Policy-Making Processes

Despite its certain imperfections, VPT has proved to be useful to study reforms in other policy fields and has become a prominent concept in political science. It has been tested predominantly in welfare and tax policy contexts, finding answers to the general reform capability of governments, providing reasons for reform delays and explaining major policy shifts. It seems plausible that media policy scholars may contribute to the further development of the concept, as VPT may provide a tangible approach to address the intricate networks of political and media actors in media reform processes.

Scholars aiming to analyse policy outcomes and process-trace policy-making need to identify the relevant actors within the power networks where political and media systems meet. VPT in small- and medium-sized case studies allows us to do this, to compare legislative processes and to assess the role of media owners as stakeholders or indirect veto players, always embedded in the broader context of a reform. In this regard VPT is a useful tool when one wants to know about the political influence of media owners in legislative processes, why crucial and pressing reforms seem to be blocked and are not being passed, why a new law or regulation differs substantially from the initial proposal or why a legal initiative does not contain certain provisions that were central to one of its proponents. The bargaining power of media owners and conglomerates needs to be assessed in any particular reform process in order to overcome a mere structural assumption of 'power' and political influence. For analyses of lobbyism, corporatism and clientelism in media policy, VPT can help to identify the addressees, to locate entry points of interest groups and evaluate their potential policy congruence with decision-makers. With a differentiated focus on veto players and the reach of their veto power, the incentives of media and political actors and the timing and sequencing of a media reform, policy research can produce substantial and differentiated findings and identify the specific actors who network, negotiate and decide – in other words: turn the light on in the black box of media policy-making.

References

Alemann, U. v. and Marschall, S. (2002), 'Editorial', in U. von Alemann and S. Marschall (eds.), *Parteien in der Mediendemokratie/Political Parties in Media Democracy*, Wiesbaden: Westdeutscher Verlag, pp. 7–13.

Andrews, J. T. and Montinola, G. R. (2004), 'Veto Players and the Rule of Law in Emerging Democracies', *Comparative Political Studies*, 37: 1, pp. 55–87.

Bagdikian, B. (2000), *The Media Monopoly*, Boston: Beacon.

Brettschneider, F. (2002), 'Wahlen in der Mediengesellschaft/Elections in Media Society', in U. von Alemann und S. Marschall (eds.), *Parteien in der Mediendemokratie/Political Parties in Media Democracy*, Wiesbaden: Westdeutscher Verlag, pp. 57–80.

Baker, C. E. (2007), *Media Concentration and Democracy. Why Ownership Matters*, Cambridge: Cambridge University Press.

Castells, M. (2009), *Communication Power*, Oxford: Oxford University Press.

Compaine, B. M. and Gomery, D. (eds.) (2000) *Who Owns the Media? Competition and Concentration in the Mass Media Industry*, Mahwah: Lawrence Erlbaum Associates.

Cukierman, A. and Tommasi, M. (1998), 'When Does It Take a Nixon to Go to China?', *The American Economic Review*, 88: 1, pp. 180–197.

Easton, D. (1965), '*A Systems Analysis of Political Life*', New York: John Wiley & Sons.

Ganghof, S. (2003), 'Promises and Pitfalls of Veto Player Analysis', *Swiss Political Science Review*, 9: 2, pp. 1–25.

Green, D. and Shapiro, I. (1996), *Pathologies of Rational Choice Theory: A Critique of Applications in Political Science*, New Haven: Yale University Press.

Gunther, R., Puhle, H.-J. and Montero, J. R. (eds.) (2007) *Democracy, Intermediation and Voting on Four Continents*, Oxford: Oxford University Press.

Katz, R. S. and Mair, P. (2002), 'The Ascendancy of the Party in Public Office: Party Organizational Change in Twentieth-Century Democracies', in R. Gunther, J. R. Montero and J. Linz (eds.), *Political Parties. Old Concepts and New Challenges*, Oxford: Oxford University Press, pp. 113–135.

McQuail, D. (1997), 'Accountability of Media to Society. Principles and Means', *European Journal of Communication*, 12: 4, pp. 511–529.

Merkel, W. (2003), 'Institutionen und Reformpolitik. Drei Fallstudien zur Vetospieler-Theorie/ Institutions and Reform Politics. Three Case Studies on Veto Player Theory', in C. Egle, T. Ostheim and R. Zohlnhöfer (eds.), *Das Rot-Grüne Projekt. Eine Bilanz der Regierung Schröder 1998–2002/ The Red-Green Project. An Assessment of the Schröder Incumbency 1998-2002*, Wiesbaden: Westdeutscher Verlag, pp. 163–192.

Meier, W. A. (2004), 'Gesellschaftliche Folgen der Medienkonzentration/Societal Consequences of Media Concentration', *APuZ (Aus Politik und Zeitgeschichte)*, B 12–13, pp. 3–6.

Meyer, T. (2002), *Media Democracy. How the Media Colonize Politics*, Cambridge: Wiley-Blackwell.

Natali, D. and Rhodes, M. (2004), 'Trade-Offs and Veto Players: Reforming Pensions in France and Italy', *French Politics*, 2: 1, pp. 1–23.

Puhle, H.-J. (2002), *Parteienstaat in der Krise: Parteien und Politik zwischen Modernisierung und Fragmentierung/Party-State in Crisis: Parties and Politics between Modernization and Fragmentation*, Vienna: Picus.

Puppis, M. (2007), 'Media Governance as a Horizontal Extension of Media Regulation: The Importance of Self- and Co-Regulation', *Communications*, 32: 3, pp. 383–389.

Sabatier, P. A. (1988), 'An Advocacy Coalition Framework of Policy Change and the Role of Policy-Oriented Learning Therein', *Policy Sciences*, 21: 2/3, pp. 129–168.

Schäfer, M. (1999), *Medienmacht macht Medienpolitik. Die Durchsetzungsfähigkeit der Interessen von Medienkonzernen/Media Power makes Media Policy. The Assertiveness of Media Comglomerates and their Interests*, Baden-Baden: Löw und Vorderwülbecke.

Tsebelis, G. (2000), 'Veto Players and Institutional Analysis', *Governance*, 13: 4, pp. 441–474.

———— (2002), *Veto Players. How Political Institutions Work*, Princeton: Princeton University Press.

Volcansek, M. L. (2001), 'Constitutional Courts as Veto Players: Divorce and Decrees in Italy', *European Journal of Political Research*, 39: 3, pp. 347–372.

Wolinetz, S. B. (2002), 'Beyond the Catch-all Party: Approaches to the Study of Parties and Party Organization in Contemporary Democracies', in R Gunther, J. R. Montero and J. Linz (eds.),*Political Parties. Old Concepts and New Challenges*, Oxford: Oxford University Press, pp. 136–165.

Notes

1   At this point, only the central claims of VPT can be sketched out, whereas large and deeply elaborated aspects have to remain uncommented on.

2   Whether constitutional courts can be considered to be veto players has remained a debated issue (Volcansek 2001).

3   An example: In Germany, with a one-chamber parliament and a president with no veto power, we find only one institutional veto player, the *Bundestag*. In the case of laws that will affect the budget of the German federal states, their collective representation, the *Bundesrat*, has to agree (*Zustimmungsgesetze*). In those legislative processes we find two veto players. However, if both *Bundesrat* and *Bundestag* are dominated by the same majority, we count only one institutional veto player and the number of the majority parties in one institution.

4   At the time of writing this chapter and in the light of several scandals involving Italy`s prime minister, it remains unclear whether Berlusconi's coalition will last until the formal end of the legislative period in 2013.

5   Direct lobbying is opposed to grassroots lobbying, which is not directed at bargaining with political elites, but to employ a 'going public' strategy and exert influence via mass mobilization.

6   Translation by Ulrike Klinger; original quote: 'Auch die Aushandlung und Gestaltung der Medienpolitik erfolgt immer stärker im Interesse von dominanten Medienunternehmen und weniger im Sinne der Öffentlichkeit bzw. einer demokratischen Gesellschaft. […] Durch konzertierte medienpolitische Einflussnahme gelingt es den Branchenvertretern immer wieder, sowohl ordnungspolitische Rahmenbedingungen als auch staatliche Maßnahmen im Mediensektor maßgeblich zu beeinflussen. Keine Regierung kann Medienpolitik gegen die Medien, sondern nur zusammen mit diesen durchsetzen.'

7   *Reform capability* is a central variable used by the sustainable governance indicators (SGI) with the intention to measure democratic quality among OECD members (see www.sgi-network.org).

8   In some countries, airtime for TV or radio spots is distributed among the competing parties by electoral authorities; in others airtime can be acquired on a free market.

PART II

NEW METHODS

Chapter 9

A Political Scientist's Contribution to the Comparative Study of Media Systems in Europe: A Response to Hallin and Mancini

Peter Humphreys

Introduction

The paper provides an overview of the development of theoretical approaches to comparing media systems since Siebert, Peterson and Schramm's classic *Four Theories of the Press* (1956). Considerable progress has been made in exploring comparatively the complex relationship between media systems and political systems. Hallin and Mancini's *Comparing Media Systems: Three Models of Media and Politics* (2004) has recently achieved a deservedly wide impact for its theoretical framework based on three distinct analytical models of media and politics:

(1) The Mediterranean or polarized pluralist model;
(2) The northern/central European democratic corporatist model; and
(3) The north Atlantic or liberal model.

The paper points to the ambitious scope but more limited usefulness of their actual classifications. In fact, Hallin and Mancini themselves were the first to admit that allocating certain countries to particular models, which are in fact ideal types, is not straightforward and unproblematic. This paper argues that these caveats hardly disguise the rather 'broad brush' character of their approach. The paper explores the way forward. It argues that it will be necessary to consider a more comprehensive range of salient political and political-economic variables. It also suggests that rather than concentrating on the production of neat typologies it is more useful to explore the patterns of congruence between particular media systems, which are often highly 'sui generis' in character, and the political and social systems within which they are embedded. This approach is informed by Kleinsteuber's (1993: 324) insight that while economic and technological developments point generally towards convergent outcomes, national specific political, social and cultural factors will explain much of the divergence. Moreover, the paper argues that application of the concepts of historical institutionalist (HI) theory – with its stress on path dependence – will be very useful for future comparative analysis.

The State of Comparative Research on the Relationship
Between Political and Media Systems in Europe

There has been a considerable amount of research done on European media systems, but relatively little of it has drawn for analytical inspiration on political science theories and concepts, and still less has it had an analytical focus on the relationship between the political system and the media system. Since the mid-1980s, there has hardly been any shortage of comparative data on the main structural characteristics of media systems. Very useful data about national media structures have been produced by the Euromedia handbooks (Kelly et al. 2004; Kleinsteuber et al. 1986), by the regular international handbooks produced by the Hans-Bredow-Institute (e.g. Hans-Bredow-Institut 2009) and by projects such as the three-volume multi-country study by the Open Society Institute's EU Monitoring and Advocacy Programme Network in cooperation with the OSI's Media Program (Open Society Institute 2005). As Thomaß (2007: 224) notes, the EU has also contributed numerous studies on a number of particular policy themes and also encouraged collaborative research projects. There have been scholarly comparative analyses of such themes as media concentration (Sánchez-Tabernero 1993; Sánchez-Tabernero and Carvajal 2002; Stock et al. 1997), press subsidies in Europe (Fernández-Alonso et al. 2006), the regulation of broadcasting (Goldberg et al. 1998; Hoffmann-Riem 1996; Jarren et al. 2002; Robillard 1995), technological and market 'forces for change in the European media' (Weymouth and Lamizet 1996), the introduction of digital television in Europe (Levy 1998), the European television industries (Iosifidis et al. 2005) and policies for public television in the digital era (Jarren et al. 2002; Iosifidis 2007). Alongside the Euromedia handbooks mentioned earlier, the Euromedia Research Group have also produced very useful edited collections of scientific comparative thematic contributions by its various national experts exploring the 'dynamics of media politics' (Siune and Trützschler 1992) and 'convergence, concentration and commerce' (McQuail and Siune 1998). Thus there is a considerable corpus of work drawing on a range of disciplinary approaches, including media and communication studies, journalism studies, law, sociology, economics, politics and history.

Yet, relatively few studies have drawn heavily on political science and focused closely on the relationship between political systems and media systems. This is perhaps surprising. In their highly influential *Four Theories of the Press*, Siebert, Peterson and Schramm (1956: 1f) maintained that: 'the press always takes on the form and coloration of the social and political structures within which it operates.' Similarly, in a ground-breaking article on the application of the comparative approach to this field, Kleinsteuber (1993: 324) observed that, whereas economics and technological developments point generally towards convergent outcomes, nationally specific political (and cultural) factors explain many of the enduring differences. Kleinsteuber's own work in this field has been prodigious (see e.g. Kleinsteuber 1982, 1993, 2002 and 2003; Kleinsteuber and Rossmann 1994; Kleinsteuber et al. 1991). A number of detailed studies of national media systems by political scientists would appear to confirm his insight. Thus, Humphreys (1994) has examined media policy in Germany, stressing the striking congruence of political institutional norms, structures and processes, the working of the media system and the making of media policies. Kuhn (1995) has produced the standard English-language work on the French media, similarly written from the perspective of a political scientist concerned with institutional norms, structures and processes. Most recently, Smith's (2007) study of the introduction of digital TV in the UK has provided a political scientist's perspective on UK broadcasting policy, applying a number of theoretical approaches from the policy analysis sub-discipline of political science, including the HI approach (more on which later). Recent years have also seen the appearance of excellent textbooks on comparative media systems and media policy (Puppis 2007; Thomaß 2007), which underline the importance of political science insights and approaches.

There have been a number of small-N comparative studies of media systems by political scientists. The advantage of such:

> 'focused comparisons' is that they allow for detailed and in-depth comparison. Analysis of similar media processes and institutions in a limited number of cases can 'illuminate the process or institution itself, or the politics of the countries in which it occurs'. (Peters 1998: 10)

The detailed case-study method allows the researcher to fully capture the context and complexities of each system. Thus, Dyson and Humphreys (1986; 1988) applied insights and concepts from political science to analyse the introduction of cable and satellite broadcasting in France, Germany and the UK during the 1980s. They drew primarily on the sub-disciplines of policy analysis and political economy, employing such concepts as national regulatory and policy styles to explain divergent outcomes. They focused on the relationship between new media policies and political institutional structures and processes. Other focused comparisons of broadcasting policies in Germany and UK have highlighted the persistence, despite strong technological and economic forces for convergent outcomes, of very distinctive policy profiles, arising from the countries' different political and legal traditions, cultures and institutional structures (Gellner 1990; Humphreys 1991; Stock et al. 1997). Comparing policies for digital television in France, Germany and the UK, Levy (1999), too, has pointed to the determinant influence of these countries' different politics and policy-making profiles.

Systematic large-N comparative studies are clearly more useful for developing theoretical generalizations and exposing false generalizations. However, large-N studies of media systems informed by political science are rare. In a study comparing media policy across a range of countries in western Europe, Humphreys (1996) pointed to the importance of such political science insights as differences between consensual 'power-sharing' systems that stressed social representativeness and more majoritarian and centralized strong executive political systems (Lijphart 1984; 1999) and also the differential impact on media policies of strong interventionist and liberal non-interventionist state traditions (Dyson 1980; Hall 1986). Humphreys also pointed to the distinctiveness of northern European democratic corporatist countries, which contrasted with liberal states such as the UK and statist ones such as France and (historically) 'Latin' Europe (Katzenstein 1985). In the northern European democratic corporatist countries, organized interests have played a strong role in media policy.

As noted, Hallin and Mancini (2004) have produced a ground-breaking, highly systematic media–politics typology that emulates Siebert, Peterson and Schramm's (1956) now outdated but still influential *Four Theories of the Press*. As is well known, Siebert et al. had produced a broad typology that distinguished between authoritarian, totalitarian, libertarian and social responsibility philosophical and political rationales for the organization of the media, a typology that clearly reflected the Cold War era in which they were writing. Hallin and Mancini's *Comparing Media Systems: Three Models of Media and Politics* (2004) is a much less general, less normative and less abstract typology, which is also far more relevant for the post-Cold-War era. It applies a more sophisticated analytical approach, exploring empirically the relationship between media systems and social/political systems.

Basing their comparative approach on the 'most similar systems' design, Hallin and Mancini chose to focus only on the media systems of the advanced capitalist countries of north America and western Europe. They posited three analytical models of media and politics: the 'Mediterranean or polarized pluralist' model, the 'northern/central European democratic corporatist' model, and the 'north Atlantic or liberal' model. Combining theories of political and media studies with empirical observations, they employed a number of indicators to assign 18 western countries into one of these three models. They introduced four main media system variables:

(1) The development of the media markets, focusing on the development of the mass-circulation press;
(2) 'Political parallelism', in the broad sense of the extent to which the media are partisan and reflect the major political positions;
(3) The development of journalistic professionalism; and
(4) The degree of state intervention in the media system.

They also explored some key political variables:

(1) The role of the state;
(2) Consensus versus majoritarian patterns of democracy;
(3) Individual versus organized pluralism, or liberalism versus corporatism;
(4) Rational–legal authority versus clientelism; and, lastly, moderate versus polarized pluralism in the party system.

To the 'Mediterranean or polarized pluralist model,' Hallin and Mancini assigned France, Greece, Italy, Spain and Portugal. The media in these countries, characterized by relatively low circulations for the press, were found to be subject to more state intervention than in the other models. The media were more aligned with highly polarized politics and were less 'professionalized'; journalism was more commentary oriented and more easily politically instrumentalized. The media systems of Scandinavia, the Netherlands, Belgium, Austria, Germany and Switzerland were commonly 'democratic corporatist.' These countries had a high-circulation press that was once closely aligned to the political parties but has since become commercialized and no longer so politicized; professionalization was strong. Lastly, Hallin and Mancini lumped together the UK, Ireland, Canada and the US as 'liberal,' with the market-predominant, medium-high circulations for the press and a politically neutral and information-oriented journalism that contrasted with the politicized and commentary orientation of the Mediterranean or polarized pluralist model.

Hallin and Mancini's (2004) 'three models of media and politics' undoubtedly provides an excellent basis for discussion about future comparative research. Although their approach has provided a highly interesting, indeed obligatory, reference point, there remain problems with their typology and models. The most obvious relates to their exclusion of post-communist central Europe and eastern Europe entirely. This omission could certainly be justified by the fact that at the time they were researching and writing their book these countries were very new democracies and not consolidated or established enough to merit meaningful comparison with the other liberal democracies under examination. Of course, these countries are now certainly worthy – indeed very interesting – candidates for comparative examination, and there is a growing literature on them. A COST supported collection edited by Jakubowicz & Sükösd (2008) has produced a detailed overview of the performance of the media systems in post-communist central and eastern Europe. Blum (2005), too, added an eastern European model and two further models from beyond Europe, to an adapted version of the Hallin and Mancini framework.

A more serious weakness is the highly questionable validity of Hallin and Mancini's attribution of some countries to a certain model. The British media system for example, with the marked partisanship of its national press and its distinctive approach towards strong public service broadcasting, obviously differs greatly from the North Atlantic liberal model to which Hallin and Mancini consign it (on the UK see Gibbons 1998). The French media system, too, appears 'sui generis,' not easily classified as 'polarized pluralist' or 'Mediterranean' (on France see Kuhn 1995). Close examination hardly merits the German media system's classification along with the democratic corporatist Scandinavian countries. Germany's affinities to the liberal model rules out press subsidies for instance. It is also distinguished by its federalism, the striking constitutional legalism of its broadcasting policy and its strong conditioning by a very particular historical experience of disjuncture: notably fascism and the Anglo-American influence in the immediate post-war occupation (on Germany see Humphreys 1994). Nor, one might add, does Canada merit easy classification alongside the US system. Its complex regulatory framework for broadcasting has been protectionist and interventionist, akin to that of France, precisely in order to preserve its cultural distinctiveness against the imposing market power of its giant continental neighbour. In other words, the broad-brush inclusiveness of the Hallin/Mancini approach is problematical, given the marked heterogeneity of liberal–democratic media systems. Admittedly, Hallin and Mancini fully acknowledged the significant difficulties presented in producing their classifications, observing that the UK and France in particular could be conceived as mixed cases. Nonetheless, as McQuail observed in reviewing Hallin and Mancini's book:

> A great many judgements in drawing the boundaries of the models are inevitably a matter of degree and often of subjective decision. The reader is continually being cautioned on this point, but it does tend to undermine confidence in the viability of the classification. (McQuail 2005: 268)

Another shortcoming of Hallin and Mancini's typology is the lack of detailed attention to what might cause change in the character of the media–politics relationship that they see as being rooted in historical development, apart from the inexorable 'triumph of the market.' They see the historical experience of late democratization and a historical experience of polarized pluralism as having left an enduring imprint on the southern European cases. Yet, as they note, the German Weimar Republic (1919–1933) was a 'classic' case of polarized pluralism. Germany was by far the most striking historical case of polarized pluralism in Europe; after all, it brought the Weimar political system (1919–1933) crashing down. Austria, too, was a similarly 'late democracy' and highly polarized in the inter-war years, to the point of having a near civil war experience, notably the serious clashes between socialists and conservatives of February 1934. Indeed, Hallin and Mancini (2004: 155f) note that this left a rather more enduring mark on the Austrian post-war press than on Germany's. Yet, for Hallin and Mancini these two countries' highly polarized pasts appear to be far less significant than their 'northern European-ness.' The question of what makes a historical legacy in one set of countries less significant for other comparable cases begs for more causal explanation. The disjuncture of Allied occupation is briefly mentioned, but no satisfactory causal explanation is offered to this question. It is suggested that the Northern European traditions of rational–legal authority and professionalization contrast with southern European clientelism. However, this might be seen as a cultural stereotype bearing rather too much of the burden of causality.

Despite Hallin and Mancini's careful attention to their chosen variables, their final classification of the countries into northern, southern and 'North Atlantic' is indeed suggestive of a degree of stereotyping. This is a common pitfall. Esping-Andersen's famous *Three Worlds of Welfare Capitalism* (1990) has been criticized for aligning Britain, with its National Health Service and (largely) state-funded higher education, alongside the US as 'liberal' (Castles and Mitchell 1993). Esping-Andersen was also criticized for leaving out of consideration the distinctive southern European welfare systems (Bonoli 1997; Ferrera 1996; Leibfried 1992). Yet the widespread notion among political scientists that there is a Mediterranean 'model of democracy,' based on the southern European countries' cultural, social, economic and historical–developmentalist similarities, has also been shown to be highly misleading when their political systems are subjected to close analysis. In terms of the institutional variables of Arend Lijphart's contrasting majoritarian and consensus models of democracy they certainly do not form a distinctive and cohesive cluster (Lijphart et al. 1988).

Accordingly, if the media system reflects the social and political system within which it is embedded, then closer inspection of the media–politics relationship in these southern European countries might be expected to reveal important differences between them. Thus, the majoritarian nature of Spanish and Greek post-dictatorship democracy has led to single-party control of public broadcasting, whereas in Italy's more consensual model of democracy for many post-war years control was shared among the main political parties, Christian Democrats, Socialists and Communists. This is certainly noted by Hallin and Mancini, but it might be considered to be a *major* point of difference, giving pause to reflect on the coherence of the model. Clearly, much depends on the choice of and weight given to particular variables. Had Hallin and Mancini chosen to place more stress on all the variables making for majoritarian or consensus-style political systems, then they would also have concentrated more on the degree to which media systems were centralized or decentralized, this being one of the main dimensions of majoritarian or consensus democracies according to Lijphart (1984), the others being the government/party dimension and the pluralist/corporatist dimension of interest intermediation, both of which are considered by Hallin and Mancini. This would, of course, affect the clusters considerably. Germany, Spain and the US are all highly decentralized; Germany's federalism, Spain's marked decentralization and US localism being highly significant media-system characteristics. By contrast, the UK and France with their metropolitan centred media are highly centralized (notwithstanding France's regional press, and the UK's Scottish press). For media policy, it can matter greatly whether policy-making is centralized or decentralized. The German case, where the *Länder* are responsible for media policy, exemplifies the importance of this variable (Humphreys 1994). Largely ignored by Hallin and Mancini, the federal-unitary variable points to another omission, namely, considerations of ethnic/linguistic homogeneity or heterogeneity. The existence of sub-state national identities has a special bearing on whether countries have opted for federal or at least decentralized media systems, as in the case of Spain, as well as Belgium and Canada. And this in turn relates to yet another variable only obliquely considered by Hallin and Mancini: media market size.

Market size is a highly significant variable for comparative analysis, the importance of which Hallin and Mancini underplay, their consideration of markets being largely confined to press markets, in particular in relation to newspaper circulation. This is, indeed, rather an odd omission given that they draw on Katzenstein's (1985) work on democratic corporatism, which focused precisely on the common problems and solutions of 'small states in world markets.' Market size obviously impacts greatly on the media and media policy. Trappel (1991) has shown how a factor market size has been a determinant for small European countries' media policies. Characterized by dependence, scarcity of resources and economic and cultural vulnerability, they argue that small states have tended to pursue corporatist policies in order to re-establish a degree of control of their own destinies. However, recent market and technological developments have put this approach under considerable pressure. In connection with small states' lack of autonomy, Iosifidis has noted:

> the size of the market usually defines the relative strength of a country in the television sector and thus the influence it can exert or is exerted on it by neighbouring countries. For small countries such as Ireland, for example, influenced as it is by a powerful neighbour (Britain), it is more difficult to develop an independent television system. (Iosifidis 2007: 18)

For this reason, Iosifidis deliberately chose the size of the country as a major criterion for his recent cross-national examination of policies for public television, including examination of three large (Britain, France and Spain) and three small west European countries (Ireland, Sweden and Greece).

A recent special issue of the journal *The International Communication Gazette*, edited by Manuel Puppis and Leen d'Haenens (2009), is devoted to media regulation in small states. In its introductory article, one of the editors Puppis (2009: 7) draws attention to the Hallin and Mancini typology's neglect of the small media system dimension and points to a significant number of ways that smallness may affect small states' media regulation, not least living next door to a 'giant neighbour' that shares the same language (e.g. Canada and the US; Ireland and UK; Austria and Germany; Belgium and France; Switzerland and France, Germany and Italy). Indeed, in a short comment piece within the same journal issue, Hallin (2009) himself makes the highly pertinent observation that 'State size clearly does matter, though like other variables that affect the character of media systems, its effects are likely to be complex, and we should not expect any simple, consistent pattern in small state systems' (Hallin 2009: 101). In this, Hallin argues persuasively that generalizations, such as those holding that small states will tend to have more interventionist and more corporatist policy approaches, simply do not stand. Of course, as Hallin (2009: 101) notes, 'Like other variables that affect media systems [...] state size interacts with other variables, and its effects are therefore not consistent.'

A more comprehensive framework of salient political and political–economic variables might appear as follows (see Table 1):

The fact that countries' political histories and cultures matter clearly comes out strongly in Hallin and Mancini's comparative analysis. However, they arguably pay too little attention to the variable impact of historical *disjuncture*. Comparative research should pay due attention, for example, to the very different legacies among European countries (e.g. Germany, Austria or Spain) of their experiences of having had a dictatorial regime in the twentieth century. Analysis of the (west) German case suggests that the disjuncture of defeat and Allied occupation combined with a self-conscious effort to learn from history has been a singularly important determinant of the development of the post-war media institutions and media policy-making (Humphreys 1994). However, the experience of democratization and its impact on the mass media have been very different in Spain. Hardly had Spain emerged from Franco's dictatorship in 1976, than broadcasting was confronted with the technological (primarily satellite in Spain) and economic pressures that led to European broadcasting systems being liberalized and commercialized. Private broadcasting developed in what might be described as a regulatory vacuum, with no national regulatory authority to oversee content standards and diversity, quite in contrast to the (west) German story (Vilches 1996: 185f). In similar light, as already suggested, the new democracies of post-communist central and eastern Europe would now make for very interesting cases. What has been the legacy of their recent experience of authoritarianism? How has that particular experience affected them? What special challenges have they faced and how have they met them?

Table 1: Key National Political and Politico–Economic Variables Bearing on the Media System.

Political History	Continuity	–	Disjuncture
Market size	Large	Intermediate	Small
Concentration (in different markets: national, regional, etc. and press, TV, cross-media, etc.)	High	Intermediate	Low
Ethnic/Linguistic Structure	Homogeneous	Regionalized	Sub-State Nationalism(s)
Ideological Polarization	High Polarization	Moderately Polarized	Low Polarization
Majoritarian or Consensual on Federal/Unitary Dimension	Unitary (Majoritarian)	Decentralized	Federal (Consensus)
Majoritarian or Consensual on Party/Government Dimension	Governmental Alternation/ Party System Dualism/ Single-Party Governments (Majoritarian)	Moderate Power Sharing/ Intermediate	Governmental Power Sharing/ Multi-partyism/ Grand Coalitions/ (Consensus)
Majoritarian or Consensual on Interest Intermediation	Pluralism (Majoritarian)	Clientelism	Corporatism (Consensus)
State Tradition	Strong ('dirigisme')	Intermediate	Weak ('liberal')
Influence of Judicial Law Making/Constitutional–Legal Rulings	Strong	Intermediate	Weak
Legal Tradition	Common Law	–	Civil (Code) Law

Another important factor arguably rather neglected by Hallin and Mancini, for all their insightful discussion of rational–legal authority versus clientelism, are legal-system traditions and attributes. Common law or civil law traditions suggest quite different approaches to media law, the former being conducive to 'judge-made law,' the latter being conducive to a codified body of special press law for instance (Humphreys 1996). This has a bearing, too, on different national approaches to such matters as protections for privacy, journalistic confidentiality and indeed journalistic employment and autonomy. It is also necessary to consider the role of judicial review in the political system and its impact on policy-making. Through its case law in this field, since its first television ruling in 1961 establishing the ground rules for the legislators and media policy-makers of the German *Länder*, the German Federal Constitutional Court (*Bundesverfassungsgericht*) has functioned, in Hoffmann-Riem's (1996: 119) words, 'much like a legislature' with respect to the development of that country's broadcasting regulation. This may be a unique feature of the German model, though constitutional courts have certainly played a significant role in media policy in other systems as well (the US and Italy).

Comparative study might also extend to examination of such interesting media policy themes as national regulatory approaches and 'styles' and their implications for, say, democratic representativeness and accountability. Thus Jarren et al. (2002) have devoted attention to exploring current regulatory trends in broadcasting, examining the balance between state and market, the mix between regulation, self-regulation and co-regulation, the degree of representativeness in different countries' regulatory structures, their varying degrees of exposure to public accountability, their differing mechanisms for this, and so forth. Another very important theme is the degree of pluralism in the media system, measured in both structural and behavioural terms. How much media concentration is there? How does it impact on editorial competition and the diversity of media content? What is the real or presumed impact on public-opinion formation? What measures are accordingly employed in different countries to counteract media concentration? Do they reflect national political (and social and cultural) factors? (For a recent analytical discussion and framework, see Lange 2008.)

Admittedly, Hallin and Mancini's study is rather more concerned with the relationship between politics and journalism, primarily news media, than with analysis of media policy. The aspects of the media system that they concentrated on were questions of the degree of neutrality or partisanship of the media ('political parallelism'), the degree of professionalization (autonomy, professional ethics and conduct, public service orientation, etc.) or, conversely, the scope for instrumentalization of the media, and the related impact of the extent of state intervention on the media system. Unquestionably, these are very important matters. Future comparative research might explore further the degree of media freedom and pluralism offered by different systems, exploring carefully the different national historical, political, legal and regulatory, and economic conditions for media freedom (e.g. Czepek et al. 2009).

In this connection, an interesting comparative research initiative – the Media and Democracy Monitor (MDM) project – is an attempt by an international research team coordinated by Josef Trappel of the University of Salzburg (formerly of the Institute of Mass Communication and Media Research, University of Zurich) to monitor the extent to which different western European media systems have fulfilled specific democratic functions such as providing a free flow of information, providing a forum for public debate, reflecting a diversity of opinions and viewpoints and mobilizing political participation, and acting as a watchdog against the abuse of power. Hallin and Mancini had made some attempt to assess the strengths and weaknesses of each of their three models in terms of supporting democracy, but really there was little systematic analysis of this aspect. The MDM project explores a comprehensive range of both structural features (external constraints on media organizations such as laws and regulations) and performance features (media organizations' actual behaviour). The project has identified an extensive range of indicators across three dimensions of democratic function: namely, information flow, interest mediation (pluralism and diversity) and watchdog. For example, the indicators for structural conditions and the information flow are the geographic distribution of news-media availability and patterns of news-media use. The performance criteria for the information flow function are internal rules for newsroom democracy, internal rules against internal influence on the newsroom by owners and internal rules against external influences (e.g. advertisers). The structural indicators for the interest-mediation/pluralism function include various measures of media concentration (national, regional cross-media, etc.) whereas the performance indicators were levels of self-regulation and public participation. The structural indicator for the watchdog function is whether there is a national instrument to monitor the performance of news media, whereas the performance indicators included the extent of commitment to journalistic training and resource indicators. In this project, discussion of structures involves a more comprehensive consideration of both market and legal characteristics than Hallin and Mancini's typology, investigating for instance differences in journalistic working conditions and differences in journalistic legal protections and how such factors might impact on journalism (see e.g. Trappel and Maniglio 2009; d'Haenens et al. 2009).

Convergence? Or Historical Institutional Path Dependencies?

Hallin and Mancini's penultimate chapter (preceding the conclusion) argues in favour of a significant degree of convergence on their North Atlantic model, what they call the 'triumph of the liberal model.' They take care to point out that some variation will certainly persist precisely because of differences in political, legal and regulatory systems. Indeed, their whole approach pays great attention to history and the way events and institutional patterns from the past have influenced the directions the media systems have taken. Nonetheless, they seem to conclude that a striking measure of 'Americanization' is resulting from a combination of socio-economic modernization, technological and media market developments. Just as their 'three models of media and politics' appear to track Esping-Andersen's (1990) 'three worlds of welfare,' this observation, too, echoes debates from the political economy literature, surrounding the notion that the Anglo-Saxon system is more congruent with globalization and that therefore other models of capitalism have had to converge on it in order to remain competitive. However, again, a number of important academic studies have refuted the convergence hypothesis. Studies by Schmidt (2002), Weiss (1998), Hall and David Soskice (2001), have all pointed to the durability of distinctive models of capitalism, stressing the crucial mediating role of national institutions.

Given Hallin and Mancini's emphatically history-informed approach, it is perhaps surprising that they do not draw on or engage more with the political-science theory of historical institutionalism (HI), though the concept of 'path dependence' does feature very briefly (Hallin and Mancini 2004: 12, 300f). HI sees institutions, defined broadly to include norms, informal rules and procedures as well as formal rules and structures, as crucially important in explaining political outcomes. The institutional features of different countries present structural constraints and opportunities for political agency (Hall 1986; Thelen and Steinmo 1992; Zysman 1983). Central to the theory is the concept of path dependency, which posits that past policy has an enduring and largely determinate influence on future policy. National institutional profiles are persistent and resistant to change, and institutions become 'locked in' to particular policies (Peters 2005).[1] Thus, historically rooted national institutional differences explain the persistence of national idiosyncrasy. According to the HI perspective, when change does occur, such as under the force of powerful exogenous pressures such as technological change and internationalizing markets, the reforms follow characteristic national paths. Thus, Steven Vogel's (1996) comparative analysis of regulatory reform in industrial societies pointed to the 'many roads of re-regulation.'

A number of other detailed empirical studies would seem to confirm the high relevance of the historical institutional perspective for explaining the persistence of diversity in media systems that are undergoing common processes of technological and market change. For example, Levy's (1998) study of the introduction of digital broadcasting at the national and EU levels found a striking resilience of distinct national 'policy styles' to erosion by either the EU or by exogenous forces of technological change and globalization of media markets, despite the commonly experienced pressures and reform agendas. Jääsaari's (2007) comparative study of Canadian and Finnish responses to technological convergence shows that policies for the introduction of digital television were largely shaped by ideas and institutional structures from the past. Iosifidis (2007), comparing policies for public television in the digital era in six European countries, comes to a similar conclusion: policies for public television varied significantly according to different past approaches to public broadcasting in the six cases. The theme of the continuity of national 'policy styles' in the face of powerful pressures for change comes across from single-country studies as well. Thus, Humphreys (1994) has demonstrated the enduring, primarily institutionally conditioned features of German media policy. Media policy-making in Germany has been strongly characterized by certain political institutional features, notably federalism and the strong role of constitutional law. Although competition among the *Länder* for media investment has resulted in a considerable amount of deregulatory *Standortpolitik*, the institutional entrenchment of a strong system of *Länder*-based public broadcasting institutions combined with repeated constitutional–legal guarantees for media structures that ensure a high degree of pluralism and diversity have strongly underpinned the central role of public service broadcasting. The importance of historically persistent and different political and regulatory structures and approaches is the theme of some of the contributors, most notably Kuhn and Stanyer (1999) and Regourd (1999), to an edited collection by Scriven and Lecomte (1999) comparing television broadcasting in France and the UK.

A recent research project, conducted by the author and colleagues,[2] has confirmed the high relevance of path dependence in explaining media policy and further substantiated the durability of national historical institutional norms, structures and processes. Funded by the UK Economic and Social Research Council (ESRC), the project examined the impact of globalization, technological pressures and (de)regulatory competition on public service broadcasting and other elements of the 'cultural policy toolkit' (Grant and Wood 2004), such as production subsidies, programme quotas and media ownership rules. It looked at Canada and France as exemplars of countries that have traditionally had a strong commitment to a markedly protectionist cultural toolkit model based on a sophisticated array of subsidies and regulatory instruments. It also looked at Germany and the UK as exemplars of countries that were much more open to free trade and globalization, but which traditionally had a very strong commitment to public service broadcasting. The project's core hypothesis was that under conditions of trans-frontier broadcasting, regulatory competition between states (or indeed sub-national jurisdictions such as the German *Länder)*, keen to maximize media investment, encourages pro-market deregulation. Our empirical research detected serious challenges, associated with changing market and technological conditions, to the cultural policy toolkits of all four cases. Policy-makers were grappling with the challenges of falling investment in home-originated high-cost/quality television content, particularly fiction, drama and children's programmes – core areas of national cultural and public service production. Although there was plainly evidence of far-reaching deregulation of the private television sector, in none of these four countries could it be said that deregulatory competition had been driving television regulation downwards, specifically with regard to their cultural policy toolkits. Despite the challenges, these countries' respective cultural policy toolkit models appeared robust and demonstrated a striking degree of path-dependent policy-making. Canada and France remained as reliant as ever on scheduling and investment quotas and subsidies and provided evidence that it was possible to hold a cultural protectionist line against strong international commercial pressures. They were also fiercely supportive of this model on the international stage, reflected in their stance in international trade negotiations and their leading role in the adoption of the UNESCO Universal Declaration on Cultural Diversity. Germany and the UK remained strongly reliant on public service broadcasting as the core element of their cultural toolkit models, and the public broadcasters were much more highly valued and supported than in Canada and France. Policy-makers in all four cases were adapting these distinct national models to the digital era in ways that very closely reflected past policy approaches (Gibbons and Humphreys 2012).

Conclusion

There can be no questioning the major scholarly contribution that Hallin and Mancini have made to the systematic comparative study of the complex relationship among media systems, society and politics. They have established an impressively high standard for approaching such complex matters. Their work is certainly one of the most important books on political communication. However, this paper has argued that their *Three Models of Media and Politics* has certain key weaknesses. The paper concludes, firstly, that Hallin and Mancini might have integrated rather more elements into their analytical framework. Secondly, it argues that media systems are not so easily fitted into identifiable models; they are more 'sui generis' than Hallin and Mancini have allowed. The paper suggests, therefore, that rather than expend time and energy on producing neat typologies, it is much more important to explore in depth a more comprehensive range of salient political, legal and economic variables that bear on the media system. It applauds Hallin and Mancini's history-informed approach but suggests that HI theory from political science might be more explicitly employed for the study of the relationship between often highly idiosyncratic national media systems and the socio-cultural and political system in which they embedded.

References

Blum, R. (2005), 'Bausteine zu einer Theorie der Mediensysteme', *Medienwissenschaft Schweiz*, 2: 1, pp. 5–11.

Bonoli, G. (1997), 'Classifying Welfare States: A Two-Dimension Approach', *Journal of Social Policy*, 26: 3, pp. 351–372.

Castles, F. G. and Mitchell, D. (1993), 'Worlds of Welfare and Families of Nations', in F. G. Castles (ed.), *Families of Nations: Patterns of Public Policy in Western Democracies*, Aldershot: Dartmouth, pp. 93–128.

Czepek, A., Hellwig, M. and Nowak, E. (eds.) (2009), *Press Freedom and Pluralism in Europe: Concepts and Conditions*, Bristol and Chicago: Intellect.

d'Haenens, L., Marcinkowski, F., Donk, A., Maniglio, T., Trappel, J., Fidalgo, J., Balčytienė, A. and Naprytė, E. (2009), 'The Media for Democracy Monitor Applied to Five Countries: A Selection of Indicators and their Measurement', *Communications*, 34: 2, pp. 203–220.

Dyson, K. (1980), *The State Tradition in Western Europe*, Oxford: Martin Robertson.

Dyson, K. and Humphreys, P. (eds.) (1986), *The Politics of the Communications Revolution in Western Europe*, London: Frank Cass.

———— (with Negrine, R. and Simon, J-P.) (1988), *Broadcasting and New Media Policies in Western Europe*, London and New York: Routledge.

———— (eds.) (1990), *The Political Economy of Communications: International and European Dimensions*, London and New York: Routledge.

Esping-Andersen, G. (1990), *The Three Worlds of Welfare Capitalism*, London: Polity.

Ferrera, M. (1996), 'The Southern Model of Welfare in Social Europe', *Journal of European Social Policy*, 6: 1, pp. 17–37.

Fernández-Alonso, I., de Moraga, M., Blasco Gil, J. J. and Almiron, N. (2006), *Press Subsidies in Europe*, Barcelona: Generalitat de Catalunya and Institut de la Comunicació, Universitat Autonoma de Barcelona.

Gellner, W. (1990), *Ordnungspolitik im Fernsehwesen: Bundesrepublik Deutschland und Großbritannien*, Frankfurt am Main, Bern, New York and Paris: Peter Lang.

Gibbons, T. (1998), *Regulating the Media*, 2nd edition, London: Sweet & Maxwell.

Gibbons, T. and Humphreys, P. (2012), *Audiovisual Regulation Under Pressure: Comparative Cases from North America and Europe*, London and New York: Routledge.

Goldberg, D., Prosser, T. and Verhulst, S. (eds.) (1998), *Regulating the Changing Media: A Comparative Study*, Oxford: Clarendon Press.

Grant, P. and Wood, C. (2004), *Blockbusters and Trade Wars: Popular Culture in a Globalized World*, Vancouver and Toronto: Douglas & McIntyre.

Hall, P. (1986), *Governing the Economy: the Politics of State Intervention in Britain and France*, Oxford: Oxford University Press.

Hall, P. and Soskice, D. (eds.) (2001), *Varieties of Capitalism: The Institutional Foundations of Comparative Advantage*, Oxford: Oxford University Press.

Hallin, D. (2009), 'Comment: State Size as a Variable in Comparative Analysis', *International Communications Gazette*, 71: 1–2, pp. 101–103.

Hallin, D. C. and Mancini, P. (2004), *Comparing Media Systems: Three Models of Media and Politics*, Cambridge: Cambridge University Press.

Hans-Bredow-Institut (ed.) (2009), *Internationales Handbuch Medien*, Baden-Baden: Nomos.

Hoffmann-Riem, W. (1996), *Regulating Media: The Licensing and Supervision of Broadcasting in Six Countries*, New York and London: Guilford Press.

Humphreys, P. (1991), 'Political Structures and Broadcasting Marketisation: A Comparison of Britain and West Germany', in M. Moran and M. Wright (eds.), *The Market and the State: Studies in Interdependence*, Basingstoke: Macmillan, pp. 200–218.

———— (1994), *Media and Media Policy in Germany: The Press and Broadcasting since 1945*, Oxford and Providence: Berg.

———— (1996), *Mass Media and Media Policy in Western Europe*, Manchester: Manchester University Press.

Iosifidis, P. (2007), *Public Television in the Digital Era: Technological Challenges and New Strategies for Europe*, Houndmills: Palgrave Macmillan.

Iosifidis, P., Steemers, J. and Wheeler, M. (2005), *European Television Industries*, London: BFI.

Jääsaari, J. (2007), *Consistency and Change in Finnish Broadcasting Policy: The Implementation of Digital Television and Lessons from the Canadian Experience*, Abo: Abo Akademi Press.

Jakubowicz, K. and Sükösd, M. (eds.) (2008), *Finding the Right Place on the Map: Central and Eastern European Media Change in a Global Perspective*, Bristol and Chicago: Intellect.

Jarren, O., Weber, R. H., Donges, P., Dörr, B., Künzler, M. and Puppis, M. (2002), *Rundfunkregulierung: Leitbilder, Modelle und Erfahrungen im internationalen Vergleich. Eine sozial- und rechtswissenschaftliche Analyse*, Zürich: Seismo.

Katzenstein, P. J. (1985), *Small States in World Markets: Industrial Policy in Europe*, Ithaca: Cornell University Press.

Kelly, M., Mazzoleni, G. and McQuail, D. (eds.) (2004), *The Media in Europe: The Euromedia Handbook*, London: Sage.

Kleinsteuber, H. J. (1982), *Rundfunkpolitik in der Bundesrepublik*, Opladen: Leske + Budrich.

———— (1993), 'Mediensysteme in vergleichender Perspektive: zur Anwendung komparativer Ansätze in der Medienwissenschaft: Probleme und Beispiele', *Rundfunk und Fernsehen*, 41: 3, pp. 317–338.

———— (2002), 'Mediensysteme im internationalen Vergleich: Ein Überblick', in K. Hafez (ed.), *Die Zukunft der internationalen Kommunikationswissenschaft in Deutschland*, Hamburg: Deutsches Übersee-Institut, pp. 39–58.

———— (2003), 'Medien und Kommunikation im internationalen Vergleich. Konzepte, Methode, Befunde', in F. Esser and B. Pfetsch (eds.), *Politische Kommunikation im Internationalen Vergleich. Grundlagen, Anwendungen, Perspektiven*, pp. 78–103.

Kleinsteuber, H. J. and Rossmann, T. (1994), *Europa als Kommunikationsraum: Akteure, Strukturen und Konfliktpotentiale*, Opladen: Leske + Budrich.

Kleinsteuber, H. J., McQuail, D. and Siune, K. (eds.) (1986), *Electronic Media and Politics in Western Europe: Euromedia Group Handbook of National Media Systems*, Frankfurt and New York: Campus.

Kleinsteuber, H. J., Wiesner, V. and Wilke, P. (1991), 'Public Broadcasting im Internationalen Vergleich', *Rundfunk und Fernsehen*, 39: 1, pp. 33–54.

Kuhn, R. (1995), *The Media in France*, London and New York: Routledge.

Kuhn, R. and Stanyer, J. (1999), 'Television and the State', in M. Scriven and M. Lecomte (eds.) (1999), *Television Broadcasting in Contemporary France and Britain*, New York and London: Berghahn, pp. 2–15.

Lange, B-P. (2008), *Medienwettbewerb, Konzentration und Gesellschaft. Interdisciplinäre Analyse von Medienpluralität in regionaler und internationaler Perspecktive*, Wiesbaden: VS.

Leibfried, S. (1992), 'Towards a European Welfare State', in Z. Ferge and J. E. Kolberg (eds.), *Social Policy in a Changing Europe*, Frankfurt: Campus, pp. 245–279.

Levy, D. (1999), *Europe's Digital Revolution: Broadcasting Regulation, the EU and the Nation State*, London and New York: Routledge.

Lijphart, A. (1984), *Democracies: Patterns of Majoritarian and Consensus Government in Twenty-One Countries*, New Haven and London: Yale University Press.

———— (1999), *Patterns of Democracy Government Forms and Performance in Thirty-Six Countries,* New Haven and London: Yale University Press.

Lijphart, A., Bruneau, T. C., Diamandouros, P. N. and Gunther, R. (1988), 'A Mediterranean Model of Democracy? The Southern European Democracies in Comparative Perspective', *West European Politics*, 11: 1, pp. 7–25.

McQuail, D. (2005), 'Review of Daniel. C. Hallin and Paolo Mancini, Comparing Media Systems: Three Models of Media and Politics. Cambridge University Press, 2004', *European Journal of Communication*, 20: 2, pp. 266–268.

McQuail, D. and Siune, K. (eds.) (1998), *Media Policy: Convergence, Concentration and Commerce*, London: Sage.

Open Society Institute (2005), 'Television Across Europe: Regulation, Policy and Independence', http://www.soros.org/initiatives/media/articles_publications/publications/eurotv_20051011. Accessed 15 November 2010.

Peters, G. (1998), *Comparative Politics: Theory and Methods*, Basingstoke: Macmillan.

——— (2005), *Institutional Theory in Political Science: the New Institutionalism*, London: Continuum.

Puppis, M. (2007), *Einführung in die Medienpolitik*, Konstanz: UVK.

——— (2009), 'Media Regulation in Small States', *International Communications Gazette*, 71: 1–2, pp. 7–16.

Puppis, M. and d'Haenens, L. (eds.) (2009), Special Issue of *The International Communications Gazette*, 71: 1–2.

Regourd, S. (1999), 'Two Conflicting Notions of Audiovisual Liberalisation', in M. Scriven and M. Lecomte (eds.), *Television Broadcasting in Contemporary France and Britain*, New York and London: Berghahn, pp. 29–45.

Robillard, S. (1995), *Television in Europe: Status, Functions and Powers in 35 European Countries*, London, Paris and Rome: John Libbey, The European Institute for the Media, Media Monograph 19.

Sánchez-Tabernero, A. (1993), *Media Concentration in Europe: Commercial Enterprise and the Public Interest*, Düsseldorf: The European Institute for the Media, Media Monograph 16.

Sánchez-Tabernero, A. and Carvajal, M. (2002), *Media Concentration in the European Market. New Trends and Challenges*, Pamplona: Servicio de Publicaciones de la Universidad de Navarra.

Schmidt, V. A. (2002), *The Futures of European Capitalism*, Oxford: Oxford University Press.

Scriven, M. and Lecomte, M. (eds.) (1999), *Television Broadcasting in Contemporary France and Britain*, New York and London: Berghahn.

Siebert, F. S., Peterson, T. and Schramm, W. (1956), *Four Theories of the Press*, Urbana: University of Illinois Press.

Siune, K. and Trützschler, W. (eds.) (1992), *Dynamics of Media Politics: Broadcast and Electronic Media in Western Europe*, London: Sage.

Smith, P. (2007), *The Politics of Television Policy: The Introduction of Digital Television in Great Britain*, Lewiston, Queenston and Lampeter: Edwin Mellen Press.

Stock, M., Röper, H. and Holznagel, B. (1997), *Medienmarkt und Meinungsmacht: Zur Neuregelung der Konzentrationskontrolle in Deutschland und Großbritannien*, Berlin und Heidelberg: Springer.

Thelen, K. and Steinmo, S. (1992), 'Historical Institutionalism in Comparative Politics', in S. Steinmo, K. Thelen and F. Longstreth (eds.), *Structuring Politics: Historical Institutionalism in Comparative Analysis*, Cambridge and New York: Cambridge University Press, pp. 1–32.

Thomaß, B. (ed.) (2007), *Mediensysteme im internationalen Vergleich*, Konstanz: UVK.

Trappel, J. (1991), *Medien, Macht, Markt: Medienpolitik westeuropäischer Kleinstaaten*, Wien und St. Johann im Pongau: Österreichischer Kunst- und Kulturverlag.

Trappel, J. and Maniglio, T. (2009), 'On Media Monitoring – The Media for Democracy Monitor (MDM)', *Communications*, 34: 2, pp. 169–201.

Vilches, L. (1996), 'The Media in Spain', in T. Weymouth and B. Lamizet (eds.), *Markets and Myths: Forces for Change on the European Media*, London and New York: Longman, pp. 173–201.

Vogel, D. (1996), *National Styles of Regulation: Environmental Policy in Great Britain and the United States*, Ithaca: Cornell University Press.

Weiss, L. (1998), *The Myth of the Powerless State*, New York: Cornell University Press.

———— (2003), 'Bringing Domestic Institutions Back In', in L. Weiss (ed.), *States in the Global Economy*, New York and Cambridge: Cambridge University Press, pp. 1–33.

Weymouth, T. and Lamizet, B. (1996), *Markets and Myths: Forces for Change in the European Media*, London and New York: Longman.

Zysman, J. (1983), *Governments, Markets and Growth: Financial Systems and the Politics of Industrial Change*, Ithaca: Cornell University Press.

Notes

1   An earlier and similar political science perspective had stressed characteristic national 'policy styles' or national 'regulatory styles' (e.g. David Vogel 1986).

2   The project (ESRC Ref: 000 23 0966) was conducted by the author together with Professor Thomas Gibbons of the Law School, University of Manchester, and Dr Alison Harcourt, of the Politics Department, University of Exeter. For further details see the ESRC Society Today website: http://www.esrcsocietytoday.ac.uk/esrcinfocentre/viewawardpage. aspx?awardnumber=RES-000-23-0966

Chapter 10

What We Talk about When We Talk about Document Analysis

Kari Karppinen & Hallvard Moe

Introduction

Most studies in communication policy research employ documents as research material in one way or another. With the growth of the Internet and computer-mediated research tools, policy researchers can access and search a wider range of documents with greater ease than ever before. As a distinctive research method, however, document analysis is not especially well explicated either in textbooks on the methodology of media and communication studies or in most actual research contributions. In fact, although the term itself is used routinely in some languages – such as German and Norwegian – 'document analysis' is not even much used in English-language contributions to the field of media and communication studies.[1]

Some of the ambiguities of document analysis as a research method can be explained by disciplinary barriers between different strands of media and communication studies, and between the field of communication studies and broader discussions in public policy analysis and political science. However, the challenges do seem to apply to social research more broadly. As John Scott (1990: ix) has noted, interviews, questionnaires and other methods figure centrally and in detail in textbooks and courses on social science research methods, but documentary research is usually considered in only a fragmentary way. Often it is as if the use of documents was self-evident, without much need for any further methodological reflection. Yet, the increasing availability and ease of accessing various sources of data that can be identified as documents also creates methodological challenges.

The purpose of this chapter is to review different uses and definitions of the terms 'document' and 'document analysis' in recent communication policy research and to point out some common methodological problems and confusions surrounding the notions. Also drawing on neighbouring disciplines and the broader field of policy studies, we argue that document analysis as a distinctive research method remains, if not under-developed, at least under-communicated in much of communication policy research. In particular, we address the problem of the implicit distinctions, found especially in textbooks, among document analysis, textual analysis and other interpretative techniques used in different strands of media studies.

As different research questions and objectives necessitate different approaches, our aim is not to define one correct way of doing document analysis. Nor will we focus in detail on the actual work of or tools involved in collecting and analysing documents.

Rather, by assessing some existing contributions and their varying methodological approaches, we argue that explicating the process from research interests and data gathering through to the actual analysis would not only strengthen the validity of communication policy research but also increase its impact both in academic and policy debates.

Within the social sciences there are several different notions of what constitutes a document. In one much-quoted definition, sociologist John Scott (1990: 5) describes a document broadly as 'an artefact which has as its central feature an inscribed text' (see also Scott 2006a: xx). For sociologist David Altheide (1996: 2), a document is 'any symbolic representation that can be recorded or retrieved for analysis.' In a textbook on media policy research, Trine Syvertsen defines documents as 'written or audio-visual remains not produced or generated by the researcher' (2004a: 215, our translation).

Two interesting issues emerge from these definitions. The first is the distinction between documents and research literature. Syvertsen introduces this distinction, which leads to a restricted definition (see also Bryman 2001: 370), while Scott and Altheide's definitions cover practically all kinds of text. As such, they include more than definitions traditionally used in the discipline of history or political science (e.g. Johnson and Reynolds 2005: 206ff). The second issue concerns the definition of 'text.' Whereas Scott is careful not to delimit his approach to texts merely in the sense of written sources, he treats other text forms as marginal: 10 of the 195 pages in his book deal with visual texts such as paintings and photographs. Audio-visual texts are implicitly left out, as they also tend to be in contributions in political science. Syvertsen and Altheide, who write more from the perspective of media studies, on the other hand, employ an explicitly media-neutral concept of text. In the following, we will use these two issues as entry points to discuss challenges with the definition and use of documents in communication policy research.

Firstly, we address the problem of the status of documents and the role of the researcher. Contrary to common assumption, we argue that documents can be reactive, in the sense that they are not 'natural' or shielded from the researcher's intervention in the field. They therefore require methodological awareness. Secondly, we discuss how different research interests influence what we are looking for in documents. We make a distinction between an interest in documents as a source and as a topic of study. In the first case, documents are understood as more or less objective sources that can reveal the interests and intentions of their authors or in other ways uncover facts about a policy process. In the second case, documents are treated as meaningful social products or cultural artefacts that have independent consequences and are worth analysing in themselves.[2] Overall, the chapter emphasizes the importance of paying greater attention to basic epistemological assumptions while making methodological choices and for being explicit about analytical practices. In closing, we discuss inter-linkages among different research interests and point to potential ways forward for communication policy research.

The Status of Documents and the Role of the Researcher

The distinction between documents and research literature seems strongly entrenched in recent contributions to communication policy research. Eli Skogerbø employs the distinction in her study of conflicts and compromises in Norwegian media policy in 1983–1993, even though, quoting David Stewart, she refers to 'traditional books and journals found in libraries' as a kind of secondary sources (Skogerbø 1996: 51). In his analysis of the decision-making process of the Television Without Frontiers directives, Daniel Krebber does the same, separating 'published scientific literature' from other sources (Krebber 2002: 13). Despite her wide definition of document analysis quoted earlier, in her methodological discussion of document analysis Syvertsen focuses on 'public documents,' that is 'documents that affect a public decision-making process' (Syvertsen 2004a: 216, our translation). In her study of Finnish broadcasting policy, Johanna Jääsaari (2007: 51f) also makes the distinction between primary sources, or the 'paper trail' left behind by state agencies, and secondary sources, which consist of academic studies. For her, policy documents and other official documents represent reliable sources of factual information about policy processes, whereas secondary sources are useful for establishing the background and the importance of events and for evaluating the process after the manifest events.

Such studies invite a dichotomy between primary documents as the actual objects of the study and secondary documents as records or accounts of primary documents (see Altheide 1996: 3). In many cases the distinction is reasonable and commonsensical, even though it is made on largely pragmatic grounds. Still, there are more fundamental problems with this distinction, as it might be in danger of replicating the divisions of traditional historical research, where documents are understood to exist for the purpose of 'action' and are not written to inform researchers or any other detached observer (see Scott 1990: 12). According to this view, documents are written by people who are active participants in the process they describe. This also explains why documents are often perceived as primary sources that represent 'facts,' whereas literature is classified as secondary or background material that offers 'interpretation.' So the idea behind the distinction is that documents reveal something real about the outside world in a more unmediated or authentic way. They are thus regarded as more reliable than research literature, as it is never possible to be sure that the latter accurately or in an unbiased way records what actually happened or what is contained in the 'original' documents (Scott 1990: 12).

Writing about the use of documents in the qualitative research process, Klaus Bruhn Jensen (2002: 243) stresses their 'relatively naturalistic and unobtrusive nature.' 'The data are "found" rather than "made" through the researcher's intervention in the field' (Jensen 2002: 243). According to sociologist Alan Bryman (2001: 370), documents 'are simply "out there" waiting to be assembled and analysed.' Similarly, Syvertsen (2004a: 216, our translation) argues that an advantage with 'public documents' is that they are 'produced under "natural" conditions in the sense that the researcher has not affected the collected material.' Such statements lead to claims that the documents we deal with are non-reactive (e.g. Bryman 2001: 370; Sommer 1995: 362). In methodological discussions, reactive effects occur for instance when an experiment is affected by a pre-test, i.e. when the research process affects the data collection.

In practice, however, the assumption that documents, as opposed to secondary sources, are more authentic or objective is problematic on several levels. To begin with, research is a social activity, and methods and data are always closely related to theoretical ideas about what is important (e.g. Altheide 1996: 2, 8f). In practice, the researcher thus always interacts with documentary materials to place specific statements in a context for analysis. In the context of policy research, it is also problematic to make categorizations based on the purpose of the documents' authors. For example, is it not the purpose of many policy documents to review and interpret other documents, to inform detached observers, or even intentionally convey a policy problem and possible solutions in a certain light for the public? Problems with inaccuracy and bias also beset documents, so they cannot automatically be given the privileged status conventionally accorded to them (Scott 1990: 12).

As a consequence, the borders between documents and literature are inevitably blurred. As Scott puts it, there is a very real sense in which reading a book by other researchers is also documentary research (Scott 1990: 37). If one wished to study the texts produced by other researchers to understand their language and assumptions, then those texts would become primary documents (Altheide 1996: 4). Moreover, we need to ask whether policy reports or discussion papers written by researchers should be considered policy documents or as 'policy analysis literature.' And what about other sources, such as a newspaper article that seeks to 'document a policy process' but that also inevitably frames a policy problem in certain way?

The broader problem with the strict distinction of documents and literature thus has to do with the role of the researcher as one of the many actors influencing the policy discourse. As Brian Fay (1975: 68) argued in his classic critique of positivist tradition in policy analysis, it is analytically myopic to view theoretical–conceptual knowledge and its practical application as separate processes. Instead, discourses, concepts and theories travel reflexively among contexts of theory, politics and policy, with different actors applying them to different purposes. Academic theories and concepts thus feed back into society and are selectively introduced to various wider audiences and, sometimes, theoretical knowledge is purposefully mobilized in 'policy documents' for the purposes of political legitimation. In this sense, policy documents can also be understood as intellectual machinery that serves to transform abstract ideas into the realm of political calculation and action.

The way ideas and discourses travel between academic and policy contexts can be illustrated with examples from communication policy research and Norwegian media policy. The first example concerns the concept of public service broadcasting. In a 1990 article, Syvertsen discussed three meanings of public service broadcasting, based both on politicians' and media researchers' uses of the concept in the 1980s (Syvertsen 1990: 183ff). In her argument, the three meanings could be associated with different time periods: the public good meaning was important in the early years of broadcasting. It was replaced by the second meaning's ideas about the public sphere, which was in turn challenged by the third meaning of servicing audiences (see Syvertsen 2004b for an updated discussion).

In 1997, these three meanings were introduced to Norwegian media policy in the Public Service Council's first report (Allmennkringkastingsrådet 1997: 6f). The Public Service Council was set up as an independent advisory unit under the Ministry of Culture to assess the practices of public service broadcasters. At the time, Syvertsen was among its members. Importantly, the Public Service Council's report does not refer to the latter shift in meanings – from the public to audiences – but it does identify the different understandings. Since this introduction, the three meanings have permeated Norwegian policy-making processes. They surface for instance in a 2001 White Paper grandly titled 'In the Service of Freedom of Speech', a 'principled review of aims and means' of media policy (Regjeringen 2001: 4, 25), and are repeated in a 2007 White Paper titled 'Broadcasting in a Digital Future' (Regjeringen 2007).

The latter White Paper includes another relevant example of travelling ideas, concerning the potential democratizing effects of media audience participation. Here the document explicitly refers to a recent study of the number of participatory programmes on Norwegian television and states that:

> This can be interpreted as an expression of an important change in relation to who gets to express themselves in the public sphere. While it used to be first and foremost members of the society's elite who could use the mass media as a channel for expression, we see today that the media to a larger extent are available for ordinary people. (Regjeringen 2007: 26)

However, the study in question does not argue for such egalitarian shifts. In fact the researchers behind the study do not make any claims about potential democratizing effects, but rather point to continued social stratification of media participation (Karlsen et al. 2009).

Both these White Papers are key documents for anyone who wants to understand recent developments in Norwegian media policy (e.g. Moe 2010). And both build on contributions in the form of a systematic analysis by media researchers and apply researchers' arguments and findings in more or less well-founded ways. Such examples might not be as prevalent in other regulatory contexts.[3] Still, they at least point to important problems for communication policy researchers in upholding a strict division between documents and research literature – and considering documents as more 'natural' than other sources. Contrary to what is often claimed in methodology textbooks (e.g. Bryman 2001: 370), such documents are thus not immune to reactive effects.

Our aim here is not to provide any correct definition of a document that would solve such challenges. Instead, we argue that there is a need for researchers to acknowledge these aspects while dealing with documents as sources and to reflect on the criteria for choosing relevant documents based on the aim of the particular study in question. In addition, we need to bear in mind that undertaking communication policy research is in a very real sense always a normative action. Our assumptions, values and interests guide our research. Moreover, as the problems with separating research literature from policy documents illustrate, our participation in a social context calls for caution when claiming the role of a neutral observer.

Different Research Interests in Document Analysis

The second issue that emerges from the definitions of documents laid out in the introduction concerns their status as texts.

Obviously, many of the sources relevant for research questions raised in communication policy research are in the form of written material. Policy documents, strategic plans, press releases, annual reports, newspaper articles – accessible either as paper or online versions – inform many of our analyses. However, there are clearly audio-visual sources of equal relevance: parliamentary debates, official speeches, talks at business conferences, advertising or commercials, propaganda films, TV talk-show appearances, or radio news commentaries. In addition, physical arrangements pertaining to media, such as artefacts, technological devices or pieces of art, might also be considered as texts (Deacon et al 2007: 15; Jensen 2002: 244). The former kind is included in Syvertsen's definition quoted earlier, whereas the latter is not. Neither is included by Scott.

Contributions to communication policy research, including all the studies mentioned earlier, overwhelmingly concentrate on written documents. Both authors of this chapter have done so in studies of different definitions of media pluralism (Karppinen 2010) and the regulation of public broadcasters online (Moe 2009). In a recent study of the liberalization of broadcasting regulations in Switzerland, Austria and Ireland and their leitmotivs, Matthias Künzler (2009) notes that a definition of documents relevant for such a study could take both written and audio-visual form, but while embarking on the actual analysis he limits his sources to the written kind. Johanna Jääsaari (2007: 52) also notes the need to supplement official documents with other sources that reflect more widely held opinions on policy issues. Yet, she only refers to newspapers, magazines and websites and not to any audio-visual sources.

Audio-visual sources, whether mediated or unmediated, have the obvious disadvantage of being harder to grasp, archive and analyse. Nevertheless, strands of media studies based in the humanities have long experience with such work. It is also worth keeping in mind that research into written texts also entails challenges of this kind, whether we are dealing with old newspaper clippings or constantly updated, amorphous web pages (e.g. Brügger 2008). Clearly, the inclusion of the audio-visual aspects of documents in a specific analysis will depend on the research question. There might, for instance, be more to gain from a study of the meanings of and the backgrounds and considerations behind a regulatory development or a specific policy approach than from a mapping and comparison of actual regulatory instruments. This, then, has to do with what we are interested in when we analyse documents.

Apart from the form of documents, a basic issue often poorly articulated in actual research practice is the distinction between analysing documents as *sources* and as *topics* or *objects* (Scott 1990: 36; Østbye et al. 2007: 47). In the former case, the researcher is interested in what documents reveal about the real (material) world, how they reflect the actions or interests of political actors or how they describe the contents of a given law etc. In the latter case, the main concern is to explain the nature of the documents themselves: they are regarded as social products that are themselves consequential objects of analysis. In the following, we argue that these two approaches are related to different epistemological assumptions. These differences need to be addressed to bring us nearer to an understanding of what we talk about when we talk about document analysis.

Documents as Sources

In traditional policy analysis, documents are usually considered primarily as sources. Rather than being interested in the documents' qualities as texts in themselves, the interest lies in using them as 'sources intended to document a process' (Skogerbø 1996: 50; also Østbye et al. 2007: 47). When considered in this way it is assumed that documents somehow reflect the interests or actions of their authors or in some other way represent the facts of the policy process they refer to. So, by analysing documents we can uncover political interests or forces and determinants behind policy developments. In other words, the aim of using documents is to move from *source* to *fact* (Scott 1990: 11).

In this kind of research, documents can have a simply descriptive function. For instance, if the aim is to provide comparative information on the types of legislation in different countries, then the task of document analysis is only to find relevant documents and provide an accurate description of their content. Documents can also be considered important statements intended to communicate political actions. For instance, if the European Commission (2007) writes 'the European Union is committed to protecting media pluralism as an essential pillar of the right to information and freedom of expression,' we conclude that this actually signals a political intention. These are probably the most common ways of employing documents in actual research practice.

This kind of use stems from historical research (see Dahl 2004: 48ff; also Syvertsen 1992: 144ff). As Richard Collins comments, 'the policy researcher's task is to be a historian of the present without the assistance time affords "real" historians by winnowing away the chaff of irrelevant data and contingent associations and revealing fundamental structures' (1990: viii).[4] Importantly, although it is sometimes downplayed in methodological discussions (e.g. Scott 1990: 6ff; Østbye et al. 2007: 46ff; also Scott 2006b: vol. 1), using documents as sources implies some form of textual analysis: to be usable at all we need to interpret them with the aid of one or several of the analytical tools developed especially within the humanities (e.g. Bryman 2001: 380ff; Gripsrud 1995: 118ff; Künzler 2009: 159).

Examples of studies that use documents as sources include the studies mentioned earlier by Skogerbø (1996), Jääsaari (2007) and most other systematic studies of recent media policy developments. Studies of this kind are undoubtedly useful for our understanding of communication policy. However, we also know that documents have a rhetorical function. They can be used to legitimize political actions that have already been taken on completely different grounds, which are harder to record. Much of the political influence also resides in practices such as lobbying, which rarely leave behind any public documents. So even when they are used as sources, a researcher needs to assess the credibility of documents and to reflect on the intentions of their authors. These kinds of problems are also typical of historical research. It is in this sense that Scott (1990: 6), to name one key contributor, discusses criteria such as genuine and unquestioned origin, freedom from distortion, representativeness, and clarity in assessing the quality of documents. For instance, in assessing the statement that 'the European Union is committed to protecting media pluralism as an essential pillar of the right to information and freedom of expression' we inevitably have to consider the context of the statement, its relation to past political action and its rhetorical function. As most documents somehow reflect the process that has produced them, there is a need to be aware of the context and the social surrounding of the document in question to grasp its meanings and significance (e.g. Altheide 1996: 9). Typical ways of familiarizing oneself with the context involve complementing document analysis with other methods, such as interviews with key policy actors or other informants.

Documents as Texts

Apart from their use as sources, documents can be treated explicitly as texts or social products that have consequences in themselves, irrespective of their authors' intentions. Recently this notion has been employed in particular in constructivist approaches to public policy (Fischer 2003). In contrast to the conventional methods of document analysis, these accounts have increasingly employed methods such as discourse analysis, narrative analysis, argument analysis and metaphor analysis, all of which focus attention precisely on the quality of the documents as texts. This does not necessarily mean that it is the language of the documents itself that is of interest. Rather it is assumed that the themes and discourses, as well as the framing of policy problems they convey, are somehow politically consequential irrespective of the traditional institutional explanations. The hypothesis is that when revised frameworks of meaning become part of the public domain and are routinely used, social reality itself has changed (Altheide 1996: 69). Central to the constructivist perspectives is thus the recognition that the activities of governments, regulators and other policy actors are always bound up with discursive power.

Often such approaches are associated with the framework of governmentality and its focus on understanding the discursive aspects of political power and public policy (see Dean 1999; Foucault 1991). As Nikolas Rose and Peter Miller (1992: 178) note, political discourse by definition is 'a domain for the formulation and justification of idealized framings for representing reality, analysing it and rectifying it.' From this perspective, analysing policy documents is not so much about their relationship with facts or the objective political reality. Instead, documentary research is seen as a tool for analysing the value-laden assumptions behind policy-making.

Documents of various kinds can thus be understood to contribute to the governing of a certain area of social life as 'intellectual machinery' that renders the world thinkable and amenable to regulation (Rose and Miller 1992). Events need to be transformed into political language, and furthermore into information, reports and position papers. And although necessary, these can never be neutral – they are always bound to specific values and political rationalities.

From this perspective, policy documents can be analysed as discourse, much in the same way as communication scholars analyse newspaper stories, for instance, with an interest in the narratives and metaphors used in the documents, or the way they portray some courses of action as commonsensical and others as nonsensical.

Treating policy documents as *texts* has also been associated with the broader critique of empiricist or rationalist policy inquiry. According to Frank Fischer (2003), policy research that is concerned with evaluating policy choices or explaining their causes often assumes that the subject matter of research is self-evident and independent of any theoretical framework. Instead, it leans on documentary sources to analyse politics in terms of a more-or-less balanced competition between different interests. Most accounts of policy-making have thus focused on the way in which policy outcomes are determined by prevailing institutional arrangements, which structure the interests and behaviour of economic agents. Policy analysis and document analysis, in a somewhat caricatured form, is thus arguably reduced to a de-politicized scientism offering no genuine alternatives to established ways of thinking (Fischer 2003: 4f). More interpretative approaches, which understand ideas and their expression in politics as a form of political action, are therefore often regarded as being more 'critical' or 'normative' (Finlayson 2004: 530f).

In this sense the constructivist approach would seem to correspond with the criticism that media policy analysis has typically been long on realism, anxious to appear economically and technologically literate and rather short on idealism and fundamental criticism (McQuail 1997). Yet, as Des Freedman (2008) has recently emphasized, although policy-makers and sometimes even policy researchers may feel that they are involved in a rather dull, disinterested process of problem-solving, media policy is a deeply political phenomenon.

In some ways, the interest in political ideas and the assumptions that underlie policies and regulation is linked with the concept of media governance, which has recently become popular in mainstream media policy research. Though it is given various definitions, and some call it a 'fashion term' (Kleinsteuber 2007: 43), the concept seems to be introduced to stress the inclusion of actors beyond national authorities and different social forces in the analysis (e.g. Donges 2007; Syvertsen 2004a: 16ff). According to McQuail (2003: 91), media governance 'covers all means by which the mass media are limited, directed, encouraged, managed, or called into account, ranging from the most binding laws to the most resistible of pressures and self-chosen disciplines.' As opposed to policy or regulation, which often refers only to formal control, media governance has thus been used as a broader concept that includes various (informal) influences, claims and demands from different interests in society as well as the guiding principles and values that they are based on. The concept may potentially lead to innovative investigations in the context of documentary research. Still, the wider scope that such investigations must have when it comes to the gathering of data from relevant documents and its subsequent analysis should not lead to less attention being given to methodological issues.

Maria Michalis' (2007) recent study on European media governance is a good example of a study that employs a governance approach. In an ambitious and innovative discussion spanning some 60 years of developments, Michalis explains that her conception of media governance incorporates how theoretical understandings shape policy discourse and how they are employed, endorsed and institutionalized by political actors to legitimate or influence the definition and framing of policy problems (Michalis 2007: 17). This conception has direct consequences for her argument. For instance, Michalis (2007: 18f) notes how the European Commission has employed concepts such as technological convergence or globalization as a rhetorical means to portray its decisions as *a*political, technology-driven and unavoidable. Although this conclusion is apparently based on textual analysis of policy documents, neither the method nor the data collection is elaborated on.[5]

Another example of this kind of research in media policy is David Young's (2003) study of Canadian and European communication policy discourses. Young identifies three hegemonic discourses of communication technology and links them to struggles between dominant and subordinate agents in media policy. In identifying the discourses, he refers to illustrative quotes in official documents as well as research literature. In stressing the power of hegemonic discourses and their relation to different institutional actors, the approach seems to go beyond the standard explanations of traditional policy analysis and to combine both discursive and institutional factors. Yet, Young explains neither the method nor the document basis for his claims. It is thus unclear whether the three discourses are derived from theoretical debates and only are illustrated by quotes from policy documents or if are they derived from a systematic analysis of the documents themselves.

Moreover, studies like these, which deal with policy discourses in a broad sense, could arguably profit from including audio-visual documents in their analysis. Analysis of different audio-visual texts such as television talk shows, records of conference addresses or informational and commercial videos could build on the insight for instance from visual rhetoric (e.g. Kjeldsen 2004: 258ff) or semiotics (e.g. Seiter 1992) to complement the analysis of hegemonic policy discourses.

As we have shown earlier, there are different ways in which documents can be used in communication policy studies. In this sense, it can be argued that documentary research does not even constitute a method, as it does not say anything about *how* one uses documents (see Platt 1981). However, this does not free us as researchers from the requirement to explain our interest and how we use which texts when we analyse documents. This is a prerequisite for a more advanced discussion about the selection of novel forms of documents, investigations into policy discourses and other innovative approaches.

Conclusion

What we talk about, then, when we talk about document analysis is various textual analytical treatments of texts as sources or objects of study. The 'documents as sources' approach treats ideas as resources that political actors possess, thereby facilitating a mapping and comparison of policy developments. Nevertheless, the approach does have limitations. The advantage of the 'documents as texts' approach is that it acknowledges how ideas and discourses can have force of their own. Words and language can be analysed as a form of political action. A key insight that constructivist approaches have contributed to policy analysis thus concerns the emphasis on social meaning and values, often through the analysis of language and discourse.

Documents are not just instrumental tools used by self-seeking agents in the pursuit of their interests; documents and the ideas, concepts and beliefs conveyed in them affect the range of policy options that actors consider as well as actors' perceptions of their interests. As Hay (2004: 504) notes, concepts and ideas provide 'interpretative schemas' that limit the scope of policy-making by defining the targets and goals of policy and delineating the range of instruments and settings that are considered legitimate. Although analyses of documents may give only limited information on the intentions and motives of political actors, they can often help us understand the process of creating political definitions and meanings and thus clarify the policy process.

However, politics is clearly not only about discourse and language games either. Even when analysed as texts or discourses, documents do have an origin in a real world of political institutions and interests. All types of documents are thus influenced by the conditions of their production, whether we are dealing with policy documents, academic studies or media texts. In all cases, the researcher must interact with documents to place them in a proper context for analysis. On the one hand, even when used as sources we need to be aware of the documents' nature as texts. On the other hand, if used as texts and analysed as discourses, we still have to acknowledge that documents are born and may have consequences in certain institutional contexts and real-world situations, and thus do not exist only in the sphere of ideas. The question, then, is how to combine the two main approaches in a constructive way.

A similar challenge also underlines the problem with the distinction between policy documents and academic literature. As we have argued, we should be careful not to overstate the 'natural' and non-reactive character of the documents we deal with as policy researchers. Instead, it is ultimately the researcher's perspective and the research question, which define the appropriate unit of analysis or the types of document that are relevant, and in many cases, too rigid a classification of documents into particular statuses can be counter-productive.

Moreover, policy documents are by no means the only site where policy problems are defined and framed. The media, expert discourses, even academic debates set policy agendas, construct narratives and portray some decisions as inevitable. So far, however, communication policy researchers have rarely engaged with other kinds of material than 'public documents,' let alone combined or compared these sources in a systematic way. One reason for this is the disciplinary distance between theoretical reflection, policy analysis and other strands of communication studies. According to the established division of labour within academia, ideas and values are considered part of 'theory' whereas policy studies deal more with the empirical and causal models that seek to explain policy-making in terms of (material) interests and behaviour. Similarly, in communication studies, 'communication policy research' is often unnecessarily detached not only from other disciplines but also from other areas of communication studies. We could profit from striving to cross these boundaries to analyse academic debates, policy documents and newspaper discourses, not as autonomous spheres but as inter-linked debates.

In the digital era our capacity to access potential documents for research purposes might well surpass our conceptual awareness of how to handle what we find. The methodological challenge for researchers therefore lies not only in the practical capacity to execute a research plan but also in developing the theoretical awareness necessary to see the possibilities.

References

Abrams, P. (1980), 'History, Sociology, Historical Sociology', *Past and Present*, 87: 1, pp. 3–16.

Allmennkringkastingsrådet (1997), *Allmennkringkastingsrådets rapport 1996*, Oslo: Statens medieforvaltning.

Altheide, D. L. (1996), *Qualitative Media Analysis*, London: Sage.

Born, G. (2008), 'Trying to Intervene: British Media Research and the Framing of Policy Debate', *International Journal of Communication*, 2, pp. 691–698.

Brügger, N. (2008), 'The Archived Website and Website Philology – A New Type of Historical Document?', *Nordicom Review*, 29: 2, pp. 155–175.

Bryant, J. M. and Hall, J. A. (2005), 'Towards Integration and Unity in the Human Sciences: The Project of Historical Sociology', in J. M. Bryant and J. A. Hall (eds.), *Historical Methods in the Social Sciences*, London, Thousand Oaks and New Delhi: Sage, pp. xxi–xxxv.

Bryman, A. (2001), *Social Research Methods*, Oxford: Oxford University Press.

Collins, R. (1990), *Television: Policy and Culture*, London: Unwin Hyman.

Dahl, H. F. (2004), *Mediehistorie. Historisk Metode i Mediefaget*, Oslo: N. W. Damm & Søn.

Deacon, D., Pickering, M., Golding, P. and Murdock, G. (2007), *Researching Communications. A Practical Guide to Methods in Media and Cultural Analysis*, London: Hodder Arnold.

Dean, M. (1999), *Governmentality. Power and Rule in Modern Society*, London: Sage.

Donges, P. (2007) (ed.) *Von der Medienpolitik zur Media Governance?*, Köln: Herbert von Halem.

European Commission (2007), *Media Pluralism in the Member States of the European Union.* Commission Staff Working Document SEC(2007)32, Brussels.

Fay, B. (1975), *Social Theory and Political Practice*, London: Allen & Unwin.

Finlayson, A. (2004), 'Political Science, Political Ideas and Rhetoric', *Economy and Society*, 33: 4, pp. 528–549.

Fischer, F. (2003), *Reframing Policy Analysis. Discursive Politics and Deliberative Practices*, Oxford: Oxford University Press.

Foucault, M. (1991), 'Governmentality', in G. Burchell, C. Gordon and P. Miller (eds.), *The Foucault Effect: Studies in Governmentality*, London: Harvester Wheatsheaf, pp. 87–104.

Freedman, D. (2008), *The Politics of Media Policy*, Cambridge: Polity.

Giddens, A. ([1979] 1995), *Central Problems in Social Theory. Action, Structure and Contradiction in Social Analysis*, London: The Macmillan.

Gripsrud, J. (1995), *The Dynasty Years. Hollywood Television and Critical Media Studies*, London and New York: Routledge.

Hay, C. (2004), 'The Normalizing Role of Rationalist Assumption in the Institutional Embedding of Neoliberalism', *Economy and Society*, 33: 4, pp. 500–527.

Hindman, M. (2009), *The Myth of Digital Democracy*, Princeton and Oxford: Princeton University Press.

Jensen, K. B. (2002), 'The Qualitative Research Process', in K. B. Jensen (ed.), *A Handbook of Media and Communication Research – Qualitative and Quantitative Methodologies*, London and New York: Routledge, pp. 235–254.

Johnson, J. B. and Reynolds, H. T. (2005), *Political Science Research Methods,* Fifth edition, Washington D.C.: CQ.

Jääsaari, J. (2007), *Consistency and Change in Finnish Broadcasting Policy*, Åbo: Åbo Akademi University Press.

Karlsen, F., Sundet, V. S., Syvertsen, T. and Ytreberg, E. (2009), 'Non-Professional Activity on Television in a Time of Digitalisation. More Fun for the Elite or New Possibilities for Ordinary People?', *Nordicom Review*, 30:1, pp. 19–36.

Karppinen, K. (2010), 'Rethinking Media Pluralism. A Critique of Theories and Policy Discourses', Ph.D. thesis, Helsinki: University of Helsinki.

Kjeldsen, J. E. (2004), *Retorikk i vår tid. En innføring i moderne retorisk teori*, Oslo: Spartacus.

Kleinsteuber, H. J. (2007), 'Rundfunkaufsicht zwischen Regulierung und Governance. Zur Rolle von Staat, Wirtschaft und Gesellschaft', in P. Donges (ed.), *Von der Medienpolitik zur Media Governance?*, Köln: Herbert von Halem, pp. 67–83.

Krebber, D. (2002), *Europeanisation of Regulatory Television Policy. The Decision-Making Process of the Television without Frontiers Directives from 1989 & 1997*, Baden-Baden: Nomos.

Künzler, M. (2009), *Die Liberalisierung von Radio und Fernsehen. Leitbilder der Rundfunkregulierung im Ländervergleich*, Konstanz: UVK.

McQuail, D. (1997), 'Policy Help Wanted. Willing and Able Media Culturalists Please Apply', in M. Ferguson and P. Golding (eds.), *Cultural Studies in Question*, London: Sage, pp. 39–55.

———— (2003), *Media Accountability and Freedom of Publication*, Oxford: Oxford University Press.

Michalis, M. (2007), *Governing European Communication. From Unification to Coordination*, Lanham: Lexington Books.

Mills, C. W. ([1959] 1969), *The Sociological Imagination*, London: Oxford University Press.

Moe, H. (2009), 'Public Broadcasters, the Internet, and Democracy. Comparing Policy and Exploring Public Service Media Online', Ph.D. thesis, Bergen: University of Bergen.

———— (2010), 'Notions of the Public in Public Service Broadcasting Policy for the Digital Era', in J. Gripsrud and H. Moe (eds.), *The Digital Public Sphere: Challenges for Media Policy*, Göteborg: Nordicom, pp. 99–116.

Platt, J. (1981), 'Evidence and Proof in Documentary Research: Part I, Some Specific Problems of Documentary Research', *Sociological Review*, 29: 1, pp. 31–52.

Postan, M. M. (1971), *Fact and Relevance: Essays on Historical Method*, Cambridge: Cambridge University Press.

Regjeringen (2001), *St.meld. nr. 57 (2000–2001) I ytringsfrihetens tjeneste. Mål og virkemidler i mediepolitikken.*

———— (2007), *St.meld. nr. 30 (2006–2007) Kringkasting i en digital fremtid.*

Rose, N. and Miller, P. (1992), 'Political Power Beyond the State: Problematics of Government', *British Journal of Sociology*, 43: 2, pp. 173–205.

Scott, J. (1990), *A Matter of Record. Documentary Sources in Social Research*, Cambridge: Polity.

———— (2006a), 'Editor's Introduction', in J. Scott (ed.), *Documentary Research*, London: Sage, pp. xix–xxxiv.

———— (ed.) (2006b), *Documentary Research*, London: Sage.

Seiter, E. (1992), 'Semiotics, Structuralism, and Television', in R. C. Allen (ed.), *Channels of Discourse, Reassembled: Television and Contemporary Criticism, second edition*, Chapel Hill: University of North Carolina Press, pp. 31–67.

Skogerbø, E. (1996), *Privatising the Public Interest – Conflicts and Compromises in Norwegian Media Politics 1980–1993*, Oslo: University of Oslo.

Syvertsen, T. (1990), 'Kringkasting i 1990-åra: Hvem er mest "public service"?', in U. Carlsson (ed.), *Medier, Människor, Samhälle – 14 artiklar om nordisk masskommunikationsforskning*, Göteborg: Nordicom, pp. 183–195.

———— (1992), *Public Television in Transition*, Oslo: Norges allmennvitenskapelige forskningsråd.

———— (2004a), *Mediemangfold – Styring av mediene i et globalisert marked*, Kristiansand: IJ-forlaget.

———— (2004b), 'Citizens, Audiences, Customers and Players. A Conceptual Discussion of the Relationship between Broadcasters and their Publics', *European Journal of Cultural Studies*, 7: 3, pp. 363–380.

Sommer, V. (1995), 'Glossar', in U. von Alemann (ed.), *Politikwissenschaftliche Methoden. Grundriss für Studium und Forschung*, Opladen: Westdeutscher, pp. 357–379.

Young, D. (2003), 'Discourses on Communication Technologies in Canadian and European Broadcasting Policy Debates', *European Journal of Communication*, 18: 2, pp. 209–240.

Østbye, H., Helland, K., Knapskog, K. and Larsen, L. O. (2007), *Metodebok for Mediefag*, 3. Utgave, Bergen: Fagbokforlaget.

Notes

1   The German term is *Dokumentenanalyse*, the Norwegian is *dokumentanalyse*. Though 'document analysis' is in use, for instance, within political science (e.g. Johnson and Reynolds 2005), English-language contributions tend to use formulations like 'the use of document sources' or 'documentary research' (e.g. Bryman 2001, Scott 1990; 2006b). On the other hand, Altheide (1996) discusses all qualitative media analysis under the concept of document analysis.

2   The distinction is made here for analytical purposes, and it must be recognized that in practice the two uses can overlap or even be conflated. See Syvertsen (2004a: 49ff) for an example of categorizations of approaches to media and communication policy studies in general.

3   One contrasting example is Georgina Born's (2008) discussion of her attempts since the late 1990s to use her academic research as a basis for intervening in media policy debates in the UK.

4   See Postan (1971:144ff) on the history of the historical method in social science. Similarities are not limited to data sources and analytical strategies. 'The social sciences are, inherently and irreducibly, *historical* disciplines', argue Bryant and Hall, as their shared subject matter is 'the transformative movement of history' (2005: xxi, italics in original). Mills contends that 'every well-considered social study […] requires an historical scope of conception and a full use of historical materials' ([1959] 1967: 145). See also Giddens ([1979] 1995: 230ff) and Abrams (1980) for different views from the debate on a 'convergence' of history and sociology.

5   To a certain extent, the lack of space given to elaboration on methods or methodological discussions can be seen as a consequence of the norms and requirements imposed by commercial publishers and the preferences and restrictions of editors of academic journals. Yet, there are ways to work with (e.g. Hindman 2009 for a recent example in political communication) or avoid such pragmatic problems (e.g. by using the web to publish background material etc).

Chapter 11

Qualitative Network Analysis: An Approach to Communication Policy Studies

Maria Löblich & Senta Pfaff-Rüdiger

Introduction

It has been observed for some time that structures of interest, influence and power in communication policy are shifting as a result of increasing digitization, economization and globalization. New information and communication structures are emerging because of changing institutional arrangements at all levels of action (Jarren 1998: 624ff; McQuail 2007: 11). Moreover, studies have shown that communication processes in communication policy are highly informal (Isenberg 2007; Wiek 1996). These developments in communication policy suggest that it is necessary to analyse methods of studying the relations between actors and their potential influences on regulation processes in greater depth.

The aim of this article is to explain qualitative network analysis as a research strategy for communication policy research. Our approach is based on an interpretative paradigm. We will discuss the advantages and the limits of network analysis and also show to some extent how it can be applied. The paper is based on a network analysis of the German youth protection system.

First, we will discuss several network theory approaches and explain the theoretical background to our qualitative network analysis. We will then suggest a methodological explanation of this research strategy and outline its characteristics and advantages, addressing several practical issues. Finally, we will summarize the importance of qualitative network analysis for communication policy research. Throughout our article, we refer to the German youth protection network.

Network Theory

Conceptions of Networks

Network research is an inter-disciplinary field with heterogeneous theoretical approaches, which has led critics to speak of a 'Babylonian spectrum' (Börzel 1998: 254). We limited our theoretical basis to approaches that focus on human behaviour and social change in a more narrow sense and excluded the methodological holism that approaches such as actor network theory provide (Law 1992; Latour 2005; Roldán Vera and Schupp 2006: 408). Without going into too much detail, we will briefly explain this decision, because there are some similarities between actor network theory and this paper with regard to research interests. Actor network theory also asks what patterned networks consist of and how power constellations and asymmetrical relations emerge within a network. But it implies particular epistemological and ontological assumptions, leading to a network conception that we consider to be too broad and finally as not suited to our purpose.

Actor network theory regards a network as comprising not simply human 'materials,' such as people, society and organizations, but also machines, animals, texts, architecture and other materials. All these 'heterogeneous materials' are effects of patterned networks that exist between them (Law 1992: 2). In this conception of network, a particular idea of 'the social' also becomes visible. Denying 'that people are necessarily special,' it does not distinguish between people and objects (Law 1992: 3).

Actor network theory is not suited to this paper's purpose because it leaves little margin for human agency. Human beings 'have no inherent qualities and take their form and acquire their attributes only as a result of their relations with other entities' (Roldán Vera and Schupp 2006: 408). On the contrary, we assume that people and their social position cannot be reduced to an effect produced by a patterned network (Law 1992: 4) but take the conception of a reciprocal relationship between individuals and society as a basis, assuming that human action affects social structures and that action is guided by meaning that actors attribute to objects and subjects in their environment. Actor network theory, on the other hand, ignores the importance of meaning for action (Couldry 2008: 103). Finally, actor network theory is more interested in the question how networks form and establish than in their later dynamics (Couldry 2008: 101–102; Law 1992: 2). With regard to the youth protection network in Germany, which has existed for decades, this theory provides little insight regarding the long-term consequences that established networks have for media control or the inclusion of new actors.

Later we will address political science conceptions, where network analysis has a long tradition (Kenis and Raab 2008: 132). These conceptions define 'network' in a more narrow sense than actor network theory. However, we do not consider studies that use the concepts 'policy network' and 'policy community' interchangeably but only those, which distinguish between them. The analytical value of the policy network concept is the study of relations among political actors: how do relations establish and change, what are their effects and how do actors use their relations in order to grapple with existing regulations and to influence policy processes? In contrast, the policy community concept focuses on the mapping of relevant actors who attempt to influence a policy process, their interests, motives and ideas (Pross 1986; see also the article by van den Bulck in this volume).

There is no agreed meaning of 'policy networks' (Christopoulos 2008: 478). One encounters at least three different ways of using 'network' in present social science literature.

(1) One concept considers that networks consist of informal relations and of horizontal and decentralized structural patterns (Christopoulos 2008: 475; Kenis and Raab 2008: 132).

(2) There is also the understanding of network as a distinct, new governing structure, as a way of coordinating action. Here the basic assumption is that the various state and non-state actors bargain and take joint action to solve collective problems. This perspective sees networks as an ideal type of governance, distinct from the two other ideal types: the hierarchy and the market. The main concern here is to ascertain the conditions under which the state is able to successfully manage networks of various actors without assuming a dominant position (Adam and Kriesi 2007: 130; Kenis and Raab 2008: 132f).

(3) The term 'network' is used in a rather general way to describe the 'different types of empirically possible patterns of interaction among public and private actors.' From this perspective, network is involved as an analytical approach (Kenis and Raab 2008: 132).

We dissociate ourselves from the first two meanings and use the term 'network' in its third all-embracing meaning of an interconnected system of social relations in which individuals, collective or corporative actors are embedded (Jansen and Wald 2007: 189). From this point of view, policy networks constitute '(more or less stable) patterns of social relations between interdependent actors, which take shape around policy problems and/or policy programs' (Kickert et al. 1997: 6). In our research example the network takes shape around the issue of protecting children and the youth from harmful media content and around the corresponding legislation *(Jugendmedienschutz-Staatsvertrag)*. The questions of how structures and processes are built and intended within a network and which actors dominate have to be answered empirically (Baumgarten and Lahusen 2006: 178). In other words, we are interested in the 'governance of networks' instead of in 'network governance' (Kenis and Raab 2008: 140). We see the term 'network' as an analytical approach and as a 'toolbox' providing orientation for (qualitative) empirical research. Later we will address the content of this toolbox and explain the assumptions that we take as a theoretical basis.

We proceed from two basic assumptions.

(1) Structures are the result of actions and of the strategies of actors who grapple with existing structures and possibilities (Jansen and Wald 2007: 193).

(2) The specific structure of actor relations in a network influences the opportunities and constraints of action and hinders or facilitates social outcomes (Christopoulos 2008: 476).

A policy network consists of two basic elements: actors and the relations among them. Following the assumption by social network analysis that the capacity of an individual to act in society does not just depend on their attributes but also on the pattern of relations within which they are located (Roldán Vera and Schupp 2006: 408), we nevertheless want to emphasize that actors should be considered as essential elements when it comes to explaining policy processes (Rhodes 2007: 1254).

Actors

Actors in regulation are in the first place corporative (Puppis 2009), and thus a corporative actor constitutes the unit of analysis in most governance studies. Corporative actors are formally organized and have resources that are distributed within the organization according to hierarchies (i.e. administrative bodies) or to majorities (i.e. parties) (Mayntz and Scharpf 1995: 49f). Although our concern is to analyse an organizational network we believe that individual actors have to be included too, because corporative actors themselves consist of interpersonal networks and, in the end, they act through individuals. Individual actors have to be studied in their function as representatives of their organizations, and they are also objects of study because institutional rules will generally not completely determine action orientation but leave room for individual interests and orientation (Mayntz and Scharpf 1995: 52). Thus, the subjectivity of relational structures has to be considered (Rhodes 2007: 1252).

- Actors can be described by the following characteristics: They have specific perceptions, preferences and interests and pursue the aims of their organization;
- They are provided with a specific amount of resources such as knowledge, money, reputation, relations;
- They build and maintain contacts with other actors by means of communication and exchange of resources (Baumgarten and Lahusen 2006: 179).

This concept is based on the utilitarian premise that actors tend to be selective and strategic when making resource investments and that each actor anticipates the strategies of the other actors when choosing his or her options (Christopoulos 2008: 477; Schneider and Janning 2006: 117).

Relations

From a relational perspective, actors are viewed as 'interdependent rather than independent, autonomous units' (Wasserman and Faust 2008: 4). A network constitutes patterns of social relations between interdependent actors. Those patterns are to some extent independent of the actors' wills, beliefs and values (Roldán Vera and Schupp 2006: 408). Different kinds of relations can appear within a network: information and communication relations and the exchange of resources or directives within hierarchies. The specific structure of relations within a network can constitute opportunities and constraints for the members of the network. Different advantages of network structures can be distinguished: information, power in the sense of autonomy and in the sense of social influence, self-organization of collectives, trust in social norms and solidarity within a group. The negative effects of a network can for instance be control and social pressure (Jansen and Wald 2007: 189ff).

There are different aspects of the structure of relations, which influence the social interaction of the network actors. Actors occupy different positions; they are connected to each other by ties of different strength and by symmetrical or asymmetrical relations. Strong ties are relations that are frequent or intense; these are often formed with actors who share similar social contexts and values. Often they produce solidarity and trust, but they also tend to involve negative effects, such as social pressure and obstacles to adaptation. Weak ties are rarer and looser than strong relations. They serve to bridge distances within networks and tend to impart new and different information (this is a function of strong ties as well) (Jansen and Wald 2007: 190ff).

Not all ties can be assumed to be positive or reciprocated with the same intensity. Networks are often the locus of conflict for competing policy ideas, thus they are often clustered and factionalized. Such an individual sub-group may be closely inter-linked within itself and share similar beliefs and policy ideas and it may be weakly tied to other sub-groups (Schneider and Janning 2006: 117, 194).

Clustered and factionalized network structures create 'structural holes' and brokerage roles (Christopoulos 2008: 477). This means that actors gain social capital when they are in a position where they are the only ones able to connect several clusters with each other (i.e. by transferring information) and to take advantage of it. The influence an actor can achieve depends on three characteristics of their network.

(1) The more singular the actor's position within the network, the more powerful they are.
(2) The more they are able to cooperate with competitors, the more autonomy and power they gain.
(3) The more various and far reaching their relations, the more independent of reference groups they are (Jansen and Wald 2007: 191).

Asymmetric relations are also reflected in the ability of actors to achieve their objectives and influence others. Within a policy network, actors are often unlikely to have the same status or resources. In most policy environments actors within a network exercise some degree of influence. 'And although influence can be perceived as diffuse, decision making is reserved for those endowed with decision authority and is therefore concentrated' (Christopoulos 2008: 477). A policy network analysis in the first place has to be concerned with whether power is concentrated in the hands of one of the dominant actors or within one coalition of actors or whether it is shared between them (Adam and Kriesi 2007: 134). We would like to add the types of interaction mentioned earlier, developed by Uwe Schimank's actor-structure dynamics, to these theoretical assumptions of network analysis. Actors within a network interact with each other by observing each other, bargaining with each other or by influencing each other (Schimank 2007).

The structure of a network may change as far as its members, positions and resource distribution are concerned when members form new contacts, maintain existing contacts or end contacts. A network may also change due to changes in its environment (Adam and

Kriesi 2007: 143–47; Jansen and Wald 2007: 193). Media and societal contexts influence communication policy actors, their perception of problems and their capabilities. The network around the protection of children and young people against harmful media content is deeply influenced by the new online media and by young people's changing use of the media. These two factors have given rise to new political problems. The network has also been influenced by the implementation of the legislation, which for example introduced a new corporative actor, the *Kommission für Jugendmedienschutz* (KJM, Commission for the Protection of Minors in the Media) in Germany (Hasebrink and Lampert 2008: 11f; Hans-Bredow-Institut 2007: 368f).

Network Analysis as a Research Strategy

Social Network Analysis

Network analysis has a long quantitative tradition known as social network analysis, which has its own distinct research perspective based on network theory. Social network analysis research started in the 1930s as an inter-disciplinary field focusing on the phenomena of social groups and has since developed a shared 'core' of concepts and methods of measurement (Butts 2008: 13). Owing to the underlying mathematical models, such as equivalence or graph theory (Wasserman and Faust 2008: 15), these are mainly quantitative methods. Social network analysis has expanded rapidly since the 1990s owing to 'a realization in much of behavioral science that the "social context" of actions matters' (Wasserman et al. 2005: 1). Methodologically, the gold standard of network analysis is a 'detailed reconstruction of the entire social network on a given population' (Butts 2008: 18), mostly using survey instruments or secondary data analysis (exception: anthropology, mainly using observation; see Jansen 2006: 69).

These statistical and mathematical approaches underline the shift that has taken place in social network analysis: it has moved from an approach based on analysing data on social relations to a *relational analysis* of data (Roldán Vera and Schupp 2006: 407). Relational approaches are nowadays used more frequently than positional approaches, the latter focusing on the structural equivalence of network members (Saunders 2007: 232). In contrast, relational approaches look for the actual *patterning of relations* (Saunders 2007: 233) (as structural variables) and the implications and the impact of these relationships (Wasserman and Faust 2008: 3). Relational approaches thus do not ask about the outcome of a (political) decision but focus on the process by which members of a network influence each other in order to make a decision (Wasserman and Faust 2008: 7). Ties and relations (developed on the basis of ties between individuals) are central to social-network analysis. Relations can, for example, consist of information exchange, resource exchange, reputation or influence, family connections, affective relations (such as friendship) or concrete interactions (Jansen 2006: 75).

Network analysis was developed to overcome explanations based *solely* on the categorical attributes of actors (Roldán Vera and Schupp 2006: 408). Nevertheless, the actor remains a category in social network analysis, but only actor variables such as gender or race are measured to describe the network *composition* (Wasserman and Faust 2008: 21).

In summary, quantitative social network analysis, as it is actually used, collects predominately structural data about the relationship and linkages between actors. But this does not suffice to describe network relations, because these regular patterns require interpretation (Saunders 2007: 233). We subscribe to the interpretative paradigm, according to which political actors interpret societal and political reality and act on the basis of their subjective perceptions, their knowledge and their values (Schindler 2006: 99). Knowledge of these subjective perceptions is necessary to analyse the process and impact of political decisions and requires a qualitative approach (which has seldom been used so far).

Network Analysis and Qualitative Research

In contrast to the long quantitative tradition, qualitative network analysis is relatively young. It lacks systematic introductions and a distinctive methodology of its own – let alone specific research tools (Franke and Wald 2006: 160). Nevertheless, qualitative methodology seems adequate for dealing with network-related questions, and in doing so, it provides a different perspective to mathematical models.

A qualitative approach makes it possible to analyse all three dimensions of a network:

(1) The actors themselves and their subjective perspectives on political problems (such as youth protection);
(2) The relations between the actors while disclosing the patterns of relations as structures; and
(3) The context of each network, since qualitative research always includes the context of acting.

According to Baumgarten and Lahusen (2006: 183ff) the qualitative approach offers three advantages:

(1) Qualitative approaches consider research as a process in which theory and methodology may change and need to be steadily adjusted to one another. This openness means that the researcher does not need to know the network as a whole (all actors, subjects and sorts of patterns of relations) before starting to analyse it.
(2) Furthermore, the complexity of possible patterns of relations can better be taken into account (by putting them in their respective contexts) than in quantitative studies, where the type of relation needs to be defined beforehand.

(3) Qualitative research reveals the subjective perceptions of the actors. The actors have their own perception of their power, of their allies and opponents in a network.

To omit these personal perspectives would provide a false image of the real balance of power in the network. Nevertheless, qualitative approaches also have their limits: first of all, owing to the effort needed for each interview a complete sampling of a network – rather than a very small part of it – is almost impossible. Furthermore, a network analysis requires interviewing the most appropriate representative of the organization (Baumgarten and Lahusen 2006: 186). A good theoretical sampling is therefore all the more necessary. It is a general characteristic of qualitative research that generalizations cannot be made statistically but theoretically, by finding and describing typical patterns (Reichertz 2005: 577). The reliability of quality data depends in particular on the naturalness of the information (e.g. the statements in an interview) and requires the interviewees to tell the truth, or at least their subjective perspective of it. Qualitative data are more valid if they are contextualized, for example if an interview with an actor is accompanied by an analysis of the relevant documents concerning the actor and his or her institution (Reichertz 2005: 577).

Network Analysis as a Research Strategy

Unlike (quantitative) social network analysis, network analysis – in our qualitative understanding – does not describe a method but a research strategy, linking network theory to specific qualitative research tools (see Figure 1). Network analysis is a qualitative design to understand social relations and their impact on policy processes (the original aim of social network analysis). By suggesting network analysis as a research strategy, we intend to overcome the absence of adequate connections between theoretical concepts and methodological operationalization (Adam and Kriesi 2007: 147). In contrast to Franke and Wald (2006: 160), there seems to be no need to develop totally new research tools. Instead, we suggest that existing research methods, such as interviews and document analyses, should be adapted to the purpose of analysing networks (by integrating special instruments such as record cards into the interviews). This should make it possible to create a methodological framework for further qualitative network analysis.

In our understanding, qualitative research is driven by theory (Pfaff-Rüdiger 2007). Consequently, network analysis is derived from network theory and governance, whose core principles are adopted and converted into categories (Löblich 2008) to guide the design and execution of the interviews and the document analysis.

According to Adam and Kriesi (2007: 133), a network analysis always contains two sets of categories: one concerning the actor and one addressing the relations between the actors. We propose that the context of a network should also be included – as a third set of categories. Theoretically, we thus derive three *main categories* from governance and network theory:

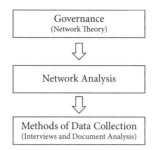

Figure 1:   Network Analysis as a Research Strategy.

(1) The actors
(2) The relations between the actors (as structures)
(3) The context of the network

Each main category needs sub-categories (what to look for?), which are then transformed into particular questions in the interview guideline.

   Actors will be regarded and questioned about:

- Their biographical background (qualification, professional motivation)
- Their position in the institution (also integrating their room for manoeuvre)
- The resources they can rely on (in their work in a special policy domain, such as youth protection in our case)
- Their perceptions of the policy domain (youth protection and media competence) with its political concepts and its regulatory system
- Their problem perceptions of the current regulatory system (concerning also the necessary adaptations caused by technological and other changes; see Adam and Kriesi 2007: 142)
- Their goals
- Their problem-solving strategies

To describe the *relations in the network*, network analysis asks about:

- The cooperation with other actors (development and density of relations)
- Shared and contrasting interests
- The perception of one's own influence and of the influence of other actors
- The actors' room for manoeuvre within the network
- The effects of the network (e.g. exchange of information and resources)

In a network analysis, context data will also be collected (either from the interview or from document analysis) in order to understand the network and the participating actors:

- The actors' institutional context and their working conditions

- The standards and rules that guide youth protection – because each policy domain has its own standards, which have to be taken into account for the analysis of the network (Adam and Kriesi 2007: 141)
- Media development
- Social development

The Research Practice of Qualitative Network Analysis

Different types of network can be studied. There are one-mode and two-mode networks, ego-centred networks and the complete range of actors within a network. With regard to the complete range of actors, it is assumed that, theoretically, all of them can have ties to all other relevant actors. The objects of study are the complete network of all members of a defined field and the ties among them. This kind of study is usually carried out using quantitative methods. An ego-centred network consists of a focal actor, termed ego, and a 'set of alters who have ties to ego' and the ties among these alters. Relations are identified solely from the perspectives of individual actors (Wasserman and Faust 2008: 35–39, 42f).

Our concept of network analysis defies this categorization, because, instead of being defined prior to data collection, types of relations and sets of actors are recorded openly, and because the aim of qualitative research is to relate to each other the structures of a network and the subjective views of the actors (Baumgarten and Lahusen 2006: 190). We do this by integrating the maximum variation in the sample until the 'theoretical saturation' is achieved (Cresswell 2007: 160).

Network Boundary Specification and Sampling

Prior to data collection, several concerns have to be addressed. Researchers have to define the boundaries of the network they want to investigate and decide how to sample actors and relations. Both steps are related. The boundary of a set of actors makes it possible to describe and identify the population being studied. It is of particular importance to decide who the relevant actors are, because a mis-specified network boundary may exclude relevant actors and their relations, and this would create a bias that would affect the research results for whole network structure (Butts 2008: 17). It is recommended to set the definition rather broadly, because irrelevant actors can be identified during interpretation (Jansen 2006: 72; Butts 2008: 17).

Both steps in defining the network boundaries – choosing the actors belonging to it and deciding on the type of relations to be investigated within the selected set of actors – have to be appropriate to the research question. In our case the second step could be dropped, because we wanted to investigate all types of relations within the field of youth protection.

There are two ways of defining network boundaries: the nominalist approach and the realist approach. While the nominalist approach is based on the theoretical concern of the researcher who defines who belongs to a network, the realist way focuses on the boundaries and membership perceived by the actors themselves. Snowball sampling is a method frequently encountered in the literature (Lauman et al. 1989: 64–67; Jansen 2006: 72ff).

In our case, it was not easy to determine the boundaries of a set of youth protection actors. In several steps, we used a combination of nominalistic and realist methods to define the youth protection network. We first used the 'medium' criterion and limited our inquiry to broadcasting and the online media network. Both media are governed by the same statutory regulations in the youth protection legislation mentioned earlier. This generates a specific interaction context with specially defined roles and positions for the actors and proceedings (Hasebrink and Lampert 2008). To determine network boundaries empirically, a joint system of symbols such as statutory regulations is taken as a basis on which interaction takes place (Franke and Wald 2006: 156). We will here apply our second criterion – the youth protection legislation – and see what special characteristics it defines for the actors: actors endowed with decision-making authority (i.e. parliaments, state governments), supervising institutions (i.e. KJM, co-regulation organizations), the subjects of protection (children, young people) and the actors against whom the statutory basis of the protection against harmful media content is directed (media organizations). Defining the network boundary from the point of view of the youth protection legislation is not unproblematic, because this only considers actors who are relevant from a legislative point of view. Parents, scientists and representatives of the educational system would be neglected. We have therefore also used the criteria of participation in political youth protection events and memberships in important committees and boards as a basis for the criteria, and we have thus added more actors to our list. In qualitative research, the definite boundaries of the network are the result of investigation (Merkens 2007: 291).

In order to identify the contacts that are of subjective importance to the actors within the network, the specification of the network has to be continued during inquiry and data interpretation until no new types of actor or relations can be added. The aim of this method, known as 'theoretical sampling,' is to embrace the 'most dissimilar cases,' which in our example means to have the most varied possible actors and relations within the defined network (Merkens 2007: 292). We included for instance both private and public service media organizations, presuming that, although both are among those who are the target of the statutory basis of the protection against harmful media content, they would differ with regard to the contacts they maintain.

Beyond these methodological aspects one has to be aware of one simple practical concern as well – there may be a large number of actors trying to influence the political process. At least seven groups of actors can be distinguished in the field of youth protection, each containing a vast number of organizations. These groups are the state, media organizations, the educational system, parents, children and young people, research institutions and the public (Hasebrink and Lampert 2008: 13). In most cases, a complete census of these would probably be a fiction.

Qualitative Research Tools: Expert Interviews and Document Analysis

Relational data can be obtained from archival records and documents, observations, questionnaires and from interviews (Wasserman and Faust 2008: 48). We carried out qualitative interviews with representatives of the chosen organizations and (additionally) we analysed documents. The advantage of a qualitative interview is to gain background information about informal contacts and about the various perceptions in the political decision-making process (Blatter et al. 2007: 60f).

Gaining Access

We had to bear in mind that organizations cannot be interviewed directly but only through individuals in their role as representatives. Individuals always have a subjective perception of their organization and its environment and they have selective access to knowledge of it (Baumgarten and Lahusen 2006: 186, 192). It is therefore all the more important to gain access to people who can best inform the researcher about the problem under examination (Cresswell 2007: 118). If the study deals with working relations, the specialist level is adequate. For studies like ours, dealing with political bargaining, the head of the organization has to be interviewed. We always tried to interview heads of department, managing directors or the authorized representatives (for instance the youth protection representative of a media organization, *Jugendschutzbeauftragter*). As soon as one tries to arrange an interview with the head of an organization or with an expert, appointment calendars tend to make it difficult (Kvale and Brinkmann 2009: 147). It can be assumed that this will be the case in all communication policy studies. Until now, all our efforts to interview the director of one of the most prominent research institutes in this field have failed. For this institute we had to carry out the interview with a member of the research team. Here there was the problem of validity. Less involved in political decisions than the director, the person interviewed could give us little information on the institute's strategic activities in the youth protection network. And she was obviously hardly in a position to assess her institute's financial situation.

Interview Guide and Record Cards

Using an interview guide ensures that all relevant topics can be covered in the interview. The guide we used contained not only a set of questions posed to all interviewees in order to ensure comparability but also questions that made it possible to raise issues concerning the interviewee's individual situation.

According to Adam and Kriesi (2007: 147), one of the major problems of network analysis is the absence of an adequate connection between the theoretical concept and the methodological operationalization. Because of this, we will not explain how we operationalized the actor and context categories but concentrate on the relation categories, which are our main interest. Few tools specifically aimed at collecting network data have been developed in qualitative network analysis so far (Franke and Wald 2006: 160ff). In line with our qualitative approach, we did not use standardized lists of names and types of relations as in quantitative studies (Butts 2008: 20). Instead, we proceeded as follows. First, we posed a hypothetical question to all of our interviewees:

Imagine you had to organize a conference on youth protection. Who would you invite?

The interviewees were instructed not only to name but also to comment their choice of actors. With this open question, we learned of all the actors who were of subjective relevance to the interviewee. In follow-up questions, we asked who should not be left out of the conference. In this way, we were given a ranking and information about the actors we had to add to our sample. We also specifically asked about (groups of) actors within the youth protection network who had not been mentioned, and we asked why they had been left out. (We knew these corporative actors from the legislation and from the literature.) Thus, we went beyond the interviewees' subjective horizons and got them to analyse (inter-subjectively) all relevant actors, including those they had no contacts with (Baumgarten and Lahusen 2006: 182f).

We used record cards as an additional instrument to collect relational data (Franke and Wald 2006: 160ff), recording the actors mentioned and using the cards to find out what the interviewee thought about hierarchies within the youth protection network. The interviewees were asked to sort the cards according to the degree of influence they thought the actors had within the network, thus making them visualize their network.

To collect further information about the relations between the youth protection actors the interview guide also contained questions about interests that were shared or contrasted with other actors, about forms and types of relations and reasons for non-cooperation, about how they perceived their own influence and what effects contacts with other actors had.

Dealing with Interview Problems

Network information may be very sensitive. Actors – particularly the most important ones – may not be prepared to be interviewed, interviews may be censored or questions may not be answered freely (Baumgarten and Lahusen 2006: 186). The topic of youth protection also raises the problem of social desirability. It is a moral topic, shaped by the existing social values and standards (Carlsson 2006). We were therefore well aware that all our interviewees would tell us that youth protection is an important political issue.

There were different types of interviewee behaviour in the nine interviews we have carried out so far. A *Jugendschutzbeauftragter* (youth protection representative) from a private TV company told us very frankly that statutory cooperation with public service representatives was a total farce, and an advertiser said that, for him, youth protection was in the first place a question of public image. In another case, it was obvious that the interviewee was avoiding addressing problems of the youth protection co-regulation system. She stressed the system's advantages for all participants.

What strategies did we apply to address validity in our interviews?

Validity in interviewing pertains to the trustworthiness of the subject's reports and to the quality of the interviewing, which should include a 'careful questioning to the meaning of what is said and a continual checking of the information obtained' (Kvale and Brinkman 2009: 249; Cresswell 2007: 207ff). We try to translate these ideas into practice by using the following strategies:

- Formulation of question: Because youth protection is a highly political topic, it was all the more important to pose well-formulated questions. On every topic, at first we posed open questions to allow the interviewees to reveal their views freely. As these are sensitive topics, questions addressing problems, informal aspects and influence structures within a policy network cannot be posed directly. For these topics, we confronted the respondents with quotations from other actors or with results of scientific studies (e.g. the evaluation of the youth media protection system; see Hans-Bredow-Institut 2007). To ask for influence structures we formulated this question:

An issue of the journal 'Medien + Erziehung' [Media and Upbringing] is about the 'inner circles' of youth protection, which are not transparent for outsiders. In your opinion, who belongs to these inner circles?

In the second question, we broached the subject again or would even word the question as a deliberate provocation if we had the impression that an answer remained too broad or elusive. In order to gain an insight into the position of a youth protection representative in a media organization we asked:

The head of the media politics department in a TV company told us that youth protection is usually not much of a topic in a broadcasting station. What's your view on that?

We usually addressed sensitive topics at the end of the interview.

- Triangulation: we made use of multiple and different sources, such as research results (e.g. Hans-Bredow-Institut 2007), position papers, internal reports, guidelines for youth protection actors, a conference, websites and many others. We used these sources not only to provide corroborating evidence (Cresswell 2007: 208) but also to shed light on interviewee statements from other points of view in order to evaluate the extent of open, specific and relevant answers (Kvale and Brinkman 2009: 164).

Qualitative Data Analysis

The analysis interpretation of qualitative data is at the core of qualitative research, a 'challenging task' (Cresswell 2007: 147) and the most criticized step in the qualitative research process, running the risk of being too subjective. The textbooks on qualitative research all require that the process of analysing and interpreting qualitative data should be thoroughly documented and disclosed. All the more so as there is no standardized analysis strategy (Cresswell 2007: 140). The analysis methods vary depending on the theoretical contexts used. As mentioned earlier, we follow a theory-driven approach that is different from any classical 'grounded theory' and different from hermeneutics. Following network theory, we analysed each of the actors separately and did this with the network as a whole in the second step. Our procedure could best be described as a 'theoretical coding,' a search for the latent meanings contained in the interviews (Kvale and Brinkmann 2009: 201).

First of all, the interviews had to be recorded and transcribed. Before starting reading *all* the transcripts, we recalled the theoretical assumptions (in our case the categories derived from network theory) (Pfaff-Rüdiger 2007: 36). While reading closely (step 2), we made notes, also called memos. In the third step, the statements were condensed by paraphrasing them (see for example Kvale and Brinkmann 2009: 206). The following coding process is the key step in analysing the data. We used concept-driven as well as data-driven codes (Kvale and Brinkmann 2009: 202) to ensure the openness of the coding process. Coding aims at winnowing out the great number of statements and texts into a manageable set of themes (Cresswell 2007: 153). Finally, we wrote a portrait of each actor, using the theoretical categories and paying special attention to silences, contradictions, double entendres, metaphors and social desirability (Cresswell 2007: 153f). Then we contextualized the given statements using the biographical, institutional and societal contexts (publicly discussed subjects and standards of youth protection), which we had gained through document analysis and integrated them into the portraits. Each interview was analysed both by researchers and by the interviewers and discussed afterwards. A shared interpretation augments the inter-subjective testability and therefore the validity of the results (Flick 2009: 405). Afterwards, we contrasted the nine portraits (looking for similarities and differences concerning the resources and the perceptions of the tie-up relations in the network).

To analyse the network, we visualized it by using the cards from the interviews as knots of the network and by drawing different lines (according to the different ties among the members of the network). Such a drawing is naturally not as elaborate as the mathematical models of social network analysis (Franke and Wald 2006: 162), but it helps understand the network dynamics nevertheless. During this visualization, we found that there were in fact two networks: one including only the media pedagogues, which is almost totally separate from the second, the network of the regulatory agents. This way of interpreting the data may be time-consuming, but it is necessary. We do not support other researchers' suggestions to minimize the systematic interpretation of the data in order to maximize the number of actors who can be interviewed (Baumgarten and Lahusen 2006: 194).

Conclusion

By using qualitative network analysis, we suggested a particular research strategy to put network theory into practice. Qualitative network analysis is suited for studies that ask:

- How do the various actors in communication policy deal with given political structures of rules and how do they interpret and evaluate the corresponding communication policy issues?
- What are the actors' relations with each other and how can the structures of their network be described?
- How do the actors try to influence the institutional framework within their network in order to advance their interests?

Qualitative network analysis makes it possible to explain the process and the outcome of communication policy because it focuses on the relations between actors. Network analysis can be applied to different levels of policy formation and implementation. It therefore captures the fragmentation of competence, which is characteristic not only of communication policy in Germany but also at EU level (Levy 1999: 26–30; Simpson 2000).

From a relational perspective, we nevertheless consider actors to be a central factor within the policy process, and they should not be excluded from analysis (Kenis and Raab 2008: 132). Unlike most (quantitative) network analyses, the network analysis proposed by us illuminates the 'black box' of interactions and actors within policy fields (Schneider and Janning 2006: 116) and thus gives an insight into the motives and mechanisms within policy-making. Because of the considerable effort involved in this kind of qualitative research, it is seldom possible to analyse the complete set of actors within a network. However, a typical selection makes it possible to obtain particularly profound results. The profoundness of the results gained with qualitative network analysis and the insight into policy-making processes justifies this approach.

References

Adam, S. and Kriesi, H. (2007), 'The Network Approach', in P. Sabatier (ed.), *Theories of the Policy Process*, Boulder: Westview Press, pp. 129–154.

Baumgarten, B. and Lahusen, C. (2006), 'Politiknetzwerke – Vorteile und Grundzüge einer qualitativen Analysestrategie', in B. Hollstein and F. Straus (eds.), *Qualitative Netzwerkanalyse: Konzepte, Methoden, Anwendungen*, Wiesbaden: VS, pp. 177–197.

Blatter, J. K., Janning, F. and Wagemann, C. (2007), *Qualitative Politikfeldanalyse. Eine Einführung in Forschungsansätze und Methoden*, Wiesbaden: VS.

Börzel, T. (1998), 'Organizing Babylon – On the Different Conceptions of Policy Networks', *Public Administration*, 76: Summer, pp. 253–273.

Butts, C. T. (2008), 'Social Network Analysis: A Methodological Introduction', *Asian Journal of Psychology*, 11: 1, pp. 13–41.

Carlsson, U. (ed.) (2006), *Regulation, Awareness, Empowerment. Young People and Harmful Media Content in the Digital Age*, Göteborg: Nordicom.

Christopoulos, D. (2008), 'The Governance of Networks: Heuristic or Formal Analysis? A Reply to Rachel Parker', *Political Studies*, 56: 2, pp. 475–481.

Couldry, N. (2008), 'Actor Network Theory and Media. Do They Connect and on What Terms?', in A. Hepp, F. Krotz, S. Moores and C. Winter (eds.), *Connectivity, Networks and Flows*, Cresskill: Hampton, pp. 93–109.

Cresswell, J. W. (2007), *Qualitative Inquiry & Research Design. Choosing among Five Approaches*, Thousand Oaks: Sage.

Flick, U. (2009), *An Introduction to Qualitative Research*, London: Sage.

Franke, K. and Wald, A. (2006), 'Möglichkeiten der Triangulation quantitativer und qualitativer Methoden in der Netzwerkanalyse', in B. Hollstein and F. Straus (eds.), *Qualitative Netzwerkanalyse: Konzepte, Methoden, Anwendungen*, Wiesbaden: VS, pp. 153–175.

Hans-Bredow-Institut (2007), 'Analyse des Jugendmedienschutzsystems – Jugendschutzgesetz und Jugendmedienschutz-Staatsvertrag. Endbericht, Oktober 2007', http://www.hans-bredow-institut.de/webfm_send/104. Accessed November 22, 2010.

Hasebrink, U. and Lampert, C. (2008), 'Jugendmedienschutz im Netzwerk. Plädoyer für eine integrative Perspektive', *medien + erziehung*, 52: 1, pp. 10–17.

Isenberg, M. (2007), *Verhandelte Politik. Informale Elemente in der Medienpolitik*, Berlin: Vistas.

Jansen, D. and Wald, A. (2007), 'Netzwerktheorien', in L. Benz, S. Lütz, U. Schimank and G. Simonis (eds.), *Handbuch Governance. Theoretische Grundlagen und empirische Anwendungsfelder*, Wiesbaden: VS, pp. 92–105.

Jansen, D. (2006), 'Erhebung von Netzwerkdaten', in D. Jansen (ed.), *Einführung in die Netzwerkanalyse*, Wiesbaden: VS, pp. 69–79.

Jarren, O. (1998), 'Medienpolitische Kommunikation', in O. Jarren, U. Sarcinelli and U. Saxer (eds.), *Politische Kommunikation in der demokratischen Gesellschaft*, Opladen: Westdeutscher Verlag, pp. 616–631.

Kenis, P. and Raab, J. (2008), 'Politiknetzwerke als Governanceform: Versuch einer Bestandsaufnahme und Neuausrichtung der Diskussion', in G. F. Schuppert and M. Zürn (eds.), *Governance in einer sich wandelnden Welt*, Wiesbaden: VS, pp. 132–148.

Kickert, W., Klijn, E. H. and Koppenjan, J. (1997), 'A Management Perspective on Policy Networks', in W. Kickert, E.H. Kljin and J. Koppenjan (eds.), *Managing Complex Networks: Strategies for the Public Sector*, London: Sage, pp. 1–13.

Kvale, S. and Brinkmann, S. (2009), *Interviews. Learning the Craft of Qualitative Research Interviewing*, 2nd edition, London: Sage.

Latour, B. (2005), *Reassembling the Social. An Introduction to Actor-Network-Theory*, Oxford: Oxford University Press.

Laumann, E. O., Marsden, P. V. and Prensky, D. (1989), 'The Boundary Specification Problem in Network Analysis', in L. Freeman, D. White and K. Romney (eds.), *Research Methods in Social Network Analysis*, Fairfax: George Mason, pp. 61–87.

Law, J. (1992), 'Notes on the Theory of the Actor Network: Ordering, Strategy, and Heterogeneity', http://www.lancs.ac.uk/fass/sociology/papers/law-notes-on-ant.pdf. Accessed 13 October 2010.

Levy, D. A. (1999), *Europe's Digital Revolution. Broadcasting Regulation, the EU and the Nation State*, London: Routledge.

Löblich, M. (2008), 'Ein Weg zur Kommunikationsgeschichte. Kategoriengeleitetes Vorgehen am Beispiel Fachgeschichte', in K. Arnold, M. Behmer and B. Semrad (eds.), *Kommunikationsgeschichte. Positionen und Werkzeuge. Ein diskursives Handbuch*, Münster: Lit, pp. 433–454.

Mayntz, R. and Scharpf, F. (1995), 'Der Ansatz des akteurzentrierten Institutionalismus', in R. Mayntz and F. Scharpf (eds.), *Gesellschaftliche Selbstregelung und politische Steuerung*, Frankfurt am Main: Campus, pp. 39–72.

McQuail, D. (2007), 'Introduction: Reflections on Media Policy in Europe', in W. A. Meier and J. Trappel (eds.), *Power, Performance and Politics. Media Policy in Europe*, Ba-den-Baden: Nomos, pp. 9–20.

Merkens, H. (2007), 'Auswahlverfahren, Sampling, Fallkonstruktion', in U. Flick, E. von Kardorff and I. Steinke (eds.), *Qualitative Forschung. Ein Handbuch*, Reinbek: Rowohlt, pp. 286–299.

Pfaff-Rüdiger, S. (2007), 'Medien im Alltag. Methodenprobleme qualitativer Nutzungsforschung', in S. Pfaff-Rüdiger and M. Meyen (eds.), *Alltag, Lebenswelt und Medien. Qualitative Studien zum subjektiven Sinn von Medienangeboten*, Münster: Lit, pp. 9–45.

Pross, P. (1986), *Group Politics and Public Policy*, Toronto: Oxford University Press.

Puppis, M. (2009), *Organisationen der Medienselbstregulierung. Europäische Presseräte im Vergleich*, Köln: Halem.

Reichertz, J. (2005), 'Gütekriterien qualitativer Forschung', in L. Mikos and C. Wegener (eds.), *Qualitative Medienforschung. Ein Handbuch*, Konstanz: UVK, pp. 571–580.

Rhodes, R. A. W. (2007), 'Understanding Governance: Ten Years on', *Organization Studies*, 28: 8, pp. 1243–1264.

Roldán Vera, E. and Schupp, T. (2006), 'Network Analysis in Comparative Social Sciences',*Comparative Education*, 42: 3, pp. 405–429.

Saunders, C. (2007), 'Using Social Network Analysis to Explore Social Movements: A Relational Approach', *Social Movement Studies*, 6: 3, pp. 227–243.

Schindler, D. (2006), 'Die Rolle von Ideen und Deutungsmustern in der Politik: Wissenspolitologische Perspektiven auf Netzwerke', in B. Hollstein and F. Straus (eds.), *Qualitative Netzwerkanalyse: Konzepte, Methoden, Anwendungen*, Wiesbaden: VS, pp. 99–123.

Schimank, U. (2007), 'Elementare Mechanismen', in A. Benz, S. Lütz, U. Schimank and G. Simonis (eds.), *Handbuch Governance. Theoretische Grundlagen und empirische Anwendungsfelder*, Wiesbaden: VS, pp. 29–45.

Schneider, V. and Janning, F. (2006), *Politikfeldanalyse. Akteure, Diskurse und Netzwerke in der öffentlichen Politik*, Wiesbaden: VS.

Simpson, S. (2000), 'Intra-Institutional Rivalry and Policy Entrepreneurship in the European Union: The Politics of Information and Communications Technology Convergence', in *New Media & Society*, 2: 4, pp. 445–466.

Wasserman, S. and Faust, K. (2008), *Social Network Analysis: Methods and Applications*, Cambridge: Cambridge University Press.

Wasserman, S., Scott, J. and Carrington, P. J. (2005), 'Introduction', in P. J. Carrington, J. Scott and S. Wasserman (eds.), *Models and Methods in Social Network Analysis*, Cambridge: Cambridge University Press, pp. 1–7.

Wiek, U. (1996), *Politische Kommunikation und Public Relations in der Rundfunkpolitik. Eine politikbezogene Analyse*, Berlin: Vistas.

Chapter 12

Towards a Media Policy Process Analysis Model and Its Methodological Implications

Hilde Van den Bulck

Stakeholder Analysis in Media Studies

Key Concepts and Methods

Media policy analysis, in the words of Hansen et al. (1998: 67), seeks to 'examine the ways in which policies in the field of communication are generated and implemented, as well as their repercussions or implications for the field of communication as a whole.' Forward-looking, policy-oriented research aims to contribute to the establishment of future media policies. Most critical academic media policy research is concerned with tracing how certain policy outcomes came about, why certain policy outcomes rather than others became dominant, what parties were involved in the decision-making process and how power was distributed amongst them (Fischer 2003; Freedman 2008). In both types of research, a policy decision is implicitly or explicitly considered as the result of a process characterized by the formulation of different views and interests expressed by actors or stakeholders who adhere to a certain logic, engage in debate and work towards a policy decision in the relevant fora (Hutchinson 1999; Blakie and Soussan 2001). As such, the policy process with regard to a specific media issue is mostly studied by means of stakeholder analysis.

Media policy studies in general show relatively little conceptual analysis of the actual research process involved in such stakeholder analysis. Yet, inspiration can be found in other fields of enquiry ranging from business management (e.g. Mitchell et al. 1997) and health care (e.g. Brugha and Varvasovsky 2000) to development and environmental studies (e.g. Prell et al. 2009). Although 'each [policy] sector poses its own problems, sets its own constraints, and generates its own brand of conflicts' (Freeman 1985: 469) and although institutions and loci of power to influence policy outcomes differ across sectors (Howlett 2004), they do provide a number of conceptual tools applicable to the field of media policy.

Stakeholder analysis starts from a general broad understanding of the formal structures and processes of decision-making as well as the main conceptual–theoretical insights into and positions on a certain policy issue. The next step is the identification of all relevant stakeholders, i.e. people, groups or organizations with a vested interest in (the outcome of) a particular policy. As media policy-making has expanded in scale and scope and has increasingly become subject to multi-level governance (EU, national, regional, local) (Collins 2008; Hamelink and Nordenstreng 2007), the number of stakeholders has increased exponentially (Freedman 2008: 82f). These can include politicians, regulatory institutions, media organizations, citizens and institutional and other representatives of civil society, as well as providers of communication services and the advertising industry, among others. Interestingly, the category of stakeholders does not entirely overlap with that of policy actors. Certain stakeholders with a distinct interest in a certain outcome may not actually take part in the policy process (e.g. audience members) whereas policy actors with no explicit stake can considerably influence the outcome of the process (e.g. academics, civil servants). Within the broad category of stakeholders, the core informants are the most-involved actors who directly influence the formation and execution of policy decisions. Stakeholders are identified on the basis of who they are/represent/belong to, their stake (or visibility) and their impact (or power). They can further be characterized on the basis of their attitude towards the policy issue and of the main logic they adhere to. The latter relates to the perception of the situation and the structure of goals and means in a certain situation (Van den Bulck 2008). As such, they can formulate their arguments within a cultural, political, technological and economic logic among others. For instance, two stakeholders can be found to be in favour of a certain policy outcome (e.g. a return to advertising-free public service television), but can come to that conclusion on the basis of a different logic (e.g. the economic logic of profit maximization in the case of commercial competitors and a cultural logic of protecting programme quality in the case of certain groups in civil society). Finally, the relevant fora in which each stakeholder can be seen to play need to be mapped. Whereas in many sectors the media is considered to be an important forum, in the case of media policy analysis this forum can be seen to overlap – or at least have considerable ties – with a number of stakeholders (Freedman 2008: 87ff).

Data collection in stakeholder analysis typically takes two complementary roads involving written and oral sources. Data is obtained, on the one hand, through the search for and analysis of relevant documents. Document analysis, according to Altheide (1996: 2), refers to 'an integrated and conceptually informed method, procedure and technique for locating, identifying, retrieving and analysing documents for their relevance, significance and meaning.' Documents can be both primary (original documents, contemporary records, records in close proximity to an issue/event) and secondary (based on primary sources) (Startt and Sloan 1989: 114; see also Altheide 1996; Bryman 2001; Deacon et al. 2007; Van den Bulck 2002). When it comes to media policy analysis, this includes published and internal policy documents and white and green papers, annual reports and other documents of the key informants involved in the policy issue (government, key media institutions, advisory committees etc.) as well as analytical documents from other stakeholders (Van den Bulck 2002: 89–94). Other sources include communication from stakeholders in relevant fora. The latter can be in oral (speeches at events) or audio-visual (interview on television) rather than written (comments and interviews in the press and other publications) documentary form (for an in-depth discussion of documents see Karppinen and Moe in this volume). These documents can be analysed through quantitative content analysis as well as qualitative discourse or semiotic analysis, using a meticulous translation of the theoretical and conceptual framework in a guide.

Document analysis is complemented, on the other hand, by elite and expert interviews with privileged witnesses who have been part of or have special insight into the policy-making process. These people have the advantage of having followed the process from close quarters and therefore knowing intricate details and/or often having an aggregate knowledge (Aberbach and Rockman 2002; Bogner et al. 2009; Dunn 2004; Seldon and Pappworth 1983; Van Gorp 2011). In-depth interviewing involves the reconstruction of meaning, beliefs or patterns of action by means of a 'conversation with a purpose' (Minichiello et al. 1992: 87) based on a (more or less structured) topic list that deals with the main issues of interest to the researcher. The combination of document analysis and expert interviews allows for the necessary triangulation of data.

Example: Stakeholder Analysis of the Policy Process Towards Flemish PSB 2006 Management Contract

An example of a stakeholder analysis in the field of media policy is the study of the role of the technological argument of digitization and its potential for PSB in the policy process leading up to the renewal of the management contract between the Flemish government and VRT, the Flemish PSB, in the autumn of 2006. The results of this study, in terms of shifting policy options and the policy outcome, are discussed elsewhere (Van den Bulck 2008). Here the focus is on the actual steps taken in this stakeholder analysis to obtain and analyse all relevant data. The research project first started with a study of the literature to distinguish potential theoretical positions with regard to the role of PSB in digital new media and to identify potential arguments and logics. This resulted in the identification of four positions with regard to media digitalization – technological determinism (TD), technological nationalism (TN), technological democracy (TDc) and technological relativism (TR) – and of potential views on the role of PSB in this (everything is legitimate (L1), attrition model/arrested development (L2a), attrition model/harmless role (L2b), attrition model/superfluous (L2c) and obsolete model (L3)) (for relevant literature, see Van den Bulck 2008).

Secondly, the exact research period was outlined, starting with the original policy statement by the Flemish media minister, released at the start of his mandate in 2004, including remarks on (the future of) PSB and on digitization. The research period ended with the signing of the management agreement in July 2006, as this contract can be considered the outcome of the policy process that was the topic of this stakeholder analysis.

Thirdly, all relevant stakeholders and fora were identified, based on prior knowledge of Flemish media structures and processes and of Flemish policy-making and on some preliminary expert interviews. Fourthly, all relevant published and internal documents from stakeholders and documents, transcripts and media coverage of discussions in relevant fora were collected. Documents were checked for authenticity and for references to further relevant sources and actors. A series of in-depth interviews with privileged witnesses were conducted. Fifthly, these documents and transcripts were analysed looking for viewpoints and logic, based on the theoretical framework. This resulted in the following matrix (see Table 1).

Table 1: Management Contract Stakeholders and Their Logic, View on Technology, View on PSB and Relevant Forum.

Actor	Forum	Logic	View on Technology	View on PSB
Media minister	cabinet, government, media	cultural logic audience logic economic logic	TD/TN/TDc	L2a&b/ L1
VRT CEO	cabinet, media, audience	cultural logic, audience logic economic logic	TD/TDc/TN	L1
PUBLIC	referendum, media	cultural logic		L1
Civil Society Culture	referendum, media	cultural logic	TD	L1/L2a
POF*	cabinet, media	economic logic	TD	L2b/L3
VMMa**	cabinet, media 'politics'	economic logic	TR	L1/L2b
SBS***	cabinet, media	economic logic	TD	L2b/L3
Media Council	cabinet	cultural logic audience logic	TD/TDe	L2b/L3

*(Lobby) organization representing all commercial audio-visual media in Flanders.

**Flemish media conglomerate including the main commercial general interest and two other television stations.

***Flemish branch of German/Swedish company, ProSiebenSat.1, which has two commercial television stations in Flanders.

To grasp the evolution of arguments and changing directions of policy intentions of various stakeholders and to understand the final outcome of the resulting policy process – the extent of the digital mandate of VRT in the contract – documents were compared in a time perspective looking for and comparing significant changes in the views of relevant stakeholders over time. For instance, we traced the way in which the media minister's original enthusiasm for a wide range of digital opportunities for PSB weakened over time, which is reflected in the final outcome of the policy process: the management contract allowed VRT one digital channel for cultural content; i.e. it obtained a very limited digital mandate (Van den Bulck 2008).

Blind Spots and Other Conceptual and Methodological Shortcomings

Although such stakeholder analyses have proved very useful to better understand how particular media policies take shape, there are a number of shortcomings. For one, such analyses tend to be inspired by an 'institutional' view of the media policy process, focusing on formal and visible points of decision-making. The potential downside of this is the danger of failing to identify key non-institutional and informal policy-making fora, such as certain stakeholders' lobby work outside of the 'official' policy channels (Freedman 2008: 93; Kingdon 1995). In the above case, the commercial competitors' lobby work outside of the formal meeting points (media council and cabinet) was insufficiently detected on the basis of documents and interviews with the key informants. This may also lead to a failure to identify all relevant actors/stakeholders, such as the role of civil servants or small and relatively invisible informal pressure groups as actors in the policy-making process. Researchers thus miss out on interesting informants who can help in explaining certain steps in the process and coding documents and interview transcripts in greater depth, resulting in richer data and analyses. It appears that there is a need for a more complex view of all those involved in the policy process, their positions and interrelations. There is a further need for a better conceptual understanding of the dynamics of the policy process as a means to identify who gets something on the policy agenda, how different stakeholders relate to one another and to the central policy-maker (e.g. media minister) and how the decision-making process works formally and informally. These new understandings, furthermore, can have methodological implications for media policy analysis, as it requires a search for tools that can expose the actual process better.

Indeed, document analysis and interviews with relevant privileged witnesses are essential methodological tools but have certain shortcomings. Firstly, the adequacy and/or completeness of the collected documents can prove problematic. How to guarantee that all key documents have been collected? For instance, an overly institutional view of stakeholders and policy can blind the researcher to bottom-up or other alternative forces, and to other crucial sources that may provide evidence of these ideas and efforts (Murphy 1980). Secondly, documents can only reveal part of the evolution of stated policies over time. Document analysis cannot always account for changes in positions of stakeholders from one document to another, such as the considerable shift in views from the media minister's original policy statements to his subsequent annual policy papers. Nor can it relate the content of a document directly to the actual policy outcome, as documents cannot account for intervening variables such as the relative impact of different stakeholders on the policy outcome. For example, the media minister's shifting views seem to indicate recognition of the claims of stakeholders other than VRT, who requested permission for eight digital channels. Yet, the available documents did not reveal which stakeholders were key in this. In other words, documents are static and usually reflect only one stakeholder's views, while the policy process is dynamic and complex, with a variety of stakeholders and views struggling to influence the policy outcome.

These shortcomings can partly be overcome by in-depth interviews with key policy actors. In the case study referred to earlier, interviews did indeed confirm the impact of the commercial competitors rather than the cultural sector on the eventual decision to opt for a single cultural digital channel in the management contract. Expert interviews, however, pose their own problems, which can hamper an understanding of the dynamics and causality of the policy process (Bogner et al. 2009; Van Audenhove 2010; Van den Bulck 2002). Interviewees may exaggerate or downplay their own role. Their answers may be inspired by grudges or other personal feelings that taint their memories or lead them to adjust their accounts. In the earlier case study, for example, in a two-hour in-depth interview with two civil servants (Uyttendaele and Braekeveld 2007), in a bid to show their professionalism the interviewees continuously downplayed the role of informal relationships or lobby work from non-institutional stakeholders, in favour of a picture of the policy process close to the official guidelines. An in-depth interview with the PSB's CEO (sacked six months after signing the management contract) was tainted by his desire for vindication and to clear his name. In other words, interviewees' stakes in and experiences with the policy process taint the information they provide. What is more, informants may simply not know 'the whole story,' as they are locked up in their own particular part of that story or are stakeholders who were on the sidelines of the process (possibly without realizing it themselves). This is confirmed by Kingdon (1995), who found that policy-makers often do not know where policies have come from. He concludes from it that the policy process is tainted by coincidence and chance as much as negotiation and insight.

To overcome these shortcomings it seems we need to look at conceptual models that can help us understand the complexities of the policy process. Likewise, there is a need to explore complementary methodologies.

Mapping the Policy Process: Alternative Frameworks and Methodologies

John (2003) contends that no 'stages' model of the policy process can guarantee a simple map. Instead, regardless of whether one advocates a pluralist consensus, a critical conflict or a mixed view of the policy process, it must be considered as complex, involving a multitude of sources of causation and feedback, a wide variety of actors and institutions involved and the complex web of networks between them.

Different Models with Regard to Stakeholders and the Policy-Making Process

A good point of departure is Paul Pross's (1986) notion of 'policy communities,' which embraces all the actors with an interest in a broad policy area such as media or a sub-area such as PSB. This concept can help to account for how and where actors/stakeholders attempt to exert influence, particularly through Pross's analytical distinction between actors located in the 'sub-government' and actors that are part of the 'attentive public.' The first consists of influential governmental institutions that develop and implement public policy. In this case it would include among others the above-mentioned media minister, his/her cabinet, the Flemish civil service media administration and others such as the Flemish Media Policy Advisory Board (SARC, before 2008: Flemish Media Council), the Flemish Media Regulator (VRM) and the parliamentary media committee. The PSB institution itself can also be seen to reside in this subset. Other stakeholders, interest and lobby groups can be expected to try and exert a strong influence on these bodies. The 'attentive public' refers to all other actors interested in this policy area, 'monitoring and criticizing prevailing policy and outcomes' (Lindquist 2001: 6). In the case of the Flemish PSB management contract, these include not only the competing media as stakeholders and/or lobby groups but also others, including the local radio federation, advertisers, academics, consultants, think tanks, civil-society organizations representing audience groups, journalists and prominent individuals. Inspired by Pross (1990, quoted in Lindquist 2001: 7), this can result in the following policy community chart for the Flemish case (see Figure 1):

The next step is to identify 'policy networks' by looking for particular relationships between actors and stakeholders both within the broad area of media policy and within specific sub-areas (e.g. PSB policy, policies on digital providers etc.). Depending on the specific issue at hand, very different networks of actors can be found within one field such as media policy. In other words, stakeholders active in one media policy sub-area (e.g. PSB) may differ considerably from the actors involved in another (e.g. telecommunications). Some actors within the media policy community may limit their activities to one specific issue (e.g. local radio), whereas others can be seen to

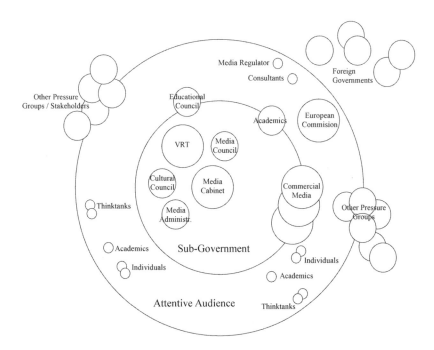

Figure 1:   Policy Community for the Flemish PSB Contract-Renewal Policy Process.

operate in many different sub-areas around which specific policy networks have formed. Commercial broadcasters, for instance, can be involved in issues regarding PSB, the press or telecommunications, although their closeness to these and other issues may vary according to their relative stake in each issue. One stakeholder can adhere to different (even opposing) views and positions depending on the issue at hand. Commercial competitors can hold a position of technological relativism when discussing the digital future of PSB (as did VMMa in the earlier case study) while at the same time taking up technological determinist stance in other policy issues or sub-areas. Identifying and analysing such policy communities allows for a better understanding of the relative positions, strength and power to influence the policy-making process of actors inside and outside of government.

A further useful development on the notion of policy networks is Sabatier and Jenkins-Smith's (1993; 1999) 'advocacy coalition framework' (ACF). This framework is based on the assumption that there are sets of core ideas about causation and value in public policy. The relationships between actors who share similar values and beliefs result in advocacy coalitions. These can be tight or loose and cut across governmental and non-governmental boundaries as well as across Pross's distinction between sub-government and the attentive audience. What links them all is a shared set of beliefs and a general agreement on the best solution to a certain policy issue. According to Sabatier, typically two to four advocacy coalitions can be found in every policy community with regard to a particular issue, and it is possible to identify these networks of actors within a policy sector. Different coalitions can be seen to fight it out until one such coalition emerges as the dominant one controlling the key instruments of policy-making and implementation. Elaborating on the case study regarding the policy process leading up to the new management contract for VRT, the Flemish PSB, and working from the available material, it is possible to distinguish between two main advocacy coalitions based on the core beliefs about the position and future of PSB in the Flemish media landscape: those in favour of a strong PSB, including in the area of new digital media platforms (L1) and those in favour of a more modest PSB to ensure a 'level playing field.' (L2) (see Figure 2):

Two further modifications to these models can be made. Firstly, Kingdon (1995) and Sabatier and Jenkins-Smith (1993) confirm the need mentioned earlier to pay attention to the influence exerted through informal networks, which are often quite invisible and subtle, but nevertheless can create considerable leverage in the policy-making process. Lindquist (2001: 13) borrows the term 'epistemic communities' to refer to such networks. Secondly, Rhodes (2007: 1254) stresses the need to pay attention to the agency of individuals within the policy process. Such a decentred approach recognizes 'that the actions of these individuals are not fixed by institutional norms […] but, on the contrary, arise from the beliefs individuals adopt against the background of traditions and in response to dilemmas' (Rhodes 2007: 1252). Lindquist (2001) refers to these individuals as 'policy entrepreneurs': advocates of certain policy causes or solutions, experienced in understanding policy

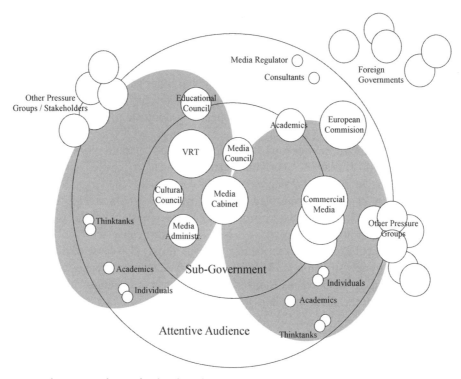

Figure 2:   Advocacy Coalitions for the Flemish PSB Contract-Renewal Policy Process.

environments and spotting policy windows. Accordingly, we should seek to identify which individuals were pivotal in bringing about policy change.

Accounting for Change

A further conceptual issue is how to account for change. In Pross's model, the push for change comes mainly from the attentive audience, as its members have no real stake in preserving the status quo and are more likely to come up with creative ideas for new policy approaches. The sub-government is expected to have an interest in maintaining the status quo. This may account for certain changes in media policy, showing the influence of academics and equal-opportunity groups in pushing certain solution paradigms for a more balanced gender portrayal in advertising. Yet, there are many other examples in media policy that point to changes originating from within the core policy-making circle.

Sabatier's ACF model provides a more complex view on change. At the macro-level, policy-making (and changes of policy) is influenced by stable, exogenous factors such as the characteristics of the problem (e.g. Flanders as a small media market), institutional structures (e.g. multi-level governance) and socio-cultural phenomena (e.g. digital age gap). It is further influenced by dynamic exogenous factors such as changes in socio-economic circumstances (e.g. the move away from the welfare state), shifts in governmental structures (e.g. shifting (media) competences from the federal state to the regions resulting in new media regulatory frameworks) and policy decisions in other sub-systems and policy areas (e.g. liberalization of the telecoms market). In general, a policy community maintains the status quo as it is built around deep core beliefs (e.g. long-standing traditions of social responsibility in broadcasting (PSB) and of liberalism in press). Particularly with regard to secondary beliefs, though, change can be seen to appear through policy-oriented learning or shocks in the system. The latter can originate externally or, as acknowledged in more recent adjustments to the ACF model (Weible et al. 2009), internally. The larger economic crisis that started late in 2008, for example, led to the failure of the traditional business model of the press; a crisis which, in turn, has impacted views of certain stakeholders on the role and position of PSB in online news provision. These shocks can cause actors in the advocacy coalitions to shift coalitions, if only for tactical reasons. It may also cause coalitions to adapt their arguments to new situations and even switch across coalition divides. Due to internal and external changes, the balance of power in policy networks changes and the structure and memberships of the coalitions alter (John 2003: 491).

Not unlike the proponents of the ACF, Rhodes (2007: 1253) analyses consistency and change in terms of 'traditions' and 'dilemmas.' Traditions explain how rule, power, order and norms arise and become sustained patterns of policy-making. Change is caused by a dilemma that 'arise[s] when a new idea stands in opposition to existing beliefs or practices and so forces a reconsideration of the existing beliefs and associated tradition' (Rhodes 2007: 1253). This suggests that in order to understand changes in media policy we need to look for the relevant dilemmas. Rhodes further specifies that the power (to change) is contingent and relational, relative to the power of other actors and stakeholders.

Methodological Implications

What methodological implications does this more elaborate conceptual toolbox have? From an analytical overview of 80 applications of the ACF (Weible et al. 2009), it appears that one in four are based on in-depth interviews and one in eight on a combination of interviews and document analysis. Interestingly, nearly half of all studies 'left their methodologies unspecified and appeared to rely on unsystematic collection and analysis of existing documents and reports' (Weible et al. 2009: 126). So at first glance, the application of the ACF has not generated new methodological approaches. Looking closer, however, it becomes clear that it provides new research strategies when using the 'traditional' policy study methods of document analysis and elite or expert interviews.

With regard to documents, conceptual attention to the process aspect of media policy leads to an additional or complementary coding of the documents to look for coalitions and changes over time. A number of ACF studies have opted for a quantitative approach to document analysis, using time-series analysis and/or cluster analysis on expressed policy positions to prove the existence of advocacy coalitions, indicating long-term developments of actors' beliefs and showing both changes in the polarization between advocacy coalitions and relative stability of beliefs of different coalitions (Bandelow 2006). Qualitative document analysis can likewise incorporate such a focus.

Apart from the identification of shared core beliefs, such document analysis does not, however, allow the researcher to prove a link among advocacy-coalition members. This is relevant if, for instance, two members may share the same beliefs but be too serious competitors to cooperate. Various commercial competitors with PSB can be united in their wish to limit PSB's development, but their rivalry over audiences and revenues will hamper cooperation. According to Bandelow (2006), the latter can, to a certain extent, be solved by focusing more on individuals than on the organizations and institutions as members of advocacy coalitions. It also adds to the importance of expert interviewing (John 2003). With the new research strategy in mind, interviews can accommodate the search for advocacy coalitions by asking experts more explicitly and elaborately about cooperation and polarization with other actors, the relative strength and density of these relationships, the position and latitude of the interviewee compared to the other actors, among others.

Finally, Rhodes' (2007: 1259) suggestion of 'a shift of *topos* from institutions to *meanings* in action' leads him to endorse an ethnographic approach to policy analysis that 'can take full measure of the processional, network and coalition aspects as well as of individual agency' (Rhodes 2007: 1252). To this end, he suggests complementing document analysis and interviews with observation, among other ethnographic methodologies. One way for a researcher to engage in participant observation is through the actual membership of a policy-making body, for instance a media policy council. A more feasible approach available to all researchers is that of transient observation – without 'disguise' and mainly as an outsider (Murphy 1980: 110ff). This can allow for a form of triangulation of the data obtained through documents and interviews and can provide additional information without relying on 'the potentially unreliable reports of others' (Murphy 1980: 113).

Conclusion

The development of media policies seems to be becoming more complicated through shifts from traditional state policy-making to governance and even multi-governance and through an exponential growth in potential stakeholders. Disentangling and analysing this intricate web is therefore becoming ever more important yet also more complex. New concepts, models and methodological tools suited to dealing with this complexity seem to be essential. It appears that a stakeholder analysis combined with a search for policy communities and advocacy coalitions through a combination of traditional methods and new inroads and strategies can provide a fruitful way forward in media policy analysis.

References

Aberbach, J. D. and Rockman, B. A. (2002), 'Conducting and Coding Elite Interviews', *Political Science and Politics*, 35: 4, pp. 673–676.

Altheide, D. L. (1996), *Qualitative Media Analysis, Qualitative Research Methods Series*, London: Sage.

Bandelow, N. C. (2006), 'Advocacy Coalitions, Policy-Oriented Learning and Long-Term Change in Genetic Engineering Policy: An Interpretist View', *German Policy Studies*, 3: 4, pp. 747–805.

Bogner, A., Littig, B. and Menz, W. (2009), *Interviewing Experts*, Basingstoke: Palgrave Macmillan.

Brugha, R. and Varvasovszky, Z. (2000), 'Stakeholder Analysis: A Review', *Health Policy and Planning*, 15: 3, pp. 239–246.

Bryman, A. (2001), *Social Research Methods*, Oxford: Oxford University Press.

Blakie P. and Soussan J. G. (2001), *Understanding Policy Processes*, Leeds: University of Leeds.

Collins, R. (2008), 'Hierarchy to Homeostasis? Hierarchy, Markets and Networks in UK Media and Communications Governance', *Media Culture and Society*, 30: 3, pp. 295–317.

Deacon, D., Pickering, M., Golding, P. and Murdock, G. (2007), *Researching Communications. A Practical Guide to Methods in Media and Cultural Analysis*, London: Hodder Arnold.

Dunn, W. N. (2004), *Public Policy Analysis: An Introduction*, New Jersey: Pearson Prentice Hall.

Fischer, F. (2003), *Reframing Policy Analysis: Discursive Politics and Deliberative Practices*, Oxford: Oxford University Press.

Freedman, D. (2008), *The Politics of Media Policy*, Cambridge: Polity Press.

Freeman, G. P. (1985), 'National Styles and Policy Sectors: Explaining Structured Variation', *Journal of Public Policy*, 5: 4, pp. 467–496.

Hamelink, C. and Nordenstreng, K. (2007), 'Towards Democratic Media Governance', in E. De Bens, C. Hamelink and K. Jakubowicz (eds.), *Media Between Culture and Commerce: An Introduction*, London: Intellect, pp. 225–240.

Hansen, A., Cottle, S., Negrine, R. and Newbold, C. (1998), *Mass Communication Research Methods*, London: MacMillan.

Howlett, M. (2004), 'Administrative Styles and Regulatory Reform: Institutional Arrangements and Their Effects on Administrative Behaviour', *International Public Management Journal*, 7: 3, pp. 317–333.

Hutchinson, D. (1999), *Media Policy: An Introduction*, London: Blackwell.

John, P. (2003), 'Is There Life After Policy Streams, Advocacy Coalitions, and Punctuations: Using Evolutionary Theory to Explain Policy Change?', *The Policy Studies Journal*, 31: 4, pp. 481–498.

Kingdon, J. (1995), *Agendas, Alternatives, and Public Policies*, Boston: Little Brown.

Lindquist, E. A. (2001), 'Discerning Policy Influence: Framework for a Strategic Evaluation of IDRC-supported Research', http://www.idrc.ca/uploads/user-S/10359907080discerning_policy.pdf. Accessed 17 November 2010.

Minichiello, V., Aroni, R., Timewell, E. and Alexander, L. (1992), *In-Depth Interviewing: Researching People*, Melbourne: Longman Cheshire.

Mitchell, R., Agle, B. and Wood, D. (1997), 'Towards a Theory of Stakeholder Identification: Defining the Principle of Who and What Really Counts', *Academy of Management Review*, 22: 4, pp. 853–886.

Murphy, J. T. (1980), *Getting the Facts. A Fieldwork Guide for Evaluators & Policy Analysts*, Santa Monica: Goodyear Publishing.

Prell, C., Hubacek, K. and Reed, M. (2009), 'Stakeholder Analysis and Social Network Analysis in Natural Resource Management', *Society and Natural Resources*, 22: 6, pp. 501–518.

Pross, P. (1986), *Group Politics and Public Policy*, Toronto: Oxford University Press.

———— (1990), 'Pressures Groups: Talking Chameleons', in M. Whittington and G. Williams (eds.), *Canadian Politics in the 1990s*, Toronto: Methuen, pp. 252–275.

Rhodes, R. A. W. (2007), 'Understanding Governance: Ten Years On', *Organization Studies*, 28: 8, pp.1243–1264.

Sabatier, P. and Jenkins-Smith, H. (1993), *Policy Change and Learning: An Advocacy Coalition Approach*, Boulder: Westview.

———— (1999), 'The Advocacy Coalition Framework: An Assessment', in P. Sabatier (ed.), *Theories of the Policy Process*, Boulder: Westview, pp. 117–166.

Seldon, A. and Pappworth, J. (1983), *By Word of Mouth: Elite Oral History*, London: Methuen.

Startt, J. D. and Sloan, W. D. (1989), *Historical Methods in Mass Communication*, Hillsdale: Lawrence Erlbaum.

Uyttendaele, C. and Braeckevelt, D. (2007), *Personal interview with Media Specialists of the Cabinet of Flemish Media Minister Bourgeois*.

Van Audenhove, L. (2010), 'Expert Interviews and Interview Techniques for Policy Analysis', www.ies.be/disknode/get/452. Accessed 17 November 2010.

Van den Bulck, H. (2002), 'Tools for Studying the Media', in C. Newbold, O. Boyd-Barrett and H. Van den Bulck (eds.), *The Media Book*, London: Edward Arnold, pp. 55–100.

———— (2008), 'Can PSB Stake Its Claim in a Media World of Digital Convergence? The Case of the Flemish PSB Management Contract Renewal from an International Perspective', *Convergence: The International Journal of Research into New Media Technologies*, 14: 3, pp. 335–350.

Van Gorp, J. (2011), 'Inverting Film Policy. Film as Nation Builder in Post-Soviet Russia, 1991–2005', *Media, Culture and Society*, 33: 2, pp. 243–258.

Weible, C. M., Sabatier, P. A. and McQueen, K. (2009), 'Themes and Variations: Taking Stock of the Advocacy Coalition Framework', *The Policy Studies Journal*, 37: 1, pp. 121–140.

Part III

NEW SUBJECTS

Convergence

Chapter 13

Battle of the Paradigms: Defining the Object and Objectives of Media/Communication Policy

Karol Jakubowicz

Introduction

The framework for communication policy can be described, as suggested by Bar and Sandvig (2008), as the interaction of four factors: the underlying goal, the medium, the technology and the policy/regulatory regime. Significant change in one or more of those elements cannot but lead to a policy change.

In their well-known analysis of media policy paradigm shifts, van Cuilenburg and McQuail (2003) indicate that the change from what they call the first paradigm (communication industry policy before World War II) to the second paradigm (public service media policy, 1945–1980/90) was driven primarily by a revision of the underlying goal. Whereas the first paradigm was mainly pursued for reasons of state interest and financial corporate benefits, the second, 'public service' paradigm, was dominated by socio-political concerns and was dedicated to the achievement of cultural and social goals (mainly in broadcasting) involved in the provision of what has been called 'communications welfare.' Thus the transition took place mainly for ideological, axiological and normative reasons, serving to redefine the underlying goal of policy and regulation.

The post-World War II public service policy model was partly undermined by technological change, but primarily by a confluence of a number of processes: geopolitical transitions (globalization, rise of transnational communities, changing foreign policy, with information and communication issues becoming a separate area of world politics); market transition (new services and actors, privatization and liberalization, mergers); social/cultural transitions (including changing concepts of public interest) and legal transitions (changing notions about the effectiveness of law, regulation and existing tools).

This led to a shift in the balance of the component political, social and economic values that shape the definition of the public interest (see e.g. O'Malley 2010). Many governments opted to break up monopolies in media and communication and to deregulate and privatize as much as possible. Competition and self-regulation were promoted. Old social-democratic media policy goals were redefined as new economic goals.

Of course, technological change – generally summed up as 'convergence' (see e.g. Lister et al. 2003) – has also had a major impact on the policy model. First of all, it challenged the old technological and institutional framework for policy formulation and implementation. Secondly, it reinforced the view of the economic significance of the media and the Information and Communication Technologies (ICTs), prompting policy-makers to give primacy to the economic goals of communication policies at the expense of social and cultural objectives. This now appears to be the case with the 'Digital Agenda' of the European Union.

Our goal here is to see whether the 'new' paradigm, as identified by van Cuilenburg and McQuail (2003), has remained in place or whether it is not being pre-empted by other concerns and policy objectives.

But if we are to discuss media policy, let us first make sure we understand the term 'media' properly. The traditional conceptual framework of media policy has broken down. With technology evolving fast and with the emergence of many 'media-like' activities, often conducted by amateur and unprofessional actors, it is no longer clear what the term 'media' means. For policy and regulatory purposes it is increasingly difficult to distinguish between 'media' and 'non-media' or to know the scope of policy and regulation and what regulatory regime to apply to which service.

Defining 'the Media'

Different definitions of 'the media' emphasize different dimensions:

(1) Material, relating to the prerequisites needed for an act of communication to take place, i.e. the physical or other infrastructure that mediates in the process of transmitting or distributing the message or content

(2) Organizational, referring to the 'media organization' that produces the content, also involving the editorial and other processes required for the development of content to be distributed to a mass audience

(3) Functional, referring to the tasks and functions of the media, such as information, education and entertainment, or any combination of these, as well as influencing public opinion (especially in the case of the news media) and availability to all potential receivers or at least significant parts of the public (see Lasota 2010).

Definitions of the media focusing on their material dimension abound in the literature (see Cardoso 2006). In this approach, any platform for the distribution of content can, erroneously, be called 'a medium.' Hence the frequent idea of the Internet as a 'medium' (Morris and Ogan 1996), though as such it lacks both the inherent organizational and functional elements that are needed for it to be considered as such. It should more properly be recognized as an infrastructural platform (Internet backbones; Internet service providers; broadband providers; portals; browser software; search engines; media-player software; and Internet Protocol telephony) for the distribution of content developed by media organizations and content providers that are extraneous to itself or for direct communication between its users. It is useful to note in this respect Noam's (2003) view that 'the Internet is today part of most organizations' activities. To encompass all of them as part of the Internet industry would equate this sector with almost the entire economy, thereby making an analysis over-broad.'

The reason the traditional approach to defining 'the media' is no longer pertinent is that social and technological change are to some extent de-institutionalizing and have largely 'dematerialized' media content (Lister et al. 2003: 16).

De-institutionalization means that mass communication content can now be produced and distributed by small groups or single individuals. Mass communicators could once be assumed to be relatively large media institutions with specialized and professional personnel, engaged in various aspects of a medium's operation. That assumption clearly no longer holds true.

'Dematerialization' of information or other media content is due to digitalization, which separates content from its physical form (roll of film, book, tape etc.) as well as from the technology traditionally used to deliver it to the public. As reshaped by convergence, the media *inter alia* acquires the features of digitality, hypertextuality, dispersal and virtuality (Lister et al. 2003) and combines interpersonal communication and mass media dimensions on one and the same platform (Cardoso 2006; see also Mueller 1999). All these new features are fundamentally remaking the traditional media and the manner of its operation.

Difficulties encountered when one looks for a replacement for 'the media' are well illustrated by six years of debate within the European Union on the scope of what ultimately turned out to be the Audiovisual Media Services Directive (AVMSD), replacing the old 'Television without Frontiers' directive.

The scope of the old directive, originally adopted in 1989, was to be extended to cover not only 'television,' but also 'television-like services' (primarily on-demand services), so a new term for them all needed to be found. The concept of 'audiovisual media services' was accordingly adopted.

The definition of 'audio-visual media service' is explained at length in recitals 16 to 25 of the preamble and is set out in Art. 1(a). It is composed of six cumulative criteria:

(1) It must be a service, thus requiring an economic activity that is under the editorial responsibility of a media service provider (hence excluding private websites, services consisting of the provision or distribution of user-generated audio-visual content for the purposes of sharing and exchange within communities of interest).

(2) The definition must cover 'audiovisual media services, whether television broadcasting or on demand, which are mass media, that is, which are intended for reception by, and which could have a clear impact on, a significant proportion of the general public';

(3) The function of the services must be to inform, entertain and educate the general public. An important feature is the 'impact of these services on the way people form their opinions,' as emphasized by recital 43.

(4) The principal purpose should be the provision of programmes (as opposed to cases where audio-visual content is merely incidental), as emphasized by recital 18.

(5) It must be a service with a audio-visual character (this does not cover audio transmission or radio services or electronic versions of newspapers or magazines).
(6) It must be a service provided by electronic communication networks (so excluding the cinema and DVDs).

This definition is useful for the regulatory purposes of the directive but inadequate when it comes to a new definition of 'the media.' Firstly, it does not cover radio or the print media. Secondly, the European Commission was subject to heavy lobbying by, and felt it needed to placate, particular media industries and interest groups wanting clear language in the document excluding them from the scope of the convention. So not only a positive but also a negative definition of 'audio-visual media services' was adopted, to signify clearly the media activities to which the directive does not refer (radio, electronic versions of newspapers or magazines, cinema and DVD, as well as new border-line cases that under some circumstances potentially could be classified as media – e.g. private websites, blogs and services consisting of the provision or distribution of user-generated audio-visual content for the purposes of sharing and exchange within communities of interest). The definition of the directive has the following features:

- Some focus on the organizational/institutional dimension of the media ('a service, thus requiring an economic activity, which is under the editorial responsibility of a media service provider'). This dimension is later considered in very considerable detail in Article 2, but for purposes of establishing jurisdiction, rather than as a criterion of media, or media-like character
- No reference in the definition itself to the production of content
- Very heavy emphasis on the functional dimension ('intended for reception by, and which could have a clear impact on, a significant proportion of the general public'; 'the function of the services is to inform, entertain and educate the general public'; an 'impact of these services on the way people form their opinions'; 'The principal purpose should be the provision of programmes') as the main distinguishing feature that turns these services into audio-visual media services
- No direct reference in the definition to the fact that these services should operate on a sustained basis, though this is clearly implied by references to the television schedule in article 1 (b) and 1 (c)
- Some elements of the material dimension ('A service with audiovisual character [...] provided by electronic communication networks'), needed for regulatory purposes.

Especially noteworthy are two elements of this definition. One is somewhat surprising. The phrase 'which are mass media, *that is*, which are intended for reception by, and which could have a clear impact on, a significant proportion of the general public' (emphasis added) would seem to indicate that this is the exhaustive list of criteria for the classification of a particular service as a mass medium. However, this is contradicted by the second remarkable feature, i.e. the heavy emphasis on the functional dimension. We should therefore perhaps combine the two, so that minimum criteria for classifying a service as part of the media would include both sets of elements: on the one hand, general reception and clear impact on at least a significant proportion of the public and, on the other – provision of media content ('programmes') that informs, entertains and educates.

Another interesting feature of the AVMSD definition is that the drafters seemed to recognize that their general definition of an audio-visual media service would not suffice. They took care to provide examples in Article 1 (b) of what is meant by a 'programme', i.e. what it is that such a service actually consists of: 'a set of moving images with or without sound constituting an individual item within a schedule or a catalogue established by a media service provider and whose form and content is comparable to the form and content of television broadcasting. Examples of programmes include feature-length films, sports events, situation comedies, documentaries, children's programmes and original drama.' And they added some material elements: 'a service with audiovisual character [...] provided by electronic communications networks.' Ironically, therefore, (perhaps only temporarily, until better definitions are developed) we are back in a situation in which media content, though 'dematerialized', must still be identified for the sake of precision and legal certainty by its material distribution platform.

All in all, the AVMSD directive has left many grave doubts as to what its provisions mean and how it should be applied (see e.g. Betzel and Lauf 2008).

A broader approach has been adopted by the Council of Europe, as shown by two versions of a Council of Europe recommendation on measures concerning media coverage of election campaigns, one issued in 1999 (No. R (99) 15) and another issued in 2007 (CM/Rec(2007)15), specifically for the purpose of updating the old one in technological terms. The difference between the concept of 'media' in the two recommendations on the same subject, adopted eight years after one another, can be seen in Table 1.

Table 1: The Concept of 'Media' in Two Council of Europe (CoE) Recommendations.

R (99) 15	CM/Rec (2007) 15
Print and broadcast media	'The term "media" refers to those responsible for the periodic creation of information and content and its dissemination over which there is editorial responsibility, irrespective of the means and technology used for delivery, which are intended for reception by, and which could have a clear impact on, a significant proportion of the general public. This could, inter alia, include print media (newspapers, periodicals) and media disseminated over electronic communication networks, such as broadcast media (radio, television and other linear audiovisual media services), online news-services (such as online editions of newspapers and newsletters) and non-linear audiovisual media services (such as on-demand television).'

Clearly, it must have seemed to the authors of the 1999 document that all the material, organizational and functional dimensions of the particular media were more or less self-evident and it was enough to identify them by the material infrastructure used for the distribution of their content. By 2007 they knew better.

This new definition of 'the media' has the following features:

- A clear focus on the organizational/institutional dimension of the media ('those responsible for the periodic creation of information and content and its dissemination over which there is editorial responsibility')
- Clear recognition that the purpose of the medium is not only to convey, but also to produce content ('the periodic creation of information and content and its dissemination')
- Acknowledgment that any definition of 'the media' must refer to its functional dimension ('intended for reception by, and which could have a clear impact on, a significant proportion of the general public') – though this could be noted in a clearer manner
- Reference to the fact that communication can potentially be recognized as part of 'the media' only when it operates on a sustained basis ('periodic creation of information and content and its dissemination')
- Recognition that media content can be delivered in a variety of formats ('this could, inter alia, include') over a range of distribution platforms ('irrespective of the means and technology used for delivery').

This definition has one striking feature: 'The term "media" refers to *those responsible* for the periodic creation of information and content and its dissemination' (emphasis added). Apart from the clear intention to focus on the organizational aspect of the media, the intention behind this choice of words may spring from an awareness of the fact that, as noted earlier, the range of mass communicators is much more extensive today than in the past and goes beyond traditional professional media organizations.

The 2007 CoE definition cited earlier was supplemented in 2009 by the resolution 'Towards a new notion of media', adopted by the 1st Council of Europe Conference of Ministers responsible for Media and New Communication Services, held in Reykjavik. Continuing the effort to define 'the media' in the new circumstances, the conference laid heavy emphasis on the functional dimension of the media as a criterion for classifying new services as media:

> The purpose of media or comparable media-like mass-communication services remains on the whole unchanged, namely the provision or dissemination of information, analysis, comment, opinion and entertainment to a broad public. The underlying objectives also remain comparable: to provide news, information or access to information; to set the public agenda; to animate public debate or shape public opinion; to contribute to development or to promote specific values; to entertain; or to generate an income or, most frequently, a combination of the above.

At the same time, it called for 'the establishment of criteria for distinguishing media or media-like services from new forms of personal communication that are not media-like mass-communication or related business activities' (Council of Europe, 2009: *passim*).

Thus, personal communication should not automatically be identified as a media or 'media-like' activity. However, this wording implies that such personal communication *may* be classified as 'media' if it satisfies the requisite material, organizational and primarily functional criteria.

There seems little doubt, for example, that 'citizen journalism' may qualify as media, if it meets the criteria we set out later, including the fact that it must be provided on a regular basis and in conditions of editorial responsibility (Jakubowicz 2009). However, few of the so-called social media (Cision and Bates 2009) can really be recognized as 'media.' Blogs potentially come closest. The European Parliament, in its 2008 resolution on concentration and pluralism in the media in the European Union (2007/2253(INI)), called for 'an open discussion on all issues relating to the status of weblogs.' Elsewhere serious, news- and opinion-oriented blogs are recognized as media (Meraz 2009) and bloggers are, in justified circumstances, accorded 'media' rights (e.g. protection of sources) in recognition of their 'media-like' character.

It is generally recognized that respect for basic legal and ethical norms and standards is a necessary condition for recognizing such activities as journalism and provision of media content (see Jakubowicz 2009).

These tortuous efforts vividly illustrate the conceptual and definitional challenges facing both scholars and policy-makers/regulators in defining the object of media/communication policy. Until these issues are resolved, it will not be possible to arrive at full and satisfactory definitions of this policy, its scope and objectives. Nor, indeed, will it be possible to answer the universally asked questions as to whether or not 'television,' or 'the press' or 'radio' will survive in the future (a frequent display of what is known as 'endism'). In their old 'material" form they may not. But in terms of the essential nature of the service they provide possibly yes, though we cannot really say until we have defined that service and its characteristics.

At this stage, we may perhaps venture the following preliminary general definition of 'the media':

Mass media are media organizations (regardless of their size, legal, professional and economic status) that conduct regular communication activity, in a potentially interactive relationship with the users, by producing and/or assembling, in an editorial process and with respect for legal and ethical norms, content serving to inform, educate and/or entertain (and – especially in the case of the news media – to influence public opinion), assume full editorial responsibility for it and arrange for its periodic dissemination to the general public via appropriate delivery and distribution platforms.

Table 2: Minimum Criteria for Recognition of a New Communication Service as Part of the Mass Media.

1. Own* content that informs, educates and/or entertains
2. Mass
3. Assembly/packaging of content
4. Editorial process
5. Legal and ethical norms
6. Intention to infuence public opinion
7. Periodic dissemination
8. Full editorial responsibility
9. Availability to the general public
10. Appropriate delivery and distribution platforms

*In-house production of content is not a necessary criterion for a service to be recognized as part of the mass media. Therefore 'own content' means that the communicator has assembled and assumes full editorial responsibility for content that may have been obtained externally.

This definition amounts to a number of criteria[1] for recognizing media and media-like activities among new communication services[2] and applying graduated policy and regulatory, self- and co-regulatory frameworks for them.

Table 2 lists criteria for recognizing a new communication service as a full-fledged media activity.

Three features are crucial if a communication service is to be recognized as a full-fledged part of the mass media: the editorial process, observance of legal and ethical norms and full editorial responsibility, including liability for the content.

The term 'media-like' services refers to communication services that lack these three features, but, as shown in Table 3, satisfy all or most of the other criteria. Functional and other features are the same (otherwise a service would not qualify as part of 'the media'), but the absence of these three features means that the service is not provided by a proper media organization, capable of delivering and assuming responsibility for quality content.

Table 3: Minimum Criteria for Recognition of a New Communication Services as a Media-Like Activity.

1. Own content that informs, educates and/or entertains
2. Mass
3. Assembly/packaging of content
4. Intention to infuence public opinion
5. Periodic dissemination
6. Availability to the general public
7. Appropriate delivery and distribution platforms

Media Policy: New Paradigm 2.0?

Now that we have a tentative idea of the object of media/communication policy, let us turn to its objectives, first in the field of regulation and then in policy as such.

Let us begin with a look at how the media landscape to which regulation and policy must refer may change in the foreseeable future.

The last 15 years have seen the emergence of a number of forecasts of how the electronic media would evolve in the future (see Andersen 2002; Forge et al. 2010; Foster 2007; Foster et al. 2002; Galperin and Bar 2002; Noam 1995; OFCOM 2009; Roel 2008). The authors list a wide variety of variables impacting on this process, but it seems that two main sets of variables will determine how the media/communication sector will evolve in the future:

(1) Economic growth
(2) Social, political, market and cultural determinants of prospects for a change of paradigm in the system of social communication (i.e. an end to the *one-to-many* mode of communication characteristic of the mass media, to be replaced by *many-to-many* communication – see later).

Economic growth and a putative paradigm shift are closely interrelated. It is economic conditions that determine the pace of the media and communication market development, the spread and uptake of new technologies and the willingness of users to invest in new equipment and to pay for information, content and services from new sources.

As for the other set of variables, political factors will determine whether the traditional mass media, with its crucial role in the operation of democracy and social cohesion, will be allowed to disappear. Economic and market factors will decide whether potential decentralization and individualization of mediated communication will indeed be possible. The key question here is whether business models can be developed that will sustain the new model or whether, instead, there will be further consolidation and concentration of the market, also on a global scale. Finally, social and cultural factors will impact the preferences of media users and consumers (linear or non-linear, stationary or mobile reception etc.) and their willingness to forsake the old, *lean-back* method of passive content consumption in favour of an active, *lean-forward* method of both consumption and production (and dissemination) of communication content.

If we develop a matrix of the various scenarios covered by these forecasts and take these two variables as a basis for this exercise, then the result can be portrayed as in Table 4.

The upper left quadrant groups scenarios that assume both rapid economic growth and good prospects for the change of paradigm. As suggested by the titles of these scenarios ('good-bye TV', etc.) this paradigm shift would amount to:

• Elimination of the basic framework whereby content is assembled into a programme and distributed by a number of dedicated organizations (broadcasters or media service

Table 4: Main Directions of Future Electronic Media Development.

		Prospects for a paradigm shift	
Fast / Economic growth / Slow	**Paradigm Shift** Anyone, anything, anywhere, anytime; extreme fragmentation; cyber-television; post-television; 'personalization'; 'good-bye TV'; transformation; radical fragmentation; infinite choice		**Rapid Technological Development without a Wholesale Paradigm Shift and with the Likelihood of Market Consolidation** Consolidation; personalized interactive television; 'interactivity'; 'digital world'
	Prospects for a paradigm shift at a time of slow economic growth None, or very limited		**Slow technological change, slow evolution of modes of mass communication; prospect of market domination** Stagnation; Gradual transformation; 'business as usual'; 'back to basics'; 'global challenge'; broadcast plus; commercial Big Brother
	High	Prospects for a paradigm shift	Low

providers), meaning that content would be produced and distributed by a large number of content providers;

- Combined with this, an end to the passive role of the audience, where all the content comes from the broadcaster/provider (Jakubowicz, 2010c).

In short, this would lead to the wholesale replacement of the old, allocutory model of mass communication (*one-to-many*) with *many-to-many* communication. This 'anyone, anything, anytime, anywhere' scenario is a staple feature of many forecasts of the future development of broadcasting and communication.

The lower left quadrant assumes a situation of slow economic growth and lack of social and cultural change favouring the paradigm shift. Hence there are no or low prospects of it happening.

The upper right quadrant assumes rapid economic growth, but low prospects for a wholesale paradigm shift. This could produce a situation of rapid technological growth, potentially also combined with concentration and consolidation of the market (i.e. control by large corporations and an oligopoly situation), but with the traditional mass media still remaining in place alongside flourishing new communication services.

And finally, the lower right quadrant assumes slow economic growth and low prospects for a paradigm change, leading to 'stagnation,' 'business as usual' and 'broadcast plus' (a strong broadcast media supplemented by new services), coupled with a strong likelihood of industry concentration, nationally and internationally.

Obviously, we should not expect future developments to conform exclusively to any one of these forecasts or scenarios. Rather we will see elements of many scenarios playing out in the future. It does not look as if we should expect a full and complete paradigm shift, leading to the total disappearance of the traditional mass media and its replacement by various forms of 'user-generated content' (Le Borgne-Bachschmidt et al. 2008; Wunsch-Vincent and Vickery 2007). Most of the authors would agree to some extent with Naughton (2006: 45), that television would not disappear:

> Broadcast will continue to exist, for the simple and very good reason that some things are best covered using a few-to-many technology. Only a broadcast model can deal with something such as a World Cup final or news of a major terrorist attack – when the attention of the world is focused on a single event or a single place. But broadcast will lose its dominant position in the ecosystem.

What we should expect, however, is the evolution of the regulatory system. The exact scope and arrangements for regulating the media and media-like services remain to be developed. The objective for regulation, if any, remains the same as ever.

The AVMSD directive has provided an example of graduated content regulation, as applied to linear and non-linear services. Another example is provided by the system developed some time ago in Germany for broadcasting and media- and tele-services. It may have changed somewhat since then, but the principle remains the same. It envisaged three tiers of regulation: the usual requirements for broadcasting (licensing requirement; concentration control; standards of journalism; programming quotas; access rights; listed events; advertising restrictions; sponsoring restrictions; youth protection; right of reply; privacy); only selected requirements for media services (such as on-demand TV services; teletext; online magazines and websites, i.e. CNN.com) and no significant content regulation for 'teleservices' (such as e-commerce transaction services, online databases, etc. (see Grünwald 2001).

Differences between statutory regulation and co- and self-regulation are shown in Figure 1, stressing growing consumer responsibility and the progressive decline in effectiveness of other regulation in the area of on-demand and audio-visual content on the new technologies.

Moving on to the question of policy, many of the policy objectives of the post-World War II public service media policy paradigm as identified by van Cuilenburg and McQuail (2003), are still relevant but, as already noted, convergence, globalization and socio-cultural change have led to a reorientation of this approach because of a fundamental change in the axiological and normative areas.

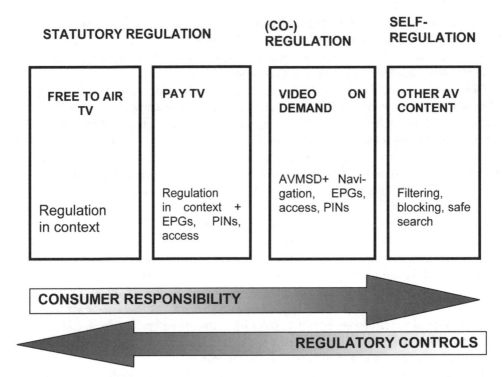

Figure 1: Graduated Content Regulation.
Source: Purvis 2008.

So we could say that, as with the transition from the first to the second media policy paradigm, the shift to the third one was also being driven primarily by a change in the underlying goal and the policy/regulatory regime. And let us also answer one of the questions posed at the outset: the 'new' paradigm as identified by van Cuilenburg and McQuail has not been superseded or pre-empted by an even newer one or a return to an earlier one. Nevertheless, the battle of the paradigms continues and, as we will argue later, a shift of emphasis in international policy can be observed.

According to van Cuilenburg and McQuail (2003), three concepts would be central to any new communication policy model:

(1) Freedom of communication: there should be provision for both negative and positive freedom (but digital technology solves some of these problems).
(2) Access: control over deciding who gets access to what communication resources, when, where, how, and on what conditions.
(3) Accountability for meeting or respecting the communication needs of others (as a society, group or individual) and for the consequences of publication.

Analysing this further, McQuail (2008) identified a number of policy concerns that he considers still relevant, although priorities and also possibilities for action have changed as a result of communication technology change. Table 5 lists the concerns that need increased attention in the new conditions, as distinct from those that require less attention (or cannot realistically be dealt with).

Two of the items (freedom of speech and accountability) appear on both lists, says McQuail, because of conflicting arguments about the trends and influence of new media technology. One could also point to another potential contradiction: 'public health and harm' are seen as needing more priority, whereas 'morals' are presented as requiring less priority. However, 'public harm' often results precisely from the violation of moral norms in the media and in cyberspace (European Opinion Research Group 2004; O'Connell and Bryce 2005).

These suggested policy objectives cannot really be assessed until we have answered two sets of questions. First, what do they mean in practice in the light of new technological developments? Second, what will be the general normative framework within which these objectives are to be pursued?

Regarding the first question, let us take 'universal service' as an example. Under the EU Universal Service Directive (European Union 2009), states must ensure that all citizens in their territory 'are provided, upon reasonable request, with a connection at a fixed location to the publicly available telephone network that allows voice and data communication, as well as basic Internet services, limited to a single narrowband connection.'

Is this enough today? Foster (2007) speaks of securing 'universal access to digital TV and high speed broadband services so that everyone benefits from them.' A number of European countries (e.g. France, Finland, Spain) have recognized access to the Internet (in some cases – broadband Internet) as a human right and have launched plans to guarantee it for everybody. In the EU, amendments to the Framework Directive adopted in 2009 amount – in the words of a European Commission press release (MEMO/09/219) – to 'recognition of the right to internet

Table 5:   Policy Concerns Needing either More or Less Priority.

More Priority	Less Priority
Public sphere needs	Universal service
Crime and security	Diversity
Public health and harm	Monopoly
Human rights	Morals
Accountability	Quality of content
Freedom of speech	Accountability
Consumer interests	Freedom of speech

Source: McQuail (2008).

access: the new telecoms rules recognise explicitly that internet access is part of fundamental rights such as the freedom of expression and the freedom to access information.'

Thus an updated definition of universal access would – and in many cases already has – put it high on the list of 'more priority' policy objectives.

As for the question of the general normative framework, let us consider two cases: those of 'monopoly' and freedom of speech.

'Monopoly' has been assigned to the 'less priority' group. However, many future scenarios show a clear risk of market consolidation and concentration, indeed domination, also on a global scale. The question would then become one of which policy framework would apply: what might be considered unacceptable and requiring public policy intervention under the public service policy paradigm ('more priority') might, under a deregulatory 'new paradigm,' be regarded as desirable or at least not warranting public intervention ('less priority').

As for freedom of expression, the reason it is given 'less priority' status is that the new technologies should facilitate exercise of free expression. However, if the trend is towards centralization of the media landscape then its assignment to the 'more priority' group would be justified. Moreover, it has traditionally been understood as a negative right to freedom from interference with free expression. However, there has long been a movement for the recognition of communication rights, including a positive right to communicate. It seems to have been gaining some traction in recent times, even leading to calls for the recognition of a 'right to public expression' (Jakubowicz 2010a; see also Nieminen 2008: 55).

Along the same lines, Tambini (2006) argues that the concept of 'access' (identified by van Cuilenburg and McQuail (2003) as central to any new communication policy model), needs to be understood as broadly including:

- A positive right to access to expression, i.e. the right to have one's speech heard or to have access to key media for expression. Citizens require a voice and access to the relevant forum in which to make themselves heard
- Access to the shared forum: citizenship practices are increasingly played out in media environments that range from key news services and discussions to web forums, chat rooms and blogs.

The public service policy paradigm would create a better framework for possible adoption and action on such ideas than the 'new paradigm' and accord freedom of expression 'more priority' status.

We may use the policy objectives identified by van Cuilenburg, McQuail and Tambini as building blocks in seeking to construct visions of future policy, depending on which process of electronic media development will predominate (Table 6).

To return to the main theme of this paper, we cannot be sure what the policy response will be, as that will depend on the more general normative framework, which gives policy objectives meaning and defines their scope.

Table 6:   Policy Responses to Media Systems Evolution.

Directions of Future Electronic Media Development	Policy Response
1. Paradigm Shift	Attempts to counteract social fragmentation and preserve the media's role in promoting social cohesion, cultural identity and the public sphere and the democratic process (e.g. by developing new forms of public service media)
2. Rapid technological development without a wholesale paradigm shift but with the likelihood of market consolidation	Efforts to curb media and information monopolies, securing public access to a wide range of media and information services, promoting freedom of expression for individuals and groups, should corporations control the market, accountability of media operators, protection of consumer interests
3. Low prospects for a paradigm shift at a time of slow economic growth	Promotion of public and private investment in the new technologies
4. Slow technological change, slow evolution of modes of mass communication; prospect of market domination	As in 2 and 3 above

Today, two broad processes are unfolding:

(1) Media/communication policy is increasingly being applied to the Internet and the ICTs and reformulated to be relevant in a new context. Padovani et al. (2010: 375) note that the master frame for discussing communication-related human rights in the digital age as regards traditional media concerns issues such as democratization of communication, the right to communicate, communication rights and for new technologies – access, interactivity and connectivity), and

(2) As has been said, the 'new' neoliberal paradigm continues to predominate, but support for a renewed public service paradigm is growing.

On the first issue, the entire Internet governance debate (Doria and Kleinwächter 2010; European Dialogue on Internet Governance 2010; MacLean 2009), including the issue of 'network neutrality' (OFCOM 2010; Valcke et al. 2008), is an area where policy is being developed. There is a growing body of binding legislation, or plans to introduce such legislation, at the national and international levels, concerning forms of regulation and supervision of Internet and other new media content. Some examples include: the CoE Cybercrime Convention and Additional Protocol; extension of the scope of broadcasting legislation to online audio-visual media services (AVMSD); laws and rules in the area of the 'war on terror' and security; intellectual property, copyright, piracy, illegal file-sharing; consumer protection and the protection of minors and human dignity. There is also a growing body of self-regulation by different types of operators active in cyberspace (Tambini et al. 2008).

Given the extension of the policy framework to cyberspace and the ICTs and the new paradigm's increased focus on the Internet and other new technologies, we may perhaps call it 'new paradigm 2.0.'

However, this new area is also the battleground on which the 'public service' and the 'new' paradigms are struggling for supremacy. This is clear from an account of the 2010 'EuroDIG' conference:

> The two leading lines of the session concerned the Internet as a market place which is driving development and the Internet as a public value space bringing more than just economic wealth to users. There were no doubts that the Internet is a platform for human development and that investments in it are adding significant financial value. Finding the right balance between the public interest and paying producers to produce even more (i.e. *finding the balance between the social and economic value of the Internet*) was highlighted. (European Dialogue on Internet Governance 2010 : 9; emphasis added)

The entire process emerging out of the World Summit on the Information Society (WSIS) in 2003 and 2005 (of which the EuroDIG meetings are an element) is an excellent case in point. The WSIS was originally intended to concentrate solely on technological and economic issues, very much in the spirit of the 'new' paradigm, but was ultimately 'reclaimed' by proponents of the 'public service' paradigm, resulting in a debate and final documents dealing with a wide range of human rights, social and cultural issues relating to the information society (Padovani 2005; Padovani and Nordenstreng 2005).

This debate has continued, notably at the Internet Governance Forum that arose out of the World Summit on the Information Society, with its focus on access, openness, diversity, security on the Internet and critical Internet resources. One of the 'dynamic coalitions' formed at these meetings is proposing the adoption of an Internet Bill of Rights (MacLean 2009: 7), which is perhaps emblematic of the 'public service' approach in this debate. This would be a globally agreed document, which would state rights and duties of the individual users of the Internet (Doria and Kleinwaechter 2010: 286).

Padovani et al. (2010: 375) confirm that in the Internet governance (IG) debate 'technical elements are still a fundamental part of the picture, but social ones are increasingly part of the ongoing conversation, where actors no longer seem to discuss the legitimacy of adding issues to the technical IG debate, but, rather, how the two sides of the coin can be adequately balanced.' At the same time, after reviewing some of the major documents in the field over the last 15 years, they note that the debate on human rights in the information society has not yet progressed to a stage of commonly agreed norm formation (see also Jakubowicz 2004; Symonides 1998).

A significant contribution to promoting the view that a human rights discourse should be prominently represented in any consideration of media/communication policy in the information society is being made by the Council of Europe. It began in 2005 with the 'Declaration of the Committee of Ministers on human rights and the rule of law in the Information Society' (CM(2005)56 final), dealing with how the ICTs can help enhance (and violate) human rights. It also deals with what governments, civil society and the private sector should do to promote the opportunities afforded by ICTs for fuller enjoyment of human rights and counteract the threats they pose in this respect.

In 2008, the Council of Europe issued 'Recommendation CM/Rec(2007)16 on measures to promote the public service value of the Internet.' An appendix to the recommendation spells out in detail how public policy can ensure that the Internet contributes to the enhancement of human rights and democracy and how the IGF themes of access, openness, diversity and security should be interpreted from a humanrights point of view. Another shot in the battle of the paradigms was the CoE 2007 'Recommendation Rec(2007)3 on the remit of public service media in the information society' (see also Geller 2003).[3]

Thus we are seeing a continuing tug of war between the two paradigms and an uneasy co-existence of elements of both. It would take another major social–cultural, normative and axiological shift on a scale comparable to the shift from a social–democratic to a neoliberal vision of society in the early 1980s for the 'new paradigm' to be replaced with something even newer (or perhaps older, if the public service paradigm were by some chance to return). Nevertheless, the new version of the 'public service' paradigm is developing momentum and gaining legitimacy in the international debate. So watch this space.

References

Andersen (2002), 'Outlook of the Development of Technologies and Markets for the European Audiovisual Sector up to 2010', http://ec.europa.eu/avpolicy/docs/library/studies/finalised /tvoutlook/finalrep.pdf. Accessed 29 November 2010.

Bar, F. and Sandvig, C. (2008), 'US Communication Policy after Convergence', *Media, Culture & Society*, 30: 4, pp. 531–550.

Betzel, M. and Lauf, E. (2008), 'Audiovisual Media Services. The Dutch Classification Concept', in EPRA (European Platform of Regulatory Authorities), *28th EPRA Meeting*, Dublin, Ireland, 29–31 October, EPRA: Strasbourg.

Cardoso, G. (2006), *The Media in the Network Society. Browsing, News, Filters and Citizenship*, Lisbon: Centre for Research and Studies in Sociology.

Cision and Bates, D. (2009), *2009 Social Media & Online Usage Study*, Washington: George Washington University and Cision.

Council of Europe (2009), 'Political Declaration and Resolutions. 1st Council of Europe Conference of Ministers responsible for Media and New Communication Services. A new notion of media?', http://www.coe.int/t/dghl/standardsetting/media/MCM(2009)011_en_ final_web.pdf. Accessed 29 November 2010.

Doria, A. and Kleinwächter, W. (eds.) (2010), *Internet Governance Forum (IGF): The First Two Years*, Paris: UNESCO, ITU and UNDESA.

European Dialogue on Internet Governance (Council of Europe) (2010), 'EuroDIG 2010. Messages from Madrid', 29–30 April, Madrid.

European Opinion Research Group (European Commission) (2004), 'Illegal and Harmful Content on the Internet', *Special Eurobarometer 203/Wave 60.2*, Brussels.

European Union (2009) Directive 2009/136/EC of the European Parliament and of the Council of 25 November 2009 amending Directive 2002/22/EC on Universal Service and Users' Rights Relating to Electronic Communications Networks and Services, http://eur-lex .europa.eu/LexUriServ/LexUriServ.do?uri= CELEX:32009L0136:EN:NOT, accessed 29 November 2010.

Forge, S. Guevara, K. Srivastava, L. Blackman, C. Cave, J. and Popper, R. (2010), 'Towards a Future Internet. Interrelation between Technological, Social and Economic Trends', *Interim Report*, Oxford: Oxford Internet Institute, SCF Associates Ltd.

Foster, R. (2007), 'Future Broadcasting Regulation', Report commissioned by DCMS. London: Department of Culture, Media and Sport.

Foster, R. Daymon, C. and Tewungwa, S. (2002), 'Future Reflections: Four Scenarios For Television in 2012. A Scenario Analysis Study of the Television Industry', http://media.bournemouth. ac.uk/research/documents/fullreport.pdf. Accessed 29 November 2010.

Galperin, H. and Bar, F. (2002), 'The Regulation of Interactive Television in the United States and the European Union', *Federal Comunications Law Journal*, 55: 1, pp. 61–84.

Geller, H. (2003), 'Promoting the Public Interest in the Digital Era', *Federal Communications Law Journal*, 55: 3, pp. 515–520.

Grünwald, A. (2001), 'What Future for Broadcasting in the Digital Era?', in Council of Europe, Expert Seminar on 'The European Convention on Transfrontier Television in an Evolving Broadcasting Environment', Strasbourg, France, 6 December, Council of Europe: Strasbourg.

Jakubowicz, K (2004), 'Human Rights and the Information Society: A Preliminary Overview', A working paper for the Preparatory Group on 'Human Rights and the Rule of Law in the Information Society', Integrated Project 1 'Making Democratic Institutions Work', Strasbourg, IP1(2004)47.

—— (2009), 'A New Notion of Media? Media and Media-Like Content and Activities on New Communication Services', http://www.coe.int/t/dghl/standardsetting/media/Doc/New_ Notion_Media_en.pdf. Accessed 29 November 2010.

—— (2010a), 'Right to Public Expression: A Modest Proposal for an Important Human Right', http://mediapolicy.siteunderdevelopment.com/wp-content/uploads/Karol-Right-to-Public _2010-05-17b.pdf. Accessed 6 December 2010.

—— (2010b), 'Analysis and Assessment of a Package of Hungarian Legislation and Draft Legislation on Media and Telecommunications', http://www.osce.org/documents /rfm/2010/09/45942_en.pdf. Accessed 29 November 2010.

—— (2010c), 'Television A.C.? Change and Continuity in Television', *Quaderns del CAC*, XIII: 34, pp. 5–16.

Lasota, A. (2010), 'Czy media są nowe. Próba polemiki', *Studia Medioznawcze*, 1: 40, pp. 169–180.

Le Borgne-Bachschmidt, F.(project manager) (2008), *User-Created-Content: Supporting a Participative Information Society*, Montpellier: IDATE, TNO and IviR.

Lister, M. Dovey, J. Giddings, S. Grant, I and Kelly, K. (2003), *New Media: A Critical Introduction*, London and New York: Routledge.

MacLean, D. (2009) (ed.) *Internet for All. Proceedings of the Third Internet Governance Forum. Hyderabad, India. 3–6 December 2008*, New York: United Nations

McQuail, D. (2008), 'Communication and Technology: Beyond Determinism?', in N. Carpentier, P. Pruulmann-Vengerfeldt, K. Nordenstreng, M. Hartmann, P. Vihalemm, B. Cammaerts and H. Nieminen (eds.), *Media Technologies and Democracy in an Enlarged Europe. The Intellectual Work of the 2007 European Media and Communication Doctoral Summer School*, Tartu: Tartu University Press, pp. 27–40.

Meraz, S. (2009), 'Is There an Elite Hold? Traditional Media to Social Media Agenda Setting Influence in Blog Networks', *Journal of Computer-Mediated Communication*, 14: 3, pp. 682–707.

Morris, M. and Ogan, C. (1996), 'The Internet as Mass Medium', http://jcmc.indiana.edu/vol1/issue4/morris.html. Accessed 29 November 2010.

Mueller, M. (1999), 'Digital Convergence and Its Consequences', *The Public/Javnost*, 6: 3, pp. 11–28.

Naughton, J. (2006), 'Our Changing Media Ecosystem', in E. Richards, R. Foster and T. Kiedrowski (eds.), *Communications: The Next Decade. A Collection of Essays Prepared for the UK Office of Communications*, London: OFCOM, pp. 41–50.

Nieminen, H. (2008), 'Towards the Democratic Regulation of European Media and Communication', in N. Carpentier, P. Pruulmann-Vengerfeldt, K. Nordenstreng, M. Hartmann, P. Vihalemm and B. Cammaerts (eds.), *Researching Media, Democracy and Participation. The Intellectual Work of the 2006 European Media and Communication Doctoral Summer School*. Tartu: Tartu University Press.

Noam, Eli M. (1995), 'Towards the Third Revolution of Television', http://www.columbia.edu/dlc/wp/citi/citinoam18.html. Accessed 29 November 2010.

——— (2003), 'The Internet: Still Wide Open and Competitive?', http://web.si.umich.edu/tprc/papers/2003/200/noam_TPRC2003.pdf. Accessed 29 November 2010.

O'Connell, R. and Bryce, J. (2005), 'Harmful Content',. Group of Specialists on Human Rights in the Information Society, Strasbourg, MC-S-IS(2005)007.

OFCOM (2009), *Converged Communications in Tomorrow's World. OFCOM's Technology Research Programme 2008/09*, London: Office of Communications.

——— (2010), *Traffic Management and 'Net Neutrality'. A Discussion Document*, London: Office of Communications.

O'Malley, T. P (2010), 'Broadcasting Policy in the 1980s: An Overview', http://www.nosuch-research.co.uk/pdfs/PaperBroadcastingPolicy.pdf. Accessed 29 November 2010.

Padovani, C. (2005), 'Debating Communication Imbalances from the MacBride Report to the World Summit on the Information Society: An Analysis of a Changing Discourse', *Global Media and Communication*, 1: 3, pp. 316–338.

Padovani, C. and Nordenstreng, K. (2005), 'From NWICO to WSIS: Another World Information and Communication Order?', *Global Media and Communication*, 1: 3, pp. 264–272.

Padovani, C. Musiani, F. and Pavan, E. (2010), 'Investigating Evolving Discourses On Human Rights in the Digital Age: Emerging Norms and Policy Challenges', *International Communication Gazette*, 72: 4–5, pp. 359–378.

Purvis, S. (2008), 'The Future of Content Regulation', in EPRA (European Platform of Regulatory Authorities), 27th EPRA Meeting, Riga, Latvia, 14–16 May, EPRA: Strasbourg.

Roel, M. (2008), 'Audiovisual Digitalization in Spain and Italy: from Neo-Television to Post-Television', *Observatorio (OBS*)*, 2: 1, pp. 95–112.

Symonides, J. (ed.) (1998), *Human Rights: New Dimensions and Challenges*, Dartmouth: Ashgate.

Tambini, D. (2006), 'What Citizens Need to Know. Digital Exclusion, Information Inequality and Rights', in E. Richards, R. Foster and T. Kiedrowski (eds.), *Communications: The Next Decade*, London: OFCOM, pp. 112–124.

Tambini, D. Leonardi, D. and Marsden, C. (2008), *Codifying Cyberspace. Communications Self-Regulation in the Age of Internet Convergence*, London and New York: Routledge.

Wunsch-Vincent, S. and Vickery, G. (2007), 'Participative Web: User-Created Content', Paris, DSTI/ICCP/IE(2006)7/Final.

Valcke P. Hou, L. Stevens, D. and Kosta, E. (2008), 'Guardian Knight or Hands Off: The European Response to Network Neutrality. Legal Considerations on the Electronic Communications Reform', *Communications & Strategies*, 90: 72, pp. 89–112.

Van Cuilenburg, J. and McQuail, D. (2003), 'Media Policy Paradigm Shifts: Towards a New Communications Policy Paradigm', *European Journal of Communication*, 18: 2, pp. 181–207.

Notes

1   These criteria still await their generally accepted definition, given that the decisive question is not superficial 'similarity' to traditional media, but functions, features and processes that replicate or approximate – possibly in new or different forms – those of the media organizations. Later, we will briefly discuss a few selected ones. 'Mass and general public' – mass communication has traditionally been defined as a case of mediated public communication addressed to a large audience (mass) and available to all ('general public'). What matters is the intention to distribute content for reception by and making it accessible to the general public without discrimination. As for 'mass,' whereas traditional mass communication consisted in making content available potentially to large numbers of receivers *at the same time*, non-linear new communication services may reach a comparable number of recipients *over time*. The 'mass' criterion therefore requires further consideration.

'Media organization' is here intended to refer to a basic unit of media operation, comprising management, media personnel and technical dimensions and operating in a field of social forces (social and political pressures, economic pressures etc.). The media organization performs a sequence of activities to obtain, select or edit content, then assembles it into a media product and disseminates it, or has it disseminated, to the public. In new communication services, the various roles of personnel and dimensions of the media organization can be telescoped into the activities of single individuals (e.g. bloggers). 'Editorial process': media-organizational functions include: securing an in-house and/or external supply of content, gate-keeping and selection of content for consideration; processing of content; decisions about presentation, structuring and packaging; preparation for distribution and assuming full editorial responsibility for the content.

'Influence on public opinion': a desire to influence public opinion manifests itself in devoting content to matters of public debate, covering news and developments of current public interest, seeking to animate the public debate and set its agenda, to promote specific views or values, to assist the public in forming opinions on matters of public concern and to follow and participate in the public debate. It also includes facilitating public scrutiny of politicians and civil servants. The intention to influence public opinion (regardless of how strong the potential impact is) is enough to take this factor into account in classifying a particular new communication service.

'Full editorial responsibility': this covers responsibility for the selection of content, for the editorial process (see earlier) and includes potential legal liability for the content provided.

'Periodic dissemination': as in the case of the traditional media, this may in practical terms mean very different frequency of publication – from daily to yearly. With electronic media delivered via the Internet on broadband networks, content can be updated or revised many times a day. This can qualify as periodic dissemination even if there is no wholesale replacement of content on a periodic basis.

2   As shown by a Hungarian draft 'Law on the freedom of the press and the fundamental rules governing media content', recognition of the subject of regulation is by no means a theoretical or academic question. The draft law adopts the concept of 'media content' as the object of regulation and defines it in Article 1(5) as 'Content provided by any media service or in printed or Internet-based press publications, whose content is the editorial responsibility of some person, and whose primary objective is the delivery of content consisting of text and images to the public for the purpose of providing information, entertainment or education through electronic telecommunication networks or in a press publication.' 'Content provider' is defined as 'the provider of media services or other media content.' It has been pointed out (Jakubowicz 2010b) that the definition of 'media content' is inadequate in distinguishing media content from other content and in providing clarity and legal certainty, as it fails to incorporate features that characterize media: regular distribution of content; the editorial process; the intention to reach and availability to the general public; the intention to exert influence on public opinion; editorial responsibility for content. The draft law would therefore extend the scope of the regulatory regime to almost all Internet content.

3   Other CoE documents in this field include: 'Human rights guidelines for Internet service providers,' 'Human rights guidelines for online games providers,' 'Recommendation CM/Rec(2008)6 of the Committee of Ministers to member states on measures to promote the respect for freedom of expression and information with regard to Internet filters,' 'Declaration on protecting the dignity, security and privacy of children on the internet,' 'Recommendation CM/Rec(2007)11 of the Committee of Ministers to member states on promoting freedom of expression and information in the new information and communication environment.'

Chapter 14

Content Control and Digital Television: Policy, Technology and Industry

Andrew T. Kenyon, Julian Thomas & Jason Bosland

Introduction: Content Management for Digital Media

From the turn of this century, with the transition to digital television in sight, the broadcasting and screen content industries called loudly for regulatory intervention to protect content on the new medium. These debates were especially prominent in the United States with the 'broadcast flag' proposal. The industries' basic claim was that valuable content would be withheld from terrestrial television broadcasters unless regulatory action was taken. If content shifted from broadcast platforms, this would undermine longstanding broadcast business models. At the same time, public interest groups called for different forms of regulation to safeguard longstanding forms of public service television (Kenyon and Wright 2006: 338). Each group argued, in quite different ways, that without regulatory intervention the cultural, political and economic roles played by broadcast television in the second half of the twentieth century would face an inevitable decline. The tradition of universally accessible, free-to-view television would be lost.

In the years since those calls first emerged, further substantial shifts have occurred in the delivery and use of television content, and the 'post-broadcast' era has generated an extensive academic literature (e.g., Bennett and Strange 2010, Kenyon 2007, Olsson and Spigel 2004, Ross 2008, Turner and Tay 2009). Highly successful new platforms for audio-visual media have appeared alongside broadcast television, including Apple's iTunes, the US networks' Hulu, and the BBC's iPlayer. Hulu and iPlayer are services offering streamed free-to-view content with Hulu supported by advertising. iTunes provides downloadable content for purchase or rent. All these new services provide television programming on demand over the broadband Internet. All three are examples of new platforms that emerged either within the television industry or in close partnership with it (iTunes). Other platforms, most notably Google's YouTube, grew out of the less-regulated, user-generated domain of the Internet and include very substantial bodies of unlicensed content. YouTube, however, has moved into the entertainment industry mainstream, with a series of alliances and agreements with both content producers and device manufacturers, taking YouTube beyond the personal computer on to smart phones, tablets and television receivers.

For our purposes, the significance of these new services is threefold: they point towards the near-term emergence of IPTV as broadband networks increase in capacity and flexibility. They point also to the power of the video-on-demand model – the pervasive idea that in the near future television viewers may expect access to the content they want to watch, at the time and in the place they choose and on the device they choose. iPlayer in the UK is an instructive example: it has evolved from a simple catch-up service into a cross-platform application, paving the way for YouView, an IPTV platform delivering a broad range of public service television channels. This idea of 'random access' television is clearly shaped by the user experience of the Internet and other digital media. It does not mean that the market for broadcast or streamed linear programming will disappear, but it plainly involves a complex re-engineering of the television business. The third point is that all these services acknowledge intellectual property rights in content and seek to manage the distribution and redistribution of material accordingly. Their approaches to content management are all quite different, but all have generated public debate and, in the case of YouTube, extended litigation with some rights holders. Conditional access is a common feature, especially the restriction of content to users in certain geographical domains. Diverse forms of digital rights management or other technical protections for content are also widely used. Both iTunes and YouTube have modified their content management systems extensively over time, as business models for broadband media have evolved.

Alongside these new broadband platforms, a parallel development has occurred in the consumer hardware viewers use to access and display digital media. Here content control has become a feature of everyday household technologies. As we explain later, new interface standards for high-definition media seek to control the circulation of licensed content between consumer devices, such as recorders, receivers and displays. Technologies such as these extend content control to popular new forms of packaged media, such as Blu-Ray discs and games.

Those observations provide the context for the analysis that follows, which is primarily concerned with digital broadcast television. Here there is a striking contrast. Whereas content control has flourished for broadband video-on-demand and high-definition video discs, the roll-out and switch over to digital broadcast television has proceeded almost entirely without content management. In this area, regulatory intervention to manage content has either failed – after legal challenge to the broadcast flag in the US – or it remains at a much earlier stage of formulation. However, that does not mean there has been no industry response to the shifts that digital transmission poses to audio-visual content markets. Even while broadcasters evolve into multi-platform content providers, industry groups have attempted to protect their traditional business models. They have relied in large part on other legal avenues, such as trademark protection, to construct their own limits to the functionality of digital reception equipment. The fact that some of the goals sought by public regulation have been pursued through these private regimes is an important illustration of the shifting conceptions of public interest and regulation in relation to audio-visual content. However, the effect of the policy legacy is a counter-intuitive situation, where the formal, highly regulated medium of broadcasting provides substantially less content control than the 'new media', whether these are mainstream Internet services or packaged discs.

The first part of this chapter considers the current state of technologies to control the reuse of content that is supplied through digital terrestrial television (DTT). In Europe, a content-control standard known as the Content Protection and Copy Management (CPCM) system is being developed by the Digital Video Broadcasting (DVB) Project. DVB standards are used by many countries for digital television across a wide variety of platforms, notably excluding the US. Although CPCM is having a 'protracted gestation' (Brennan 2007: 214, 219), there have been recent advances towards its development and deployment. The current US situation, where there appears to have been no recent public policy movements, is also examined. (Similarly, in Australia, interest in the technological control of DTT content appears to have been minimal. On this point see Wright et al. 2007: 2f).

The chapter's second section considers the trend of limiting the functional features of DTT reception equipment through restrictive trademark and certification mark licensing terms. This de facto regulatory 'solution' has been used in places such as Europe, Australia and New Zealand. It involves requiring receiver manufacturers to limit features (such as restricting analogue and digital outputs from reception equipment) or to install technological measures, such as the high-definition content protection (HDCP) system, to prevent unencrypted digital content being released from reception equipment. This de facto approach also provides a possible avenue for industry adoption of the CPCM standard without the need for regulation.

Technical Challenges and Technical Solutions

The concerns of content owners, producers and distributors stem from two features of free-to-air DTT. First, broadcast television has traditionally been 'in the clear', without any form of technological protection limiting its reuse. From the 1970s onwards, viewers could easily record analogue content, a situation which led to its own legal debates (see Sony Corporation v University City Studios 1984).[1] Free-to-air television signals are not encrypted at the point of broadcast and are not subject to the conditional access systems commonly used on subscription services to limit access to subscribers. This means that content can be accessed by anyone located within the broadcast signal's footprint using an appropriate receiving device. Secondly, digital transmission without technological measures over content allows content to be captured from the DTT signal. This content can then be distributed over the Internet and associated networks via peer-to-peer file sharing technology. Faced with this situation, content owners argued that content would be withheld from broadcast television, especially valuable high-definition content, unless DTT content was protected by technical measures (Center for Democracy and Technology 2003; McClintock 2002). Testifying before the US Congress, a representative of the Motion Picture Association of America (MPAA) stated:

> Without [content control technologies], the market will respond to the increasing threat of unauthorized redistribution by migrating high-quality programming away from broadcast television to other, protected distribution channels. (Attaway 2003)

At least on the predictions of the MPAA and associated interests, withholding content would result in the demise of the quality – and popularity – of free-to-air DTT. Content, and along with it the mass audience of viewers, would move to more secure platforms such as satellite and cable services, which can be made subject to conditional access and where broadcasters have greater legal and technical scope to control how consumers use content.

In light of these concerns, there has been a series of attempts in the US and Europe to develop technological measures to control the use of DTT content. The attempts have not yet been implemented, even while objections from content owners have continued, as have significant levels of illicit online redistribution of broadcast content. Even so, digital broadcasting being 'in-the-clear' does not appear to have moved much content from broadcast to more secure platforms. Instead, valuable content has been broadcast on DTT without technological control in key markets, such as the UK and US, for over a decade. And during that time, the lack of control has appeared to do very little to slow development of DTT, especially in Europe and the UK. Wider regulatory aspects of conversion and switching off analogue signals have received academic attention (e.g., Galperin 2004, Given 2003, Starks 2007), but issues of content control remain for consideration.

Although the transition to DTT appears to have been relatively successful, discussions about content control technologies have not disappeared. Instead, pressures for the adoption of technological controls have now gained renewed momentum with the introduction of high-definition (HD) DTT in the UK and other parts of Europe. Old arguments have returned, with rights holders threatening to withhold content from broadcast on HD DTT unless technological measures are put in place. With the commencement of HD DTT in the UK and elsewhere, broadcasters are reconsidering how content control technologies might be implemented.

Technological control over digital broadcast content can take one of two general forms. The first involves protection 'at the source' and requires the broadcast stream to be encrypted at the *point of transmission*, preventing *access* by those without appropriate authorization. This type of control or 'scrambling' is used by subscription broadcasters to limit reception of content to paying customers, but could also be used for free-to-air content. In that event, contractual terms on which descrambling equipment was offered could limit viewers' rights in relation to reusing content and allow their activities to be monitored by providers. Alternatively, reception equipment might provide technological means to monitor and control viewers' use of content (Carlson 2006). For example, in Japan free-to-air broadcast signals are encrypted and viewers must enter a contract with the national broadcaster, NHK, for the supply of reception and decryption equipment. The reception equipment complies with content controls, including the requirements that content be copied only once and that it cannot be redistributed beyond the domestic environment. In this way, control measures are imposed via the encrypted nature of the broadcast.

Elsewhere, however, the free-to-air environment usually lacks any contractual relationship between broadcaster and viewer and the content is not usually protected at source. Indeed, many countries, such as the UK and Australia, specifically provide that free-to-air content must not be encrypted – a person must be able to receive the service with commonly available reception equipment and without a special agreement with the service provider (Commonwealth of Australia 1992).[2] This means that any measures to control content reuse must be imposed by reception equipment *post-broadcast* rather than by the broadcaster at source. Different avenues have been pursued in the US and Europe – the broadcast flag and CPCM, respectively – to develop and implement restrictions on viewers' ability to reuse DTT content broadcast in the clear. In both these systems, control measures are imposed *at the point of reception* – content is 'flagged' with metadata that informs reception devices that the use of content should be limited according to controls contained within the receiving hardware. The flag, however, does not affect the functionality of receiving devices that do not contain content controls or do not recognize the metadata. Legacy reception equipment would still function, and there is no technical requirement that all reception devices limit content copying and redistribution. This is a challenge for flag systems. Reception devices that implement the limits appear likely to be commercially disadvantaged, with viewers likely to prefer devices allowing greater functionality over devices that restrict their ability to use content. Equipment manufacturers, therefore, have an incentive to make receivers that will not recognize or obey flag metadata. The lack of any contractual relationship between broadcaster and viewer and the market pressures towards greater functionality in equipment led to the view, common in existing policy and academic debates, that flag-based systems require public-law regulation. Such regulation is needed to ensure that reception equipment will comply with the system in question and to prevent the production, importation and distribution of non-compliant reception devices.

It should be noted that existing multi-lateral copyright agreements and domestic copyright laws do not provide legal support for the systems. Flags *in and of* themselves do not, for example, provide 'effective technological measures' as that term is used in the WIPO Copyright Treaty (Brennan 2007; Butler and Rodrick 2007; WIPO 1996), the treaty which requires parties to enact laws granting legal protection of and effective remedies against the circumvention of technological protection measures used by copyright owners to protect their content. Nor does it appear that the anti-circumvention provisions of the European Information Society Directive (European Parliament 2001) or of domestic laws apply to the flag systems. Under the current law, it is only manufacturing or distributing devices that circumvent the *compliant* features of reception equipment that would breach the provisions. The manufacture of non-compliant reception devices does not circumvent the protection offered by compliant devices. In addition, whereas flag metadata would likely amount to 'electronic rights management information' under the WCT and other laws, it is only the *removal or alteration* of such information that is targeted. A non-compliant device does not remove or alter the data; it simply does not recognize it.

All of this leads to the idea that specific regulation over DTT reception equipment is required for flag-based systems. It should also be noted, as David Brennan (2007) points out, that the current draft of the WIPO Treaty of the Protection of Broadcasting Organizations does not touch on the regulation of receiver and associated electronic equipment or on the protection against the circumvention of these flag-based protection systems. The imposition of a public law mandate over reception equipment is the reason the broadcast flag system stalled in the US and appears to be a major hurdle facing the introduction of the CPCM in Europe and elsewhere. It is the reason the proposed use of flag-based systems has been so controversial, with opponents arguing that a mandated standard will harm viewers by hindering technological innovation and limiting competition and by limiting the continued role for certain public value attributes of traditional broadcasting.[3]

The Broadcast Flag in the United States

In the US, it was recognized that withholding high-value content could delay digital conversion and result in significant loss of revenue that would otherwise be expected from auctioning vacated spectrum (the so-called digital dividend). Without high-quality programming on free-to-air digital, viewers would have few incentives to invest in the new equipment needed for DTT reception (House of Representatives Committee on the Judiciary 2003). In 2003, following an industry report by the Broadcast Protection Discussion Subgroup (Perry et al. 2002) and a Notice of Proposed Rulemaking from the Federal Communications Commission (FCC 2002), the FCC issued the Broadcast Flag Order to implement the broadcast flag.[4]

The stated aim was to control the 'indiscriminate redistribution of DTT content' (FCC 2002). The broadcast signal was to include a code that would instruct reception devices whether or not to restrict content reuse. The broadcast flag, however, was short lived. Nine non-profit organizations, representing consumer, research, educational and library interests, sought judicial review of the FCC's Broadcast Flag Order. In American Library Association v FCC (2005: 689) the US Court of Appeals for the District of Columbia found the FCC had exceeded its statutory powers. In particular, the FCC did not have jurisdiction to regulate 'consumer electronics products [...] when those devices are not engaged in the process of radio or wire transmission.' The FCC only had power to regulate the transmission of broadcast communication, not their reception. Because the broadcast flag does not affect transmission equipment and only comes into effect at the point of reception, the Broadcast Flag Order fell outside the FCC's statutory remit. The decision meant that manufacturers were not required to comply with the order.

Following the decision, attention turned to Congress to provide the FCC with the power to implement the broadcast flag. After several attempts to legislate lapsed, the broadcast flag appeared to fall off the policy agenda. At a more practical level, however, the flag persists. Microsoft's Windows Vista Media Center software recognizes the broadcast flag and prevents the recording of flagged programmes to viewers' computers. There are also reports that broadcasters such as NBC have continued to 'flag' premium content (Sandoval 2008).

Europe and CPCM

In Europe, there has been less focus on legal processes and more on the development of technological responses by industry. However, as with the broadcast flag, the proposed technology has been thought to require public-law support to be effective. CPCM, a 'European broadcast flag' (Doctorow and EFF 2005), has been in development since 1999 by the DVB project, an industry consortium responsible for developing the digital broadcasting technical standards (DVB-T and the subsequent DVB-T2) that are used for DTT in the EU, Russia, Australia, New Zealand, India and many other countries. The development of CPCM has been lengthy, with widely different interests implicated – content owners, equipment manufacturers, viewers, commercial and public service broadcasters. As just one example, it took three years to reach consensus regarding the system's commercial requirements, let alone its technical specifications (see Brennan 2007).

CPCM, like the broadcast flag, includes an electronic notice in the broadcast signal to 'instruct' receiving devices. However, unlike the broadcast flag, which is a simple 'on/off' notice, reuse of content under CPCM is restricted according to the 'usage state information' (USI) that is contained within the broadcast metadata. This system offers greater flexibility for broadcasters and rights holders to determine how the content is to be reused, if at all. It would also offer interesting options for regulators who could, for example, require that the use of certain forms of public interest content not be restricted in particular ways (see also Kenyon and Wright 2006). The first three planned specifications for the CPCM system were published in 2005 in the CPCM 'Bluebook': *Digital Video Broadcast (DVB): Content Protection & Copy Management* (Digital Video Broadcasting 2005). The Bluebook contains USIs regarding five areas of content control:

(1) Copy and movement control (to control the number of copies of content that could be made).
(2) Consumption control (for example, use of content could be limited to a set period or a number of views).
(3) Propagation control (ability to restrict content to a 'defined realm' such as a domestic environment).
(4) Output control (for example, to limit the resolution of digital outputs or prevent analogue outputs).
(5) Ancillary control (ability to prevent the scrambling of content as it travels between devices).
(6) A further six planned specifications were published in 2007, including the System Specification and the Security Toolbox.

The completed specifications were submitted to the European Telecommunications Standards Institute and were approved and published by that body in July 2008. DVB is currently working on four final specifications for CPCM, including a compliance framework and an extension to limit the number of times content can be played (called 'play counts') (Digital Video Broadcasting 2009a). The compliance framework sets out components for a 'compliance and robustness regime' to ensure that CPCM technical specifications are correctly implemented in reception devices. The compliance rules define the behaviour and characteristics required of CPCM-compliant devices, whereas the robustness rules specify the level of protection necessary to ensure that the CPCM system cannot be circumvented or compromised (Digital Video Broadcasting 2009b). It is only when compliance and robustness rules are satisfied that a compliance body will authorize the issuing of device certificates to be included within CPCM-compliant devices. These certificates essentially perform the technical function of ensuring that CPCM devices can confirm that connecting devices are also CPCM compliant (or contain alternative content protection systems). At the time of writing, there appears to have been no formal announcement regarding the development of compliance and robustness regimes for the CPCM. However, there have been a number of recent demonstrations of CPCM and ongoing trials (see for example Moscheni 2008). It has also been suggested that DVB is trying to have CPCM included in the next EU Copyright Directive (Leeming 2007).

De Facto Regulation: High-Bandwidth Digital Content Protection

In the absence of regulatory intervention to support flag-based systems, content and broadcasting industries have pursued alternative avenues. These de facto solutions involve using various intellectual property rights to ensure that HD equipment manufacturers adopt the High-Bandwidth Digital Content Protection (HDCP) standard. HDCP, developed by Intel Corporation, prevents content from being intercepted as it travels between devices where high-bandwidth digital video interfaces are used. These include the High-Definition Multimedia Interface (HDMI) and the Digital Video Interface (DVI), which are current industry standards for data transmission between high-definition digital devices. HDCP therefore protects digital transmissions in the last stages of distribution – for example, transmission between a digital receiver and display screen or digital video recorder.

HDCP is initiated where content is protected 'upstream' by a content-control system and that system indicates that it desires HDCP. The system then encrypts data streams between HDCP-compliant devices to prevent interception of content during transmission. Once data have been sent, they are decrypted by the receiving device. However, transmission only occurs where, through the exchange of keys, the source device has authenticated all other devices within a system as being HDCP-compliant. Each HDCP-compliant device has a unique set of keys, which can be revoked where a device has been compromised, for example where keys have been cloned or have been disclosed in violation of the HDCP licence agreement (DCP 2009). Revoked keys are included in a list stored within HDCP compliant devices. The list can be updated, either from content sources such as DVDs or broadcast streams or through a connection with a device containing a more recent list.

The HDCP system, however, has broader effects for viewers and device manufacturers than simply protecting high-bandwidth digital links. This is because of the compliance rules imposed on equipment manufacturers who want to license HDMI and HDCP technologies for their products (which is, effectively, all device manufacturers) (Evain 2007). The compliance rules in the licence agreement set out a range of requirements depending on the nature of the device. For 'presentation devices' such as screens and monitors, the rules state the device must not make any copies of decrypted content for any purpose other than temporary buffering (cl. 7.2). In addition, the device must not permit the digital output of any decrypted HDCP content; the audio portions of decrypted audio-visual content may be output in analogue form or in a compressed digital form that cannot be copied (cl. 3.3). 'Source devices' such as DTT receivers and DVD players must not permit any digital output that is not HDCP operational (cl. 4). There is no prohibition on source devices having analogue outputs; the rules are not seeking to close the so-called analogue hole (cl. 4.2). However, 'repeaters' – devices located between the source and presentation devices, such as digital video recorders – must not have analogue outputs and their digital outputs must be HDCP operational (cl. 5.4. 5.5). Where HDCP is not wanted, no limitations are imposed on how the content can be used or redistributed (cl. 5.6).

In various regions, broadcast interests have used trademark licensing to ensure that manufacturers adopt HDCP. For example, Digital Europe (the European information and communication technology industry association) only licences the use of the 'HD Ready' and 'HDTV' logos, which are certification marks designed to inform viewers that receivers are HD compatible, where equipment manufacturers agree to use HDCP (Digital Europe 2006a, 2006b). Similar requirements are planned by UK free-to-air broadcasters for the use of the 'Freeview HD' logo on HD set-top boxes when HD transmissions commence (British Broadcasting Corporation 2009, OFCOM 2009a). Although the licences are not publicly available, similar requirements appear to have been imposed in New Zealand for the 'Freeview HD' logo as well as in Australia where receivers with built-in digital video recorders must not be able to ad-skip (Turner 2009). Of course, the limitation of this strategy, from the perspectives of broadcasters and content owners, is that it does not require manufacturers to incorporate the technology. Manufacturers remain able to forego using the applicable logo and develop more functional equipment. But what is particularly notable, given the earlier trajectory of debate on the broadcast flag and CPCM, is the way in which a high level of compliant devices among viewers has been achieved through marketing the relevant logos to potential equipment purchasers and licensing the use of those logos to equipment manufacturers.

Alternative avenues that would effectively mandate the adoption of relevant technologies are also being pursued. The BBC on behalf of all UK terrestrial broadcasters announced a plan in 2009 that would require the adoption of HDCP or a similar technology such as Digital Transmission Content Protection (DTCP) by all HD equipment manufacturers wanting their equipment to operate fully within the UK. Multiplex B is currently being prepared to carry HD terrestrial television signals using the DVB-T2 and MPEG 4 standards. Content owners, through the Digital Transmission Licensing Administration (DTLA), the body responsible for licensing the DTCP standard, have asked broadcasters to ensure that HD receivers implement industry-specified content-control standards (British Broadcasting Corporation 2009, OFCOM 2009a). Rather than using a 'flag' technology, the solution proposed by the BBC involves compressing the service information data using look-up tables developed by the BBC. Without these Huffman look-up tables, receivers will be unable to access electronic programme-guide information. This would make it more difficult for users to programme devices to record material, and it may make access to content more complicated for average consumers (see O'Brien 2009; Smith 2009; Watson 2009). Although the compression algorithm is freely available to equipment manufacturers, the BBC has copyright and database rights in the look-up tables required for the algorithm to work. (The table would also appear to be confidential information that could be protected by law.) The BBC plans to limit licensing the look-up table to receiver manufacturers who agree to implement content-control standards specified in the 'HD D-Book' issued by the Digital TV Group, the industry body responsible for recommending DTT standards in the UK.

The UK media regulator OFCOM's view is that the BBC's proposal would require amendments to the terms of the Multiplex B licence. At the time of writing, OFCOM has released a consultation paper seeking stakeholder views on the BBC proposal and its own preferred options, and the BBC has provided a more detailed explanation of what it wants to do and why it believes content management on free-to-air HD television is in the interests of television viewers (OFCOM 2010). The BBC's argument can be summarized briefly: there is a strong public interest in free-to-view broadcasting, but without the capacity to offer content management, some rights holders will not license valuable content for Freeview transmission, effectively reducing the range and quality of public service broadcasting, especially in comparison with rival subscription television services. The proposal is to enable rights owners to designate one of three 'content management states' for a programme:

(1) Unrestricted copy: the digital receiver output is unencrypted and unrestricted copies of HD content can be made onto any digital device. There are no restrictions imposed on Internet distribution.
(2) Multiple copy: the digital receiver output is encrypted and unrestricted copies of the content can be made onto digital devices that are compatible with the copy-management technology. Internet distribution is not permitted.
(3) Managed copy: the digital receiver output is encrypted and only one copy of the content can be made onto a DVR and one external digital device, which is compatible with the copy-management technology. Internet distribution is not permitted (OFCOM 2010: 9).

In all three states, HDCP is applied to the HD display output on receivers; no restrictions are placed on consumer recordings of HD programmes onto integrated digital recorders; no restrictions are placed on down-converted SD versions of HD content; and no restrictions are placed on the number of times copies of HD content can be accessed or the period of time it can be stored (OFCOM 2010: 10).

OFCOM's provisional finding is that the BBC's proposal represents a reasonable compromise between the interests of rights owners and those of citizens and consumers. However, OFCOM is concerned that viewers' 'fair dealing' rights under copyright law should not be prejudiced and, among other conditions, proposes a requirement that the BBC 'respect current usage protections under copyright law and any future extension of these protections,' including those proposed by ongoing review of intellectual property in the UK (2010: 32).

Conclusion

The language of the UK regulator is cautious, for good reason given the recent history of copyright law reform. But clearly content management has now emerged as an important new domain of audio-visual policy and regulation. In the establishment and early transition period of digital television, regulators and legislators did not provide a solution. The focus was on the complex logistics and dynamics of converting the underlying transmission technology of a universal medium. In the absence of a regulatory solution, industry groups developed their own approaches, supported by private law such as trademarks and contract, to achieve some of the objectives of content owners and of major media content providers. It should be clear how similar methods might be used for systems like CPCM.

As broadcast becomes just one among a plethora of platforms for accessing and using television content, it will be interesting to see what becomes of arguments about the role of public regulation and the traditional qualities of broadcast television – its free availability and general accessibility to audiences. For decades, public service television has been widely available without technical limitations on the use of content by viewers, while other platforms have evolved and adopted technologies for controlling and limiting what viewers might be able to do with the content they paid to see. With OFCOM's most recent deliberations over Multiplex B, a complete digital public television service will no longer be available and accessible to everyone with a standard receiver. People who have contributed to the cost of the digital transition through their licence fees and taxes will now have to enter into a new bargain with broadcasters if they are to enjoy one of the main benefits of that conversion – the capacity to see and make use of detailed service information alongside the transmitted programme. A large part of the reason for this transformation lies in the fact that broadcasting is now part of a broader audio-visual ecosystem and content licensed to broadcasters must also retain real value for what are, for the time being, termed 'secondary usages,' such as Blu-ray discs and video-on-demand applications for broadband Internet (OFCOM 2010: 7).

We can conclude by observing how far the music and screen industries have now diverged on this issue. Although the trend in music is towards a reduction or elimination of content management, the screen industries, arguably with more now at stake, are pursuing a combination of technical, legal and, to a lesser extent, regulatory strategies to curtail the re-use and re-circulation of broadcast content. Of course, it is possible that in the audio-visual environment attitudes towards content control may turn out to be more favourable than in music, and the technology may be better implemented. Broadcasters are relying on the fact that people use television content and music in different ways. Faced with the challenge of digital copying and redistribution, broadcasters and programme makers have decided, on the whole, to rely much more on technology and private law than on conventional broadcasting law and policy. This has left copyright law as the major focus for public policy debate, an outcome that may in turn lead to new and unexpected articulations of the cultural, political and economic roles of television, whatever its platform of delivery.

Acknowledgements

The authors would like to acknowledge the support of the Australian Research Council Centre of Excellence for Creative Industries and Innovation. An earlier version of this paper appears in 'Digital Television: Emerging Markets and Challenges for Policy Making', a themed issue of the journal *Communication, Politics and Culture*, 43: 2.

References

Anderson, N. (2007), 'DVB broadcast flag will require government support, but may not get it', http://arstechnica.com/tech-policy/news/2007/03/dvb-broadcast-flag-will-require-government-support-but-may-not-get-it.ars. Accessed 16 November 2010.

Attaway, F. (2003), 'Hearing Before the Subcommittee on Courts, The Internet and Intellectual Property of the Committee on the Judiciary: House of Representatives', http://ftp.resource.org/gpo.gov/hearings/108h/85490.pdf. Accessed 16 November 2010.

Bennett, J. and Strange, N. (eds.) (2010), *Television as Digital Media*, Durham: Duke University Press.

Brennan, D. (2007), 'Flag Waving in the Digital Jungle', in A. T. Kenyon (ed.), *TV Futures: Digital Television Policy in Australia*, Carlton: Melbourne University Press.

British Broadcasting Corporation (2009), 'Letter from BBC to OFCOM, 27 August', http://www.ofcom.org.uk/tv/ifi/tvlicensing/enquiry/ofcom_bbc.pdf. Accessed 16 November 2010.

Commonwealth of Australia (1992), 'Broadcasting Services Act. Act No.110 of 1992 as amended', http://www.comlaw.gov.au/ComLaw/Legislation/ActCompilation1.nsf/0/204764F6E03D1B86 CA257767000A574A/$file/BroadServ1992Vol1_WD02.pdf. Accessed 16 November 2010.

Butler, D. and Rodrick, S. (2007), *Australian Media Law*, 3rd edition, Pyrmont: Thompson.

Carlson, M. (2006), 'Tapping into TiVo: Digital Video Recorders and the Transition from Schedules to Surveillance in Television', *New Media and Society*, 8: 1, pp. 97–115.

Center for Democracy and Technology (2003), 'Implications of the Broadcast Flag: A Public Interest Primer (Version 2.0)', http://www.cdt.org/copyright/broadcastflag.pdf. Accessed 16 November 2010.

Crawford, S. P. (2003), 'The Biology of the Broadcast Flag', *Hastings Communications and Entertainment Law Journal*, 25: 2, p. 559.

Digital Content Protection (2009), 'HDCP Licence Agreement', http://www.digital-cp.com/files/static_page_files/77E11069-C938-A30E-9B3B0F1736565D2C/HDCP%20 License%20Agreement102109final.pdf. Accessed 16 November 2010.

Digital Europe (2006a), 'HD TV Logo License Agreement', Annex A, cl. 8', http://www.eicta.org. Accessed 16 November 2010.

——— (2006b), 'HD READY Logo License Agreement', Annex A, cl. 4', http://www.eicta.org. Accessed 16 November 2010.

Digital Video Broadcasting (2005), 'Content Protection and Copy Management', DVB Document A094, November 2005, http://www.dvb.org/technology/dvb-cpcm/a094. Accessed 16 November 2010.

——— (2009a), 'Digital Video Broadcasting (DVB) Content Protection & Copy Management Specification; Part 14: CPCM Extensions', http://www.dvb.org/technology/standards/A094r4_CPCM_Part_14_Extensions.pdf. Accessed 16 November 2010.

——— (2009b), 'Digital Video Broadcasting (DVB) Content Protection & Copy Management Specification; Part 13: DVB-CPCM Compliance Framework', http://www.dvb.org/technology/standards/A094r4_CPCM_Part_13_Compliance_Framework.pdf. Accessed 16 November 2010.

Doctorow, C. and Electronic Frontier Foundation (2005), 'Europe's Broadcast Flag. The Digital Video Broadcasting Project Content Protection and Copy Management: A Stealth Attack on Consumer Rights and Competition', http://w2.eff.org/IP/DVB/dvb_critique.php. Accessed 16 November 2010.

European Parliament (2001), 'Directive 2001/29/EC of the European Parliament and the Council of 22 May 2001 on the Harmonisation of Certain Aspects of Copyright and Related Rights in the Information Society, OJ L 167, Article 6', http://eur-lex.europa.eu/smartapi/cgi/sga_doc?smartapi!celexapi!prod!CELEXnumdoc&lg=EN&numdoc=32001L0029&model=guichett. Accessed 16 November 2010.

Evain, J.-P. (2007), 'HDCP – The FTA Broadcasters' Perspective', http://www.ebu.ch/fr/technical/trev/trev_312-evain_hdcp.pdf. Accessed 16 November 2010.

Federal Communications Commission (2002), 'Notice of Proposed Rulemaking Re Digital Broadcast Copy Protection', 9 August, Washington D.C., No 02-231.

Galperin, H. (2004), *New Television, Old Politics: The Transition to Digital TV in the United States and Britain*, Cambridge: Cambridge University Press.

Given, J. (2003), *Turning Off the Television: Broadcasting's Uncertain Future*, Sydney: UNSW Press.

Kenyon, A. T. and Wright, R. (2006), 'Television as Something Special', *Melbourne University Law Review*, 30: 2, pp. 338–369.

Kenyon, A. T. (ed.) (2007), *TV Futures: Digital Television Policy in Australia*, Carlton: Melbourne University Press.

Leeming, R. (2007), 'DRM – "Digital Rights" or "Digital Restrictions" Management?', http://www.ebu.ch/en/technical/trev/trev_309-digital_rights.pdf. Accessed 16 November 2010.

McClintock, P. (2002), 'Viacom's Ultimatum – CBS Parent: No Piracy Protection, No Hi-Def', http://www.variety.com/article/VR1117877531?category1d=1237&cs=1. Accessed 16 November 2010.

Moscheni, F. (2008), 'DVB-CPCM: The Solution for Valued-Added and Customer-Oriented Business Cases in Home Networks, with no Compromise with the Security', in CCP(Centre for Content Protection), Digital Future Symposium 2008, 10 December, Singapore, CCP: Singapore.

O'Brien, D. (2009), 'License to Kill Innovation: the Broadcast Flag for UK Digital TV?', http://www.eff.org/deeplinks/2009/09/broadcast-flag-uk. Accessed 16 November 2010.

OFCOM (2010), 'Content Management on the HD Freeview Platform', http://www.ofcom.org.uk/consult/condocs/content_mngt. Accessed 16 November 2010.

——— (2009a), 'Enquiry to OFCOM from BBC Free to View Ltd Concerning Its DTT High Definition Multiplex Licence', http://www.ofcom.org.uk/tv/ifi/tvlicensing/enquiry/ofcom_bbc.pdf. Accessed 16 November 2010.

——— (2009b), 'The Communications Market – 2009', http://www.ofcom.org.uk/research/cm/cmr09. Accessed 16 November 2010.

Olsson, J. and Spigel, L (eds.) (2004), *Television After TV: Essays on a Medium in Transition*, Durham: Duke University Press.

House of Representatives Committee on the Judiciary (2003), 'Piracy Prevention and the Broadcast Flag: Hearing Before the Subcommittee on Courts, the Internet, and Intellectual Property. 108th Congress. 6 March 2003', http://frwebgate.access.gpo.gov/cgi-bin/getdoc.cgi?dbname=108_house_hearings&docid=f:85490.pdf. Accessed 16 November 2010.

Perry, P., Ripley, M. and Setos, A. (2002), *Final Report of the Co-Chairs of the Broadcast Protection Discussion Subgroup to the Copy Protection Technical Working Group*, http://www.cptwg.org/Assets/TEXT FILES/BPDG/BPDG Report.DOC. Accessed 16 November 2010.

Ross, S. M. (2008), *Beyond the Box: Television and the Internet*, Malden: Blackwell.

Sandoval, G. (2008), 'Microsoft confirms Windows adheres to broadcast flag', http://news.cnet.com/8301-10784_3-9946780-7.html?tag=nefd.riv. Accessed 16 November 2010.

Smith, P. (2009), 'Call to Copy-Protect HD Shows', http://www.guardian.co.uk/media/pda/2009/sep/16/bbc-feeview-signal-encryption-drm. Accessed 16 November 2010.

Starks, M. (2007), *Digital Television: UK Public Policy and the Market*, Bristol: Intellect.

Turner, A. (2009), 'Freeview – The Great Aussie Swindle?', http://digihub.smh.com.au/node/275. Accessed 16 November 2010.

Turner, G. and Tay, J (eds.) (2009), *Television Studies After TV*, Abingdon: Routledge.

Watson, T. (2009), 'Personal Video Recorders: OFCOM Consultation Indicates that the BBC Wants to Make Yours Obsolete', http://www.tom-watson.co.uk/2009/09/personal-video-recorders-ofcom-consultation-indicates-that-the-bbc-want-to-make-yours-obsolete. Accessed 16 November 2010.

Wright, R., Kenyon, A. T. and Bosland, J. (2007), 'Broadcast and Beyond: An Industry Snapshot of Content Control Technologies and Digital Television in Australia,' (April 2007), http://papers.ssrn.com/sol3/papers.cfm?abstract_id=978703. Accessed 16 November 2010.

WIPO (1996), 'Copyright Treaty, (adopted in Geneva on December 20, 1996), Article 11', http://www.wipo.int/export/sites/www/treaties/en/ip/wct/pdf/trtdocs_wo033.pdf. Accessed 16 November 2010.

Notes

1 Sony Corporation v Universal City Studios (1984) 464 US 417.
2 In the UK, the requirement is contained in licence agreements made with broadcasters.
3 An example from the US broadcast flag debates concerned the question as to whether public domain material and news content would be subject to the flag: see further Anderson 2007, Crawford 2003.
4 Broadcast Flag Order, 18 FCCR 23550, [4] (4 November 2003), codified at 47 CFR §§ 73, 76 (2005).

Chapter 15

Regulating and Monitoring Online Activities of Public Service
Broadcasters: The Case of Switzerland

Natascha Just, Michael Latzer & Florian Saurwein

Research Questions and Context

Since the mid-1990s, public service broadcasters in Europe have developed online services in addition to their traditional radio and television programmes. These activities have from the outset led to controversial discussions regarding their legitimacy and extent as well as their financing and control. In reaction to complaints by private media companies, the European Commission, for example, has used state aid policy to put pressure on the member states and their public service broadcasters to clarify the extent of online activities (Donders and Pauwels 2008; Humphreys 2008; Just and Latzer 2011). Although the discussions within Europe are similar, the regulatory responses by national governments differ. Various European Union states, for example Germany and the UK, have implemented public value tests. Switzerland specified the rules for the provision of online content by the Swiss public broadcaster (SRG) with the *SRG charter*, which entered into force in 2008.[1] The provision of online services is part of its remit and Art. 13 clarifies which content is permissible. The rules require the content to closely relate to specific broadcasts, allow self-promotion solely with the aim of audience bonding and the setting of external links on a non-commercial basis. With a few exceptions, there is also a total ban on online advertising and sponsoring.[2]

In 2009, the Swiss Communications Regulator (BAKOM) commissioned the first study on the SRG's compliance with these regulatory requirements. This paper presents the results of this study. It analyses the SRG websites according to three research questions:[3]

RQ1. Do the individual parts of the online service comply with one of the legal requirements of Art. 13(1) of the charter?

RQ2. What areas are critical in the sense of being a *grey area*? Are there offers that do not relate to the programme directly or indirectly (thematic connection)?

RQ3. Do the websites contain links that are not journalistically but commercially motivated?

RQ1 requires an examination of the online content according to Art. 13(1) lit. a–d of the charter. Accordingly, the SRG's online presence is intended to deepen and supplement the traditional programme and not to substitute or extend it. The following content is allowed:

a. Programme-related, multimedia-based content that relates thematically and temporally directly to broadcasts/programmes.
b. Background and context information that served as basis for broadcasts/programmes.
c. Basic knowledge information related to educational broadcasts if it serves an improved or more purposeful fulfillment of the remit.
d. Audience forums and games connected to broadcasts and with no independent meaning.

The grey area of RQ2 is accordingly defined as all content that does not comply with at least one of the criteria given earlier and further covers all types of advertising, self-promotion and online sales that are not expressly permitted by law.[4]

RQ3 refers to Art. 13(2) of the charter, which prohibits the SRG from electronically linking to other web pages for money or other benefits of monetary value.

Methods and Context

The goal of this study is to examine the SRG's online offers regarding the structure and properties of its websites and the extent to which they comply with regulatory requirements. The study looks into these questions by applying a content analysis and a link analysis, which are complemented by qualitative explorations:

- *The content analysis serves to assess the conformity of the websites with the charter*: this shows the structure and properties of the websites and to which extent and in what areas there is content for which compliance with regulations is unclear (grey area).
- *The link analysis serves to capture the intensity and patterns of electronic linking between the SRG and third parties*: this shows the type of external websites and the extent to which these are interlinked with the SRG and assesses – by way of classification of these links – the potential for their commercialization.
- *The qualitative exploration and case studies complement the quantitative analyses*: this helps in understanding the findings and patterns within the grey area and the link structure.

The Internet is a 'moving target for communication research' (McMillan 2000: 80), a 'unique mixture of the ephemeral and permanent' (Schneider and Foot 2004: 115). These characteristics pose various challenges for scholars doing online research. The extreme depth and breath of online content, the dynamic non-linear structure, the extensive linking of pages and the myriad of new interactive communication means all require attention and the adaptation of traditional research tools, probably even the development of novel approaches suited to individual research. Weare and Lin (2000), for example, claim that the WWW (World Wide Web) opens additional realms for content-analytic research and necessitates the development of new empirical techniques. Content analysis, a prominent tool in traditional communication research, is rarely employed for online research as compared to other methods such as web surveys, for example.[5] Welker and Wünsch (2010) apply the term 'shadow existence' to it.[6] McMillan (2000) and Zhang (2005) both assess content analysis research of the WWW prior to 2000 and from 2000 to 2004, and identify 19 and 39 papers respectively from various sources such as the Social Citation Index. The analyses of these papers show variations with regard to research questions and methodological approaches and highlight potential problems for researchers at all stages of content-analysis research: from the formulation of research questions to sampling and data collection, from the definition of units of analysis to the coding and the interpretation of data (also Wang 2006; Weare and Lin 2000). A theoretical and methodological review of communication research into the Internet by Kim and Weaver (2002) indicates that – contrary to traditional communication research – articles employing qualitative methods outnumber quantitative ones by five to one. They further conclude that there is a lack of theoretical applications in Internet research, an assessment shared by McMillan (2000) and Zhang (2005), who find that most articles and results are descriptive.

Link analysis is widely neglected in communication science, although Jackson (1997) early on pointed to the strategic nature of the link, which raises important questions for the interpretation and representation of web structures, and suggested using network analysis to study it. Alongside webometrics, which derives from information science, hyperlink network analysis, which derives from social network analysis, has in fact become a prominent approach to link analysis. In the field of Internet research, link analysis has proliferated in recent years and has been applied, among other disciplines, by computer science, statistical physics and information science (Park and Thelwall 2003). Despite this surge, Schneider and Foot (2004: 116) argue that there is a 'paucity of analytical tools for making sense of the links among web pages and between websites.' Link analysis has thus far been applied to investigate various types of connections between websites, e.g. the connectivity structure between universities (Park and Thelwall 2003) and hyperlinked environments in politics and media to analyse emerging power relations on the web (Escher et al. 2006; Hindman 2009), but never to the question of whether links are established for commercial reasons.

Although the Internet allows researchers easy access to huge amounts of previously inaccessible data, this also raises questions as to the methods and quality of data collection and the reproducibility of data and approaches applied. In a study on mediated interaction Wouters and Gerbec (2003) conclude that the use of publicly available search engines is unsuitable for creating data sets because of the instability of results. Consequently, they urge researchers to develop their own software for data collection. However, in recent years various new and fairly inexpensive software products have been developed. For this study, a combination of various available products was chosen after testing and the data for content and link analysis directly collected by webcrawling processes.[7] Thelwall (2002) argues that the increasing use of crawlers and search engines necessitates that researchers clarify their methodological decisions, so as to allow replication of studies. This paper builds upon selections regarding SRG enterprise units, addressing elements/domain names, the compilation of sample frames and definitions of the basic unit of analysis.

Table 1: Object of Investigation: Websites of Five SRG Enterprise Units.

Language		German	French		Italian
Medium	TV	Radio	TV	Radio	TV & Radio
Website	sf.tv	drs.ch	tsr.ch	rsr.ch	rsi.ch
Included URLs	sf.tv	drs.ch	tsr.ch	rsr.ch	rsi.ch
		drs1.ch	tsr.blogs.com	couleur3.ch	
		drs2.ch	tsrboutique.ch		
		drs3.ch	moncinema.ch		
		radiokiosk.ch	tsremploi.ch		
			tsrdecouvertc.ch		
Examples of URLs not included	drs4news.ch, drspirando.ch, drsmusikwelle.ch, drsmusigwaelle.ch, virus.ch, radioswissclassic.ch, radioswissjazz.ch, radioswisspop.ch, rtr.ch, mx3.ch, pactemultimedia.ch, publisuisse.ch, rtsr.ch, sortir.ch, srg.ch, srgdeutschschweiz. ch, srg-ssr.ch, srg-ssr-idee-suisse.ch, swissinfo.ch, swisstxt.ch, teletext.ch, vxm.ch, worldradio.ch				

The paper analyses the websites of five SRG enterprise units from three language regions: *Schweizer Fernsehen* (Swiss Television–SF) and *Radio DRS* (DRS) for the German-speaking area, *Télévision Suisse Romande* (TSR) and *Radio Suisse Romande* (RSR) for the French-speaking area, and *Radiotelevisione svizzera di lingua italiana* (RSI) for the Italian-speaking area.[8] The addressing of the enterprise units is inconsistent and therefore – for comparison – requires a decision regarding what domain names should be included. SF, for example, uses only the domain sf.tv whereas other enterprise units also use sub-domains. Such sub-domains are included in this study if they refer to online shops or if they appear with the same header and logo (branding) as the investigated website of an enterprise unit. The study surveys a total of 15 domains and sub-domains, summarized in Table 1.

The sample frame for the quantitative content analysis covers all web pages available at the time of crawling via a maximum of 5 links starting from the 15 domains. Accordingly, the research includes six levels with a total of 350,000 web pages. The totality of theoretically reachable pages was restricted on three dimensions:

Data format: Web pages may be composed of various data sets. The sample frame contains only URLs (Uniform Resource Locators) of web pages. URLs that form parts of these pages, such as audio and video files or style sheets, are downloaded and archived but not included individually. As part of the web page, they are, however, part of the analysis.

Time frame: Only pages available during the time of crawling are included.[9]

Levels: The research includes six levels of a website. The crawler starts at the homepage of a website (level one), saves all URLs of pages that are linked with it (level two), visits these pages, and continues with saving all URLs of these pages (level three). This procedure is continued until the crawler has gathered all URLs of the six levels or until no new URL is identified.

The sample of the content analysis is a representative random sample of 2,000 web pages stratified according to enterprise unit, i.e. 400 web pages per unit.

The sample frame for the link analysis comprises all links in the form of *http://requests* contained in the content analysis' sample frame. This totals approximately 850,000 URLs from about 17,000 different domain names.[10] The analysis includes:

(1) All links in the from of content and technologies that are embedded in the SRG websites by http://requests, such as Youtube Player, AdBanners, iFrames; and

(2) All sorts of clickable links through which users access other websites. The sample is an intentional selection of the 500 most linked-to domain names, i.e. 100 per enterprise unit.

The 2,000 web pages were content analysed on the basis of a codebook[11] comprising *control variables* for technical administration (e.g., enterprise unit, URL, coder information, date), *formal variables* for analysing the structure of SRG websites, *content-related variables,* and *assessment variables* for controlling the conformity of web pages with regulations. Different regulations require separation for assessment: editorial content is appraised by a different variable than games, for example.

The complex structure of a web page composed of various textual or graphic elements, video and audio content etc. requires a definition of the basic *unit of analysis,* i.e. a specification of what part of the page is inspected for conformity. For this analysis the basic unit is the centrally displayed content that is reached by the URL. All other content is only considered to the extent that it aids in understanding whether the central content complies with regulations or not.

The *link analysis* tackles RQ3 and scrutinizes whether the SRG links to other websites for purely commercial purposes (in exchange for money or benefits of monetary value), which is prohibited by law. A definite assessment of whether the links are purely commercially motivated is difficult, due to a lack of insight into contracts and because linking in the Internet economy assumes various more or less transparent forms of potential benefits. The Internet has special economic characteristics that complicate the assessment of whether the exchange involves benefits of monetary value (Varian et al. 2004). Internet business models allow several often non-transparent forms of potential benefit for both referring and referenced sites. For the referenced sites, the practice of linking or embedding creates non-monetary value for the third party through the attention and the eyeballs of users (Davenport and Beck 2001). Linking leads to PageRank (Page et al. 1998), a measure of website relevance in search results and creates 'Google Juice' (Jarvis 2009), one of the important currencies in the digital economy. In return, websites that link to or embed third-party content may receive a broad set of potential benefits. First, there are direct monetary benefits. Revenues can be generated by brokering new customers to third-party e-shops (affiliate marketing) or by embedding online advertising such as banner ads, sponsoring, classifieds or sponsored links. Second, there are potential benefits where no direct payments are involved. These are typical examples of market transaction in Anderson's (2009) 'free economy' – an emerging economic system that allows high-quality products to be obtained without direct payments, made possible through business models including cross-subsidies, three-party markets, freemium or non-monetary markets. This study identifies further benefits such as free technology services, for example streaming, hosting or content-management systems, technically integrated, free third-party content (e.g., Youtube-videos), the added journalistic value of linking to third-party offerings, and the reputational effect of image transfer and branding. The business models in the Internet economy lead to difficulties in assessing the compliance with the charter: the charter states that all kinds of commercially motivated links are forbidden. Using a narrow interpretation, this would also include links that create potential benefits where no direct payments are involved. This study, therefore, approaches this question by analysing the links according to their potential for commercialization. All links contained in the sample frame of the content analysis are first extracted, then the frequency of the domain names is assessed and the links ranked accordingly. The frequency of connection is labelled as *intensity of linking* and provides information on the most referred-to domains in the sample frame. Subsequently, the sample of 100 most-linked domains per enterprise unit is grouped according to five categories with a varying potential for commercialization:

(1) Links to e-shops;
(2) Links to ad-serving technology providers;
(3) Links to content sites of third parties;
(4) Links to technology suppliers with no content; and
(5) Links to suppliers of technically integrated content.

Results

Content Analysis: Formal Structure of Websites

The paper distinguishes five formal categories to describe the general structure of SRG websites: editorial contributions, advertisement, interactivity, company information and overview pages. Table 2 shows the results of the structure and points to significant differences among the SRG enterprise units.

Table 2: Structure of SRG Websites According to Enterprise Units and Formal Categories (in percentage).

Overview pages	26.5	18.3	21.8	13.0	13.3	18.6
Company information	2.8	4.0	1.8	1.0	1.0	2.1
Advertising/Self-promotion	9.0	9.8	18.5	29.3	8.8	15.1
Interactivity	25.0	3.3	19.5	20.8	8.5	15.4
Editorial contributions	36.8	64.8	38.5	36.0	68.5	48.9
Enterprise unit	SF	DRS	TSR	RSR	RSI	Total
N	n = 400	n = 400	n = 400	n = 400	n = 400	n = 2000

- The SRG websites are dominated by editorial content. Almost half of the pages (48.9%) contain editorial contributions in the form of written articles/text, audio and video files, pictures and picture galleries.
- Interactive content, e.g. user-generated content, editor-generated interactivity (mostly blogs), games, and user platforms amounts to 15.4%, and is followed in almost equal parts by advertising (15.1%), like programme and event promotion, sales in online shops and self-promotion to maintain and strengthen the audience bond; 18.6% are overview pages for navigation and orientation. Finally, company information amounts to 2.1%.
- A comparison of the five enterprise units points to noticeable differences. RSI and DRS display a higher share of editorial contributions compared to RSR, TSR and SF, which have more interactive content. Further, there is a large amount of advertising on the RSR website resulting from many pages describing and promoting its radio programmes.

Content Analysis: Content Structure of Websites

The programming remit of the SRG as detailed in the charter (Article 2(4), a–d) specifies four content categories: information, culture, education and entertainment. Table 3 shows the patterns of content provision across the SRG enterprise units and the differences among them.

Table 3: Structure of SRG Websites According to Enterprise Units and Content Categories (in percentage).

	SF	DRS	TSR	RSR	RSI	Total
Other content (Advertising/ Self-promotion etc.)	19.3	18.3	30.0	38.5	13.0	23.8
Entertainment/Popular culture	24.8	17.3	12.8	18.0	17.3	18.0
Education	7.0	8.8	7.8	7.5	11.0	8.4
Culture/Arts	3.0	11.0	6.8	8.0	15.0	8.8
Information	46.0	44.8	42.8	28.0	43.8	41.1
Enterprise unit	SF	DRS	TSR	RSR	RSI	Total
n	n = 400	n = 400	n = 400	n = 400	n = 400	n = 2000

- The SRG online content is dominated by information. More than 40% of the pages in the sample contain information on a wide range of issues such as politics, the economy /finance, sports, health/social issues, media/Internet/telecommunications, or law/justice /criminal affairs.

- Considerably fewer pages are devoted to entertainment (18%), including popular music, fictional entertainment (series, movies), talk shows, cabaret/comedy and reporting on lifestyle, celebrities and gossip.
- Little space is dedicated to culture/arts (8.8%) and to educational content (8.4%).

A comparison between the enterprise units points to some differences in content coverage.

- The proportion of *information* in the case of RSR (28%) is considerably below the SRG average (41.1%). This may be explainable by the large amount of programme promotion on its website. DRS reports politics more often than any other enterprise unit, and SF stands out with a strong sports coverage.
- The proportion of *entertainment/popular culture* content is low in the case of TRS (12.8%) and above the SRG average for SF (24.8%), which covers lots of fictional entertainment and celebrities/gossip. RSR dominates in the popular music sub-category.
- *Culture and Arts* are more strongly represented on the websites of RSI (15%) and DRS (11%) than on the other sites. For DRS, findings show many pages related to classical music; RSI reports on literature comparatively often. The proportion of arts and culture on the SF website is significantly low (3%).
- *Educational content* is spread more or less equally across the enterprise units (between 7% and 8.8%), with only RSI (11%) showing a remarkably higher proportion of educational content, with articles on philosophy, theology, history, technology, zoology/nature and geography as well as educational reporting on the country and the people.

Content Analysis: Compliance of SRG Websites with Regulations

This section shows the extent to which the SRG websites comply with the charter and the proportion and types of pages for which compliance is unclear (grey area). It is important to stress that pages in the grey area may not necessarily violate charter requirements. These web pages may comply but the analyses are inconclusive due to a lack of researchable indications to the contrary (non-transparency) or to legal rules that allow for wide interpretation. The verifiability is partly restricted, for example, because some video or audio material that might indicate a relation to the programme is explicitly only available online for a limited time or because topics of broadcasts are not researchable retrospectively. This raises problems for compliance assessment, especially for older online contributions, and increases the research efforts disproportionately. Moreover, the charter remains vague in various respects, for example regarding how closely connected the background and context information is to be grasped, or also with regard to sales of broadcasts. There are no indications of whether the SRG is allowed to sell broadcasts only in their original form or also in parts (e.g., a single song from a music programme) or even a product that is only partly connected to a broadcast (e.g., a whole album although the broadcast aired only one song).

The assessment of the websites with the applicable regulations results in three groups of pages:

(1) Pages for which compliance with regulations can clearly be *verified*;
(2) Pages for which compliance with regulations can be *assumed*; and
(3) Pages for which compliance with regulations remains *unclear.*

Table 4 provides an overview of the extent of compliance across the SRG websites and for the five enterprise units separately.

Table 4: Conformity of SRG Websites According to Enterprise Units (in percentage).

Compliance not assessed (overview pages)	26.5	18.3	21.8	13.0	13.3	18.6
Compliance unclear (grey area)	14.5	3.5	15.3	5.8	7.3	9.3
Compliance assumed	7.5	5.3	5.0	6.0	1.5	5.1
Compliance verified	51.5	73.0	58.0	75.3	78.0	67.2
Enterprise unit	SF	DRS	TSR	RSR	RSI	Total
n	n = 400	n = 400	n = 400	n = 400	n = 400	n = 2000

- The SRG websites largely comply with the charter requirements. For more than two-thirds of the pages, the compliance can clearly be *verified* (67.2%). For an additional 5.1% of all the pages compliance can be strongly assumed, because the contents deal with major news (political elections or referendums, major sports events, etc.); 18.6% of the online offer covers overview pages for navigation and orientation.[12] In total, more than 90% of the online content complies with the charter.
- The grey area amounts to 9.3%, i.e. for almost one in eleven pages compliance cannot be verified and there are no indications to assume compliance.
- Here again, a comparison shows differences among the enterprise units. The extent of the grey area is above average in the cases of TSR (15.3%) and SF (14.5%), and significantly low for DRS (3.5%).

Content Analysis: Compliance of SRG Websites According to Formal Categories

A major objective is to identify the kind of pages that form the grey area. What formal categories have a higher proportion of potentially problematic content? What kind of content is more prone to violations of regulations? Table 5 displays the grey area according to formal content categories.

Table 5: Conformity of SRG Websites According to Formal Categories (in percentage).

Formal categories	Editorial contributions	Editor-/User-generated interactivity	Games/Audience forums	Sales/Shop	Self-promotion/Company information
Compliance unclear	7.1	40.9	12.4	16.7	1.2
Compliance assumed	7.1	15.8	0	0	0
Compliance verified	85.9	43.3	87.6	83.3	98.8
N	n = 978	n = 203	n = 105	n = 102	n = 241

- The grey area is strongly pronounced in the case of interactive content. For more than 40% of user-generated and editor-generated interactivity (e.g. blogs, readers' comments), compliance with legal requirements remains unclear as there is no direct link between the online and broadcasting content. This indicates that the SRG uses interactivity as an independent content outlet instead of as means to deepen its traditional broadcasting services as stipulated by law.
- Compared to interactivity, all other formal categories are less problematic. The extent of the grey area is 16.7% for online shops, 12.4% for online games and user platforms and 7.1% for editorial content. Self-promotion and company information show hardly any problems – only 1.2% of the pages are inconsistent with regulations.

The comparison among the five websites exhibits several differences and points to specific problem zones (see Table 6):

- There is no common pattern in the grey area across the SRG enterprise units and each website has its particular problem areas, resulting in part from the varying formal structures of the websites.
- There are unclear cases of *editorial content* on all SRG websites but to differing extent. These are more comprehensive on the website of RSI (7.3%) than in other units. DRS in particular has only a small amount of editorial content where compliance is unclear (0.3%). A qualitative analysis of unclear pages shows that they are prominently placed in the main categories of the websites (e.g., information rubric, sports rubric). Moreover, a remarkable number of unclear cases originate from online offers related to movies

Table 6: Extent of Grey Area According to Enterprise Units and Formal Categories (in percentage).

Enterprise unit	SF	DRS	TSR	RSR	RSI	Total
Advertising/Self-promotion & Company information	0.5	1.8	2.0	0.8	0	1.0
Games/Audience forums	2.3	1.0	0	0	0	0.7
Editor-/User-generated interactivity	8.8	0.5	8.5	3.0	0	4.2
Editorial contributions	3.0	0.3	4.8	2.0	7.3	3.5
n	n = 400	n = 400	n = 400	n = 400	n = 400	n = 2000

(e.g. movie reviews). The remaining cases are spread over various categories such as columns, advisory services and picture galleries.

- *Interactivity* forms the dominant problem area for SF (8.8%) and TSR (8.5%) and to a lesser extent for RSR (3%). In contrast, the interactive content of DRS (0.5%) and RSI (0%) does not pose significant problems. A qualitative review indicates that various *editor's blogs* of SF, TSR and RSR cause problems with regard to compliance. Editors often use their personal blogs to provide background information about their professional working practice and to report on private events and personal impressions, which are not always related to the traditional broadcasting content. Moreover, selected *user-platforms*[13] for music and video uploads on TSR and SF are identified as major problem sources as they hardly relate to broadcast programmes. Finally, the interactive services also comprise *online games, quizzes* and *polls* for entertainment as well as *online forums* for user debates, which mostly relate to broadcasts.

- Finally, but to a lower overall extent, *advertising* is a problematic area across all SRG websites apart from RSI. The grey area is predominately concentrated on the websites of TSR (1.8%) and DRS (2%), where the analysis locates three-quarters of all inconclusive advertising content (mostly products for sale in the online shops). The online stores offer DVDs, books, games and music CDs. The sale of such articles is allowed under certain conditions (e.g. merchandising products for audience bonding, broadcast of programmes) and most products comply. Apart from the online shops, there are only a few individual cases of problematic forms of advertising, e.g. event calendars with inter-linked ticket sales functions (DRS, RSR).

Link Analysis

The link analysis is to assess RQ3, namely whether the websites contain links that are not journalistically but commercially motivated, which is prohibited by law. For this the 500 most referred-to external web domains (100 per enterprise unit) are categorized according to their functionality, the intensity of linking and their potential for commercialization. For the latter the external URLs are classified into five functionally different categories. The first two categories (e.g. links to e-shops and to ad-serving technology providers) have a high potential for commercialization in the Internet economy.

Links to e-Shops

There are 24 domains of different e-shops in the sample frame.[14] Three of them contain affiliate IDs, which indicate an affiliate marketing relationship between two websites – an Internet business practice where a retailer rewards website owners for every customer they bring who is identified through the affiliate ID. They are found in the links between SF and Exlibris.ch (popular Swiss e-shop for music, DVDs etc.), RSR and iTunes Music Store, as well as RSR and Cede.ch (popular Swiss music e-shop). Exlibris.ch also receives a substantial number of links from DRS; however, by a form of technological integration that should be distinguished from the affiliate programmes. DRS does not direct its users to the Exlibris. ch website, but has Exlibris.ch run the shop under a DRS-owned domain (radiokiosk.ch). The immense intensity of electronic linking derives from album cover images and sound bites integrated via http://request from Exlibris.ch's website. A range of other e-shops selling event tickets, books, DVDs and other merchandise are also found in the sample frame.

Links to Ad-Serving Technology Providers

The SRG charter prohibits most advertising. The sample frame does not contain any links with ad-serving technology providers apart from pages of *SF-Wissen*, where online advertising is allowed.[15] *SF-Wissen* contains a number of links to Adition.com, a service provider that hosts and places online advertising.

The remaining domains that are neither e-shops nor ad-service providers are classified into three functionally different categories: links to content sites of third parties, to technology suppliers with no content and to suppliers of technically integrated content. Compared to links to e-shops and to ad providers, these three categories have a less explicit potential for commercialization. For this reason, other indicators allowing conclusions regarding commercialization are presented.

Links to Content Sites of Third Parties

This category consists of sites users are taken to when clicking a link. The evaluation of the potential for commercialization is difficult here, because there are no explicit indicators other than the intensity of linking. Therefore, qualitative case analyses are conducted to identify formalized partnerships. The most-linked-to domains generally include official partners, broadcasting partners and co-producing partners. Furthermore, there is a substantial intensity of linking from SRG websites to activities not covered by the charter. These activities have to be notified in advance if they impair the position and activities of other Swiss media companies.

Links to Technology Suppliers with no Content

Links not only take users away to third-party content sites, they also embed third-party technologies in the SRG's websites. Technology service-providers are among the domains with the highest intensity of linking in the sample frame. These links exhibit a varying potential for commercialization. They refer to branded technology, such as plug-ins and media players (Adobe Flash Player, Real Player), external distribution channels for SRG's own content (Twitter.com, Youtube.com, Photobucket.com, Facebook.com), content-management systems (Wordpress.org, Drupal.org, Plone.org, Blogspot.com) and design templates that link to designers' web pages. Branded technology extends the functionality of a website and is usually free of charge for website owners. The trade-off is the placement of the supplier's brand, logo and links. This slightly raises the potential for commercialization as compared to white-label (non-branded) technologies, which are also contained in the sample.

Links to Suppliers of Technically Integrated Content

This category contains links to suppliers who provide content and dedicated distribution technology to embed in the SRG's websites. The domains can be classified into customized and standardized solutions. SF uses customized solutions where picture galleries from Tillate.com (nightlife portal), stock-exchange data from Swissquote.ch (online trading service), and personality tests from Alpha-Test.de are embedded using SF's look and feel. Furthermore, all SRG enterprise units make extensive use of standardized embeddable content such as videos (via Youtube.com, Brightcove.com), maps (Google Maps) or pictures (Flickr.com).

To sum up, a definite assessment of whether links are purely commercially motivated is difficult without insights into contracts and because the Internet has special economic characteristics that complicate the assessment of whether the exchange involves benefits of monetary value. The assessment of links in this study therefore focuses on the structure and intensity of linking and the potential for commercialization of links with indicators such as affiliate IDs, customized technical solutions, formalized partnerships and ad-serving technologies. One of the characteristics of the Internet economy is the need for links and integration of third-party services. Third parties often offer their services as branded technology or branded content (i.e. plug-ins, media players, distribution channels, content-management systems, design templates or embeddable content). The use of such services is usually free of charge for website owners but the suppliers demand that their logo, brand or link appears on the website. When assessing the potential for commercialization of such links one has to take into account that without such non-monetary countertrade – which, however, often involves benefits of monetary value that in a strict sense are prohibited by the charter – a state-of-the-art webpage would often not be possible.

Discussion of Results and Regulatory Implications

The *central question* of this paper that is based on a research project conducted in 2009 is whether the SRG websites comply with the provisions of the SRG charter, whether the websites supplement and deepen the traditional programme. This question was specified accordingly:

(1) Do the websites directly relate to broadcasts;
(2) Is there a grey area with uncertainties regarding compliance; and
(3) Are there links that are solely commercially motivated, i.e. does the SRG receive money or benefits of monetary value for linking?

A *preceding question* here is whether such an assessment is accomplishable by external expertise. As discussed earlier, the characteristics of the Internet evoke various challenges for the monitoring and control of online activities and there are no approved approaches for assessing compliance with regulatory requirements of websites of public service broadcasters to which regulatory authorities can resort to by default. The two-tiered approach developed here is a novel way of assessing the SRG's websites and linking practice using a combination of content and link analyses, the data for which were directly collected by webcrawling processes. This study is the first to systematically assess compliance of a European PSB's online offer with regulations ex post and on a large scale. The developed analytical approach – coupled with computer-assisted webcrawling – contributes to methodologically furthering online research in the fields of data collection, online content and link analyses. It further provides innovative and instructive findings on *questions* of ex post controllability and regulatory implications. With the enactment of law (rule making) regulatory challenges do not end and the question of how to control compliance with regulations (rule enforcement) moves centre stage together with the role and strategies of regulators (Latzer et al. 2010a; 2010b). This question will become increasingly relevant with regard to online activities of PSBs, in particular for European Union member states where the recently revised European Broadcasting Communication[16] from now on requires a prior (ex ante) evaluation of new online services with consideration of public value and market impact at the national level (Just and Latzer 2011). In Switzerland, to the contrary, regulatory requirements do not demand an ex ante evaluation, but allow for alternative modes of control, for example, ex post monitoring.

From a methodological point of view the results of this study show that an ex post assessment is accomplishable by external expertise. The SRG largely complies with regulations but compliance remains unclear for almost one in eleven web-pages and linking generates non-monetary value. Although no common pattern of grey area across the SRG enterprise units is discernible, Internet-typical activities (e.g. interactive content, links to technology suppliers) appear problematic.

The content analysis allows a fine identification of the formal and content structures of the websites, assessment of the compliance of the pages with regulations and captures a grey area where compliance remains unclear. The limits to final verification result from legal rules that allow for wide interpretation (e.g., is the SRG allowed to re-bundle broadcasts in any way it likes and thus sell broadcasts in different versions than originally aired?), from missing regulations (e.g., treatment of user generated content apart from audience forums) and from varying non-transparencies on the web-pages (e.g., regarding the extent to which the content relates to specific broadcasts and programmes).

The link analysis makes it possible to assess the functionality, the structure and intensity of linking and the potential for commercialization of links. The limits are mostly in the assessment of factual commercialization that is not provable without insights into contracts and in the assessment of non-monetary exchange generated by linking and integration of third-party content, essentially to determine whether this exchange amounts to benefits of monetary value as stated by the charter. Here one has to consider the need for linking and integration of third-party services in the Internet economy and that a state-of-the-art website is often impracticable without such countertrade.

Finally, the results raise questions of regulatory implications, e.g. whether there is the need for rules clarification or regulatory intervention given the extent of grey area. At the level of rule-making, clarifications may be appropriate regarding the questions of whether non-monetary benefits resulting from linking amount to benefits of monetary value or whether user platforms and editorial blogs that hardly relate to programmes are permissible. Moreover, it may be appropriate to actively implement additional regulations, such as transparency rules that disclose the relationship to broadcasts. As for regulatory reactions at the enforcement level, various strategies remain: from a passive approach of awaiting complaints and then reacting case by case (fire alarm oversight), to soft pressures to increase awareness and maybe stimulate self-regulation on the part of the SRG (institutional checks), to pro-active compliance assessments (police patrol oversight) (McCubbins and Schwartz 1984; Kiewiet and McCubbins 1991). The different strategies involve different costs, advantages and disadvantages for regulatory authorities and have to be chosen in accordance with existing law. Fire alarm oversight requires little direct centralized involvement by regulatory authorities and relies on third parties (e.g. citizens, organized interest groups, competitors such as publishers) to monitor the SRG's online activities. In cases of non-compliance with regulations, redress is sought through appeal, judicial review and case-by-case assessments of potential infringements. This rather passive regulatory approach does not provide incentives for the SRG, however, to actively increase the efforts to adhere to regulatory requirements more strictly.

The enforcement regime may also be modified towards shared responsibilities for monitoring and control *(institutional checks)*. For example, the role of the SRG may be strengthened by means of self-regulation, which is an increasingly preferred solution in the media domain. The SRG itself could implement monitoring procedures in order to assure and increase compliance with regulatory requirements. The regulatory authority may contribute to the initiation of self-regulation by means of information and dialogue to increase problem awareness. Theoretical arguments suggest that strategies of soft pressure are typically successful if state regulatory authorities can resort to strong intervention capacities when industry self-regulation fails, as self-regulation often works best in the shadow of hierarchy (Ayres and Braithwaite 1992; Héritier and Lehmkuhl 2008; Latzer et al. 2002; Newman and Bach 2004).

Police patrol oversight comprises active monitoring by regulatory authorities with the aim of detecting and remedying violations and – by its surveillance – discouraging them. Examples from other regulatory domains (e.g., film rating) show that periodic reviews increase the efforts of the industry to comply with regulatory requirements (Saurwein and Latzer 2010). Such modes of pro-active control may be applied before a service or product is launched in the market (ex ante control), or alternatively regulatory compliance may be assessed ex post for already introduced offers as was done in this study. This mode of ex post control enables the SRG to launch new services without time lags, avoids long-winded ex ante authorization procedures and does not compromise the monitoring and enforcement obligations of the regulator.

Beyond these insights into regulatory implications of the status quo, one has to bear in mind that the existing regulations for the online activities of the SRG are not undisputed and possible reforms are frequently being discussed. Issues for discussion include the lifting of advertising restrictions and questions regarding the general regulatory approach that restricts the online offer of the SRG to a supplementary and deepening role to traditional broadcasting by demanding a close relationship between online and broadcasting content. This approach constrains the SRG's abilities to offer an added value on the Internet, which is characterized, among other things, by usage patterns that differ from traditional broadcasting and may require innovative approaches. As a result of the stipulated online-broadcasting relationship, the SRG is limited in its ability to fully explore the potentials of the Internet to provide a public added value online. An easing of regulatory restrictions could, however, entail the danger of distortions of competition, and the implementation of accompanying measures is therefore indispensable for reducing possible risks to fair competition. The regulatory focus would thus shift to questions regarding the justification of public funding and public added value, which is provided by the SRG as compared to available private/commercial offers. Determination of such a public added value is far more difficult than the assessment of compliance with precise regulatory restrictions. As such, the required *ex ante evaluations* of new online services with consideration of public value and market impact as required by the European Union guidelines are not unproblematic. The added value of innovations is often not fully assessable in advance, as many innovations unfold their benefits to society neither straight from the beginning nor in the way intended by the innovator. Many valuable aspects of innovations develop in the ongoing process of diffusion in which providers and users are likewise involved. *An ex post evaluation* of an added value, on the other hand, can only be accomplished by elaborate comparative assessments of the public and private/commercial services. This involves difficult methodological questions for which no standard instruments have been developed thus far. The approach developed here, which will from now on be periodically applied in Switzerland for a regulatory compliance assessment, may also serve as a methodological basis for the comparison of public and private Internet offers and thus contribute to the development of comprehensive comparative evaluation approaches.

Acknowledgements

The paper presents the results of a research project commissioned by the Swiss Office of Communication (BAKOM) in 2009. Since 2010 this study has been conducted annually as part of the regulator's continuous analysis of SRG programs.

References

Anderson, C. (2009), *Free: The Future of a Radical Price*, New York: Random House.
Ayres I. and Braithwaite, J. (1992), *Responsive Regulation*, Oxford: Oxford University Press.

Davenport, T. H. and Beck, J. C. (2001), *The Attention Economy: Understanding the New Currency of Business*, Boston and New York: Harvard Business School Press.

Donders, K. and Pauwels, C. (2008), 'Does EU Policy Challenge the Digital Future of Public Service Broadcasting?', *Convergence: The International Journal of Research into New Media Technologies*, 14: 3, pp. 295–311.

Escher, T., Margetts, H., Petricek, V. and Cox, I. (2006), 'Governing from the Centre? Comparing the Nodality of Digital Governments', http://www.allacademic.com/meta/p_mla_apa_research_citation/1/5/2/5/8/p152580_index.html. Accessed 30 November 2010.

Héritier, A. and Lehmkuhl, D. (2008), 'The Shadow of Hierarchy and New Modes of Governance', *Journal of Public Policy*, 28: 1, pp. 1–17.

Hindman, M. (2009), *The Myth of Digital Democracy*, Princeton: Princeton University Press.

Humphreys, P. (2008), 'Digital Convergence, European Competition Policy, and the Future of Public Service Broadcasting: The UK and German Cases', in ICA (International Communication Association), *58th Annual Conference of the International Communication Association*, 22–26 May, Montreal, Canada, ICA: Washington.

Jackson, M. H. (1997), 'Assessing the Structure of Communication on the World Wide Web', http://www3.interscience.wiley.com/cgi-bin/fulltext/120837720/HTMLSTART. Accessed 30 November 2010.

Jarvis, J. (2009), *What Would Google Do?*, New York: HarperCollins.

Just, N. and Latzer, M. (2011), 'Medienpolitik durch Europäische Wettbewerbspolitik: Druck auf öffentlichen Rundfunk durch Beihilfenpolitik – Public Value Konzepte als Lösungsansatz', in H. Gundlach (ed.), *Public Value in der Digital- und Internetökonomie*, Cologne: Herbert von Halem, pp.79–100.

Kiewiet, D. R. and McCubbins, D. M. (1991), *The Logic of Delegation. Congressional Parties and the Appropriations Process*, Chicago: University of Chicago Press.

Kim, S. T. and Weaver, D. (2002), 'Communication Research about the Internet: A Thematic Meta-Analysis', *New Media & Society*, 4: 4, pp. 518–538.

Latzer, M,. Braendle, A., Just, N. and Saurwein, F. (2010a), 'SRG Online Beobachtung: Konzessionskonformität von Webseiten und elektronischen Verbindungen', *medialex*, 15: 2, pp. 77–83.

—— (2010b), *SRG Online Beobachtung: Konzessionskonformität von Webseiten und elektronischen Verbindungen*, Zürich: Rüegger.

—— (2010c), 'Public Service Broadcasting Online: Assessing Compliance with Regulatory Requirements', *International Telecommunications Policy Review*, 17: 2, pp. 1–25.

Latzer, M., Just, N., Saurwein, F. and Slominski, P. (2002), *Selbst- und Ko-Regulierung im Mediamatiksektor*, Wiesbaden: Westdeutscher.

McCubbins, D. M. and Schwartz, T. (1984), 'Congressional Oversight Overlooked: Police Patrols Versus Fire Alarms', *American Journal of Political Science*, 28: 1, pp. 165–179.

McMillan, S. J. (2000), 'The Microscope and the Moving Target: The Challenges of Applying Content Analysis to the World Wide Web', *Journalism and Mass Communication Quarterly*, 77: 1, pp. 80–98.

Newman, A. L. and Bach, D. (2004), 'Self-Regulatory Trajectories in the Shadow of Public Power', *Governance*, 17: 3, pp. 387–413.

Page, L., Brin, S., Motwani, R. and Winograd, T. (1998), 'The Pagerank Citation Ranking: Bringing Order to the Web', http://ilpubs.stanford.edu:8090/422/1/1999-66.pdf. Accessed 30 November 2010.

Park, H. W. and Thelwall, M. (2003), 'Hyperlink Analyses of the World Wide Web: A Review', http://jcmc.indiana.edu/vol8/issue4/park.html. Accessed 30 November 2010.

Saurwein, F. and Latzer, M. (2010), 'Regulatory Choice in Communications: The Case of Content-Rating Schemes in the Audiovisual Industry', *Journal of Broadcasting & Electronic Media*, 54: 3, pp. 463–484.

Schneider, S. M. and Foot, K. E. (2004), 'The Web as an Object of Study', *New Media & Society*, 6: 1, pp. 114–122.

Thelwall, M. (2002), 'Methodologies for Crawler Based Web Surveys', *Internet Research: Electronic Networking Applications and Policy*, 12: 2, pp. 124–138.

Varian, H. R. Farrell, J. and Shapiro, C. (2004), *The Economics of Information Technology: An Introduction*, Cambridge: Cambridge University Press.

Wang, X. P. (2006), 'Exploring Sample Sizes For Content Analysis of Online News Sites', http://www.stpt.usf.edu/journalism/showcase/documents/wangSampleSizesPaper.pdf. Accessed 30 November 2010.

Weare, C. and Lin, W. Y. (2000), 'Content Analysis of the World Wide Web: Opportunities and Challenges', *Social Science Computer Review*, 18: 3, pp. 272–292.

Welker, M. and Wünsch, C. (2010), *Die Online-Inhaltsanalyse. Forschungsobjekt Internet*, Cologne: Herbert von Halem.

Witte, J. C. (2009), 'Introduction to the Special Issue on Web Surveys', *Sociological Methods & Research*, 37: 3, pp. 283–290.

Wouters, P. and Gerbec, D. (2003), 'Interactive Internet? Studying Mediated Interaction with Publicly Available Search Engines', http://jcmc.indiana.edu/vol8/issue4/wouters.html. Accessed 30 November 2010.

Zhang, J. (2005), 'Content Analysis of Web Sites from 2000 to 2004: A Thematic Meta Analysis', http://txspace.tamu.edu/bitstream/handle/1969.1/2639/etd-tamu-2005B-STJR-Zhang.pdf?sequence=1. Accessed 30 November 2010.

Notes

1 *Charter for the SRG SSR idée suisse* of November 28, 2007; in force since 1 January 2008.

2 Online adverting is, for instance, permissible on pages that are produced in cooperation with non-profit organizations, e.g. *SF Wissen*, an educational platform. Besides the advertising and sponsoring rules of the SRG charter, those contained in the law and ordinance on radio and television also apply. Federal law on radio and television of 24 March 2006; Radio and television ordinance of 9 March 2007.

3 The Swiss Federal Office of Communication (BAKOM) specified the research questions and the five enterprise units to be analysed. The regulator named 5 domain names to be analysed, which were here extended to 15 for comparative reasons.

4 Rules providing for exemption are contained in the Art. 11, 13, 22, and 23 of the Ordinance and Art. 10 and 13 of the SRG charter.

5 The literature on web surveys is manifold. See e.g. the special issue on web surveys in *Sociological Methods Research* 2009 (Witte 2009, and other articles in issue).

6 See book announcement of Welker and Wünsch 2010.

7 *Meta Products Offline Explorer* was used for copying and downloading the websites, *Karen's Directory Printer* for generating lists of URLs and data files, *Microsoft Excel* for filtering data to be excluded, and *Spadix Extract Link* for extracting URLs from web documents.

8 The SRG online offer of the fourth Swiss language region (Rhaeto-Romanic) is not covered by this study.

9 Because of the time-consuming crawling process the sample could not be generated in one day. The websites of SF were generated from 22 to 23 April, 2009; of DRS from 15 to 18 May, 2009; of TSR from 6 to 7 May, 2009; of DRS from 14 to 15 May, 2009, and of RSI on 7 May 2009.

10 Twelve URLs of websites that exceed 50,000 links are not included numerically in the sample frame, e.g. w3.org, which refers to technical specifications and wemfbox.ch or webtrendslive.com, which produce online access statistics.

11 The codebook was developed in a multi-stage process. Preliminary coding for testing and improvement of the codebook were conducted twice, followed by a pilot test of inter-coder reliability. Two coders for each of the three language regions coded 50 web pages. At the beginning the mean inter-coder reliability was 0.77 and therefore not sufficient, but by additional training and refinement of coding instructions it was raised to a mean of 0.89. To ensure the quality of the results, all codes were double-checked by the researchers and corrected if necessary. At the end of the coding process the mean inter-coder reliability among the researchers was at an excellent level of 0.98.

12 Compliance is not checked for each item on overview pages separately as each item could be part of the sample. If the page displays 'critical' content this is subsequently assessed in the qualitative analysis.

13 *TSR*: moncinema; *SF*: Musicnight myStage.

14 The analysis was in part extended to the whole sample frame.

15 See endnote 3.

16 The Broadcasting Communication clarifies the application of state aid rules to public broadcasting. The revision of this Communication entered into force in October 2009.

State Aid

Chapter 16

Conditional Access for Public Service Broadcasting to New Media Platforms: EU State-Aid Policy vis-à-vis Public Service Broadcasting – the Dutch Case

Jo Bardoel & Marit Vochteloo[1]

Background: Developments in EU Media Policy

The development of state-aid rules for public service broadcasting is not just a legal matter. It highlights steady changes in broadcasting policy in western Europe. Initially, public service broadcasters were seen as a national matter entirely and as a better alternative to radio and television being controlled either by state agencies or by commercial companies. Roughly, this tradition stems from the inter-war period and reached its apex somewhere between 1970 and 1980 (Michalis 2007). Eventually PSBs became one of many services of general interest in European welfare states. They were designed to serve democracy, culture and social cohesion of societies and their output was associated with standards such as independence, diversity, quality and reach. For a long time western European countries shared such general ideals on broadcasting, although their actual systems differed (Bardoel 2007).

In the 1980s and 1990s most countries were in the midst of reforming the welfare state, involving a downsizing of the public sector and deregulation of markets. The broadcasting sector was affected by rapid technological changes, leading to a proliferation of channels, distributed across national borders. This spurred the liberalization of the broadcasting sector, making it subject to the single European market. Relevant European policies were primarily directed towards more competition in telecommunication markets and ensuring free reception and redistribution of television within the EU. The 1989 Television without Frontiers directive set out a number of harmonized provisions concerning advertising, sponsoring, the protection of minors, and (quotas for) European production. According to Michalis (2007) the original aim of using the advent of trans-frontier television for democratic ideals and creating a direct link between the EU and its citizens was rapidly overshadowed by cultural and industrial policy considerations at a time when the broadcasting market was transforming from public and national to private and transnational.

Towards the turn of the century, public service broadcasting became affected by competition law and state-aid rules of the EC Treaty. In 1997, a series of complaints by the commercial media culminated in the Amsterdam Protocol. Member states tried to shield their public broadcasters from a harsh interpretation of the EC Treaty, and they succeeded. The Broadcasting Communication of the European Commission (2001) reaffirmed the significance of public service broadcasting and left member states in control, as long as they met procedural requirements. In recent cases, however, the commission has indeed moved into the delicate matters of the public service remit and funding (Depypere 2004; Donders and Pauwels 2008; Loisen 2008).

Although the commission leaves member states to decide on the content provided by public broadcasters, it does encourage procedures that tend to narrow the public service remit in the new media to offerings not already available on the market. According to Collins (1994 162), 'the internal market is hostile to public service broadcasting [...] as seen from the vantage point of the neo-classical economic theory underpinning the EEC Treaty, public service is aberrant and offensive.' In the periodization proposed by Michalis (2007) the period of defensive Europeanization, roughly the 1980s, was followed by a pro-competitive market restructuring, starting in mid/late 1980s to the late 1990s, leading to a liberalized telecommunications market and a multi-channel television order, making this period in her opinion the most intense regulatory reform period of Europeanization.

Revision of the Broadcasting Communication

Since the 2001 Broadcasting Communication, the European Commission has handled 23 separate cases of state aid for PSBs: 5 were notifications by member states, 15 involved complaints from commercial media and 1 was both a notification and a complaint.

The application of state-aid rules – mainly articles 86 and 87 of the EC Treaty – for public service broadcasting involves a number of tensions. First, there is a tension between 'liberalization' of broadcasting markets and 'harmonization' of rules to remove barriers to free trade across member states versus the principle of 'pluralism,' which stands for the preservation of national cultures and languages in the media (Bardoel and Van Cuilenburg 2003; Wheeler 2004). Associated with this tension between the single market and cultural pluralism is the conflict between supra-nationality and subsidiarity (Biltereyst and Pauwels 2007: 44), affecting both the European institutions (Commission, Parliament, Court) and the member states. In addition, public broadcasters and private media companies have high stakes in the application of state-aid rules. No wonder that a revision of the Broadcasting Communication caused heated debate among all stakeholders.

According to the consultation documents of the European Commission (10 January 2008), the reasons for an update were twofold. First, the ongoing digitalization and convergence of media markets forced a rethinking of state-aid rules for PSB. Second, the commission wanted to consolidate its case practice in new general guidelines, thereby increasing legal certainty. The revision process took one and a half years.[2] Member states quickly joined forces; responding to a Dutch initiative 19 member states expressed their views in a common position paper (Common position paper of member states 2008). In the multi-lateral meeting of 5 December 2008, the first draft encountered opposition from 22 member states (out of 27). At that time, the European Parliament also took an interest in the discussion. The commission channelled the concerns through a second round of consultation on a (second) draft text, which is unusual.

At first sight, subsidiarity was the main subject of debate. Most member states felt that translating the commission's case-by-case practice into rules applying to all would limit the room for national broadcasting policies. In particular, member states opposed detailed requirements for a full-fledged market-impact assessment for every new PSB media activity.[3] At second sight, there is an underlying (political) dispute about the future role of PSB. As worded in the position paper:

> The benchmark for public services lies in criteria such as diversity, independence, quality, accessibility and reach. The Broadcasting Communication can not limit the public service remit to services which are not available on the market, neither by criteria with regard to content nor by rules concerning the entrustment procedure. (ibid.)

Thus, member states once again indicated that they oppose a marginalization of PSB that is based on purely economic reasoning.

The final text of the Broadcasting Communication (European Commission 2009) is a compromise. Compared to the first draft, the final text contains a warmer recognition of PSB's role in the digital age. In addition, the guidelines became less detailed and less prescriptive. A compromise was reached on the issue of market impact by trading form and matter. Member states got form: the original layout for a market-impact test was replaced by 'open consultation', an 'internal supervisory body' could do the job too, and the test would only concern 'significant new services' as defined in national regulation. The commission got matter: there had to be a prior evaluation taking into account 'existing offerings' and 'interests of market players.'

The 2009 Broadcasting Communication: Prior Evaluation of New Media Services

As before, the 2009 Broadcasting Communication requires a precise definition of the public remit, effective supervision of the fulfilment of the public service obligations and transparency of financial accounts. The new ones are more detailed requirements on financial control to prevent overcompensation and cross-subsidy. The main innovation concerns the prior evaluation and approval of new media services of public broadcasters:

> Member States shall consider, by means of a prior evaluation procedure based on an open public consultation, whether significant new audiovisual services envisaged by public service broadcasters meet the requirements of the Amsterdam Protocol, i.e. whether they serve the democratic, social and cultural needs of the society, while duly taking into account its potential effects on trading conditions and competition. (European Commission, Broadcasting Communication 2009)

This sentence reflects that a compromise was struck. The commission got substance; member states got leeway to design their own procedures. Below, we sum up the main requirements.

- The commission may still prefer an elaborate and independent market-impact test, as OFCOM does for the BBC Trust. The communication allows other variants too, such as the Flemish procedure (involving advice of the national Media Council) and the Dutch procedure (allowing the commercial media to comment on a draft decision by the minister).
- Prior evaluation is required whenever a public broadcaster wants to offer 'significant new services.' The communication is vague on the meaning of this concept. ·Whether a service qualifies as 'new' may depend on distribution technology, content, financing and modalities of consumption. Its 'significance' may depend on the financial resources required and the expected impact on demand.[4] In any case, it is up to member states to determine what services qualify for prior evaluation. As a result, new services via old broadcasting technology (e.g. a new linear television channel) can come under scrutiny, whereas public broadcasters' vested interests in the Internet may not.
- The communication leaves room for experiments without prior approval, as long as they are limited in time and scope. Again, it is up to member states to define the precise conditions. During negotiations with the commission the Dutch agreed on a very short time frame: within one year (!) the broadcaster must start and run the experiment, evaluate and decide on its continuation.
- Approval of new services must come from a body that is independent of the management of public broadcasting. The commission prefers a decision by the government or the media regulator, but it gave in to pressures to allow prior approval by internal supervisors, such as the BBC Trust in the UK and the *Rundfunkräten* in Germany.

For a better understanding, one needs to read the commission's case decisions on public service broadcasting in Germany (2007), Ireland and Belgium (2008), Austria (2009) and the Netherlands (2010).[5] In all countries, a prior evaluation procedure for new media services has now been established. Note that national developments and interests interfered with the negotiations between the national authorities and the European Commission, influencing the end result.

The Dutch System since the 2008 Media Act

We refer to Dutch public broadcasting as a single organization, but the system is made up of a number of separate organizations. Currently, there are 11 broadcasting associations representing 3.6 million members (roughly half of Dutch households); 3 organizations with specific tasks in the fields of news and sport, culture and education, and 8 smaller religious broadcasters. These organizations are working together and led by the board of directors of the umbrella organization *Nederlandse Publieke Omroep* (NPO), which is ultimately responsible for the fulfillment of the public service remit.

The Dutch public broadcasting system became the object of investigation by the European Commission in 2004, following complaints by commercial broadcasters and press companies. The investigation was split into two cases, one concerning (alleged) ad-hoc financing and one concerning existing aid.[6] In the case of new state aid the commission reached a decision in 2006 requiring the Dutch government to recover €80 million from the public service broadcaster. The Dutch government has appealed to the European Court of Justice against this decision. In January 2010, the Dutch government and the commission reached an agreement in the case on existing state aid. By then the 2008 Media Act had incorporated most of the appropriate measures required by the commission.

The net result is the following system for the definition, entrustment and supervision of the public service remit:

- The 2008 Media Act introduces a new definition of the public service remit, which abolishes the distinction between main tasks (three television and five radio stations) and side tasks (thematic channels, websites, mobile services etc). The scope of the public service remit and thus public financing is limited to electronic offerings (images, sound and text) in the areas of information, education and entertainment. Hence, other services such as print media, DVDs, merchandising and e-commerce are treated as commercial activities. Furthermore, qualitative criteria regarding variety, quality, independence and reach continue to determine the public service remit.
- Every five years the public service broadcaster sets out how it will carry out its duties in a strategic plan, the *Concessiebeleidsplan*. This describes overall programme strategy, including quantitative and qualitative objectives. In addition the plan must describe 'the nature and number' of programme and distribution channels, the required spectrum and the required financial means. Changes to the plan can be made annually as part of the budget procedure.
- In the strategic plan, the public broadcaster also has to describe what significant *new* channels it plans to offer. Before new services can be launched, they are subject to prior evaluation and approval by the minister, taking into account the interests of commercial media companies. This was a much-disputed element in the agreement between the Dutch authorities and the commission. In the next paragraph, the procedure is discussed in greater detail.
- On the basis of the strategic plan, the NPO and the minister conclude a performance agreement (*Prestatieovereenkomst*). This contract contains a selection of measurable objectives to be achieved and seeks to ensure the variety of public media offers in the digital age. The performance agreement replaces former programme requirements that only covered the three general television channels. The public service broadcaster reports annually to the minister on the implementation of the agreement. Besides its regular

supervisory tasks, the *Commissariaat voor de Media* verifies the annual performance reports for the minister. If the public broadcaster fails to deliver, the minister can impose (financial) penalties.

- Every five years, the entire public broadcasting system is subject to evaluation by an independent committee, established by the board of governors of the NPO. Evaluation reports came out in 2004 and 2009. A recent amendment to the 2008 Media Act made renewal of the licences of individual broadcasting associations (partly) dependent on a positive evaluation.

Complying with the 2009 Broadcasting Communication, the 2008 Media Act limits the financial reserves of PSB to 10% of the annual budget; any excess will be recovered by the government. The commission accepted the existing regulation of 'side activities,' which should be carried out under market conditions.

The Dutch Procedure for Prior Evaluation of New Media Services

The procedure for prior evaluation starts every five years with the strategic plan of the NPO. One appendix to the plan gives the required overview of the 'nature and number of channels.' This includes general and thematic radio and television channels, web channels, larger umbrella websites or portals and online catch-up services (*Uitzending Gemist*) – some are of course available on different distribution devices. There is no obligation to list all individual programmes and websites, as this would hamper creative and journalistic operations and bring government too close to editorial content. In legal terms, the overview should refer to 'a coherent clustering of media offerings under a recognizable (brand) name.'[7] The overview of all channels serves three purposes:

(1) Entrustment: the minister determines whether the NPO can indeed carry out the public service remit though the described portfolio of channels. Any significant *new* channels are subject to a prior evaluation and approval procedure.
(2) Transparency: the overview helps third parties, such as commercial media, to plan their activities taking public offerings into account if necessary.
(3) Underpinning of extra claims on spectrum for public service broadcasting.

The second appendix to the strategy plan contains the proposal for new media services; that is, any new channels in the portfolio (of old and new channels). Besides channels that did not previously exist or that carried completely different content, prior approval is needed when an existing channel is distributed through another network or platform with distribution scarcity or when payment by end users is introduced. In the proposal the public broadcaster must explain why the new channels would fit into the strategy, paying attention to qualitative aspects of the remit, audience behaviour and needs, existing market offers and so on. The public broadcaster's proposal is the first step in the evaluation and approval procedure, which is based on general administrative law, the *Algemene Wet Bestuursrecht*. The next steps are:

- The *Raad voor Cultuur* (Council for Culture) and the *Commissariaat voor de Media* (Media Authority) advise the minister on the strategic plan, including the proposal for new media services. The role of these two independent and expert bodies is to evaluate new offerings against the public service remit as defined in the Media Act. Moreover, they validate the arguments for new offerings in relation to the wider programme strategy and objectives set out by the public broadcaster.
- Based on the advice and his own assessment, the minister then draws up a draft decision, which summarizes the planned new media services. In this phase, the minister may already decide to discard the proposal partially or entirely.
- The draft decision is then submitted to an open public consultation. Interested third parties can submit comments within six weeks of the publication of the draft decision and the ministry will hold a general public hearing and/or bilateral meetings with stakeholders. This consultation allows commercial media and other market players to bring forward whether and how planned new media services of the public broadcaster may entail negative effects on their operations.
- In his final decision, the minister will balance the value of a new PSB media service for society against its negative effects on the market, as required by the Broadcasting Communication. The minister's final decision may reject, amend or approve a new service. The decision will be published.
- Third parties as well as the public broadcaster can appeal against the decision in the administrative court.

New services will thus be entrusted by means of a three-step prior approval procedure – evaluation of public value, evaluation of market effects and balancing of the two – which culminates in a decision of the media minister approving (or rejecting/amending) the launch of new services by the public broadcaster. Changes to the services approved can be made annually as part of the budget cycle, in which case a similar procedure is followed. The public broadcaster also needs government approval when it wants to end approved services. Experiments can start without prior approval if they are limited in duration (one year), size (up to 2% of annual budget) and scope (restricted audience).

First Experiences with Prior Evaluation in the Netherlands

The prior evaluation procedure has been carried out once in the Netherlands. With its annual budget proposals for 2008 and 2009, the public broadcaster requested the launch of thematic radio channels for digital cable and an audio-visual service on screens in public transport and train stations. Commercial broadcasters and newspaper publishers gave their comments on the minister's draft decision. In essence, they argued that any expansion of public service broadcasting would harm their operations. Negative effects on the market were hardly substantiated. The comments criticized the evaluation procedure, claiming that it would not present a 'market-impact assessment' as required by the 2009 Broadcasting Communication.

In response to the views of third parties, the minister set limits on the proposed new media services. Approval was given for a short period, effectively turning them into experiments to be evaluated before September 2010. Furthermore, the presence of public broadcasting on public screens is not to exceed half of the distribution capacity. The commercial media were not satisfied and appealed against the final decision in court. A trial has not yet taken place.

The strategic plan for 2010–2016 from the NPO is the first to be handled entirely according to the new rules of the 2008 Media Act. At the time of writing, the plan had just been sent to the minister (March 2010). Interestingly, the NPO envisages a streamlining of its new media policy. So far, the decentralized organization of Dutch public broadcasting has led to a proliferation of digital offerings. Although the NPO board of directors controls all channels, in practice it has given individual broadcasting organizations considerable freedom to pioneer the new media. This fosters pluralism and innovation but it also leads to waste and sub-optimal performance. Now the pioneering days seem to be over. The NPO does not propose any new channels but only asks for renewed approval for a delayed start to the 2008/2009 experiments. The NPO promises to rearrange existing channels according to their public value and audience reach, which should result in a more concentrated portfolio by 2012. There are many good reasons for this strategy, but the new rules of the 2008 Media Act might play a role too. Only when the NPO gains a grip on total supply can it deliver proposals for future new services that can survive a prior evaluation procedure.

Benefits and Risks of Prior Evaluation

The commission has promoted prior evaluation by calling it the 'Amsterdam Test.' Just like the Amsterdam Protocol (1997), the 2009 Broadcasting Communication is indeed another temporary appeasement in the battle between commerce and culture within the EU. But this time member states have far less autonomy to shape their national broadcasting policies. One cannot predict the outcome, but possible benefits and risks are discussed later.

During the revision of the Broadcasting Communication, member states opposed a marginalization of PSB that was based on purely economic reasoning. The argument of market failure seems indeed less valid for sustaining and even widening the scope of public service broadcasting. Digitalization of networks, a proliferation of special-interest channels and on-demand services, the convergence of audio-visual media and print – all this feeds the argument that scarcity has come to an end and that the market provides for most of society's needs. On the other hand, high production costs, low to zero reproduction costs, problems with protecting copyright, and high uncertainty of success all tend to limit diversity and quality of audio-visual output – and this would remain so if the Internet were to replace television as the dominant distribution platform, especially in smaller and/or poorer countries. Leaving economic interests aside, the strongest case for public service broadcasting surely rests upon the impact of television on society and the political – some call it 'paternalistic' – wish to maintain standards on society's main channels of communication. Thus, the role of PSB, its budget and the scope of its activities are essentially a matter of political choice.

Prior evaluation of new PSB media services implies that administrative and legal procedures will gain influence over the role of PSB in society. We call this *depoliticization of (national) media policy*. Of course, there are possible benefits. Prior evaluation encourages public broadcasters to use new media in a more selective and effective manner. At the same time, the commercial media are gaining opportunities to underline their interests. In order to serve their respective needs, all stakeholders need to invest in research and intelligence to substantiate either positive public value or negative market impact of new PSB media services. This will serve the legitimacy of public broadcasting and at the same time protect commercial media from disproportionate competition in the marketplace. The flipside of the coin is a growing administrative burden. The commission reasons that both elements of the Amsterdam Protocol are now truly accounted for whilst ensuring subsidiarity for member states: member states have control over the remit and test the impact on competition too (Kroes 2008). In case of complaints, the commission would be able to refer to a rigorous national approval procedure. On the other hand, one might predict that the 2009 Broadcasting Communication will not discourage but promote complaints from commercial media companies, as they now have more precedents to follow. Complainants might first go to the national government and national courts. But eventually the commission cannot absolve itself of its duties under the treaty; complaints are bound to draw the commission back into the details of national procedures. At best, member states will have to go to greater lengths to demonstrate that their PSB systems remain within the EU rules. At worst, administrative and legal procedures will come to overshadow political choices about the role of PSB in society. Moreover, EU regulation might prevent member states from developing their own national media policies in the future. A recent example in the Netherlands is the advice from a high-ranking commission on the future of the press (Commissie-Brinkman 2009) to stimulate the cooperation between public broadcasting and the private newspaper press, as both sectors share a social responsibility for maintaining a sound journalistic infrastructure in the country. Supporters as well as critics, however, state that such a new policy direction might well be in conflict with EU regulations, which prioritize an open market system over a vital public sphere.

At the same time, prior approval by the government might lead to a *politicization of editorial strategies*. Germany was especially eager to amend draft versions of the 2009 Broadcasting Communication to protect the independence of its public service broadcasters. There is indeed a real risk. Some southern European countries and many post-communist countries are showing features of 'state paternalism' or 'political clientelism,' where politics pervades other social systems, including business, the judicial system and indeed the media, and where the development of liberal institutions, critical journalism and an independent public sphere is weak (see Jakubowicz 2007 and reports by the Open Society Institute). Other European countries are not immune, as they are witnessing emerging of populist styles in politics. All in all, the power balance within the EU might be shifting from the liberal and democratic corporatist media cultures to more state paternalist and clientelist media cultures (Bardoel 2007; also Baldi and Hasebrink 2007; Hallin and Mancini 2004). In this context, a prior evaluation of new media services can become one of the instruments for exerting political influence over editorial decisions within public broadcasting – alongside budget cuts, appointments and performance agreements.

Let us go back to the example that inspired the 2009 Broadcasting Communication, the BBC's public value test. This is not only designed to accommodate pressures from commercial media, it is also meant to shield the BBC from political pressure by improving internal accountability and control. We will have to wait and see what the actual effects of prior evaluation and approval procedures in the various member states will be.

Conclusion and Discussion

The struggle over state aid for public service broadcasting mirrors a general dilemma about the scope of the European Union (Harrison and Woods 2001; Moe 2008). Initially the European Union started as an economic project; the idea was to prevent another war on European soil by building a common market. In later years, the scope of the EU extended to other areas, such as immigration and justice. However, on the whole the EU's emphasis is still on the economy, whereas member states remain in control of the social, cultural and democratic needs of their respective communities. Moreover, the EU delegated great powers to the European Commission to ensure member states' compliance with the treaty's rules on competition and state aid. Consequently, the commission can act rather independently in this area, based on 'soft law' – case practice, communications – without a formal role for the Council of Ministers and the European Parliament. When member states do want to counter the commission's powers on the internal market, they have to join forces and express strong political will.

Precisely because member states are unwilling to delegate cultural interests to the EU and leave the core competence of the EU with competition policy, national media and PSB policies come under increased scrutiny from Brussels' competition approach, in which commerce may eventually beat culture (see also Harcourt 2005; Michalis 2007). Bardoel and Lowe (2007: 12) conclude that:

> The question is how the European Union can so blithely treat PSB from a deterministically economic perspective when the entire enterprise isn't about that and is in fact explicitly about the countervailing importance of the socio-cultural dimension. How can PSB be treated as an 'exception' when it is so obviously central to the European media ecology and a European invention that remains a cultural institution that greatly contributes to the heritage and richness of European social life?

In conclusion, the traditional model of European public service broadcasting seems to have become an endangered species in the context of the European Union. In the digital era, it rests more strongly on the political will to sustain a public institution that enjoys a wide mandate and true independence from the state and commercial interests. Such political will is present in most western and northern parts of Europe, but certainly not – as already indicated – in most eastern countries or in Italy. At EU level, public service broadcasting presents a distortion of the market, which is inevitably under constant scrutiny from the European Commission. As a result, state-aid rules for public service broadcasters may become ever stricter over time, depoliticizing the definition of the role and remit of PSBs whilst politicizing their actual editorial strategy. In such a scenario, a simple 'procedure' can have far-reaching consequences for public service broadcasting in Europe.

References

Baldi, P. and Hasebrink, U. (eds.) (2007), *Broadcasters and Citizens in Europe. Trends in Media Accountability and Viewer Participation*, Bristol: Intellect Books.

Bardoel, J. (2007), 'Converging Media Arrangements in Europe', in G. Terzis (ed.), *European Media Governance. National and Regional Dimensions*, Bristol: Intellect, pp. 445–459.

Bardoel, J. and Lowe, G. (2007), 'From Public Service Broadcasting to Public Service Media: The Core Challenge', in G. Lowe and J. Bardoel (eds.), *From Public Service Broadcasting to Public Service Media*, Gotenburg: Nordicom, pp. 9–26.

Bardoel, J. and van Cuilenburg, J. (2003), *Communicatiebeleid en communicatiemarkt. Over beleid, economie en management voor de communicatiesector*, Amsterdam: Otto Cramwinckel.

Biltereyst, D. and Pauwels, C. (2007), 'Our Policies in Reinventing the Past: An Overview of EU Policy-Making in the Audiovisual Domain', in L. d'Haenens and F. Saeys (eds.), *Western Broadcast Models: Structure, Conduct and Performance*, Berlin and New York: Mouton de Gruyter, pp. 25–61.

Collins, R. (1994), *Broadcasting and Audio-Visual Policy in the European Single Market*, London: John Libbey.

Commissie-Brinkman (2009), *De Volgende editie*, Den Haag: Tijdelijke Commissie Innovatie en Toekomst Pers.

Common Position Paper of Member States (2008), 'Main Principles for a Revision of the Broadcasting Communication', addressed to the European Commissioner Kroes, 24 September, (See also letter to Dutch Parliament of 10 October 2008, Kamerstukken II 2008–2009, 21 501–534, nr 106, www.tweedekamer.nl.)

Depypere, S. (2004), 'Responsibilities for Public Service Broadcasters', in D. Ward (ed.), *The Key Role of Public Service Broadcasting in European Society in the 21st Century*, The Hague: Ministry of Education, Culture and Sciences, pp. 132–135.

Donders, K. and Pauwels, C. (2008), 'Does EU Policy Challenge the Digital Future of Public Service Broadcasting?', *Convergence: The International Journal of Research into New Media Technologies*, 14: 3, pp. 295–311.

European Commission (1997), 'Treaty of Amsterdam Amending the Treaty on European Union, the Treaties Establishing the European Communities and Certain Related Acts', 2 October, Amsterdam, – C. Protocols annexed to the Treaty establishing the European Community, *Official Journal of the European Communities*, C340/109.

—— (2001), 'Communication from the Commission on the Application of State Aid Rules to Public Service Broadcasting', *Official Journal of the European Communities*, C320, pp. 5–11.

—— (2008), 'Revision of the Communication from the Commission on the Application of State Aid Rules to Public Service Broadcasting – Questionnaire for public consultation and Explanatory memorandum', 10 January.

—— (2009), 'Communication from the Commission on the Application of State Aid Rules to Public Service Broadcasting', *Official Journal of the European Union*, C257, pp. 1–14.

Hallin, D. and Mancini, P. (2004), *Comparing Media Systems. Three Models of Media and Politics*, Cambridge: Cambridge University Press.

Harcourt, A. (2005), *The European Union and the Regulation of Media Markets*, Manchester and New York: Manchester University Press.

Harrison, J. and Woods, L. (2001), 'Defining European Public Service Broadcasting', *European Journal of Communication*, 16: 4, pp. 477–504.

Jakubowicz, K. (2007), 'The Eastern European/Post-Communist Media Model Countries. An Introduction', in G. Terzis (ed.), *European Media Governance. National and Regional Dimensions*, Bristol: Intellect, pp. 303–315.

Kroes, N. (2008), 'The Way Ahead for the Broadcasting Communication', Speech made at an expert meeting on PSB, 17 July, Strasbourg.

Loisen, J. (2008), 'Staatsteun en de VRT', Working Paper.

Michalis, M. (2007), *Governing European Communications. From Unification to Coordination*, Lanham: Lexington.

Moe, H. (2008), 'Between Supranational Competition and National Culture? Emerging EU Policy and Public Broadcasters' Online Services', in I. Bondebjerg and P. Madsen (eds.), *Media, Democracy and European Culture*, Bristol: Intellect, pp. 215–239.

Wheeler, M. (2004), 'Supranational Regulation. Television and the European Union', *European Journal of Communication*, 19: 3, pp. 349–369.

Notes

1   Marit Vochteloo is a senior policy adviser with the Ministry of Education, Culture and Science in the Netherlands. The article does not necessarily reflect the views of the Dutch government.

2   For consultation documents, drafts and reactions, and the final text revised Broadcasting Communication of 2009 see http://ec.europa.eu/competition/state_aid/reform/archive .html#broadcasting.

3   Another important conflict between the commission and member states involved the conditions for paid services of PSBs.

4   In a footnote, the communication considers that simultaneous transmission of the evening television news on other platforms, such as the Internet and mobile devices, may be qualified as not being 'new.'

5   Decisions of the European Commission on state aid for public service broadcasting since 2000 can be found in an online register: http://ec.europa.eu/competition/state_aid/register/. Norway has introduced a prior evaluation procedure in reaction to complaints with the EFTA surveillance authority. See the EFTA decision of 3 February 2010 on the Norwegian Broadcasting Corporation. Decision no 36/10/COL. EFTA monitors compliance with European Economic Area rules in Iceland, Liechtenstein and Norway, enabling them to participate in the European internal market.

6   When new aid violates the treaty, the commission can require member states to recover funds from organizations that have profited. When existing aid is found incompatible with the treaty, the commission can only require appropriate measures to ensure future compliance. Existing aid includes all aid that existed prior to the entry into force of the treaty (1958) in the respective member states.

7   To enhance transparency, the NPO counted the number of websites at the reference date of 1 March 2010. There were just above 1000 websites; 90% were directly related to radio and television programmes, another 10% had substantial extra offerings or were produced only for the Internet.

Chapter 17

Film Support in the EU: The Uteca Case and the Future Challenges for the 'Main Characters'

Lucia Bellucci

Introduction

The European Commission (in the following, commission) enjoys significant discretion with regard to aid that may be considered to be compatible with the EU internal market.

It assesses national film-support schemes on the basis of state-aid provisions outlined in Articles 107[1]–109 of the Treaty on the Functioning of the European Union (formerly Articles 87–89 of the treaty establishing the European Community (i.e. the EC Treaty)). These provisions are based on the principle that state aid is incompatible with the internal market and it has to be approved in advance by the commission.

In this context, Article 107 (3)(d) TFEU (formerly Article 87(3)(d) EC) provides for a 'cultural derogation,' an additional discretionary exemption for 'aid to promote culture and heritage conservation where such aid does not affect trading conditions and competition in the Union to an extent that is contrary to the common interest.'

Furthermore, Article 167(4) TFEU (formerly Article 151(4) EC) imposes a transversal character on cultural issues (Karydis 1994: 559),[2] providing that: 'The Union shall take cultural aspects into account in its action under other provisions of the Treaties, in particular in order to respect and to promote the diversity of its cultures.'

In March 2010, we published (Bellucci 2010: 211) the results of a qualitative content analysis of the commission decisions in the field of state aid to cinematographic works,[3] from December 1988 to March 2008, which showed that the Commission Decision of 3 June 1998[4] marked a turning point in its decision-making practice.

In this decision the commission set out some specific compatibility criteria to assess national film-support schemes; these criteria were laid out and clarified in a 2001 communication, the Cinema Communication,[5] and will be applied in all the following decisions on the subject.

During the related case, which concerned France, the member state with the strongest film-production industry and the richest film-support system, the commission fully realized the political implications of state aid to film and its repercussions on the commission's relationships with the member states.

After this decision, the commission referred more to the cultural importance of state aid to cinematographic works and in some cases to its influence on European identity. Recently, it has also recognized the essential role of this aid in the promotion of cultural diversity. The expression 'cultural diversity' has in fact become part of the community lexicon (Bellucci 2006: 320) and it is now recognized by the Convention on the Protection and Promotion of the Diversity of Cultural Expressions, adopted on 20 October 2005 by the General Conference of the United Nations Educational, Scientific and Cultural Organization (UNESCO) (in the following, UNESCO Convention).

Nevertheless, the commission continued to draw a clear-cut distinction between cinema as a cultural expression and cinema as an industry, between the cultural and the industrial nature of the aid.

The study mentioned earlier revealed that the commission's approach is the source of two conflicts: one within the commission itself and the second between the commission and the member states.

The conflict within the commission is between the Directorate General for Competition and the DG for Education and Culture (whose competence in the field of cinema now belongs to the DG Information Society and Media), two bodies that have quite different goals. The DG Competition must ensure the development of a market that respects competition rules, whereas the DG Education and Culture must promote culture within the EU. For example, the 2001 Cinema Communication, which is the main EU text in the field of state aid to cinematographic works, was the fruit of collaboration between the DG Education and Culture and the DG Competition. It was also the outcome of a conflict – *latent* (rather than *declared*) – that needed to be treated to enable the commission to adopt the Cinema Communication, which represents the commission as a whole (for the expression 'declared conflict' see more extensively Ferrari 1987: 95ff and Abel 1973: 227).

Furthermore, the analysis of the commission decision-making practice pointed to a *declared* conflict between the commission, particularly the DG Competition, and the member states. This conflict has multiple facets and revolves around the commission's economic analysis of the cinematographic market. Even though, according to the member states, this analysis does not consider the peculiarities of the cinematographic market and the different features of this market in each member state, it explains the clear-cut distinction drawn by the commission between cinema as a cultural expression and cinema as an industry. This distinction has been softened since the Decision of 3 June 1998, but it is still a constant in the commission decision-making practice.

This article seeks to further explore these conflicts, highlighting some of the challenges that the 'main characters' in these conflicts will face in the treatment of them. By 'main characters,' we are referring to the commission, also considered as the DG Competition and DG Information Society and Media, and the member states. By 'conflict treatment' we are referring to the thesis that law 'treats' conflicts rather than 'solves' them (Abel 1973: 228; Ferrari 1987: 95f; Galanter 1975: 363).

To this end, we present a case analysis of the case of Unión de Televisiones Comerciales Asociadas (Uteca) v. Administración General del Estado[6] (in the following, the Uteca case), ruled by the European Court of Justice (in the following, ECJ).

Although the ECJ ruled that the measures at issue in the main proceedings did not constitute state aid in favour of the cinematographic industry of the member state in question (Spain), the Uteca case is relevant to our purpose. In fact, this case, particularly the Opinion of the Advocate-General Kokott, touches upon some of the issues that may determine the future developments of the conflicts mentioned earlier. These issues continue to be controversial, and hence they may be future challenges for the 'main characters' of these conflicts and may have a noticeable impact on the latter.

Three challenges will be explored: the relationship between cinema and television with particular reference to television broadcasters' involvement in film production; the different interpretations of the expressions 'cultural product,' 'quality/cultural film' and 'difficult film'; and the UNESCO Convention.

Section II analyses the Uteca case and television broadcasters' involvement in cinematographic production, with a focus on the legal obligations member states impose on television broadcasters to invest in audio-visual[7] production. With the support of some commission decisions, section III discusses the divergent interpretations of the expressions 'cultural product,' 'quality/cultural film' and, although not mentioned in the Uteca case, the related expression 'difficult film.' Section IV considers the provisions of the UNESCO Convention relevant to state aid and highlights the weaknesses of this convention as well as the obstacles to its implementation. Section V concludes the analysis of the challenges for the 'main characters' in the conflicts and suggests further research on cultural tests.

The Uteca Case and TV Broadcasters' Involvement in Film Production

In April 2007, the Spanish Tribunal Supremo referred to the ECJ for a preliminary ruling under Article 234 EC (now Article 267 TFEU).

The reference was made in an action brought by Uteca, an association of commercial television companies, against Royal Decree 1652/2004,[8] which imposes legal obligations on television broadcasters to invest in audio-visual production. In particular, the decree requires television broadcasters to allocate 5% of their annual revenue (precisely, their operating revenue from the previous year) to the pre-funding of European cinematographic films and films made for television (on this topic see Troya and Enrich 2007) and to reserve 60% of that funding for the production of films in which the original language is one of the official languages of Spain.[9] In the main proceedings, Uteca aimed to have the decree and the legislative provisions it is based on declared inapplicable. Uteca's claims were opposed by the Administración General del Estado, the central government administration, and by the Federación de Asociaciones de Productores Audiovisuales Españoles and the Entitad de Gestión de Derechos de los Productores Audiovisuales, two organizations representing producers' interests.[10]

Legal obligations imposed by member states on television broadcasters compelling them to invest in audio-visual production are one of the instruments they have to use the power of television to support cinema (Bellucci 2006: 201–224).

European countries had different reactions to the changing relationship between cinema and television: after being the most popular *medium* for many years, cinema has been progressively replaced by television.

Italy and France are paradigmatic of two opposite attitudes. In France, this phenomenon appeared at the end of the 1950s (Bonnell 1978: 88), whereas in Italy, it appeared during the 1960s,[11] but it increased during the following years. In Italy the absence of regulation until the mid-1980s and the limited effectiveness of the provisions that were finally adopted allowed television, with a peak between 1975 and 1985, to definitively take away the audience from cinema (Castagna 1989: 89). The following statement about the vigour of Italy's film industry, made in 1966, now seems unbelievable: 'Except for the very first years [...] Italian cinema is the only one that did not suffer from the competition with television. It is the third [cinema] in the world after US and USSR cinemas and – also taking [international] co-productions into account – it produces 180–200 films per year'[12] (Perez 1966: 1016, n. 85).

In France, in contrast, during the 1980s television broadcasters' role in the cinematographic sector began to grow (Vernier 1991: 46). Soon French law extensively and effectively used the competition from television in favour of cinema. It involved television broadcasters in film production to the extent that it imposed legal obligations on them to invest in the sector.

The model of legal obligations imposed on television broadcasters has been imported to different degrees by other states and it has been one of the issues at the heart of the declared conflict between the commission and the member states.

This model, and more generally the relationships between cinema and television, are now so important with regard to the cinematographic production and to cultural policies that in the Uteca case a large number of member states' governments participated in the procedure before the ECJ.[13]

In this case, the reference for a preliminary ruling relates to the interpretation of Article 3 of the Television Without Frontiers Directive,[14] Article 12 EC (now Article 18 TFEU), concerning the prohibition of discrimination on the grounds of nationality, and Article 87 EC (now Article 107 TFEU) on state aid. The ECJ was therefore asked to assess the compatibility of the Spanish provisions with the directive, the fundamental freedoms of the Treaty and the EU provisions on state aid.

With regard to Article 87 EC, the ECJ ruled that it 'must be interpreted as meaning that a measure adopted by a Member State, such as the measures at issue in the main proceedings, does not constitute state aid in favour of the cinematographic industry of that Member State.'[15]

The commission stated[16] that legal obligations imposed on television broadcasters by member states do not involve any transfer of state resources and do not constitute state aid within the meaning of Article 87(1) EC[17] as they can be considered as purchase obligations between private undertakings, comparable to those the ECJ ruled upon in the *PreussenElektra* case.[18] It did not seem to question the legal obligations on television broadcasters to invest in audio-visual production. Nevertheless, according to the commission these obligations 'do not constitute State aid, where these investments provide a reasonable compensation to broadcasters.'[19] For example, the considerable public funding of television broadcasters that France provides more than any other European country (CNC 2005–2006), could be considered reasonable compensation, even though funding for the public service broadcasting in France is undergoing significant changes. This is leading the cinema sector to worry (Herzberg 2008) that the public TV networks will not be able to invest in cinematographic production as much as they currently do[20] if the state financial compensation is no longer guaranteed.

Given that the study 'Identification and evaluation of financial flows within the European cinema industry' (IMCA 2001: 131), ordered by the commission, shows that cinema has become a less attractive product to generalist television networks, it is possible that, in the absence of reasonable compensation, the commission might have reconsidered the obligations in question in a way that would have been unfavourable to the cinema sector. The brief period for the approvals for the aid schemes did not guarantee legal certainty on this topic.

The ECJ's interpretation in the Uteca case[21] with regard to Article 87 EC is therefore very important to member states' cultural policies.

The Expressions 'Cultural Product,' 'Quality/Cultural Film' and 'Difficult Film'

The Advocate General assists the ECJ in providing reasoning that the ECJ can follow or reject in coming to its decision. What matters is the dialogic relationship between the Advocate General and the ECJ, which takes place over time and space. It continues after the outcome of a case as part of the ongoing discourse on the interpretation of EU law and it can continue outside the ECJ (Burrows and Greaves 2007: 293). Some of the Opinions of Advocates-General have given rise to debates among academics and practitioners at the European and international levels. They also have been widely influential, particularly in academic works. Very often academics would use these opinions as a starting point for a critique of the case law of the ECJ (Burrows and Greaves 2007: 10, 293).

In considering the proportionality of the means by which the Spanish legislation pursues its legitimate aim, particularly whether it 'is necessary to achieve the aim pursued or whether it exceeds the bounds of what is necessary,'[22] the Opinion of the Advocate General Kokott approached the problem of the definitions of culture, cultural product and quality [cultural] film, considering that, apart from some extreme cases, it is practically impossible to lay down objective and fair criteria on what is culture and to an even lesser extent on what is a cultural product that can be supported. This would favour traditional cultural patterns over more recent cultural trends and minorities' cultural activities.[23] Even if objective criteria as to whether a film can be considered a 'cultural product' or a 'quality [cultural] film' were defined, their implementation would involve a degree of bureaucracy that would give producers and artists the impression of being subjected to a state system of prior censorship: 'It does not follow from Community law or from fundamental freedoms in particular that there is an obligation on Member States to inevitably base the promotion of culture on substantive and quality criteria.'[24]

Advocate General Kokott recalled that the commission decision-making practice in the field of state aid is characterized by a restrictive approach that authorizes measures related to 'cultural products' if defined in detail.[25] To clarify the Advocate General's words one needs to remember that the Cinema Communication formalized a general legality criterion and four specific compatibility criteria to assess whether aid schemes to cinematographic production may be declared compatible with the internal market. According to the first criterion, the aid must concern a specific film-making project, namely a cultural product, rather than an industrial activity: that is to say, it must support a film rather than a business. Furthermore, in compliance with the application of the subsidiarity principle,[26] the commission did not impose a definition of culture.[27] It did not mention the characteristics upon which a work is to be considered a cultural product. It left it to each member state to ensure that the content of the production benefiting from aid is cultural according to national criteria that must be verifiable.[28]

Advocate General Kokott held that the commission decision-making practice in the field of state aid, and therefore its approach with regard to state-aid provisions, does not prejudice the interpretation of other provisions of the EC Treaty, in particular concerning the fundamental freedoms. This approach is to be considered as limited to the state-aid sector. Outside this sector, the promotion of culture can be pursued as broadly as possible. The scope of application of a pre-funding system such as the Spanish one therefore does not have to be restricted to films that appear suitable for support as 'cultural products' or 'quality [cultural] films' by objective and verifiable criteria.[29]

Nevertheless, it is important to remember that, even with regard to state aid to film production, the expressions 'cultural product' and 'quality/cultural film' are far from being unanimously shared. They are still at the heart of the conflict between the commission and the member states. In particular, they are related to two issues raised by the European national film agencies' joint declarations on state aid:[30] the clear-cut distinction between commercial and cultural works and the definition of a difficult film.[31]

Although the declarations represent the national film agencies of all member states, each state interprets these issues in a different way. With regard to the issue of a clear-cut distinction between commercial and cultural works, French authorities, in particular, refuse to distinguish between 'cultural' cinema, which would benefit from the aid, and 'commercial' cinema, which would not benefit from it, starting from the assumption that every film is a cultural product.[32] This policy, which they have tried to spread among other member states and at the EU level, is in line with the French film-support system, which provides that part of the revenue from blockbusters is used to support the production of films that *a priori* do not seem to be blockbusters. The note from the French authorities within the commission's public consultation on plans to extend the state-aid assessment criteria under the Cinema Communication until 31 December 2012 is a good example of this policy. In this note they underlined that the introductory paragraph of the press release concerning the public consultation was incorrect, as it stated that state support for film production must concern 'cultural films' (European Commission 2008). It replaced the concept of 'cultural product' mentioned in the Cinema Communication[33] by the concept of 'cultural film' and introduced the idea that some films might not be cultural, which is counter to the thesis defended by French authorities (French authorities 2008).

In line with the French position, the present Centre National de la Cinématographie et de l'image animée (CNC), the French national film agency, has blamed cultural tests for introducing a difference between films called 'cultural' and the others (CNC 2007a).

Following the recent trend to use incentives to attract large-budget productions, some member states have adopted cultural tests, with significant differences according to the national aid scheme[34] (Broche et al. 2007: 45). These have been approved by the commission. Actually, even the European national film agencies have expressed their concerns about cultural tests. They are concerned that the automatic introduction of these tests will lead the commission to adopt 'a restrictive and reductive approach towards culture and film.'[35]

With regard to the issue of the definition of a difficult film, following the third criterion established by the Cinema Communication, it is important to note that aid intensity must be limited to 50% of the production budget, except for difficult and low-budget films or, when proven necessary, for films from geographic areas whose language and cultures have a limited circulation within and outside the EC market. This communication states that under the subsidiarity principle, it is up to each member state to define the concepts of 'difficult and low-budget films' according to national parameters.[36] Nevertheless, member states did not unanimously welcome the request to define a difficult film, as they each have different policies on the matter.

The French and UK responses are good examples of the current orientations. On the one hand, French authorities consider it counter-productive to establish a definition of a difficult film, and they give as minimalist a definition as possible, stating that difficult films are those that must have a 'culturally ambitious character and [...] must fulfil conditions of quality, diversity and risk taking.'[37] On the other hand, UK authorities favour a detailed definition of a difficult film, which also includes a list of objectives, related for example to the improvement of new technologies or the engagement with minority languages. Besides affirming that a 'difficult film is one which would have little if any prospect of commercial success because of its experimental nature or because it represented a high level of creative risk,'[38] they also require that it contributes to achieving one or more objectives set out in the list.[39]

The UNESCO Convention on the Protection and Promotion of the Diversity of Cultural Expressions

While considering the legitimacy of the aim of the Spanish legislation, Advocate General Kokott referred to some recitals in the preamble and to some articles of the UNESCO Convention. Articles 1(a)(h),[40] 2(2),[41] 5(1)[42] and 6(a)(b)[43] are particularly significant for the topic of state aid to film production. These concern the objectives and guiding principles of the convention, and the rights and obligations of the parties. Their formulation implies that state aid can be included among the measures that the UNESCO Convention allows the parties to adopt with the aim of fostering film production. This possibility is strengthened by the recognition of the principle of sovereignty (Article 2(2)) among the guiding principles of the convention.

Although the European Union ratified the UNESCO Convention,[44] the analysis of the commission decisions showed that this convention only partially influenced the commission decision-making practice in the field of state aid to film production.

State aid to film production in fact has pros and cons[45] that affect cultural diversity within the state, the EU and relationships with third countries. The UNESCO Convention implicitly imposes finding a good balance between those cons and a number of other issues related to cultural diversity. More relevant to the impact on the commission decision-making practice, the UNESCO Convention is vague in many ways and shows some weaknesses. The provisions of a convention, although binding on the parties, often have some weaknesses and are difficult to implement.

In particular, it is important to note that the main UNESCO Convention provisions are expressed in aspirational terms (Craufurd-Smith 2007: 24). The convention is not to 'be interpreted as modifying rights and obligations of the Parties under any other treaties to which they are parties' (Article 20(2)), and therefore of the EU Treaties. Its dispute settlement procedures[46] are not legally binding, and there is 'no provision for formal sanctioning and therefore for a dispute settlement system that will produce concrete interpretations of its terms and concepts with the aim of making its rules more predictable and transparent' (Bellucci and Soprano 2010: 168f; Germann 2010b: 68).

Furthermore, empirical research showed obstacles to implementation. The most important of these are related to the UNESCO Convention's lack of obligations for implementation, and therefore a lack of consequences for non-implementation, and to insufficient resources and funding (e.g. the minimal contribution to the International Fund), which has been heightened by the global economic crisis. Other factors that create obstacles to implementation include: a lack of specific mechanisms to support civil society in implementation practices; inadequate institutional measures at the state level to coordinate the dialogue between trade and cultural agencies; a failure of coordination and promotion of the UNESCO Convention at the international level (Germann Avocats et al. 2010: 22ff; Jakubowski and Henriques 2010: 57ff), and a lack of information and coordination with regard to the measures and actions taken by the member states to implement this convention (Schramme and Vander Auwera 2010: 292).

On the one hand, the weaknesses related to the provisions of the UNESCO Convention do not challenge the commission, particularly the DG Competition, to focus on the cultural nature of state aid to film production. Much as the WTO Panel and Appellate Body are not oriented to allow cultural issues to prevail over trade issues (Bellucci and Soprano 2010: 168, 170), so the DG Competition is not willing to allow cultural issues to prevail over competition issues.

On the other hand, removing the obstacles to implementation, even by informing civil society about its potentialities, will increase the impact of the UNESCO Convention on the commission decision-making practice in the field of state aid to film production and therefore on its conflict with the member states.

Conclusion

The Commission draws a clear-cut distinction between cinema as a cultural expression and cinema as an industry, between the cultural and the industrial nature of the aid.

Empirical research has shown that this approach is the source of two conflicts in the field of state aid to film production: a *latent* conflict within the commission itself and a *declared* conflict between the commission and the member states.

The commission and the member states, considered as the 'main characters' of the conflicts, will face several challenges in the treatment of these conflicts.

Although the Uteca case concerns provisions that according to the ECJ do not constitute state aid, it offers an opportunity to explore some of these challenges.

One of them is the relationship between cinema and television and the involvement of television broadcasters in film production. This is a crucial issue, because through various different legal instruments the main sources of funding to cinematographic production in member states currently come from television broadcasters. As a key actor in cinematographic production, television is both a strong economic and financial power and an influence on the freedoms of expression and information as well as on cultural pluralism. Legal obligations on television broadcasters to invest in audio-visual production are one of the means of diverting this power for the benefit of cinema.

Another challenge relates to the different interpretations of the expressions 'cultural product' and 'quality/cultural film.' In the Uteca case, they are not treated with regard to state aid. However, not only are they far from being unanimously shared in this field but also they are still at the heart of the conflict between the commission and the member states. They relate particularly to the issues of the clear-cut distinction between commercial and cultural works and the definition of a difficult film, issues that were both raised by the European national film agencies' joint declarations on state aid. 'Difficult film' is therefore one of the controversial expressions the 'main characters' will have to confront.

This challenge is related to the topic of cultural tests, which was not broached by the Uteca case. It is now questionable whether the issue of these tests will partially weaken the unity that the European national film agencies have achieved by overcoming different traditions of cultural policy – as they did when, looking for a consensus among member states, they polarized the conflict (member-states commission) and set up a dialogue with the commission. Further research, especially empirical, is needed to monitor the impact of cultural tests on this unity and, therefore, on the polarization of the conflict, as well as to compare the cinema and television sectors more generally (for a comparison between these sectors see Craufurd-Smith 2008: 51f).

The last challenge revealed through the analysis of the Uteca case is the UNESCO Convention. This implicitly includes state aid among the measures that the parties can adopt within their cultural policies. Nevertheless, it also implicitly requires them to balance public support with cultural diversity, within an individual member state, the whole European Union and relationships with third countries. Moreover, the UNESCO convention has some weaknesses with regard to the content and the form of its provisions and to its implementation.

As Article 167(4) TFEU provides that culture must be taken into account to balance policies such as competition, characterized by economic concerns, the 'real issue with regard to maintaining cultural diversity in the film sector [...] is not whether it is a legitimate goal but rather how it can be achieved' (Herold 2008: 35).

The weaknesses of the UNESCO Convention do not encourage the DG Competition to stress the cultural nature of state aid to film production, thus reversing the trend in the commission decision-making practice. The commission itself recognized the importance of 'mainstreaming culture in all relevant policies [...] in order to strike the right balance between different legitimate public policy objectives, including the promotion of cultural diversity [...].'[47] Nevertheless, a stronger implementation of Article 167(4) TFEU (on this topic see European Parliament 2007 and Smiers 2002), as well as of the UNESCO Convention, is necessary to reverse this trend.

References

Abel, R. L. (1973), 'A Comparative Theory of Dispute Institutions in Society', *Law&Society Review*, 8: 2, pp. 217–347.

Angelopoulos, C. (2009), 'Court of Justice of the European Communities: Uteca v. Administración General del Estado', *IRIS*, 4: 3/2, http://merlin.obs.coe.int/iris/2009/4/article2.en.html. Accessed 19 November 2010.

Bellucci, L. (2006), *Cinema e aiuti di Stato nell'integrazione europea. Un diritto promozionale in Italia e in Francia*, Milano: Giuffrè.

——— (2010), 'National Support for Film Production in the EU: An Analysis of the Commission Decision-Making Practice', *European Law Journal*, 16: 2, pp. 211–232.

Bellucci, L. and Soprano, R. (2010), 'Study Paper 3A: The WTO System and the Implementation of the UNESCO Convention: Two Case Studies', in Germann Avocats (Geneva) and Multidisciplinary Research Team, *Implementing the Unesco Convention of 2005 in the European Union*, Long Version of the Study for the European Parliament, Directorate General for Internal Policies. Policy Department B: Structural and Cohesion Policies. Culture and Education, Brussels: European Parliament, pp. 165–170, http://www.diversitystudy.eu. Accessed 19 November 2010.

Bollero, M. (1965), 'Le fonti della legislazione sul cinema', *Ulisse*, IX: LVI, pp. 86–94.

Bonnell, R. (1978), *Le cinéma exploité*, Paris: Ed. du Seuil.

Burrows, N. and Greaves, R. (2007), *The Advocate General and EC Law*, Oxford: Oxford University Press.

Broche, J., Chatterjee, O., Orssich, I. and Tosics, N. (2007), 'State Aid for Films – a Policy in Motion?', *Competition Policy Newsletter*, 1, pp. 44–48.

Castagna, M. (1989), *La produzione cinematografica italiana: industria o artigianato? Imprenditorialità o avventura?*, in M. I. Boni (ed.), *L'economia dietro il sipario. Teatro, opera, cinema, televisione*, Torino: EDT.

CNC (Centre National de la Cinématographie) (2005–2006), 'La lettre # 30', http://www.cnc.fr. Accessed 19 November 2010.

—— (2007a), *Communiqué de presse. Les agences nationales européennes réunies, le 21 mai dernier à Cannes, adoptent une déclaration commune sur le nouvel agenda culturel européen*, http://www.cnc.fr. Accessed 19 November 2010.

—— (2007b), 'Les agences nationales européennes adoptent une déclaration commune', *La lettre # 45*, http://www.cnc.fr. Accessed 19 November 2010.

Craufurd-Smith, R. (2007), 'The UNESCO Convention on the Protection and Promotion of the Diversity of Cultural Expressions: Building a New World Information and Communication Order?', *International Journal of Communication*, 1, pp. 24–55.

—— (2008), 'Balancing Culture and Competition: State Support for Film and Television in European Community Law', in C. Barnard (ed.), *The Cambridge Yearbook of European Legal Studies*, 2007–2008, 10, Oxford and Portland: Hart, pp. 35–67.

European Commission (2008), Rapid Press Release, 'State Aid: Commission Consults on Three Year Extension of Film Support Criteria', http://europa.eu/rapid/pressReleasesAction.do?reference=IP/08/1580&format=HTML. Accessed 19 November 2010.

—— (2009), Rapid Press Release, 'A Member State Can Require Television Operators to Earmark Part of Their Operating Revenue for the Finding of European Cinematographic and TV Films', http://europa.eu/rapid/pressReleasesAction.do?reference=CJE/09/18&format=HTML. Accessed 19 November 2010.

European Parliament. Directorate-General for Internal Policies of the Union. Policy Department Structural and Cohesion Policies (2007), 'Briefing Paper on the Implementation of Article 151.4 of the EC Treaty', http://www.europarl.europa.eu/activities/expert/eStudies.do?language=EN. Accessed 19 November 2010.

Ferrari, V. (1987), *Funzioni del diritto. Saggio critico-ricostruttivo*, Rome and Bari: Laterza.

Ferri, D. (2009), 'Nota a Corte di Giustizia, 5 marzo 2009, causa C-222/07, Unión de Televisiones Comerciales Asociadas (Uteca) c. Administración General del Estado', *Rivista di Diritto pubblico comparato italiano ed europeo*, 3, pp. 1381–1388.

—— (2010), 'Study Paper 2D: New Ideas for Implementing Article 11 of the UNESCO Convention', in Germann Avocats (Geneva) and Multidisciplinary Research Team, *Implementing the UNESCO Convention of 2005 in the European Union*, Long Version of the Study for the European Parliament, Directorate General for Internal Policies. Policy Department B: Structural and Cohesion Policies. Culture and Education, Brussels: European Parliament, pp. 146–164, http://www.diversitystudy.eu. Accessed 19 November 2010.

French Authorities (2008), 'Note pour la Commission Européenne', http://ec.europa.eu/competition/consultations/2008_cinema/france.pdf. Accessed 19 November 2010.

Galanter, M. (1975), 'Afterword: Explaining Litigation', *Law&Society Review*, 9: 2, pp. 347–368.

Germann Avocats (Geneva) and Multidisciplinary Research Team (2010), *Implementing the UNESCO Convention of 2005 in the European Union*, Short Version of the Study for the European Parliament, Directorate General for Internal Policies. Policy Department B: Structural and Cohesion Policies. Culture and Education, Brussels: European Parliament, http://www.europarl.europa.eu/studies. Accessed 19 November 2010.

Germann, C. (2008), *Diversité culturelle et libre-échange à la lumière du cinéma*, Basel, Paris and Brussels: Helbing Lichtenhahn, L.G.D.J and Bruylant.

—— (2010a), 'Study Paper 2B: Intellectual Property and Competition', in Germann Avocats (Geneva) and Multidisciplinary Research Team, *Implementing the UNESCO Convention of 2005 in the European Union*, Long Version of the Study for the European Parliament, Directorate General for Internal Policies. Policy Department B: Structural and Cohesion Policies. Culture and Education, Brussels: European Parliament, pp. 72–115, http://www.diversitystudy.eu. Accessed 19 November 2010.

—— (2010b), 'Legal Action Against Asserted Cultural Genocide and Piracy in China: The Strength of the WTO and the Weakness of the UNESCO', *International Journal of Intellectual Property Management*, 4: 1/2, pp. 65–95.

Herold, A. (2008), 'European Film Policies and Competition Law: Hostility or Symbiosis?', in D. Ward (ed.), *The European Union and the Culture Industries. Regulation and the Public Interest*, Aldershot and Burlington: Ashgate, pp. 33–57.

Herzberg, N. (2008), 'Le monde du cinéma redoute la réforme de France Télévisions', http://www.lemonde.fr/cinema/article/2008/12/10/le-monde-du-cinema-redoute-la-reforme-de-france-televisions_1129222_3476.html. Accessed 19 November 2010.

IMCA (2001), Study No DG EAC/34/01, 'Identification and Evaluation of Financial Flows within the European Cinema Industry by Comparison with the American Model', http://ec.europa.eu/avpolicy/docs/library/studies/finalised/film_rating/sum_en.pdf. Accessed 19 November 2010.

Jakubowski, A. and Henriques, J. (2010), 'Study Paper 1A: Fact-Finding Analysis on the Implementation of the UNESCO Convention', in Germann Avocats (Geneva) and Multidisciplinary Research Team, *Implementing the UNESCO Convention of 2005 in the European Union*, Long Version of the Study for the European Parliament, Directorate General for Internal Policies. Policy Department B: Structural and Cohesion Policies. Culture and Education, 2010, pp. 54–60, http://www.diversitystudy.eu. Accessed 19 November 2010.

Karydis, G. S. (1994), 'Le juge communautaire et la préservation de l'identité culturelle nationale', *Revue trimestrielle de droit européen*, 30: 4, pp. 551–560.

Perez, R. (1966), 'La nuova disciplina legislativa della cinematografia', *Rivista trimestrale di diritto pubblico*, pp. 978–1052.

Schramme, A. and Van der Auwera, S. (2010), 'Study Paper 4B: The UNESCO Convention in EU's Internal Policies', in Germann Avocats (Geneva) and Multidisciplinary Research Team, *Implementing the UNESCO Convention of 2005 in the European Union*, Long Version of the Study for the European Parliament, Directorate General for Internal Policies. Policy Department B: Structural and Cohesion Policies. Culture and Education, 2010, pp. 270–308, http://www.diversitystudy.eu. Accessed 19 November 2010.

Smiers, J. (2002), *The Role of the European Community Concerning the Cultural Article 151 in the Treaty of Amsterdam. Sustaining the Development of Intercultural Competence within Europe*, Utrecht: Centre for Research Utrecht School of the Arts.

UNESCO (2005), 'Convention on the Protection and Promotion of the Diversity of Cultural Expressions', http://www.unesco.org/culture/en/diversity/convention. Accessed 19 November 2010.

Troya, C. and Enrich, E. (2007), 'Spain. Recent Developments Regarding Cinema Law', *IRIS*, 10: 11/18, http://merlin.obs.coe.int/iris/2007/10/article18.en.html. Accessed 19 November 2010.

Vernier, J-M. (1991), 'Cinéma et Administration: le rôle du Centre national de la cinématographie', *Administration*, 151 – L'Etat et la Culture, pp. 45–47.

Notes

1 Under Art. 107 TFEU (ex-Art. 87 EC) 'Save as otherwise provided in the Treaties, any aid granted by a Member State or through State resources in any form whatsoever which distorts or threatens to distort competition by favouring certain undertakings or the production of certain goods shall, in so far as it affects trade between Member States, be incompatible with the internal market.'

2 See also European Council, Resolution of 20 January 1994 on Community policy in the field of culture, [1994] OJ C 44/184; Council resolution of 20 January 1997 on the integration of cultural aspects into Community actions, [1997] OJ C 36/4; Council decision of 22 September 1997 regarding the future of European cultural action, [1997] OJ C 305/1.

3 Although the aid schemes assessed by the commission are often not limited to film production, only support to film production, understood in the sense of cinematographic production, was considered in that publication.

4 In Case No. N 3/98 – France. The author analysed the related decision through a copy of the original one given by the CNC.

5 Communication from the Commission to the Council, the European Parliament, the Economic and Social Committee and the Committee of the Regions on certain legal aspects relating to cinematographic and other audio-visual works (Cinema Communication), COM(2001) 534 final, [2002] OJ C 43/6.

6 ECJ, Case C-222/07, *Unión de Televisiones Comerciales Asociadas (Uteca) v. Administración General del Estado* [2009] OJ C 102/4. On this case see also European Commission (2009); Angelopoulos (2009: 3/2); Ferri (2010: 262).

7 For what concerns the legal obligations imposed by Member States upon TV broadcasters, the commission understands the term 'audio-visual' in its broadest sense, including both cinema and television.

8 Real Decreto 1652/2004, de 9 de julio, por el que se aprueba el Reglamento que regula la inversión obligatoria para la financiación anticipada de largometrajes y cortometrajes cinematográficos y películas para televisión, europeos y españoles, in BOE No. 174 of 20 July 2004, p. 26264.

9 See ECJ, Case C-222/07, *Unión de Televisiones Comerciales Asociadas (Uteca)*, n. 6 *supra*, at para. 2 and Opinion of the Advocate-General Kokott delivered on 4 September 2008, [2009] ECR I-01407, at para. 2.

10 See ECJ, Case C-222/07, *Unión de Televisiones Comerciales Asociadas (Uteca)*, n. 6 *supra*, at paras. 13–14.

11 Even though in Italy, cinema consumption did not decrease until the 1960s, in those years several film production companies failed and many film distribution companies closed down. See Bollero (1965: 90).

12 The translation from Italian is mine.

13 See Opinion of the Advocate-General Kokott, n. 9 *supra*, at para. 4.

14 Council Directive 89/552/EEC of 3 October 1989 on the coordination of certain provisions laid down by law, regulation or administrative action in member states concerning the pursuit of television broadcasting activities (in [1989] OJ L 298/23), as amended by Directive 97/36/EC of the European Parliament and of the Council of 30 June 1997 (in [1997] OJ L 202/60).

15 ECJ, Case C-222/07, *Unión de Televisiones Comerciales Asociadas (Uteca)*, n. 6 *supra*, at para. 2. The ECJ also ruled that Art. 3 of the Directive and Art. 12 of the EC Treaty 'must be interpreted as meaning that they do not preclude a measure adopted by a Member State such as the measures at issue in the main proceedings.' ECJ, Case C-222/07, *Unión de Televisiones Comerciales Asociadas (Uteca)*, n. 6 *supra*, at para. 1.

16 See Cinema Communication, n. 5 *supra*, at para. 2.3(b).

17 This statement is reaffirmed in the Commission Decision of 22 March 2006 in Cases Nos. NN 84/04 and N 95/04 – France, at para. III.H.35.391, available at http://ec.europa.eu /comm/competition/state_aid/register. Accessed 19 November 2010.

18 ECJ, Case C-379/98, *PreussenElektra* [2001] ECR I-2099, at paras. 59–61.

19 Cinema Communication, n. 5 *supra*, at para. 2.3(b).

20 On the one hand, Art. 28 of the Law No. 2009-258 of 5 March 2009, concerning broadcasting communication and the new public service broadcasting (Loi No. 2009-258 du 5 mars 2009 relative à la communication audiovisuelle et au nouveau service public de la télévision, JORF No. 56, 7 Mars 2009, p. 4321, text No. 2) provides that advertisement on public television networks will be totally banned after the television public service's transition to digital technology. It provides for state financial compensation for the loss of advertisement revenues, partially funded by two taxes introduced by Arts. 32–35. On the other hand, Art. 55 increases the sources of funding for film production, including on-demand audio-visual media services, covered by the Audiovisual Media Services Directive (AVMSD) (Directive 2007/65/EC of the European Parliament and of the Council of 11 December 2007, [2007] OJ L 332/279), among the media that need to contribute to the independent cinematographic production.

21 According to Ferri (2009: 1381–1388) this case clears up the misunderstanding with regard to the pre-funding of European films.

22 Opinion of the Advocate General Kokott, n. 9 *supra*, at para. 106.

23 Advocate General Kokott referred to the Case C-17/92, *Distribudores Cinematográficos* [1993] ECR I-2239. In this case the ECJ rejected justification for Spanish legislation in the film promotion sector, as *inter alia* it promoted national films without considering their content or quality. Furthermore, Advocate General Van Gerven argued that this legislation did not have any quality control. According to Advocate General Kokott, this case is not comparable with the Uteca case, because in the latter the pre-funding legislation cannot *ab initio* be dismissed as a protectionist measure adopted only on economic grounds. See Opinion of the Advocate General Kokott, n. 9 *supra*, at paras. 108, 110 and 112.

24 Ibid., at paras. 113 and 114.

25 At para. 107 of her Opinion Advocate General Kokott recalled that, according to the commission, 'the Spanish legislation is too general and too vague. The Commission criticizes the absence of objective and verifiable criteria from which it is possible to ensure that the pre-funding rule only extends to cinematographic feature films and TV films that can be categorized as "cultural products."'

26 See European Commission, Communication on Stronger Community Action in the Cultural Sector, (1982) Bull EC, Supp 6/82, at para. 4 and Cinema Communication at para. 2.3(b)(1).

27 See also European Commission, 1st Report on the consideration of cultural aspects in European Community action, COM(96) 160 final, at para. 3.

28 See, for example, Commission Decisions: of 13 May 2003 in Case No. N 410/02 (ex-CP 77/02) – Belgium, at para. 22, available at http://ec.europa.eu/ comm/competition/state_aid /register; of 22 November 2006 in Case No. N 461/05 – United Kingdom, available at http:// ec.europa.eu/comm/competition/state_aid/register and http://ec.europa.eu/community_law /state_aids/comp-2005/n461-05.pdf at paras. 4.2.2.32 and 4.2.2.55; of 20 December 2006 in Case No. N 695/06 – Germany, at paras. 4.2.2(28) and 4.2.2(34), available at http://ec.europa .eu/comm/competition/state_aid/register. Accessed 19 November 2010.

29 See Opinion of the Advocate General Kokott, n. 9 *supra*, at paras. 115–116.

30 See Déclaration commune des 15 organismes publics européens en charge du cinéma sur la nécessité des aides nationales, published in March 2003, given to the author by the CNC; Déclaration commune des agences européennes en charge du cinéma sur les règles relatives aux aides d'état au cinéma et à l'audiovisuel, published in February 2004, available at http://www.bellefaye.com/Fr/actualite/liste_flash.asp? ID_actualite=1024. Accessed 30 September 2006. See also 'Déclaration des agences européennes du cinéma', (March 2004) 12 *CNC Info. La lettre du CNC*, available at http://www.cnc.fr. Accessed 19 November 2010; Déclaration commune des agences européennes publiques en charge du cinéma, of May 2005, available at http://www.cnc.fr/b_actual/25/ ssrub1/EFAD-Declaration-2005-fr.rtf. Accessed 30 September 2006.

31 See, for example, Déclaration commune des 15 organismes publics européens en charge du cinéma sur la nécessité des aides nationales, n. 30 *supra*, at para. 4.

32 See, for example, Commission Decision of 22 March 2006, n. 17 *supra*, at para. III.B.4.2.2.41.

33 See Cinema Communication, n. 5 *supra*, at para. 2.3(b)(1).

34 See Commission Decisions of 22 November and 20 December 2006, n. 28 *supra*.

35 European Film Agency Directors, Cine-Regio, Capital Regions of Cinema, Common Declaration on the new European culture agenda, of May 2007, available at http://www .cnc.fr. Accessed 30 September 2006. See also CNC (2007b).

36 See Cinema Communication, n. 5 *supra*, at para. 2.3(b)(3).

37 Commission Decision of 22 March 2006, n. 17 *supra*, at para. III.E.20.2.1.237. For a generic definition of a 'difficult film' as well as of a 'small film,' see Commission Decision of 20 December 2006, n. 28 *supra*, at para. 4.2.4(39).

38 Commission Decision of 2 April 2003 in Case No. N 753/02 – United Kingdom, at para. 5, available at http://ec.europa.eu/comm/competition/state_aid/register. Accessed 19 November 2010.

39 This choice is confirmed by the Commission Decision of 22 November 2006, n. 28 *supra*, at para. 3(22)(a)–(j).

40 Art. 1(a)(h) includes among the objectives of the convention 'to protect and promote the diversity of cultural expressions' and 'to reaffirm the sovereign rights of States to maintain, adopt and implement policies and measures that they deem appropriate for the protection and promotion of the diversity of cultural expressions on their territory.'

41 Art. 2(2) provides that 'States have in accordance with the Charter of the United Nations and the principles of international law, the sovereign right to adopt measures and policies to protect and promote the diversity of cultural expressions within their territory.'

42 Art. 5(1) provides that 'the Parties, in accordance with the Charter of the United Nations, the principles of international law and universally recognized human rights instruments, reaffirm their sovereign right to formulate and implement their cultural policies and to adopt measures to protect and promote the diversity of cultural expressions and to strengthen international cooperation to achieve the purposes of this Convention.'

43 According to Art. 6(a)(b), the measures that the parties may adopt to protect and promote the diversity of cultural expressions include regulatory measures and measures 'that, in an appropriate manner, provide opportunities for domestic cultural activities, goods and services among all those available within the national territory for the creation, production, dissemination, distribution and enjoyment of such domestic cultural activities, goods and services, including provisions relating to the language used for such activities, goods and services.' Art. 6(2) also mentions measures fostering independent cultural industries and activities (letter (c)) and 'measures aimed at enhancing diversity of the media, including through public service broadcasting' (letter (h)).

44 See Council Decision of 18 May 2006 on the conclusion of the Convention on the Protection and Promotion of the Diversity of Cultural Expressions (2006/515/EC), [2006] OJ L 201/15.

45 They cannot be analysed in this paragraph. For a critique, in particular of selective aid, see Germann (2010a: 107–113; 2008: 152–154, 273–278) and Germann Avocats et al. (2010: 65–74).

46 Negotiation, mediation and conciliation.

47 Communication from the Commission to the European Parliament, the Council, the European Economic and Social Committee and the Committee of the Regions on a European agenda for culture in a globalizing world, COM (2007) 242 final, at paras. 2.1 and 4.4.

Chapter 18

New Approaches to the Development of Telecommunications Infrastructures in Europe? The Evolution of European Union Policy for Next-Generation Networks

Seamus Simpson

Introduction

Since the publication of its 1987 Green Paper on the establishment of the Single European Market in telecommunications, EU telecommunications policy has developed overwhelmingly along market lines. Policy energies have been concentrated on the replacement of the old, nationally idiosyncratic, state-run monopolistic systems with a differentiated, competitively ordered, series of markets of significantly homogeneous character across EU member states. The consequent elaborate policy apparatus developed as a system of regulatory governance at national and EU levels aimed almost exclusively at the opening of markets and the cultivation of competition therein. The use of interventionist non-market-based public policy levers has been modest, manifest for the most part in measures for the maintenance, and then extension at the margins, of universal service obligations.

However, recent EU policy developments in the area of very high-speed broadband – or next-generation – networks (NGNs) suggests, on the surface, evidence for the potential to develop a significant change of approach. This paper explores the reasons behind the possibilities for such a potential shift and considers the chances of its likely materialization. The creation of NGNs – and in particular the upgrading of the local part of the telecommunications network to establish what are known as next-generation access (NGA) networks – is seen by the EU as being an essential driver of economic and social progress in the coming decade and beyond. The desire to create such infrastructural development has been heightened by the severity and likely persistence of the current economic downturn. As a broad policy response, the European Commission recently put forward 'A European Economic Recovery Plan' urging significant public-sector investment in ten core areas, one of which is broadband infrastructures (European Commission 2008a). Beyond this, concerns exist about the extent to which the by now extensive regulated market competition in telecommunications, fashioned since the mid-1980s, can deliver sufficient investment in network upgrades within appropriate timescales, even if it might be deemed to be functioning appropriately in competition policy terms.

In this vein, in May 2009, the commission released a draft consultation document – followed by a finalized set of guidelines in September (European Commission 2009a) – on the application of state aid rules to broadband network deployment, leaving open the possibility for significant public-sector intervention (European Commission 2009b). However, the core argument of this chapter is that the nature and essential features of its now well-embedded telecommunications policy apparatus, as well as the EU's legal remit in telecommunications, militate strongly against such a move, even if the commission's desire to see it occur is more than rhetorical. This is the case because EU telecommunications policy, normatively and practically, is devised through a neo-liberal policy lens. The paper attempts to show, using state aid to NGAs as the example, that this dominant policy perspective not only de-limits at the outset the extent of state intervention for public policy reasons, but it also fundamentally shapes the character of any such intervention that might occur.

The chapter proceeds as follows. The next section briefly outlines the neo-liberal character of EU telecommunications policy, thereafter providing some basic coverage of the main features of the growth of broadband communication across the EU. The subsequent sections of the chapter turn to the EU's recent consideration of the role of state aid in broadband development, moving in the process to an analysis of the European Commission's policy on NGNs and specifically NGA networks. The final two sections of the chapter attempt briefly to contextualize the recent policy activity of the EU on state aid to NGA networks in the core arguments posited at the outset.

The Neo-Liberal Character of EU Telecommunications Policy Development and Its Implications for State Aid

Historically, the state across what is now constituted as the EU played a very important role in telecommunications, a series of state-owned monopoly postal, telegraph and telephone (PTT) companies being responsible for the provision of basic telephony services. Telecommunications across much of Europe was state-owned, state-funded, state-operated and state-led (Grande 1994). Since approximately the beginning of the 1980s, however, the state gradually and systematically withdrew itself from these key roles in telecommunications. The monopoly service provider was at least partly, and sometimes completely, privatized. The governance of the sector's functioning and evolution was placed in the hands of a series of new independent, national regulatory authorities (NRAs) (Thatcher 1999). Both telecommunications infrastructures and services old and new were structured along (often not very) competitive lines, the regulatory parameters of which were the responsibility of these NRAs to police. Very importantly, as the latter part of the 1980s proceeded, the EU began to play an important role in setting a broad common regulatory framework for the newly evolving telecommunications sectors of its member states (Humphreys and Simpson 2005). This involved agreement on and implementation of a battery of EU legislation of a liberalizing and harmonizing kind, which has evolved through successive phases of refinement (see Goodman 2006; Thatcher 2001). The current EU Electronic Communications Regulatory Framework is the most recent version of this process, epitomizing the classic transition of telecommunications in the EU from the corporate to the regulatory state (see Majone 1996; Seidman and Gilmour 1986;) and cementing further the significance of the EU in the governance landscape of European telecommunications (Simpson 2009).

A key concern of the (neo-) liberalizing agenda of telecommunications across the EU has been to ensure that markets develop and function free from the distortions to competition that can occur through what is viewed as unjustifiable state influence. This has manifested itself in a number of ways in telecommunications. A major issue, raised extensively by the European Commission, has been the independence of the NRA from the state. Another has been the degree of possible state ownership of and influence in the daily affairs of telecommunications incumbent (ex-PTT) operators, though the EU has not gone as far as to mandate the (partial) privatization of PTTs. Much less high profile has been the general powers held by the EU, and the commission specifically, to take action against state-aid provision made in respect of one or more telecommunications company. Over the last 20 years or so, this has not been a controversial aspect of the development of an otherwise often fractious telecommunications policy package at EU level (see Simpson 2010). Two likely reasons lie behind this. First, the acceptance of the neo-liberal policy agenda has been more or less widespread and universal across EU member states in telecommunications. Though the European Commission has taken great pains to highlight any exceptions through a careful monitoring of the evolution of competition in telecommunications across the EU, on the whole the state has willingly and relatively obediently withdrawn from operational and regulatory functions in telecommunications. Secondly, whereas the development of EU telecommunications legislation has been overwhelmingly market liberalizing and harmonizing in character, a significant aspect of successive regulatory packages has been the provision made for, albeit basic, universal service elements in telecommunications. The issue of universal service, and in particular the extent to which the currently defined level might rise as technological and service sophistication proceeds, does, however, tie in with the possible kinds of role that the state might play even in an out-and-out neo-liberal telecommunications sector. Here, the issue of economic development and relative social equity within specific state jurisdictions emerges to prominence. Beyond these matters of 'safety net' telecommunications policy, the efficacy of the neo-liberal telecommunications model in delivering appropriate levels of electronic communication networks and services is also an important issue, the key corollary being that the only likely source of resources necessary to rectify any deficiencies in the neo-liberal market mechanism is likely to be the state. In the present fiscal climate experienced by EU states, however, this too has been cast into doubt.

An until now under-addressed matter in the study of the evolving telecommunications sector across the EU has been the extent to which state involvement, in terms of resource allocation to the sector, has continued in spite of the move towards a regulated liberal market economy in telecommunications. Such an analysis draws in the well-developed general powers, which the EU is able to exercise to address state-aid measures, which might potentially distort competition in the Single European Market and the extent to which these have been applied to the telecommunications sector. As this chapter will go on to illustrate, despite the EU having been fairly active in decision taking regarding state aid measures notified to it in respect of telecommunications, it is only recently that it has begun, through the European Commission, to articulate the parameters of a clear policy on state aid to the infrastructural aspects of telecommunications. The key issue prompting this appears to have been the extent to which state aid intervention can be permitted by the EU in the relative 'leading edge' infrastructural aspects of electronic communication network evolution, specifically in respect of broadband technology. Beyond this, the EU has also recently concerned itself with future infrastructural (and related service-based) contexts in the shape of so-called NGAs. The potentially controversial debate on the role of state aid here has been sharpened by the recent global economic crisis, which has raised considerable doubt about the long-term stability and efficacy of the global neo-liberal model of regulated capitalism, not least because of the dramatic, substantial and sustained direct intervention by the state to save it from outright collapse. Before exploring in some detail the recent approach that the EU has taken to developing a policy on state aid to broadband and NGA infrastructures, the next section of the chapter provides some context on the evolution of broadband networks and services across the EU.

The State of Broadband Deployment in the EU: Opportunities and Challenges

Fixed-network broadband communication has become increasingly prevalent across the EU in the last decade. However, in 2008 the European Commission calculated that the average fixed-network broadband penetration rate, measured as the number of broadband lines per 100 of the population, was still only 21.7% (European Commission 2008a: 6).[1] In terms of information download speeds, a key issue in current and next-generation services, merely 12.8% of broadband lines delivered speeds beyond a very modest 10Mbps. Since 2006, growth in the number of new broadband lines installed across the EU had actually fallen. As might be expected, broadband lines were present in greatest number in the most populous and strongest of the EU's economies: Germany (20.1%), the UK (15.5%), France (15.4%) and Italy (10%) (European Commission 2008a: 10). The fixed broadband line market, unsurprisingly, showed less evidence of incumbent domination than traditional fixed-link networks. However, in 2008, on average across the EU, incumbent ex-PTTs still accounted for 45.6% of fixed broadband access lines, which rose to 52.1% if resale lines in the ownership of these companies are taken into account. Although this figure had been falling since 2003 (from 58.7%), evidence suggested that the rate of market-share reduction has been flattening out since 2005. Though the percentage of digital subscriber lines (DSL) provided by incumbents had fallen from 77.9% in 2003 to 55.9% in 2008, the rate had barely decreased since 2006. Incumbent fixed broadband access lines domination varied considerably across the EU, from 22% to 83% in 2008 (European Commission 2008a: 13f).

This level of incumbent domination in the broadband market led the commission to launch a consultation on future regulatory principles to be applied to NGA networks based on a draft recommendation. Highlighting the seriousness with which it viewed the development of NGAs, the commission noted that whilst 'a number of operators, both incumbent and "alternative", have launched large-scale roll-outs of new broadband infrastructure [...] Europe appears to be still lagging behind other economies, notably the United States and Japan' (European Commission 2008b: 2). The commission's approach to NGA access has at its basis the desire to ensure EU-wide lowest cost, most flexible levels of access based on the assumption that this will incentivize competitive entry into the market thereby ensuring timely, low-cost, high-quality roll-out of new networks and (by association) new services. The former Information Society and Media Commissioner, Viviane Reding, expressed the concern that 'uncoordinated or even contradictory action of national regulators as regards Next Generation Networks could seriously damage competition and undermine Europe's single market' (European Commission 2008b: 1). However, concerns over the ability of the EU to invest adequately, and according to an appropriate timescale, in broadband, has focused attention on the possible role of state aid in the development of NGAs as a supplement, though not an alternative.

The EU's Involvement in State Aid to 'Traditional' Broadband Network Development

The commission's State Aid Action Plan (European Commission 2005) has highlighted the role that state-aid intervention can play in eradicating market failures and improving the functioning of markets and competitiveness. Significantly, the commission has also more recently claimed that 'where markets provide efficient outcomes but these are deemed unsatisfactory from a societal point of view, state aid may be used to obtain a more desirable, equitable market outcome' (European Commission 2009b: 2). The presence or otherwise of state aid is assessed within the meaning of article 87(1) of the EC Treaty and its compatibility determined under the stipulations of article 87(3). There are four cumulative conditions that have to be met for a measure to qualify as state aid: it must come from state resources; it must confer an economic advantage on the beneficiary/ies; it must be selective and distorting or potentially distorting of competition; and it must affect intra-Community trade (European Commission 2009b: 3). In investigations of state aid undertaken by the commission in specific respect of article 87, state aid must be found to be well justified in terms of pursuit of social or economic development or as a rectifying measure for clear market failure. The measure in question must be proportionate to its objective/s and have a demonstrably positive effect on welfare and competition (Papadias et al. 2006: 14). It is also possible for the state to get involved in equity participation and capital injection into a company that might be involved in broadband deployment, in our case, and the EU Court of Justice has ruled that direct or indirect activity of this nature is permissible as long as normal market conditions are found to pertain.

Key indicators of abnormal market conditions, thus calling forth an aid compatibility assessment under article 87, would be situations where there was no medium- to long-term possibility of profitability from a venture and where private participants in a venture do not assume the same risk as public participants. This so-called principle of the market economy private investor has been illustrated in the case of broadband in the Amsterdam decision (2007). It is also possible to consider the provision of broadband networks and services as services of general economic interest (SGEI) or public services as defined by article 86(2) of the EC Treaty. Here four so-called Altmark criteria must be met to ensure that the measure in question falls outside the scope of article 87(1). These are: the recipient of state funding must be formally entrusted with the service, whose obligations must be clearly articulated; the means of calculating compensation for providing an SGEI must be established before the act and must be transparent and objective; the compensation must not be excessive; and, where not chosen through a public procurement procedure, the level of compensation must be determined through an analysis of the typical costs to a company of providing the service while ensuring a reasonable profit (European Commission 2009b: 5f).

A 1999 EU Council Regulation specifies a process of involvement of the commission in the investigation of possible infringements of state aid rules by member states (European Council of Ministers 1999). The commission's involvement in any case comprises two phases. In Phase 1, it may decide that the measure under investigation does not constitute state aid. Alternatively, it may decide that the measure is aid but raises no doubts in respect of it falling within article 87(1) of the EC Treaty. Finally, the commission may decide to launch a more detailed investigation in the light of compatibility doubts raised by its initial appraisal of the measure. The compatibility assessment (also called the balancing test) is based on the stipulations of article 87(3) of the treaty and may result in a number of decisions. The aim is to compare the positive impact of any state aid measure to realise an objective of common interest with any potential negative impact on trade and competition in the specified area that might ensue. A positive decision is one where, as a result of modifications undertaken by a member state, initial doubts raised about a measure have been eradicated. Another possibility is a conditional decision, wherein permission for a state aid measure is granted subject to a member state in fulfilment of a number of specified conditions. If the commission delivers a negative decision, thus finding an aid measure incompatible with the single market, this may have the condition of recovery attached to it, where the member state is required, because of the illegality of the measure, to ensure the return of the aid given to the beneficiary.

Between 2003 and 2010, the European Commission made no fewer than 64 decisions in respect of state aid to broadband (European Commission Competition DG, 2011). Of the 22 decisions taken until 2006, the commission adopted a negative conclusion in only one case,[2] though it is important to note that most of the projects it has considered concern the so-called white areas in which a population tends to be rurally located and sparse (see later). However, concern has been expressed by the commission about the possible intervention of states in 'black' areas (Papadias et al. 2006), something that is indicative of the underlying neo-liberal and potentially contradictory approach of the commission (see later).

In undertaking compatibility assessments in respect of article 87(3), the commission has permitted broadband support measures that are considered to be aid to develop key economic activities or areas where the aid is judged not to adversely affect trading conditions contrary to the common interest. In undertaking its balancing test in respect of the broadband market, the commission proposed the designation of three types of area to reflect the level of broadband deployment in existence prior to the measure under consideration having been deployed. Here, white areas have no broadband infrastructure with none likely to be developed in the near future. These areas are likely to qualify for state aid. By contrast, black areas are defined as those where at least two broadband networks exist and where services are provided competitively. In these areas, the commission has argued that there is unlikely to be evidence of market failure and thus no scope for state intervention. Third, so-called grey areas are those with only one broadband operator in existence. This monopoly situation may allow state aid measures to be permitted under certain conditions, namely that no adequate services are offered to satisfy private or business customers and where it is proven that the state aid measure would be the least distorting of a range of measures – not least among these market regulation – available to rectify the situation. In its far from expansive 2009 guidelines, in these cases the commission stipulated a consideration of overall market conditions, network access conditions, barriers to market entry and the potential efficacy of regulatory measures as an alternative. In particular, in respect of designated white and grey areas, the commission laid out a set of criteria to ensure that the level of state aid and any consequent distorting effects on competition have been minimized, pointing clearly to the primacy afforded to competition-policy considerations over social-policy concerns in communication.

Recent EU Policy Developments in Next-Generation Networks: Policy Coherence and Contradictions

The development of the fixed-link telecommunications network across Europe has taken the best part of a century to construct, a process that is arguably likely to be ongoing in some form or other as long as electronic communication remains a cornerstone of human communication. In recent years, a more prosaic, though key, challenge has been to upgrade traditional copper-based networks with fibre-optic technology, providing the bandwidth capacity and speed of communication promised to users for almost 20 years. A key problem is that although much of the trunk telecommunications network has been upgraded, the vast and complex copper communication nexus between users' homes or premises (or close to them) and nearest local switching centre has proven exceptionally time consuming and costly to refurbish.[3] Thus, the creation of this local, NGA network remains a major telecommunications policy goal, with attendant challenges, across most of the EU. According to the European Commission (2009c: 13), 'NGA networks are access networks which consist wholly, or in part, of optical elements and which are capable of delivering broadband access services with enhanced characteristics (such as higher throughput) as compared to those provided over existing copper networks.'[4] In its revised September 2009 guidelines, however, the commission defined NGAs rather more sparingly, as consisting 'wholly or in part of optical elements and which are capable of delivering broadband access services with enhanced characteristics' (European Commission 2009c: 19). The commission, however, claimed that these networks would be able to support a future converged electronic communication service environment delivering high-definition video and television content, as well as a range of high-bandwidth audio-visual on-demand service applications.

Although the use of state aid funding for the development of 'traditional' broadband networks has, as noted earlier, a fairly well-established, if short, history in EU telecommunications policy, the funding of NGNs through state aid has barely been considered and represents a potentially important landmark in the development of the EU's approach to future electronic communication network environments. In its May 2009 draft guidelines, the commission highlighted the funding of NGA networks as a key matter. The initial tone was set by the then EU Competition Commissioner, Neelie Kroes (who has since become the Information Society and Media Commissioner), who noted that 'investments in this important infrastructure may both help economic recovery in the short term and allow long-term benefits for European competitiveness' (European Commission 2009d: 1). In a recent speech, Philip Lowe, also from the Competition Directorate, made the potentially significant assertion that it was likely that state aid would play a more significant role in the creation of NGAs than it had done in previous phases of broadband network roll-out. Significantly, he noted that the commission would consider sanctioning state aid where there is considered to be market failure, meaning inadequate private investment and inadequate coverage, even where the level in existence might be seen to satisfy some economic goals. Specifically, the commission would take into account equity and cohesion considerations where market forces may not produce socially desirable results.

Unlike 'traditional' broadband networks, the economics of NGAs may militate against their deployment in urban areas as well as in rural areas with low-density populations. The commission has stated in its guidelines that, in respect of NGAs, 'Member States may decide to invest themselves or provide financial support to private operators in order to obtain NGA network connectivity, or to obtain connectivity earlier than anticipated' (European Commission 2009c: 20). The commission has noted that, as in the case of state aid to broadband networks, the market-economy investor principle, public service compensation and Altmark criteria also apply in the analysis of state aid to NGAs. It is important to note, however, that some crucial work required in the deployment of NGAs can be undertaken by the state without it being considered as state aid. This refers to public or civil works such as digging and cable laying. However, this activity, if conducted by the state, would need to be of a non-sector-specific nature and could provide facility to other types of utility providers beyond electronic communication.

In its assessment of state aid to NGAs, the commission decided to continue to use, on a definitional basis, a refined version of the white, grey and black areas. Here, white NGA areas are defined as those where NGAs do not exist currently and are not likely to be created through market investment in the near future. NGA 'grey' areas are those where only one such network is currently in place or is likely to be deployed by the private sector in the near future. This area may be without basic broadband infrastructure beyond that available through the NGA or it may be an area in which one or more basic broadband providers are operational, i.e. a traditional grey or black area (European Commission 2009a: 22). In determining whether a particular measure is compatible, the commission has stated that it will consider the effects of the proposed aid on existing broadband networks (given current levels of service substitutability) as well as the elements of the balancing test (see earlier). In respect of white NGAs where one basic broadband network already exists, states must demonstrate that broadband services already provided 'are not sufficient to satisfy the needs of citizens and business users' (European Commission 2009a: 22) and that the intended goals cannot be achieved by other means, notably ex ante sector-specific regulation. This appears a rather conservative vision of the development of new electronic communication services and stands in contrast to other more expansive rhetoric from the commission about the potential of new electronic communication networks and services in Europe's future development, as well as, more immediately, the role of the communication sector as a dynamic driver of economic recovery in a time of severe recession.

In respect of NGA grey areas, in a similar vein, the commission concluded in its guidelines that for state aid for the purpose of creating another NGA to be sanctionable the state would have to show that the existing or planned NGA network is insufficient to satisfy business and private-user needs. This tightly circumscribed, modest prescription appears to contradict the aversion of neo-liberalism to the existence of network monopoly. The commission further qualified its view by asserting that there may exist less distorting means to address user requirements than sanctioning state aid. This refers explicitly to the role of ex ante regulation and competition policy in ensuring attractive and effective access conditions under network monopoly circumstances. Here, the commission appeared to be arguing that regulated monopoly is more favourable than state-led efforts to create competitively based network competition.

In the case of NGA black areas, the commission argued in its guidelines that any state aid to provide a new NGA network would have unacceptably distorting consequences on competition. However, in developmental terms the commission has focused on the process of migration of competitively ordered broadband black areas to NGA black areas. Here, it argued that there is potential for state intervention in circumstances where broadband investors do not plan to invest in NGAs in the near future. Thus, states can demonstrate to the commission that 'the historical pattern of the investments made by the existing network investors [...] in upgrading their broadband infrastructures to provide higher speeds in response to users' demands was not satisfactory' (European Commission 2009a: 23). In these cases, the compatibility test would have to be undertaken. In addition, the beneficiaries of aid must make wholesale access to their network available to competitors for at least seven years, the access conditions to be set in conjunction with the relevant communications NRA. On top of this, the NGA network architecture benefiting from state aid 'should support effective and full unbundling.' The commission's preference here was expressed for '"multiple fibre" architecture,' which it considers a suitable vector to allow independence between parties requiring access as well as being supportive of point-to-point and point-to-multi-point technology (European Commission 2009a: 24). Though not stated explicitly, the requirements listed earlier will also be applicable to NGA grey areas. This would seem to indicate that the commission's preference is for open-access infrastructure. However, the extent to which state aid would be enough to make private companies invest in return for having to provide medium-term open access is a moot point. The final agreed guidelines, published in September 2009 (European Commission 2009a), contained an important modification of the commission's definition of what is the 'near future' in respect of the examination of the likelihood of infrastructural investment in NGAs in a given area. Originally defined as a five-year period, in the final guidelines this was reduced to three years, suggesting a loosening of the criteria that might permit the granting of state aid. Beyond this, in respect of NGA white areas, should three-year private-sector investment plans be found to exist in a given area (thus pointing towards a negative decision in respect of the granting of any state aid), these plans would nevertheless have to be able to guarantee measures to put them into practice. The current economic climate would suggest that companies will have few immediate short-term plans for major investments, so state aid might be the best way of stimulating the perceived necessary move towards NGA deployment. However, the extent to which state budgetary finances will be able to sustain significant funding of NGAs is open to question in the current economic climate, no matter how important and useful an investment in the future it might be. The contrast between aspiration and capability appears stark, therefore.

Towards a Future Electronic Communication Infrastructure and Service Environment in the EU: The Domination of Regulated Market Competition Perspectives

Consideration of the extent to which EU policy on NGAs might sanction the role of state aid has in many ways been overshadowed and arguably (pre-) determined by a simultaneous ongoing debate on the role that the EU's by now well-established Electronic Communications Regulatory Framework should play in creating the conditions for NGA development to flourish. The growth of EU telecommunications policy according to the neo-liberal parameters of harmonized, regulated competition since the mid-1980s has set a path in which the 'default' context for NGA policy-making is the use of regulated competition to achieve policy goals. It is also the case that the EU's political powers stem very much from its legal–economic remit. This has conditioned EU thinking on social matters related to telecommunications policy to such an extent that, from its techno-economic perspective, the so-called digital divide raises as many commercial-competitive policy issues as it does social-equity policy issues. The underpinning expectation, articulated since the EU's Bangemann Report (1994), has been that appropriately regulated and competitive communication markets will yield social goods. Within this context, only at the margins, where regulated competition has not developed, has direct state aid been considered palatable. Even in these circumstances, however, state action is tightly circumscribed as not to be competition distorting.

Consistent with this approach, in September 2008, the commission launched a specific initiative to create an agreed regulatory strategy among member states regarding NGA networks. Addressed to NRAs, a draft recommendation dealt with a series of matters from common definition of next-generation services to the setting of access conditions to them. Here, the principle of lowest-level access was enunciated such that regulators were encouraged to make mandatory the opening of access to competitors the ducts of incumbent network operators, so these competitors might install their own fibre. Beyond this, however, if deemed necessary to deal with a lack of competition, further higher-level access arrangements could be created to forge competition, such as access to existing-but-unused fibre owned by the incumbent, as well as access to 'active' elements, notably the bitstream capacity of the incumbent (European Commission 2008b). After a consultation period, in June 2009, the commission published an updated version of its draft recommendation. In this, it was stressed that the regulatory framework would be mostly asymmetric, that is, it would address incumbent operators' market power specifically. Though analysis of its fine detail goes beyond the scope of this chapter, it is important to note that the draft recommendation has been subject to criticism, not least from the European Telecommunications Network Operators, a collective body of which most telecommunications incumbents are members. ETNO argued that 'the recommendation would lead to disproportionate regulation as [...] strictly cost based prices for regulated access products would make it almost impossible for operators to negotiate access conditions on reasonable terms and [would] undermine the NGA business case' (EurActiv.com, 12 June 2009). Given the high investment costs, the draft recommendation endorsed the possibility of co-investment schemes, not least in low population density areas. However, in order to be sanctioned, such co-investment schemes have to demonstrate their pro-competitive nature and potential. Significantly, in the draft recommendation, no direct reference to the role that the state might play as a co-investor was made.

The economics of NGA broadband infrastructures, like their fixed-network predecessors, militate against a contestable market – and thus the deployment of the neo-liberal model successfully – in competing infrastructure terms. The commission itself has noted that as much as 80% of the total investment costs here are assigned to what it describes as civil works such that 'in most cases [...] the deployment of parallel fibre networks is not viable because no ducts are available or because the population density is too low for a sustainable business model' (European Commission 2009c: 2). In addition, opting to implement the neo-liberal model of regulation-mandated competition in the context of significant incumbent presence in a market faces the delicate challenge of creating enough incentive for the incumbent to invest in a context of imposed, regulated access requirements. The commission has argued that although the marginal costs to the incumbent of installing extra fibre in any act of investment are low relative to the gains that might be accrued from renting it to access seekers, there may be no incentive to do so should the access conditions be deemed too punitive by the incumbent. At best, this might result in short- to medium-term delay in NGA roll-out or, at worst, a serious retardation of NGA development and damage to the EU's competitive position in the long term.

There are, however, alternatives to the commission's suggested optimal solution – put forward in its recommendation on regulated access to NGAs – of cost-oriented non-discriminatory sharing of legacy physical infrastructure (European Commission 2009c). These might be pursued, at least in part, outside the parameters of the neo-liberal model of regulated competition. This policy option is brought into focus more sharply once the future electronic communication service context in which NGNs will be used is explored. It is here that the long-heralded promises of ICT service convergence are likely to be fulfilled for users on a large scale. Thus, a range of audio-visual services, incorporating high-definition television and interactive multimedia services will be available. The debate on precisely how to govern this new context is complex and has been ongoing at EU level and beyond for at least a decade, often controversially (see Michalis 1999). More recently in respect of state aid to the public service elements of audio-visual media, the EU has appeared to develop a policy from the same legal origins and underpinned by the same operational principles as its emerging state-aid policy on broadband infrastructures. Here, neo-liberal concepts such as 'transparency, proportionality, cost-efficiency, the market-investor principle and technological-neutrality' (Donders and Pauwels 2008: 296) have dominated the policy agenda. Thus, the EU's policy on the role of the state in future electronic communication infrastructural and service contexts appears destined to set out a tight legal circumscription of the degree of future government involvement in the sector viewed through a market-based, competition-dominated lens. In this neo-liberal model, state intervention is likely to be minimal, marginal and effected through a liberal-market modus operandi and policy-goal structure. That this may not be the commission's intention, given the ambiguities in the recently articulated NGN policy explored in this chapter, is a further cause for concern.

Conclusion

EU telecommunications policy has for more than 20 years been underpinned by the goal of creating a system increasingly characterized by independent public regulation of across-the-board market-based competition. Here, the directly interventionist role of the state, although far from absent, has been exercised at the margins of the sector's functioning and development. Recent policy activity of the European Commission aimed at setting harmonized conditions for the creation of NGA networks is suggestive of a more expansive view of the role of the state in the infrastructural development of upgraded fixed-link communication networks as a policy goal. In fact, the commission has argued that state aid to broadband 'may also be viewed as a tool to achieve equity objectives [...] as well as freedom of expression to all actors in society' (European Commission 2009b: 16).

However, this chapter has argued that this perspective is likely to remain largely rhetorical. The explanation lies in the fact that NGA network policy is 'hidebound' within the practical constructs of the neo-liberal system, which has characterized the last 20 years of telecommunications policy at EU level. Thus, the recent commission proposals on state aid to NGA networks articulate any state aid involvement through the policy practices and goals of marketization. Such activity should be marginal and even competition promoting in nature. In tandem with this, related recent draft proposals on regulated access to NGA networks clearly illustrate the faith that regulated market capitalism will cater to future electronic network communication requirements. In a system where the pursuit of competition has been the end goal in itself, however, this leaves the realization of social benefits to the vagaries of a market mechanism whose outcomes are often less than serendipitous in this respect. It is also the case that private-sector network infrastructural roll-out may not proceed at the pace desired by the commission or EU member-state governments, due to the current economic downturn as well as to disincentives to investment and access sharing for incumbent operators in fixed-network infrastructure environments. The case of state aid, NGA network policy at EU level illustrates clearly the narrow economic–legal parameters of the 'acquis' held by the latter – and thus the available degrees of freedom for policy manoeuvre – in the electronic communication sector. The alternative of developing more powers regarding the social policy aspects of electronic communication at EU level is unlikely to occur, due to distinct member-state reticence if not outright opposition. This was no more clearly illustrated than through the EU's last major thwarted policy foray aimed at creating a common convergence regulatory framework for communication networks and services of a decade ago. The commission, at the time damaged by the episode (see Simpson 2000), is unlikely to pursue it again with the vigour displayed initially in the late 1990s.

References

Donders K. and Pauwels, C. (2008), 'Does EU Policy Challenge the Digital Future of Public Service Broadcasting – An Analysis of the Commission's State Aid Approach to Digitization and the Public Service Remit of Public Broadcasting Organizations', *Convergence: The International Journal of Research into New Media Technologies,* 14: 3, pp. 295–311.

EurActiv.com (2009), 'EC Recommendation on the Regulation of Next Generation Access Networks', http://pr.euractiv.com/print/press-release/ec-recommendation-regulation-next-generation-access-networks-10055. 12 June 2009. Accessed 8 November 2010.

European Commission (2005) 'State Aid Action Plan – Less and Better Targeted Aid: A Roadmap for State Aid Reform 2005–2009', SEC(2005)795, Com(2005)107, 7.6.2005.

European Commission (2008a), 'Communications Committee Working Document: Broadband Access in the EU: Situation at 1 July 2008', 28 November, Brussels, DG INSO/B3, COCOM08/B3.

——— (2008b), 'Broadband: Commission Consults on Regulatory Strategy to Promote High Speed Next Generation Access Networks in Europe', 18 September, Brussels, IP/08/1370.

———— (2009a), 'Community Guidelines for the Application of State Aid Rules in Relation to the Rapid Deployment of Broadband Networks', 30 September, Brussels, 2009/C 235/04.

———— (2009b), 'Community Guidelines for the Application of State Aid Rules in Relation to the Rapid Deployment of Broadband Networks', 19 May, Brussels.

————(2009c), 'Draft Commission Recommendation of 12 June 2009 for Second Public Consultation on Regulated Access to Next Generation Access Networks (NGA)', Brussels, C(2009).

———— (2009d), 'Commission Consults on Regulatory Strategy to Promote Very High Speed Internet in Europe', 12 June, Brussels, MEMO/09/274.

European Commission Competition DG (2011), 'Commission Decisions on State Aid to Broadband 2003–10', 11 January, http://ec.europa.eu/competition/sectors/telecommunications/broadband _decisions.pdf. Accessed 4 April 2011.

European Council (1999) 'Council Regulation (EC) No 659/1999 of 22 March 1999 Laying Down Detailed Rules for the Application of Article 93 of the EC Treaty', 27.3.1999, OJL83/1-9.

Goodman, J. (2006), *Telecommunications Policy-Making in the European Union*, Cheltenham and Northampton: Edward Elgar.

Grande, E. (1994), 'The New Role of the State in Telecommunications: an International Comparison', *West European Politics*, 17: 3, pp. 138–158.

Humphreys, P. and Simpson, S. (2005), *Globalisation, Convergence and European Telecommunications*, Cheltenham and Northampton: Edward Elgar.

Majone, G. (1996), *Regulating Europe*, London and New York: Routledge.

Michalis, M. (1999), 'European Union Broadcasting and Telecoms: Towards a Convergent Regulatory Regime?', *European Journal of Communication*, 14: 2, pp. 141–171.

Papadias, L., Alexander, R. and Gerrit Westerhof, J. (2006), 'Public Funding for Broadband Networks', *EC Competition Policy Newsletter*, No3 Autumn, ISSN 1025-2266, pp. 13–18.

Seidman, H. and Gilmour, R. (1986), *Politics, Position, and Power: From the Positive to the Regulatory State*, 4th edition, New York: Oxford University Press.

Simpson, S. (2000), 'Intra-institutional Rivalry and Policy Entrepreneurship in the European Union: The Politics of Information and Communications Technology Convergence', *New Media and Society*, 2: 4, pp. 445–466.

———— (2009), 'Supranationalism and Its Limits in European Telecommunications Governance – The European Electronic Communications Markets Authority Initiative', *Information, Communication and Society*, 12: 8, pp. 1224–1241.

———— (2010), 'New Governance as Political Compromise in European Telecommunications: The Amended European Union Electronic Communications Regulatory Framework', in ITS (International Telecommunications Society), *18th Biennial Conference*, Tokyo, Japan, 25–27 June, ITS: Calgary.

Thatcher, M. (1999), *The Politics of Telecommunications: National Institutions, Convergence, and Change*, Oxford: Oxford University Press.

———— (2001), 'The Commission and National Governments as Partners: EC Regulatory Expansion in Telecommunications 1979–2000', *Journal of European Public Policy*, 8: 4, pp. 558–584.

Notes

1 The range stretches from only 9.5% in Bulgaria to 37.4% in Denmark.
2 In respect of Dutch government support for the construction of a fibre-optic network in the town of Appingedam.
3 Fibre To The Home (FTTH) and Fibre To The Building (FTTB) in the case of direct access; Fibre To The Node (FTTN) or Fibre To The Cabinet (FTTC) in the case of what the commission describes as 'an intermediary concentration point' (European Commission 2009c: 1).
4 Higher throughput here means optical fibre with downstream bandwidth of 40 Mbps minimum and upstream bandwidth of 15 Mbps (current downstream speeds available from ADSL and ADSL2+ technologies are 8 and 24 Mbs maximum respectively; upgraded cable networks delivering speeds up to and above 50 Mbps (current maximum speed is 20 Mbps); connect newly built homes and offices with new fibre-optic connections with 100 Mbs+ services – source European Commission 2009a: 14).

Participation, Power & the Role of Gender

Chapter 19

Public Service Television in European Union Countries:
Old Issues, New Challenges in the 'East' and the 'West'

Peter Bajomi-Lazar, Vaclav Stetka & Miklós Sükösd

Informed Citizenship and the Public Service Media

It is a widely held view in the member states of the European Union and most Anglo-Saxon countries that the existence of public service media is imperative for democracy. Few outlets other than public service media provide the balanced coverage and in-depth analysis of current affairs that citizens need in order to make informed decisions when casting their ballot. Most of the market-driven commercial media outlets do not meet this expectation: quality newspapers may tend to cover current affairs in an ideologically biased way and reach only elite audiences, whereas many of the tabloid newspapers, commercial radio stations and television channels are preoccupied with entertainment, scandals, stars, sex and sport.

In order to create media outlets that provide the whole public with a balanced and in-depth coverage of public interest stories, all EU member states as well as Australia, Canada, New Zealand and the United States have launched public service television channels at some point in the post-war decades (Barendt 1995; Dragomir 2005; Mendel 2000). Empirical research evidence confirms that the relationship between public service television and informed citizenship is more than a normative idea or speculation. Based on a comparison of several countries with varying shares and traditions of public service television (Denmark, Finland, the United Kingdom and the United States), James Curran et al. found that:

> the public service model of broadcasting gives greater attention to public affairs and international news, and thereby fosters greater knowledge in these areas, than the market model. [...] It also tends to minimise the knowledge gap between the advantaged and the disadvantaged, and therefore contributes to a more egalitarian pattern of citizenship. (Curran at al. 2009: 22)

After the political transformations in 1989–1991, the emerging democracies of central and eastern Europe attempted to transform what had basically functioned as propaganda television channels into public service outlets. Whereas the introduction and gradual development of public service media took decades in western Europe, the countries of central and eastern Europe had just a few years to adopt such changes. In most western European countries, dual media systems were introduced after a long period marked by the monopoly of public service broadcasters. By contrast, the establishment of public service media institutions and the introduction of commercial television took place simultaneously in most of the central and eastern European countries (Bustamante 2008; Jakubowicz 2008; Splichal 2000).

This chapter aims at assessing how far the adoption of the public service model of television had gone by 2010 in the post-communist countries by comparing the status of public service television in the European Union's old and new member states and placing the public service television channels of Bulgaria, the Czech Republic, Estonia, Hungary, Latvia, Lithuania, Poland, Romania, Slovakia and Slovenia in the general European public service television landscape. We assess the status of public service television in several dimensions, including the number of public and private television channels and the technology used to receive television signals, as well as the audience market share, the revenues and funding, the supervisory mechanisms and political contexts of public service television. We also evaluate the challenges that the public service media have encountered since the rise of commercial broadcasters and attempt to define the role of public service television in a new period marked by increased commercial competition from liberal, radical democratic and ecological perspectives, respectively.

What Really Is Public Service Television?

The television landscape in general and public service television in particular have repeatedly been studied in a comparative perspective (Barendt 1995; Bustamante 2008; Dragomir 2005; Dragomir and Thompson 2008; Hoffman-Riem 1996; Humphreys 1996; Iosifidis 2010; Jakubowicz 2008; Mendel 2000; Mungiu-Pippidi 2003; Nikoltchev 2007; Siune and Hultén 1998; Sparks and Reading 1995; Sükösd and Isanović 2007). More precisely, analysts have focused on what the law of the land defines as public service television, as the very term 'public service' has no consensual definition. When media policy analysts and regulators use this term to describe the theory and practice of public service television, they in fact refer to a range of different theories and practices.

The theory of public service broadcasting has largely been influenced by the early British Broadcasting Corporation (BBC) and developed in the belief that the media had the power to significantly transform public opinion, values, and behaviour (Siune and Hultén 1998). The BBC's first constitution and statutes, issued in 1927, prescribed that the institution (a public service radio at the time) was to inform, educate and entertain, to report the proceedings of parliament, to preserve a balance between political points of view and to broadcast the government's messages in a national emergency. The BBC was neither to advertise nor to editorialize. To this, John Reith, the first Director General of the BBC, added that the public service radio was to give the listener 'something a little better than she thought she wanted,' i.e., to educate and to elevate her (Reith quoted in Crisell 1994: 21f). This concept has largely persisted as the dominant theory of public service media to date. For example, Eric Barendt suggests in an oft-quoted work written in the mid-1990s that:

> the principal features [of public service broadcasting] can be defined as the following: 1. general geographical availability; 2. concern for national identity and culture; 3. independence from both the state and commercial interests; 4. impartiality of programmes; 5. range and variety of programmes; 6. substantial financing by a general charge on users. (Barendt 1995: 52ff)

Others stress that the public service media is to provide programmes of 'quality' and 'creativity' (Humphreys 1996: 121), to 'empower' all citizens of the state (Keane 1991: 126), to hold the political elites accountable (Siune and Hultén 1998) and to enhance social cohesion (Brants 1999). Yet others add to the public service remit the presentation and the preservation of universal culture, providing a service to minorities (Blumler and Hoffman-Riem [1992] 2002) and strengthening national and European identity and citizenship (Sükösd and Jakubowicz 2011). Similar functions have been defined as integral parts of the public service remit by the European Broadcasting Union (the organization of European public service television channels) in 2003, which, in addition to the functions listed earlier, underlines the need to provide discussion forums on both the regional and the local levels (Bustamante 2008). A largely identical mission has been identified in some EU policy documents as well as the Council of Europe's 1994 Prague Resolution, which states that public service broadcasters must enhance social cohesion, integration and tolerance, fight discrimination, provide impartial and independent news, deliver diverse programming, preserve cultural heritage on both the national and the European levels and offer programmes not provided by commercial media outlets (Council of Europe 1994). According to the Recommendation of the Committee of Ministers on the remit of public service media in the information society (2007), the public service media in the EU are:

> to promote the values of democratic societies, in particular respect for human rights, cultures and political pluralism; [as well as] social cohesion, cultural diversity and pluralist communication accessible to everyone (Council of Europe 2007).

However, the public service remit is arguably problematic for at least two reasons. First, some of the functions traditionally associated with public service broadcasting mirror the peculiar context of the United Kingdom in the 1920s and may be obsolete today. In particular, the idea of preserving national culture was derived from the then strong position of a culturally homogeneous nation state, to educate the public from the then low level of literacy and to broadcast diverse programmes from the then monopoly position of BBC Radio. None of these conditions holds today. Increased transnational migration of the workforce, the globalization of production technology, the resulting cultural heterogeneity and the cultural empowerment of minorities have undermined the axiom of the nation state, the general level of education has significantly increased in the post-war decades and the mushrooming of commercial media outlets has improved programme choice. It is an open question whether public service media should still legitimately be required to perform all of the functions traditionally prescribed to them.

Secondly, some of the functions associated with public service media could be seen as contradictory. Normative expectations such as the search for both balance and the pluralism of opinions, the representation of social cohesion and minority views, the provision of entertainment and quality programming, the preservation of the cultural heritage and the introduction of creative and innovative programming, or the strengthening of national and European identity and citizenship are arguably difficult to put into practice in unison.

The practice of the public service media seems as puzzling as its theory. The term 'public service television and radio' is used equally to describe, for example, the BBC in the UK, widely recognized as a provider of quality programming and balanced news coverage, and the RAI in Italy, known to have aired commercial programmes and biased news (Bustamante 2008; Hallin and Mancini 2004; Siune and Hultén 1998). In an era of fusion and hybridization, public service and commercial media are no longer diametrically opposed but rather two ideal typical endpoints of the same continuum. Public service television channels do broadcast an increasing amount of entertainment and, frequently, commercial advertisements, just as commercial television channels do air public service programmes such as news and current affairs (a well-known example of this is the Independent Television network in the UK).

Further, students of public service television tend to focus on television channels that are partly or entirely funded by licence fees and the state budget and ignore channels that are commercially financed. But then again, the UK's Channel 4 is publicly owned but relies largely on commercial revenues and airs a great deal of public service programmes. In short, analysts who compare what the law defines as public service television in the various countries are dealing with *de jure* public service television channels only, some of which are *de facto* commercial channels; and they fail to include in their analyses *de jure* commercial channels, some of which could be seen, at least partly, as *de facto* public service institutions. However, for the sake of simplification necessary for comparative research, we will follow this tradition and define public service television channels in line with the law, regardless of their actual programming output and funding mechanisms.

From Monopoly to Competition: Changing Television Landscapes and Audience Trends

Before proceeding with the discussion of the role of the public service media in contemporary societies and the related implications for future media policy, let us briefly summarize the broader structural processes that have contributed to a dramatic change of the mass communication landscapes across Europe in the last three decades. Despite the obvious differences between the public service model of television in the 'west' on the one hand, and the state-controlled media systems in the 'east' on the other, broadcasters on both sides of the late Iron Curtain largely operated as national monopolies until about the mid-1980s. Before 1984, national commercial television existed as an exception in three European countries only and was bound by significant public obligations (Brants and de Bens 2000).[1] In other words, for most of the European history of broadcasting in the twentieth century, the vast majority of television audiences watched programmes made and aired by only one national public service institution.

However, the development of cable and satellite technologies and the subsequent liberalization and deregulation of television industries that started in the 1980s in western Europe and continued in the 1990s in central and eastern Europe[2] (Barker 1999; Hesmondhalgh 2002) has altered this picture. All this brought about a dual system of public and commercial television channels as the default model for national television in both parts of Europe. With the rise of satellite, cable, digital and online distribution technologies, an increasing number of households can now access and watch these channels (see Table 1).

Table 1 shows that only 41% of all European households on average accessed programmes through analogue terrestrial broadcasting in 2007; i.e., 59% could watch television channels on other platforms. Since then, the ratio of new platforms could only have increased, as is shown by the adjacent column mapping the diffusion of digital broadcasting (distributed on any platform) in European households at the end of 2008. These figures reveal substantial gaps in the process of digitalization across Europe. Whereas in some countries (namely Finland, Sweden, the UK) all or nearly all television households can receive digital signals, in others fewer than a third of them can. Most of the countries of central and eastern Europe are listed in the lower part of the table (with Latvia and Lithuania remaining the least digitalized countries in the European Union); in many of them, the process of digital terrestrial switch-over, already completed in some parts of Europe, has only just begun.

Subsequent to the exponential growth of commercial broadcasters, public service television channels, the once undisputed hegemons of the air, now constitute just a small minority among a multitude of channels. According to the most recent data collected by the European Audiovisual Observatory, there are around 7700 television channels licensed in the European Union, half of them regional or local.[3] Adding to the extra-European channels (broadcasting from non-EU states), this number grows to about 8600 channels currently available to European audiences (see Table 2).

Table 2 also indicates that public service television channels currently amount to only about 10% of all European television channels. According to the European Audiovisual Observatory, a similar ratio applies on both the national and the regional levels (European Audiovisual Observatory 2010b). There are some exceptions (in the Netherlands, public service television stations account for a third of the total number of channels, and in France for a quarter, mainly because of a highly regionalized and localized system of public service media in these countries). On the whole, however, the data shows that public service television in Europe is encountering a vast and rapidly growing commercial competition. The radical structural change of the television landscape puts the public service media in a new situation, as they must not only (re-) define their mission but also keep increasingly fragmented audiences tuned to their channels.

The market position of public service television as measured by audience share has indeed been declining in most European countries (see Table 3). European public service

Table 1: Reception of Television Signal and Process of Digitalization in the EU.

Country	Analogue terrestrial	Cable	Satellite	Digital Terrestrial (DTT)	Telephone Network and Modem	Digital TVHH (%)	DTT service Launch[c]	ASO Date[d]
	2007, per television households (multiple responses, %)[a]					31.12. 2008[b]		
Austria	6	49	**42**	5	1	56.7	2006	2010
Belgium	2	**87**	6	10	2	32.8	2002	2010
Bulgaria	27	63	7	3	–	22.7	2010	2012
Cyprus	91	7	10	7	1	30.7	2010	2011
Czech Rep.	66	17	16	6	2	36.7	2005	2011
Estonia	45	40	9	5	4	34.6	2006	2010
Finland	43	38	4	21	1	100	2001	2007
France	67	8	22	21	6	65.9	2005	2011
Germany	2	55	40	4	0	57.8	2002	2008
Greece	98	0	5	1	–	22.1	2006	2012
Hungary	25	61	12	3	0	22.3	2008	2011
Ireland	39	31	31	5	1	59	2010	2012
Italy	79	10	18	8	0	55.2	2003	2012
Latvia	42	47	15	1	0	15.8	2009	2012
Lithuania	59	37	4	1	1	16.9	2008	2012
Luxem-bourg	6	71	25	2	1	100	2006	2006
Malta	17	70	15	9	1	54.7	2005	2010
Netherlands	–	83	8	12	1	46	2003	2006
Poland	53	33	16	1	0	42.2	2009	2013
Portugal	64	33	4	1	0	33.8	2009	2011
Romania	14	77	2	8	–	34.6	2010	2012
Slovakia	49	41	17	5	1	30.4	2009	2012
Slovenia	36	54	12	2	5	33.3	2006	2010
Spain	77	11	7	12	3	66.2	2006	2010
Sweden	14	43	19	36	5	96.1	1999	2007
United Kingdom	43	16	31	31	1	90.7	1998	2012
EU average	*41*	*34*	*22*	*12*	*2*	*48.4*	*–*	*–*

[a] Source: European Commission (2008).

[b] Percentage of television households receiving any form of digital signal (terrestrial, cable, satellite, IPTV). Source: European Audiovisual Observatory Yearbook (2009).

[c] Introduction of digital terrestrial television. Source: Observatory Yearbook (2009).

[d] Scheduled analogue terrestrial switch-off. Source: Observatory Yearbook (2009).

channels lost 3.3% of their audience share on average in the period 2004 to 2009. The drop was more significant in France (–6.3%), in Slovenia and in Sweden (both –7.4%), in Poland (–9.5%), in Austria (–11.2%), in Bulgaria (–11.1%) and most notably in Romania, where public service channels lost 22% of their audience within this five-year period. The only

Table 2: Number of Licensed Television Channels in the European Union (2009).[4]

Country	Public	Private	Total
Austria	18	130	148
Belgium	20	89	109
Bulgaria	6	126	132
Cyprus	3	40	43
Czech Republic	5	174	179
Denmark	28	218	246
Estonia	2	14	16
Finland	7	62	69
France	133	360	493
Germany	53	347	400
Greece	8	176	184
Hungary	11	ca. 544	ca. 555
Ireland	4	14	18
Italy	35	973	1008
Latvia	2	36	38
Lithuania	3	65	68
Luxembourg	4	40	44
Malta	2	27	29
Netherlands	219	ca. 424	ca. 643
Poland	25	322	347
Portugal	13	49	62
Romania	12	130	142
Slovakia	3	103	106
Slovenia	6	66	72
Spain	126	1079	1205
Sweden	19	245	264
United Kingdom	60	1032	1092
Total	827	*ca. 6885*	*ca. 7712*

Source: European Audiovisual Observatory (2009, ECE countries are marked grey).

country where public service television's share increased significantly, i.e., by more than 3% between 2004 and 2009, was Spain (+8.3%).

These data suggest that the decline has affected much less the old EU member states than the new ones. In fact, the average share of public service channels in the EU-14 countries (i.e., the old member states, not counting Luxembourg, which does not have a national public service television) remained virtually the same (they dropped from 38.1% to 36.7%). At the same time, the shares of the ten new member states of central and eastern Europe fell from 26.5% to 19.8% between 2004 and 2009. In 2009, the average audience share of public service television was much larger in western Europe: it was twice as high as that of the post-communist democracies in central and eastern Europe (36.7% versus 19.8%).[5]

Table 3 also shows that the combined share of commercial television channels currently exceeds that of public service channels all across Europe (with the exception of Denmark, where the two public service broadcasters, DR and TV-2, had a total of 66.5% audience share in 2009). However, in some countries, the competition is almost balanced (particularly in the UK, Germany, Finland and Poland) and in several other countries the main public service channel continues to be the single most watched television (which is the case in Austria, Italy, the Netherlands and Ireland).

Table 3: Combined Audience Share of Public Service Television Channels in Europe (percentage, 2004–2009).

Country	2004	2006	2009	Difference 2004–2009
Denmark	71.9	72.4	66.5	−5.4
United Kingdom	n. d.	47.8	47.5	n. d.
Finland	44.9	43.8	43.8	−1.1
Germany	49.3	48.5	43.1	−6.2
Poland	51.1	49.8	41.6	−9.5
Italy	44.3	43.6	40.7	−3.6
Austria	51.3	48.1	40.1	−11.2
Ireland	41.3	41.5	37.0	−4.3
Spain	28.2	38.7	36.5	+8.3
Netherlands	38.3	34.9	35.7	−2.6
France	40.7	38.6	34.4	−6.3
Sweden	40.3	38.2	32.9	−7.4
Malta	27.3	29.7	30.8	+3.5
Belgium[6]	29.5	30.0	30.3	+0.8
Slovenia	37.2	32.4	29.8	−7.4
Portugal	29.1	29.9	29.8	+0.7
Czech Republic	30.5	30.8	28.1	−2.4
Cyprus	19.4	22.4	21.7	+2.3
Slovakia	24.6	24.7	19.7	−4,9
Estonia	18.0	17.3	16.8	−1.2
Greece	16.1	16.6	16.6	0
Latvia	18.7	16.4	14.6	−4.1
Lithuania	13.1	15.7	13.7	+1.6
Hungary	19.1	18.6	13.6	−5.5
Bulgaria	23.9	17.1	12.8	−11.1
Romania	29.1	22.0	7.1	−22.0
EU-26 average	*33.5**	*33.4*	*30.2*	−3.3
EU-14 average	*38.1**	*39.0*	*36.7*	−1.4
ECE average	*26.5*	*24.5*	*19.8*	−6.7

Source: European Audiovisual Observatory (2009; 2010a).
*without the UK

The majority of the countries of central and eastern Europe, however, are at the very bottom of Table 3, which is, again, an indicator of a comparatively weaker market position of public service television in the new EU member states as opposed to the old ones. Their audience shares are particularly low in the Baltic countries as well as in Hungary and Bulgaria, where the public broadcasters have only a 14% to 16% share of the audience; and especially in Romania, where the TVR share had dropped to a mere 7% by 2009.

The declining audience share of public service television indicates that some functions traditionally associated with the public service media did not meet audience expectations. As Kees Brants puts it, public service television 'is caught between programming in the public interest and programmes the public is interested in' (Brants 1999: 240). Enrique Bustamante argues in a similar vein while observing that public service television channels had to make a 'choice between ratings and quality' (Bustamante 2008: 192). This identity crisis, whose roots go back to at least the 1980s, eventually generated a legitimacy crisis, as some actors, including those on the political right and commercial television lobbies, questioned the public funding of the public service media and called for its privatization. The BBC in the UK was nearly privatized under the premiership of Margaret Thatcher. Télévision Françaises' first channel, TF1, was effectively sold in 1986–1987 under the 'cohabitation' of Premier Jacques Chirac and President François Mitterrand (Barendt 1995). Denmark's second public service television, TV2, was also converted into a private company in 2003, although its shares are still owned by the state (Jakubsen 2007) and it must abide by 'certain PS obligations with respect to news and current affairs and a continued financial commitment to Danish film,' and it currently sees itself as a 'hybrid PSB-commercial broadcaster' (Iosifidis 2010: 30).

Public service television's efforts to provide quality programming, i.e., to offer the public with 'something a little better than she thought she wanted,' has repeatedly been criticized for its alleged 'elitism' and 'paternalism' (Keane 1991: 56ff) or even 'enlightened despotism' (Bustamante 2008: 210). As a result of the constantly changing general media landscape and the subsequent waves of criticism, and in search of a new identity and legitimacy, many public service institutions have in recent decades gone through what some analysts call a 'never-ending reform' (Bustamante 2008: 186ff). The dominant pattern of transformation has not been clearly identified. Some analysts observe a *convergence* of public service and commercial broadcasters, as indicated by the tabloidization of current affairs programmes and an increasing amount of entertainment on public service television; others find evidence of *divergence,* marked by the launch of several new, specialized, public service television channels (Siune and Hultén 1998).

Despite the evident signs of crisis as well as various attempts at institutional innovation and policy answers, mainstream policy analysts have not questioned the need for public broadcasting institutions. Public service media may especially be needed for an informed citizenship in those former communist countries where much of the commercial media is used to promote particular political interests (e.g., in Romania). The dual media system, consisting of large public and commercial sectors, has remained the exclusive media model in Europe (community/non-profit media constituting a smaller, third sector in several countries).

Changing Funding Mechanisms: From Public Sources to Advertising (and Back?)

Segmented markets, intensifying competition and declining audience shares are not the only challenges the European public service media must face today. Another issue is the changing approach to funding. Although the initial BBC model was built on the licence fee as the only source (which was supposed to safeguard its independence from both commercial and political pressures; see Brants and de Bens 2000), most European public service television has gradually introduced advertising as an additional source of income. In some cases, however, this has become as important as public funding. This is the case of, for example, Ireland's RTÉ, which gets about 35% of its revenues from advertising (on both its television channels and radio stations), or Telewizja Polska, where the share of advertising revenues (62% in 2009) is nearly four times as much as its income from public sources. Some countries, particularly the Scandinavian ones, nevertheless still do not allow public service television to air commercial advertisements. This is the case in Finland, Sweden, and to some extent in Denmark, as well as in the UK. The only post-communist country following this model is Estonia, which abolished advertising on Eesti Television in 2002 (see Table 4).

Interestingly, if we compare the data on public service television funding with that on audience share, we can find no correlation between the two variables. On the one hand, there are broadcasters with a high audience share and no funding from advertising (such as the BBC in the UK or YLE in Finland) as well as broadcasters with a high audience share and with significant advertising revenues, such as Telewizjia Polska, RTÉ in Ireland and RAI in Italy. On the other hand, a fifth of the revenues of LRT in Lithuania are generated by advertisements, yet its audience share is as low as 14%.

Recently, however, a return to the original ad-free model has been considered in several countries where a new model of funding has been discussed and, in some cases, introduced. Advertising is to be completely abolished and the licence fee is to be supplemented by a new tax system. France, for example, announced a move towards an 'ad-free public TV model' in January 2009, following a law that removed commercial advertising from France Télévisions and imposed a new tax on Internet service providers and mobile-phone operators, which should go to France Télévisions. Hailed by President Sarkozy as an attempt to free public service television from the 'tyranny of ratings' and to create a French-style BBC, the reform was allegedly adopted in an attempt to 'help the big private channels prosper in the more competitive digital environment and to create French media groups capable of competing in European and global markets' (Kuhn 2010: 164).

Similarly, in 2009 the Spanish government decided that advertising on RTVE should be replaced by a 3% tax on the revenues of all free commercial televisions (1.5% for pay TVs) and also by a 0.9% tax on revenues of all telecommunications operators (Ibarra 2010; León 2010).[8] In the UK, the British regulator OFCOM, is deliberating on 'the end of the licence fee as an exclusive resource for the BBC' (Iosifidis 2010: 27) and a new model of funding public service television, including the 'top-slicing' principle, i.e., the idea that a portion of the licence fee should be given to channels other than BBC in return for

Table 4: The Main Public Service Broadcasters' Revenues in Europe (percentage, 2009).

Country	Total Public Income[7]	Income from Advertising	Other Income	Audience Share (2009)
Austria (ORF)	52.1	27.2	20.7	38.2
Belgium (RTBF)	73.3	20.9	5.8	19.3
Belgium (VRT)	82.2	8.1	9.7	41.2
Bulgaria (BNT)	74.2	3.4	22.4	12.8
Czech Republic (CT)	79.2	6.4	14.4	28.1
Denmark (DR)	90.2	0	9.8	26.4
Denmark (TV-2)	0	59.2	40.8	40.1
Estonia (ERR)	89.8	0	10.2	16.8
Finland (Yleisradio OY)	95.9	0	4.1	43.8
France (France Télévisions)	79.5	14.2	6.3	34.4
Germany (ARD)	87.9	3.7	8.4	30.1
Germany (ZDF)	85.6	6.2	8.2	14.3
Greece (ERT)	81.2	13.8	5	16.6
Hungary (MTV)	88.3	8.1	3.6	13.6
Ireland (RTÉ)	53.4	35.1	11.5	34.4
Italy (RAI)	56.9	30.1	13	40.7
Lithuania (LRT)	64.5	21.6	13.9	13.7
Netherlands (NPO)	97.4	2.3	0.3	35.7
Poland (Telewizja Polska)	17.1	62.2	20.7	41.6
Portugal (RTP)	77.1	15.8	7.1	29.8
Romania (TVR)	87.2	6.2	6.6	7.1
Slovakia (STV)	89.1	7.1	3.8	19.7
Slovenia (RTVSLO)	72.6	14.4	13	29.8
Spain (RTVE)	62.2	34.6	3.2	22.6
Sweden (STV)	92.7	0	7.3	32.9
United Kingdom (BBC)	77.2	0	22.8	36.4

Source: European Audiovisual Observatory (2010a).

the public service content that they deliver (Iosifidis 2010: 27). In the Czech Republic, advertising on public service television is to be abolished from 2012 onwards and many in the political elites are also calling for the replacement of the licence fee by a direct state subsidy. In Hungary, the government abolished the licence fee in a populist move in 2002. In Slovakia, the government that emerged from the 2010 elections is planning to do the same. This makes public television extremely vulnerable to political pressures as funding comes directly from the state.

It still remains to be seen whether the trend to replace advertising revenues and/or licence fees paid by viewers with taxes on the telecommunications industry or by state subsidies will spread to other European countries and how public service television will adjust to the new funding regime. However, concerns have already been raised with regard to the narrowing of the types of financial resources and to the growing role of governments in determining the amount of funding, which may increase the political vulnerability of the public service media. This has traditionally been an issue of particular relevance for the countries of central and eastern Europe, where the independence of the public service media has been regularly undermined by subsequent post-communist governments:

> In this respect, the crisis of public service broadcast funding in almost all countries of Central and Eastern Europe may be prophetic for Western Europe. Countries without a long tradition of the licence fee – and of respect for it – face a lack of stable funding for PSB, due to large-scale evasion. The quest for more viable models of independent public funding has barely begun. (Dragomir and Thompson 2008: 21)

One danger is that if commercial revenues are not replaced by some sort of automatic funding (e.g., industry taxes or a certain percentage of the national GDP), shrinking resources may make the public service media directly dependent on government. The other threat may come with automatic funding itself, as this may conveniently result in a lack of motivation for institutional innovation and competition, which in turn may lead to marginalization.

The Selection of Board Members and Political Influences

National legislators have made several efforts to ensure the editorial autonomy of public service television, a key condition for balanced news and current affairs reporting. Broadly speaking, there are three marked regulatory approaches aimed at ensuring the independent supervision (boards) of public service institutions. Some countries have created a *parliamentary mechanism* whereby different political actors such as the government, parliament and the president of the republic jointly or separately select the board members (Bulgaria, Estonia, Italy, Poland, the UK and Sweden). Others have established a *corporate mechanism* whereby different political actors and representatives of civil society jointly or separately select the board members (Czech Republic, Hungary, Lithuania, and Slovakia). A third group of countries has introduced a *professional mechanism* of supervision whereby the governing bodies of public service institutions are either jointly or separately selected by political actors, non-governmental organizations (including, in some cases, representatives of the churches, academia, the arts and culture) and journalists' organizations (Latvia, Romania and Slovenia).

Table 5 indicates selection mechanisms for board members in central and eastern European countries. The table also includes Italy, Sweden and the UK from the old European member states as three benchmark cases representing Daniel C. Hallin and Paolo Mancini's polarized pluralist, democratic corporatist and liberal media models (Hallin and Mancini 2004; for the countries of central and eastern Europe, see Dobek-Ostrowska et al. 2010).

These three distinct selection mechanisms are based on different rationales. The *parliamentary* system is rooted in the view that elected politicians have a greater mandate and legitimacy to represent and to enforce the public interest than non-elected civil

Table 5: The Major Governing Bodies of the Main Public Service Television Channels in Selected EU Member States.

Country and Institution	Major Governing Body and Number of Members	Appointment Procedure
Bulgaria/BNT	Management Board (5)	Appointed by the Council for Electronic Media,[9] at the proposal of BNT's Director General
Czech Republic/CT	Czech TV Council (15)	Appointed by the Chamber of Deputies, at the proposal of NGOs
Estonia/ETV	Management Board (up to 5)	Appointed by the Broadcasting Council,[10] in a public contest
Hungary/MTV	Joint Boards of Trustees of Hungarian Television, Hungarian Radio, Danube Television and the Hungarian Wireless Agency (8)	Eight-person executive committee delegated by: • The Media Council (chair) • Parliament (7 members)
Italy/RAI	Board of Directors (9)	Appointed by: • Ministry of Economy and Finance (7) • Parliamentary Commission for Broadcasting (7)
Latvia/TV	Board (8)	General Director of the Board appointed by: • National Radio and Television Council[11] Other seven members of the board appointed by: • General Director of the Board
Lithuania/LRT	Council of Lithuanian Radio and Television (12)	Appointed by: • The President of the Republic (4) • Parliament (4) • Lithuanian Science Council (1) • Lithuanian Board of Education (1) • Lithuanian Association of Art Creators (1) • Congregation of Bishops (1)
Poland/TVP	Supervisory Council (9)	Appointed by: • National Broadcasting Council[12] (8) • Minister of Treasury (1)
Romania/TVR	Council of Administration (13)	Appointed by: • Parliamentary groups (8) • President of Romania (1) • Government (1) • TVR's personnel (2) • National minorities' parliamentary groups (1)
Slovakia/STV	STV Council (15)	Elected by parliament upon nomination by: • The Committee for Education, Science, Sport and Youth, Culture and Media ion Parliament • MPs • NGOs

(Continued)

Table 5: (*Continued*)

Country and Institution	Major Governing Body and Number of Members	Appointment Procedure
Slovenia/ RTV Slovenia	Council of RTV Slovenia (25)	Appointed by: • NGOs and academia (17) • Parliament (5) • RTV Slovenia staff (3)
Sweden/SVT	Board (7)	Five members are appointed by • An independent foundation[13] The chairperson of the board and one deputy member are appointed by • The government
United Kingdom/ BBC	BBC Trust (12)	Appointed by the British monarch on advice of government ministers

Sources: Dragomir (2005); European Audiovisual Observatory (2007).[14]

organizations. The *corporate* system is based on the belief that political parties would not exert self-restraint but attempt to influence media content by nominating partisan board members in an attempt to pursue their own interests, and therefore their powers must be countered by civil society. As a general rule, the corporate model has been more popular in countries where memories of the late authoritarian and totalitarian regimes are still vivid (Barendt 1995; Humphreys 1996), and where influential intellectuals maintain a largely idealized concept of an 'innocent' civil society as opposed to 'corrupt' political elites (Sparks and Reading 1995). The *professional* system is similar to the corporate one but involves a belief in a sound and democratic journalism culture embracing the objective of political independence and the ideal of self-regulation.

The corporate and the professional models usually pursue the proverbial principle of not putting all one's eggs in one basket. They aim at excluding uneven political influence by involving a large number of actors in the work of the boards – but they may blur responsibility for the decisions taken. By contrast, the parliamentary model is based on the alternative, Mark-Twainian principle of 'put all your eggs in one basket and watch that basket,' as board members whose numbers are limited are more accountable. The former mechanisms may in theory be better designed to ensure editorial autonomy than the latter, but we may not find such correlation in practice. Of the countries studied, Sweden and the UK are considered to provide their public service media institutions with a great deal of political independence, despite the fact that their supervisory bodies are based on the parliamentary mechanism (Humphreys 1996). The overall picture is further complicated if we consider Italy, whose system is also based on the parliamentary nomination mechanism but has failed to provide for the political independence of public service television, RAI. The outcome is the same (i.e., pro-government bias of public service media) in Hungary, another example of the parliamentary nomination mechanism. At the same time, countries that have implemented the corporate mechanism (such as Germany, which served as a model in this respect to some of the central and eastern European countries), have also been criticized for failing to ensure their broadcasters' editorial autonomy in the face of political pressure (Barendt 1995; Jakubowicz and Sükösd 2008). Non-governmental organizations may be formally independent but informally politicized. Their representation in the supervisory boards may only conceal the political bargains and decisions made behind closed doors that aim at influencing the editorial content of public service media.

It is notable that all three western European model countries, Italy, the UK and Sweden, use the parliamentary mechanism, whereas the majority of the central and eastern European countries (with the exception of Bulgaria, Estonia, Hungary and Poland) have adopted the corporate and the professional selection mechanisms (Humphreys 1996).

However, legal regulations and the realities of implementation, including the politically motivated (mis-)use of such regulations differ significantly. No matter what selection mechanism central and eastern European states have adopted, political parties in government often determine the outcome of the election of the board members as well as the general directors of public service media. After national elections and changes in government, politically motivated replacement of general directors and other top personnel in public media institutions usually spill over and then trickle down into editorial offices, as news directors, programme hosts and other journalists are regularly replaced by loyal, partisan, media professionals.

The comprehensive *Television Across Europe* research project by the Open Society Institute mapped the state of television in 20 European countries in 2005. The report concluded that in the transition societies of central and eastern Europe:

> public service TV was still associated by the general public with State TV, due to the long history of communist State monopoly on TV, and because of the numerous disclosures of State interference in the public broadcasters' activities and programmes (quoted by Dragomir and Thompson 2008: 38f).

The project exposed and criticized the widespread government control and the consequent democratic deficit of these formally public service institutions.

A follow-up study in 2008, focusing on nine countries (Albania, Bulgaria, the Czech Republic, Italy, Lithuania, the Republic of Macedonia, Poland, Romania and Slovakia) found that the degree of political control had not decreased but actually become worse in most countries in the region since 2005. The sequel report *Television Across Europe: More Channels, Less Independence* found, among other things, that the public service media is subject to growing politicization and pressure, flawed funding models and disintegrating reputation. Public service content has not been boosted by incentives or obligations, broadcast regulators are also increasingly politicized and civil society is rarely involved in the public discussion of media policy (Dragomir and Thompson 2008).

In the area of public service media:

> with regulatory control over audiovisual content rapidly eroding, and the number of channels about to multiply out of sight, the political elites in many of the new democracies are determined to keep control of PSB. In the early 2000s, when their countries had recently joined the Council of Europe and in many cases were pursuing accession to the European Union, these elites showed signs of willingness to refrain from influencing these media. Today, by contrast, they openly strive to restore and maintain tight control, usually by appointing loyal people to the governing bodies. (Dragomir and Thompson 2008: 39)

In 2008, the 'pattern of the re-politicization of public service media' was:

> evident in all countries, and clearest in Poland, Romania and Slovakia. [...] The only exceptions are the Czech Republic, which has seen progress, and Italy, where the degree of politicisation has hardly fluctuated despite changes of government. The Polish TVP (Polish Television, *Telewizja Polska*), which has been a cockpit of political infighting for a decade, is passing through major changes this year. The members of TVP's Supervisory Board continue to be drawn from party ranks and lack professional expertise. They have included the owner of a local hippodrome, a close associate of the mayor of Warsaw, a retired lawyer and a purveyor of herbal remedies to the former Prime Minister's mother. (Dragomir and Thompson 2008: 38f)

In Hungary in 2010, the government passed a media law that put public service media under a unified government organization, the National Media and Communication Authority, which would also widely regulate Internet content and distribute commercial media frequencies under government control. 'Laws like this have only been known in totalitarian regimes where governments are restricting free speech,' according to Dunja Mijatovic, Representative on Freedom of Media of the Organization for Security and Co-operation in Europe (OSCE):

> These laws are not in compliance with OSCE standards, and Hungary signed up to them so now it is up to them to accept my recommendations or refuse to cooperate. The new legislation would concentrate too much power in the hands of Premier Viktor Orban government's and would give it complete control over the media and the Internet. (Mijatovic 2010)[15]

To sum up the regional trends, a significant decrease in audience share, unstable funding and increasing government control characterize most public service media in central and eastern Europe. This results in political bias, decreasing independence, quality and credibility, which eventually lead to falling audience shares. In this vicious circle, politicians in central and eastern Europe (as well as western Europe) who undermine the political independence of public service media, also destroy the long-term credibility and quality of public media programming and eventually undermine the very future of public service media institutions.

Taking a historical perspective on post-communism, since 1990, when the communist one-party systems in central and eastern Europe fell (and after 1991 when the former Soviet Union dissolved), hopes were high for a transition to pluralist democracy, including free and democratic media systems with a robust public service media sector. Twenty years later, we may be witnessing a backlash, a wave of new authoritarianism sweeping over central and eastern Europe. This may be due to growing populism, economic problems related to globalization, the decreased influence of an enlarged European Union (Rupnik 2007), weak democratic traditions and civil society and other factors (Jakubowicz and Sükösd 2008).[16]

Summary and Conclusions

The European television landscape has changed significantly in recent decades. Public service television channels have lost their monopoly and encountered increasing competition from commercial channels and online media. Before the rise of their commercial counterparts, they sought to cater for all audiences and hence offered mixed programming. Today, commercial television channels provide viewers with a wide variety of programmes ranging from pure entertainment to educational broadcasts and documentaries. Some of the latter programmes, traditionally associated with public service broadcasting, are now also offered by such private commercial channels as Viasat History, NatGeo and Spectrum, as well as the online media. The new public service remit must take this new reality into account.

If we compare the situation of public service media in western and in central and eastern Europe, public service television in the east never enjoyed the same high prestige as it did in the west. One also finds a significant difference in terms of the market position and audience share of public service television. On average, audience shares in the west are about twice as high as those in the east.

As regards the funding of public service broadcasters, media policy analysts and regulators are still struggling to find the ideal solution. Although reliance exclusively on subscription fees or taxes may be a solution in well-populated and financially healthy countries such as France and the UK, smaller and/or economically worse-off countries, and especially those in central and eastern Europe, may also need to involve other sources such as advertising revenues.

As for the future, digitalization and convergence – despite the further multiplication of television channels and the fragmentation of the audiences – creates various opportunities for public service media. Some of them have actually been leading the process and have established themselves as pioneers in digital convergence (certainly in the UK but also in the Czech Republic).[17] One may suggest that it is not just public service television, which finds itself under a challenge of reinventing itself, but the whole television sector, or indeed television as a medium. Convergence can be a chance for public service media to win a competitive advantage by developing thematic channels and a rich array of online content and services. Audience participation, online crowd-sourcing, the involvement of bloggers and citizen journalists as well as new thematic channels should contribute to the new models of public service media in the digital age (Jarvis 2006; Legrand 2009; Rosen 2006, 2010; Stray 2010).

The supervision of public service media also continues to raise concern. Again, there seems to be no universally suitable appointment mechanism for the boards of trustees capable of eliminating political interference with editorial content under all circumstances. The political independence of public service television vis-à-vis parliamentary majorities seems to be a matter of political culture rather than of political institutions. Institutional arrangements, no matter how carefully designed, may always remain open to misuse if political elites and a widespread social consensus do not support them. Should this be the case, institutional amendments alone may not be able to improve the public service media's editorial independence, especially in the new member states of the European Union where consolidation of a democratic political culture has only just begun.

The question of how the mission of public service media should be redesigned so that they can regain legitimacy may be answered in different ways. The *liberal approach* stresses the need for a small and ideologically neutral state whose role is limited to protecting basic liberties (including the freedom to seek and to impart information) and to correcting market imperfections. From this perspective, public service media could provide an alternative to the content offered by private television channels (and the Internet) and fill the gaps in the market currently unfilled by their commercial counterparts. In particular, public service media could seek to offer creative content, community programming and a critical coverage of news and current affairs. They could develop a public service test that helps them decide whether the production and distribution of a particular content is warranted by its distinctive nature in the market. At the same time, they could consider ceasing to offer programmes that their commercial counterparts also provide on a regular basis, especially entertainment that is widely available on other airwaves and platforms.

The *radical democratic approach* offers a different answer. It stresses the distinctiveness of the public service media in terms of the holistic way it conceives of its audience and its mission to serve the public interest (Jakubowicz 2006). Public service media, it is argued:

> perceives its audience as composed of complete human beings, with a full range of needs and interests (as citizens; members of different social groups, communities, minorities and cultures; consumers; and seekers of information, education, experience, advice and entertainment), also seeking to broaden their horizons and enrich their lives. Other broadcasters – whether commercial, community, alternative or 'civic' – may also deliver worthy, high-quality programming. However, none of them addresses the audience as composed of 'complete human beings' and seeks to meet every need. (Jakubowicz 2006: 109)

How might all this be implemented in reality? A viable strategy could be indicated by a renewed focus on high-quality content in five editorial areas: news and journalism; knowledge, music and culture; drama and comedy; children's content; and 'events that bring the nation together' (BBC 2010). High performance in these priority areas, coupled with economic efficiency, market impact, citizen involvement, efforts to tackle the global environmental crisis and a rich array of online content and services may ensure the robustness of public service media in the twenty-first century both in western and in central and eastern Europe. Such a robust public service media may then also offer viable models for democratic communication in other transition countries, including Russia and China.

Our chapter utilized well-established concepts of media policy and democratic communication when exploring problems of public service media. There is, however, a third approach to answering the question how the mission of the public service media should be re-defined, namely the *ecological perspective*. One may note that the very term 'public interest,' which lies at the heart of public service media, could be reinterpreted if we take into consideration the global environmental crisis as a major challenge to humankind as a whole. The concept of 'public interest' could be 'ecologized,' as a key trend (or the 'great narrative') of the twenty-first century includes global warming, the massive extermination of animal and plant species, the shortage of drinking water, the overuse of non-renewable energy, widespread pollution of air, soil and water, the waste management crisis etc. How could 'the public interest' be defined in this situation? Media policy-makers should consider ways of tackling how the media in general and the public service media in particular can contribute to alleviating these problems. A synergic, multi-sectoral media policy agenda should put high on the agenda and address issues of environmental concerns and the media industry (from the education of environmental journalists and promoting responsible, 'smart consumption,' to standards of ecological footprint in media organizations, hardware to ensure energy savings and recycling of electronic waste, including television sets, computers, mobile phones etc.). Besides guaranteeing conditions for media freedom and media democracy (including a robust public service media), the greening of media policy and public service media content and institutions is also the responsibility of media policy-makers and practitioners if they want to contribute to the survival and the quality of life of present and future generations (Bajomi-Lazar and Sükösd 2008). In serving the public interest, public service media should be at the forefront of promoting sustainable lifestyles and utilizing sustainable communication technologies.

Whichever scenario media policy-makers decide to follow (and there are certainly further approaches and scenarios to consider), one thing is for sure. The autonomy and independence of public service media cannot be achieved without the support of the public that it seeks to serve – and it seems that earning, or regaining, public support might be the greatest challenge for public service television for decades to come both in the 'east' and the 'west.'

References

Bajomi-Lazar, P. and Sükösd, M. (2008), 'Media Policies and Media Politics in East Central Europe: Issues and Trends 1989–2008', in I. Fernández Alonso and M. de Moragas (eds.), *Communications and Cultural Policies in Europe*, Barcelona: Generalitat de Catalunya, pp. 249–270.

Barendt, E. (1995), *Broadcasting Law. A Comparative Study.* Oxford: Clarendon.

Barker, Chris (1999), *Television, Globalization and Cultural Identities.* Buckingham: Open University Press.

BBC (2010), 'BBC Strategy Review. March 2010', http://downloads.bbc.co.uk/aboutthebbc /reports/pdf/strategy_review.pdf. Accessed 24 November 2010.

Blumler, J. G. and Hoffman-Riem, W. (2002), 'New Roles for Public Service Television', in D. McQuail (ed.), *Reader in Mass Communication Theory, London,* Thousand Oaks and New Delhi: Sage, pp. 202–217.

Brants, K. (1999), 'Public Broadcasting and Open Society: A Marriage under Threat', in Y. N. Zassoursky and E. Vartanova (eds.), *Media, Communications, and the Open Society,* Moscow: Faculty of Journalism/Publisher ICAR, pp. 228–242.

Brants, K. and De Bens, E. (2000), 'The Status of TV Broadcasting in Europe', in J. Wieten, G. Murdock and P. Dahlgren (eds.), *Television Across Europe. A Comparative Introduction.* London: Sage, pp. 7–22.

Bustamante, E. (2008), 'Public Service in the Digital Age: Opportunities and Threats in a Diverse Europe', in: I. Fernández Alonso and M. de Moragas (eds.), *Communications and Cultural Policies in Europe,* Barcelona: Generalitat de Catalunya, pp. 185–216.

Council of Europe (1994), 'The Media in a Democratic Society. Resolutions and Political Declaration', http://www.ebu.ch/CMSimages/en/leg_ref_coe_mcm_resolution_psb_07_081294 _tcm6-4274.pdf. Accessed 25 November 2010.

—— (2007), 'Recommendation CM/Rec(2007)3 of the Committee of Ministers to Member States on the Remit of Public Service Media in the Information Society', https://wcd.coe.int /ViewDoc.jsp?id=1089759&BackColorInternet=9999CC&BackColorIntranet=FFBB55& BackColorLogged=FFAC75. Accessed 25 November 2010.

Crisell, A. (1994), *Understanding Radio,* London and New York: Routledge.

Curran, J., Iyengar, S., Brink Lund, A. and Salovaara-Moring, I. (2009), 'Media System, Public Knowledge and Democracy. A Comparative Study', *European Journal of Communication,* 24: 1, pp. 5–26.

Dobek-Ostrowska, B., Głowacki, M., Jakubowicz, K. and Sükösd, M. (eds.) (2010), *Comparative Media Systems. European and Global Perspectives,* Budapest and New York: Central European University Press.

Dragomir, M. (ed.) (2005), *Television across Europe: Regulation, Policy and Independence,* Budapest: Open Society Institute.

Dragomir, M. and Thompson, M. (eds.) (2008), *Television across Europe: More Channels, Less Independence. Follow-Up Reports 2008,* New York and Budapest: Open Society Institute.

European Audiovisual Observatory (2007), *The Public Service Broadcasting Culture. IRIS Special.* Strasbourg: European Audiovisual Observatory.

——— (2009), *Yearbook 2009. Film, Television and Video in Europe. Volume 2: Trends in European Television,* Strasbourg: European Audiovisual Observatory.

——— (2010a), *Yearbook 2010. Film, Television and Video in Europe. Volume 1: Television in 36 European States,* Strasbourg: European Audiovisual Observatory.

——— (2010b), 'Growth of the Number of Television Channels and Multi-Channel Platforms in Europe Continues Despite the Crisis', http://www.obs.coe.int/about/oea/pr/mavise_end2009 .html. Accessed 25 November 2010.

European Commission (2008), 'Special Eurobarometer 274. E-Communications Household Survey', http://ec.europa.eu/public_opinion/archives/ebs/ebs_293_full_en.pdf. Accessed 24 November 2010.

Farah, D. and Mosher, A. (2010), 'Winds from the East: How the People's Republic of China Seeks to Influence the Media in Africa, Latin America, and Southeast Asia. A Report to the Center for International Media Assistance. Washington', http://cima.ned.org/sites/default /files/CIMA-China-Report_1.pdf. Accessed 24 November 2010.

Hallin, D. C. and Mancini, P. (2004), *Comparing Media Systems: Three Models of Media and Politics,* Cambridge: Cambridge University Press.

Hesmondhalgh, D. (2002), *The Cultural Industries,* London: Sage.

Hoffmann-Riem, W. (1996), *Regulating Media. The Licensing and Supervision of Broadcasting in Six Countries,* New York and London: Guilford.

Humphreys, P. (1996), *Mass Media and Media Policy in Western Europe,* Manchester University Press.

Ibarra, K. A. (2010), 'The Autonomy of Professional Television Journalists in Spain: A New Regulation to Promote Independence', in MDCEE (Media and Democracy in Central and Eastern Europe), *Public Service Broadcasting as a Vehicle for Democracy: Comparing the Mediterranean and East Central Europe,* St. Anthony's College, Oxford, England, 12–13 March, ERC (European Research Council): Oxford.

Iosifidis, P. (2010), 'Pluralism and Funding of Public Service Broadcasting across Europe', in P. Iosifidis (ed.), *Reinventing Public Service Communication. European Broadcasters and Beyond,* Basingstoke: Palgrave Macmillan, pp. 23–35.

Jakubowicz, K. (2006), 'Keep the Essence, Change (Almost) Everything Else: Redefining PBS for the 21st Century', in I. Banerjee and K. Sebeviratne (eds.), *Public Service Broadcasting in the Age of Globalization,* Singapore: Asian Media and Information Centre (AMIC), pp. 94–116.

——— (2008), 'Finding the Right Place on the Map: Prospects for Public Service Broadcasting in Post-Communist Countries', in: K. Jakubowicz and M. Sükösd (eds.), *Finding the Right Place on the Map. Central and Eastern European Media Change in Global Perspective,* Bristol and Chicago: Intellect, pp. 101–124.

Jakubowicz, K. and Sükösd, M. (2008), 'Twelve Concepts Regarding Media System Evolution and Democratization in Post-Communist Societies', in K. Jakubowicz and M. Sükösd (eds.), *Finding the Right Place on the Map. Central and Eastern European Media Change in Global Perspective.* Bristol and Chicago: Intellect, pp. 9–40.

Jakubsen, S. S. (2007), 'Denmark', in: S. Nikoltchev (ed.), *The Public Service Broadcasting Culture,* Strasbourg: European Audiovisual Observatory, pp. 51–60.

Jarvis, J. (2006), 'Networked Journalism', http://www.buzzmachine.com/2006/07/05/networked-journalism. Accessed 24 November 2010.

Keane, J. (1991), *Media and Democracy,* Cambridge: Polity.

Kuhn, R. (2010), 'France: Presidential Assault on the Public Service', in P. Iosifidis (ed.), *Reinventing Public Service Communication. European Broadcasters and Beyond,* Basingstoke: Palgrave Macmillan, pp. 158–170.

Legrand, R. (2009), '5 Ways a Community Manager Can Help Your Media Outlet', http://www.pbs.org/mediashift/2009/06/5-ways-a-community-manager-can-help-your-media-outlet163.html. Accessed 24 November 2010.

León, B. (2010), 'Spanish Public Service Media on the Verge of a New Era', in P. Iosifidis (ed.), *Reinventing Public Service Communication. European Broadcasters and Beyond,* Basingstoke: Palgrave Macmillan, pp. 197–208.

Mendel, T. (2000), *Public Service Broadcasting: A Comparative Legal Survey,* Malaysia: UNESCO.

Mijatovic, D. (2010), 'Hungarian Media Law like in "Totalitarian Regime"', http://www.france24.com/en/20100921-hungarian-media-law-like-totalitarian-regime-osce. Accessed 24 November 2010.

Mungiu-Pippidi, A. (2003), 'From State to Public Service: The Failed Reform of State Television in Central and Eastern Europe', in M. Sükösd and P. Bajomi-Lázár (eds.), *Reinventing Media. Media Policy Reform in East Central Europe,* Budapest: CEU, pp. 31–62.

Nikoltchev, S. (ed.) (2007), *The Public Service Broadcasting Culture,* Strasbourg: European Audiovisual Observatory.

OSCE (2010), 'Analysis and Assessment of a Package of Hungarian Legislation and Draft Legislation on Media and Telecommunications', http://www.osce.org/documents/rfm/2010/09/45942_en.pdf. Accessed 24 November 2010.

Price, M. E. (1995), *Television: The Public Sphere and National Identity,* Oxford, New York: Oxford University Press.

Rosen, J. (2006), 'The People Formerly Known as the Audience', http://journalism.nyu.edu/pubzone/weblogs/pressthink/2006/06/27/ppl_frmr.html. Accessed 24 November 2010.

———— (2010), 'The Journalists Formerly Known as the Media: My Advice to the Next Generation', http://jayrosen.posterous.com/the-journalists-formerly-known-as-the-media-m. Accessed 24 November 2010.

Rupnik, J. (2007), 'From Democracy Fatigue to Populist Backlash', *Journal of Democracy,* 18: 4, pp. 17–25.

Siune, K. and Hultén, O. (1998), 'Does Public Broadcasting Have a Future?', in D. McQuail and K. Siune (eds.), *Media Policy. Convergence, Concentration and Commerce,* London, Thousand Oaks and New Delhi: Sage, pp. 23–37.

Sparks, C. and Reading, A. (1995), 'Re-Regulating Television after Communism: A Comparative Analysis of Poland, Hungary and the Czech Republic', in F. Corcoran and P. Preston (eds.), *Democracy and Communication in the New Europe: Change and Continuity in East and West,* Cresskill: Hampton, pp. 31–50.

Splendore, S. (2009), 'Italy', in Hans-Bredow-Institut (ed.), *Internationales Handbuch Medien,* Baden-Baden: Nomos, pp. 384–395.

Splichal, S. (2000), 'Imitative Revolutions. Changes in the Media and Journalism in East-Central Europe', *Javnost/The Public*, 8: 4, pp. 31–58.

Stray, J. (2010), 'Drawing Out the Audience: Inside BBC's User-Generated Content Hub', http://www.niemanlab.org/2010/05/drawing-out-the-audience-inside-bbc's-user-generated-content-hub. Accessed 24 November 2010.

Sükösd, M. and Isanović, A. (eds.) (2007), *Public Service Television in the Digital Age: Strategies and Opportunities in Five South-East European Countries*, Sarajevo: Media Center.

Sükösd, M. and Jakubowicz, K. (2011), *Media, Nationalism and European Identities*, Budapest and New York: Central European University Press.

Sumiala-Seppänen, J. (1999), 'A Longstanding Experiment. The History of the Finnish Broadcasting Model' http://www.jyu.fi/viesti/verkkotuotanto/broadcasting/index.html. Accessed 24 November 2010.

Notes

1　The first commercial television station in Europe was Luxemburg's CLT (later RTL), which started broadcasting in 1954. Britain followed suit in 1954, launching ITV as a commercial counterpart to BBC, but with a strong public service remit. In Finland, Oy Mainos-TV-Reklam Ab (later known as MTV Finland) was established in 1957 as an independent private company, which however had to pay one-fifth of its profits to the public service broadcaster YLE (Brants and de Bens 2000; Sumiala-Seppänen 1999). In Italy, commercial television started on a local level as early as 1976, and extended its operation on a national scale in 1984 (Splendore 2009).

2　National commercial television channels emerged in 1990 in Slovenia, in 1992 in Lithuania, in 1994 in the Czech Republic and Poland, in 1995 in Albania and Romania, in 1996 in Latvia and in Slovakia, in 1997 in Hungary, and in 2000 in Bulgaria.

3　As the European Audiovisual Observatory notes, it is difficult to obtain an exact number of existing channels as hundreds of new channels are launched every year but many others are closed down at the same time (see http://www.obs.coe.int/about/oea/pr/mavise_end2009.html. Accessed 25 November 2010).

4　Including terrestrial, cable, satellite, IPTV and mobile broadcasters and including national, regional, local and local windows of national channels as well as broadcasters targeting foreign markets.

5　One should add that traditional modes of television watching are declining, especially among those under the age of 30. However, this also means that some of the television output (including public service television content) reaches audience niches through news aggregators, YouTube posts and other distribution systems on the Internet (Dragomir and Thomson, 2008). This secondary use of television content is not reflected in traditional audience share statistics, including Table 3.

6　Figures for Belgium calculated as an average of PSB shares in the Flemish- and French-speaking territories.

7　Including both licence fee and taxation systems.

8 Both cases are currently investigated by the European Commission as regards the compatibility of the new tax with European law.

9 Five members of the Council for Electronic Media are appointed by the national assembly (3) and the President of the Republic (2).

10 Members of the Broadcasting Council are appointed by parliament, on the proposal of the Parliamentary Cultural Affairs Committee.

11 Members of the National Radio and Television Council are appointed by parliament, upon nomination by at least five MPs.

12 Members of the National Broadcasting Council are appointed by parliament (2), the senate (1), and the President of the Republic (2).

13 The foundation has 11 members nominated by parliament on the basis of consensus among the political parties.

14 The information regarding Sweden is based on SVT's information leaflet available at http://svt.se/content/1/c6/33/03/52/engelska-total.pdf. Accessed 2 March 2010.

15 For a detailed analysis and critique of the Hungarian media law, see OSCE (2010).

16 Looking at the whole post-communist and late-communist world, authoritarian politics and media policies have also strengthened in Russia since President Putin took power in 1999, and there are no significant signs of political and media democratization in China. Moreover, old and new authoritarian systems are gaining political and media power as the economy grows at unprecedented rate in China and at a steady rate in Russia. The economic might of China is transforming into global media power by a strategic build-up of international soft power by the Chinese state media institutions (Farah and Mosher 2010) in search of global 'markets of loyalty' (Price 1995). The strategic efforts of the Chinese government aim at reshaping a significant part of global media in their interest. These efforts usually result in supporting authoritarian governments' control over their national media, and countering western models of media freedom and independent media organizations (Farah and Mosher 2010). Other authoritarian countries may follow suit. In the post-communist world, on the whole, as central and eastern Europe seem to experience a democratic backlash, media freedom (including independent public service media), seems to be on the defence, whereas the global power of authoritarian media institutions in China and Russia is increasing. It is within this wider political context that public service media in post-communist central and eastern Europe seem unable to offer a viable institutional model for other transition countries.

17 The case is very different in other countries in central and eastern Europe, where visions and strategies concerning how public service media could benefit digitalization are largely absent (Sükösd and Isanović 2007). Although Hungarian Television (MTV) sponsored the creation of a comprehensive digital multimedia strategy, it was neither publicly discussed nor implemented.

Chapter 20

Civil Society and Media Governance: A Participatory Approach

Pietro Rossi & Werner A. Meier

Introduction

This article starts from the assumptions that firstly we are moving from a hierarchical form of government to a more heterarchical one and secondly that media policy and politics display some lack of democratic accountability. The first assumption can be extrapolated from most scientific articles and discourses on governance that have been published since the 1990s (Benz 2004; Kooiman 1993; Mayntz 2005; Pierre and Peters 2000; Rosenau and Czempiel 1992). In fact, from corporate governance to public and good governance the participation and involvement of all relevant stakeholders in the decision-making process is a pivotal principle on which the analysis of the argument is based. The second assumption is more political and relates to the lack of representation of civil society in media policy matters. On the one hand, few if any of the academic articles have analysed the participation of civil society organizations in media policy processes. On the other hand, and in light of the growing participation of media companies in the (self-) regulation of media matters, one could provocatively ask if we are moving towards a completely self-regulated media system.

In the following parts of this article we will first outline some aspects of the democratic deficit in media policy. Secondly, the concept of media governance and the related forms of regulation will be sketched out from the perspective of different media scholars. We will then introduce a participatory approach to media politics and use it to analyse two case studies where civil society organizations participate in media governance institutions. Finally some problems related to the participation of civil society in the regulation of media systems will be outlined.

The Democratic Deficit in Media Policy

From a public interest standpoint the last 10 to 15 years of media policy and media regulation have not been a success story at all. Both in Europe and the US the public interest in media regulation seems to have been relegated to a matter of secondary concern, whereas the economic interests within the different media systems are at the top of the policy agenda. Integration and ownership concentration have strengthened the leading media corporations. They have successfully defended every attempt to limit their economic growth. Looking at the deregulation measures in the area of the media, one could even talk of the state promotion of concentration. The state and its subordinate authorities tend to promote mergers and acquisitions rather than attempt to restrain them. Since the 1990s, politicians and policy-makers in Europe and the US have favoured the deregulation of media ownership rules without having looked more closely at the democratic consequences of such moves.

According to the analysis by Van Cuilenburg and McQuail (2003), the emerging paradigm has shifted the core values of media policy away from a (desirable) balance between political, sociocultural and economic values towards a predominance of the latter. Issues such as competition, employment and innovation are central to media policy, whereas societal or political concerns are objects of regulation only in the case of consumer protection or 'where issues of morality, taste, human rights and potential harm to young people and society are concerned' (Van Cuilenburg/McQuail 2003: 200f).

For McQuail (2008: 18f) the transition to the new order from the old order of media governance, characterized by strong public control of broadcasting and a clear separation between print and electronic media, can be explained through the greater degree of commercialization and marketization of all forms of public communication, by the higher 'centrality and pervasiveness' of electronic media and by the decline of national sovereignty over the content and flow of media content.

This perceived decline in public control over the mass media, of media accountability to society and the lack of public control over the new technological developments within media systems determine the continuity between the old and the new order concerning a 'set of perennial problems arising from the nature of communication and the important (and probably increased) role it plays in organized social life, from global to local' (McQuail 2008: 25). McQuail lists a set of issues with both international and national dimensions that should be addressed by media governance. These are (McQuail 2008: 25):

- Achieving due accountability for ethical, moral and professional standards of media performance, as decided by the larger community
- Protecting individuals and society from many kinds of potential harm that can take place through communication systems
- Setting positive expectations and goals for public social and cultural communication and steering the development of systems accordingly
- Maintaining essential freedoms of communication under conditions of total surveillance and registration
- Managing relations between state and political power on the one hand and communicative power on the other according to democratic principles.

The political values of access, freedom, diversity, information, control and accountability of media companies to society are meant to be implemented through market principles and competition law. In our view, however, the application of general competition legislation alone is insufficient. Competition law indeed emphasizes the dangers of market dominance, but for media regulation anti-trust mechanisms alone ensure neither media pluralism nor the democratic accountability of media companies to civil society. The global concentration of the media companies in the hands of few big multinational corporations is a paradigmatic result of national and international media policies. Even in the different national media systems the trend is towards the concentration of media power in the hands of a few companies.

These developments raise some fundamental questions about the agglomeration of media power. How much media power concentration is democratically tolerable and where does the abuse of power begin? Or from another perspective, how is this power to be held accountable to society? This is where the democratic deficit in media policy is situated, i.e. where media companies' accountability to society is a matter of economic principles ensuring the interests of shareholders rather than those of the stakeholders. One should not forget that the mass media are central to the democratic functioning of modern societies, as their work ensures the publication of relevant information that forms the basis of every political debate.

Due to the growing democratic deficit at a national as well on an international level, further options for new policies have to be developed in order to promote better accountability of media companies towards their stakeholders. Besides active intervention by the state, transparency of media ownership data has to be improved, so that the public is able to recognize potential conflicts of interests and the abuse of power. Regulatory and self-regulatory mechanisms to ensure editorial independence should be vital. The mechanisms for lodging complaints and judging them should also be enhanced in such a way that they include journalists, owners and the public as equal participants.

And it is at this point that the concept of governance comes into play. We have followed the scientific discourse on governance and media governance and analysed the extent to which the core values of the discourse, i.e. participation of the relevant stakeholders and a shift from hierarchical to heterarchical decision-making processes (Smisman 2008: 874f), are being implemented in media governance agreements in the various European countries. The assumption behind this is that the democratic deficit in media policies can be overcome through the new governance approach by implementing new decision-making processes, where civil society can bargain for its interests as a main stakeholder in media companies. The main questions are thus: how can civil society participate in media policy decisions? And how do civil society organizations perceive their participation?

Towards a Definition of Media Governance

The assumption underlying governance research is that we are moving from government to governance. From a political science perspective the shift to new governance approaches is characterized by participation and power sharing, multi-level integration, diversity and decentralization, deliberation, flexibility and revisability, experimentation and knowledge creation (Scott and Trubek 2002: 5f). However, the state is and remains a central actor in the institutionalization even of non-governmental approaches (Pierre and Peters 2000: 133ff).

In media politics the involvement of actors other than the media companies and the state may help to counter the democratic deficit in media policy. The concept of (media) governance is not simply a further development of steering theories but represents a shift of perspective (Mayntz 2005: 13ff). The shift towards a governance discourse is also seen as a consequence of the growing complexity of modern societies, where the state, the market, social networks and communities together are considered as institutional regulation mechanisms (Benz 2004: 20).

In general the governance debate shifts the focus from steering theories and the role of the state in regulating different sectors of society to the importance of different forms of regulation, to the involvement of more actors in the regulation process and to the emergence of new forms of governance not only at the nation state level, but also at local, regional, transnational and global levels as well as in the private and public spheres (Van Kersbergen and Van Waarden 2004: 143). The state and its actions are no longer the pivotal point of analysis, but rather the *modus* of regulation itself is examined.

From this perspective, media governance looks beyond governments, markets and corporate media managements as traditional regulating actors. Media governance focuses in particular on non-governmental modes of institutionalization and organization, as media regulation in particular may take advantage of new modes of regulation that are less state centered and accordingly less politicized.

Freedman (2008: 14) differentiates among media policy, media regulation and media governance and defines them as follows:

- Media policy refers to the development of goals and norms leading to the creation of instruments that are designed to shape the structure and behaviour of media systems.
- Media regulation focuses on the operation of specific, often legally binding tools that are deployed on the media to achieve established policy goals.
- Media governance refers to the total sum of mechanisms, both formal and informal, national and supranational, centralized and dispersed, that aim to organize media systems according to the resolution of media policy debates.

Another definition of media governance is given by Denis McQuail, who defines it as covering 'all means by which the mass media are limited, directed, encouraged, managed, or called into account, ranging from the most binding law to the most resistible of pressures and self-chosen disciplines' (McQuail 2003: 91).

Hamelink and Nordenstreng (2007: 232) note that 'media governance encompasses the governance of a professional group, of the commons, of productive processes, of content distribution, and of media–society relations.' In the authors' opinion, media governance, due to its complexity, 'will have to be a mixture of different governance modalities such as: self-governance, cooperative governance and interventionist governance' (Hamelink and Nordenstreng 2007: 233).

In our view, media governance has to focus both on the highly institutionalized and less institutionalized power relations within the media organizations and on the relationship between society and the media as a political, economic and cultural institution. The main benefit of the debate on governance and its application to media politics is the shift of the discourse from a state-centred and ideologically loaded perspective to a less political and more process-oriented discussion of media regulation. However, there is the risk of moving in the direction of less democratic control of media systems, especially if the organized interests of civil society are not taken into account.

Media Governance as a Form of Regulation

Governance is seen as an answer to the growing complexity of social systems that have traditionally been regulated by the state. Due to this complexity, the state has increasingly been confronted with lack of knowledge on how to undertake effective regulation. Media governance scholars assume that there has been a shift from hierarchical to horizontal control. For Puppis (2007: 331) the concept of media governance 'encompasses both developments and stands for a horizontal as well as vertical extension of government'. Regarding the horizontal extension of government, Puppis notes that the term 'media governance' covers both statutory media regulation as well as self- and co-regulation in the media: 'While the state is not involved in self-regulatory organizations (apart from presumable pressure on the industry), co-regulation takes place within a framework provided by the state and refers to a mix of statutory regulation and self-regulation' (Puppis 2007: 332).

By co-regulation, it is meant that private actors, both in business and civil society, and the state coordinate the formulation of a specific policy, whereas through self-regulation the media actors and industry associations are left to themselves and can decide and propose their own internal regulations. The rationale for such a shift in the form of regulation lies in the dilemma of reconciling media regulation with media freedom. Puppis (2007: 332) describes the dilemma of media regulation as always being 'between a rock and a hard place', i.e. between the liberal ideals of media freedom and the normative needs of modern societies for a democratically viable media system. In Puppis's words, although there are legitimate societal, economic and technical justifications for media regulation, in democratic societies the media should be free of governmental influence. Accordingly, media freedom restricts the scope of media regulation. In this sense non-statutory media regulation is seen as a solution to the dilemma of media regulation: media freedom is respected because the media can regulate itself.

There are some problems in self-regulation, however, which Puppis (2007: 333) recognizes. Firstly, the self-regulation of mass media may indeed favour private interests. Secondly, there are legitimacy problems with the self-regulation of media companies, i.e. the democratic control of media systems would be abolished. Finally, without the threat of sanction it is questionable whether self-imposed rules would be followed or would remain only at the level of good intentions. On the side of co-regulation, some of these problems could be better handled through the involvement of other stakeholders in media policy than the media companies. However, as Held (2007: 360f) points out, there should be sufficient incentives for the media industry to participate in the co- or self-regulation institutions and 'the different regulatory cultures have to be kept in mind when designing a co-regulatory system. While the broadcasting industry, for example, seems to welcome co-regulation as a form of deregulation, the internet industry is more skeptical about it because there is more state intervention than in pure self-regulation.'

By pointing out the importance of interactions, coordination and presumptive participation that in fact is no more than a simple consultation, the literature on media governance oversimplifies the power structures in the media system. Of course participation does not equal influence, but without access to power or the possibility of holding media power to account for deficits in the provision of public goods, the new governance regime can offer civil society only a freedom of speech within consultation forums. By holding participation in consultative bodies as a new form of democratic bargaining, media governance trivializes democratic bargaining theory. In fact, without the possibility to expose, criticize or sanction media power for unsatisfactory provision of public goods, mere consultation structures represent no more than a protest channel. In fact, media governance scholars seem to tolerate more self-regulation on the industry side, without providing civil society with an institutional setting to criticize the results of self-regulation.

One should ask who the stakeholders of media policy are, because the involvement of the majority of stakeholders affected by media policy should help the policy-makers to formulate more efficient regulations of the media system. Moreover, the legitimacy of the decision should be enhanced through this direct participation in the policy-making process. As Meier and Perrin (2007: 337) point out, 'media governance is supposed to mediate rising conflicts of interest by creating a platform that empowers previously neglected stakeholders, mainly civil society, and at the same time encourage the state and media organizations to assume their obligations to society.' The authors emphasize that media governance may foster the democratization of media and society 'by asking whose interests dominate media companies, to whose end they operate, and by integrating the "neglected" interests into the media organization' (Meier and Perrin 2007: 337).

In the following, the concept of participatory media governance will be firstly outlined. In the second step, two case studies of the participation of civil society in media governance regulatory bodies will be presented in order to understand whether participatory governance can resolve the democratic deficit of media policy identified earlier.

Participatory Media Governance

The rationale behind the involvement of actors other than the one that actually holds the decision-making power lies on the one hand in the necessity for a legitimated input and output process through the participation of all actors involved. Although it should be noted that civil society participation in media policy-making does not, of course, equal influence in media policy. On the other hand, according to the argumentation, the growing complexity of societal and political matters forces the decision-makers to open their consultation and decision-making process to other actors, who can contribute to the decision-making process on the basis of their specific expertise.

From a democratic point of view, governance can be defined as a new form of participation of all relevant stakeholders in a specific societal matter. As an overall concept, participatory governance in this sense may represent the evolution of the decision-making process from a formal institutionalization, which is the classical executive–legislative–judiciary decision process, to a more informal institutionalization, which is a new, non-hierarchical decision-making, where the actors involved sit at the decision table as equally legitimate stakeholders and assume the role of the regulators together with the regulated actors.

According to Meier and Perrin (2007: 338) the fact that media governance is based on a systematic, comprehensive, and institutionalized multi-stakeholder approach makes it possible to integrate (neglected) stakeholder interests on various levels, i.e. civil society organizations should participate in media governance processes alongside established stakeholders such as media organizations, economic interests and state authorities.

Why is such a participatory framework important for media policy? The involvement of civil society in policy decisions remains a central issue in participatory media governance. Yet, the aim should not be a simple consultation of civil society groups but full participation in the decision-making process. This can only be achieved by according the participants some form of decision-making rights. Grote and Gbipki (2002: 25) point out that 'participatory governance also and still requires some kind of democratic institutional settings. As a matter of fact, if participatory governance is a matter of ensuring that relevant actors participate in all the various governance arrangements, their quality must depend on their representativeness, as well as upon the decision-making procedures chosen by them to perform the arrangement.' They stress the fact that, with respect to the quality of the governance arrangement, it is important 'that every holder community has a real opportunity to be involved in the decision and that every holder in his or her collectivity feels properly represented' (Grote and Gbikpi 2002: 25).

From the standpoint of mass-media communication it is clear that every social group in modern society is a relevant actor that should participate in the definition of media policy frameworks, as the mass media plays an important role in delivering information about important political and social issues. Leaving the private media sector unregulated or with weak self-regulation agreements does not conform with the assumption about the involvement of relevant stakeholders. Moreover, if the mass media is an important factor in the building of an informed citizenship, it is arguable whether it would be necessary to involve more groups representing the different societal interests in the definition of media policy frameworks. As political and societal information are in some form public goods, the market alone may not be able to respond to the needs of the public, in particular where these needs cannot be expressed in market values or cannot be identified through classical supply–demand formulas.

In this article we focus on the participatory approach of Fung and Wright (2003), who developed an understanding of a participatory *modus* of governance. They proposed a model of empowered participatory governance by analysing four institutional reforms aimed at improving citizens' participation in local political matters. On the basis of these participatory experiments they identified three general principles that are fundamental to outlining the participatory approach. These are:

(1) A focus on specific, tangible problems;
(2) The involvement of ordinary people affected by these problems and officials close to them; and
(3) The deliberative development of solutions to these problems (Fung and Wright 2003: 15ff).

The first principle relates to the practical orientation of participatory governance, i.e. the problem to be solved through the participation of all important stakeholders must have a direct and substantial impact on the conditions of the actors involved. Secondly, the bottom-up participation should 'establish new channels for those most directly affected by targeted problems' (Fung and Wright 2003: 16). Consequently, the participants may bring their knowledge and particular interest in the formulation of possible solutions. Finally, the third principle aiming at a 'deliberative solution generation' (Fung and Wright 2003: 17) is based on the assumption that 'in deliberative decision-making, participants listen to each other's positions and generate group choices after due consideration.' The three principles highlighted by Fung and Wright are linked to three institutional design features intended to 'stabilize and deepen the practice' (Fung and Wright 2003: 15) of participatory institutions. These are (Fung and Wright 2003: 20ff):

(1) The administrative and political devolution of decision-making power to local action units,
(2) The centralized supervision and coordination of the governance institutions, which the authors define as new form of coordinated decentralization, and finally
(3) The design should remain state-centred by reforming existing official institutions based on the principles of practicability, participation and deliberation.

On the subject of deliberation processes, Blomgren Bingham et al. (2005: 553) note that 'participants consider multiple points of view, think critically about problems and potential solutions, and, in certain processes, try to render collective decisions that best meet the public good.' These preconditions can be found only in participatory governance institutions, because of their collaborative nature. Every participant has an interest in the functioning of the governance institution and, through repeated deliberation, all the stakeholders involved get to know each other's long-term positions.

Innes and Booher (2004), too, focus on the collaboration within participatory governance institutions, stating that 'participation must be collaborative and it should incorporate not only citizens, but also organized interests, profit-making and non-profit organizations, planners and public administrators in a common framework where all are interacting and influencing one another and all are acting independently' (Innes and Booher 2004: 422). They describe such processes as a multi-dimensional model, where one-way communication from government to citizens and vice versa becomes mutual to involve learning and action so that 'the polity, interests and citizenry co-evolve' (Innes and Booher 2004: 422).

One problem with the literature on participatory governance when applied to media regulation is that most of the time participation is seen as enhancing governmental effectiveness in the regulation of specific issues. Media policy and the regulation of media systems, however, are characterized by the dilemma of state intervention. In fact, one of the most problematic issues when discussing the regulation of mass media is how to find an appropriate balance between democratic state regulation and the freedom of press. As Hamelink and Nordenstreng (2007: 232) point out, 'the issue of media governance is quite complicated because media are both the object of societal governance as well as the key agents in the formation of images about governance in society.'

Participatory media governance therefore differentiates itself from other forms of participatory governance by keeping the state exterior to the governance agreements. This does not mean that the state has no role to play. Indeed, the state remains an important player, but only in establishing the institutional setting where private actors and civil society can meet in order to discuss and regulate the media.

Case Studies

The case studies presented here were chosen based on the given participation of civil society. It should be noted that the two governance institutions presented here are not the result of a modern shift from top-down government to horizontal governance. In fact, both advertising regulation institutions in France and the United Kingdom were founded long before the beginning of the governance debate (although both have been reformed in recent years and bottomed-up at the initiative of the industry). The analysis is based upon both documentary analysis and semi-structured expert interviews with representatives of civil society involved in the decision-making process and institution officials.[1, 2]

It should be pointed out that the advertising regulation in France and the UK is not a strict co-regulation between media industry and civil society, because in both cases the codex is formulated by councils made up only of media professionals. Nonetheless, in both cases civil society is involved in a consultative manner, i.e. every change in the regulation codex is discussed first with the representatives of the civil society, who cannot change the codex though their opinions are in fact taken seriously. So in both cases we can speak of self-regulation with a sort of deliberative cooperation. Where civil society plays a role is in the implementation of the codex by judging the advertising content either *a priori* in a pre-clearing manner or *a posteriori* in response to complaints registered.

French Advertising Regulation

The history of France's advertising regulation is a long one. Regulation began as early as 1935, with the creation of the Bureau de Verification de la Publicité (Advertising Review Office) and has recently been reformed. From the perspective of civil society it was an important reform, as representatives of civil society organizations were involved in the regulatory agency for the first time. The reform was initiated following the EU *White Paper on Governance* (EU 2001) and the recommendations proposed in the EU document 'Better Regulation' (EU 2003) and culminated in 2008 with the creation of the *Autorité de Regulation Professionnelle de la Publicité*, ARPP (Professional Advertising Regulatory Agency), which is chaired by Jean-Pierre Teyssier, who was interviewed as an expert, and the three related institutions: the *Conseil de l'Ethique Publicitaire*, the *Jury Deontologique de la Publicité* and the *Conseil Paritarie de la Publicitè*. The last of these is where civil society participates, and is at the centre of the analysis in this article.

The *Conseil Paritaire de la Publicité* (CPP) is a place for dialogue and cooperation between representatives of civil society (mostly consumers' and environmental associations) and representatives of the advertising and media industry. The CPP has 18 members – 9 professionals and 9 civil society representatives – and is chaired by one of its members from the associative sphere. Currently the CPP is chaired by Michel Bonnet, who was interviewed for the purposes of this research. The mission of the CPP is to alert the ARPP Board of Directors to the expectations of various associations or bodies concerning the content of advertisements. It also contributes to the discussion on the constant re-evaluation of the self-regulatory codes.

UK Advertising Regulation

In the UK advertising is regulated by two codes, which are administered by the Committee of Advertising Practice (CAP) and the Broadcasting Committee of Advertising Practice (BCAP). Both committees are self-regulatory, i.e. the participating parties are exclusively media-industry actors. However, the complaints are judged by the Advertising Standards Authority,[3] which is composed of one-third industry representatives and two-thirds independent members. Independence is a very important feature of the ASA non-industry members, meaning that even if the members are in some cases representatives of civil society organizations they cannot participate in deliberations involving their organizations. Every member of the ASA is expected to act as an individual and to 'exercise moral authority rather than [...] act as representatives of any particular industry or interest' (interview with Olivia Campbell, ASA spokesperson).

The rationale behind British advertising regulation is based on the assumption that, due to the high number of advertisements, verification *a priori* is not possible. Any citizen in the UK is entitled to file a complaint, which must firstly be judged as receivable. If the complaint passes the receivabilty test, and after an informal mediation talk with the affected parties, the ASA council is charged with instructing an investigation. Finally, if it is ruled that the advertisement infringes the advertising codes then it must be withdrawn from public view. In addition, the deontological infringement is made public on the basis of what in the UK is known as the *name and shame* strategy.

Evaluation

In order to assess the participatory characteristics of the two case studies we rely on five[4] critical questions that Fung and Wright (2003: 30) developed to analyse their cases of participatory governance. The answers to the following questions are extrapolated from the documents and interviews with experts from the two governance institutions. However, it must be noted that some questions cannot be answered on the same basis as Fung and Wright, because in the field of media regulation there are always some restrictions related to the freedom of the media.

1. *How genuinely deliberative are the actual decision-making processes?*
Fung and Wright (2003: 30) point out that 'equitable decisions depend upon parties agreeing to that which is fair rather than pushing for as much as they can get.' Every expert interviewed for this article emphasized how the discussions within the councils were agreeable and that no one found that there were remediless clashes of interest within the councils. Neil Watts from the ASA Council noted that:

> You often forget who is representing industry and who is representing society. In five years experience within the ASA the decisions were rarely taken with disagreement between the media side and the society side.

Speaking about how he perceives the deliberation process within the ASA Council he goes further and states that:

> We are just a team of people. Sometimes the media representatives say something from their background which is useful to us to know and the other way around. We simply bring bits of information to the discussion table.

On the same line of thought was Michel Bonnet from the Conseil Paritaire de la Publicité, who underlines how even the media representatives were astonished at how fair and balanced the deliberation process within the CPP was. Both sides learned how to learn from the other side and in the end it is a win–win situation.

2. How effectively are decisions translated into action?

Both governance institutions in France and the UK are very effective in translating their decisions into action. However, in France there is a more comprehensive procedure, where the advertisers are pre-advised about the content of their advertisements, whereas in the UK the ASA Council acts only in response to complaints made by individuals or organizations. Nevertheless, in the UK a company or advertising agency may be forced to ask for copy advice, which is like the a *priori* check in France, if it has previously been punished for other advertisements. The pre-publication control in France is carried by a group of lawyers and experts on advertising deontology within the ARPP, whereas in the UK the advertiser may freely choose to seek advance 'copy advice' in order to be sure they are not infringing the advertising codes.

Neil Watts notes that the ASA is successful, quick to respond and less expensive than using the law, but clearly dependent on industry (financial) support and government influence. Speaking about how the ASA decisions influence and regulate the advertising industry he stated that:

> In the United Kingdom it is very clear that the publication of one assessment of judication against an advertiser will appear on national news and national newspaper. In fact not having a complaint being upheld by the ASA is very important for industry representatives and media companies. The assessments are regularly given attention in the broadcast programmes. The public judication of a decision of the ASA is very powerful.

On this basis the best way to effectively auto-regulate the industry is thought to be a public and independent judgement of problematic advertisements, which could seriously damage the image of the brands concerned.

3. To what extent are the deliberative bodies able to effectively monitor the implementation of their decisions?

According to Fung and Wright (2003: 31) the implementation of deliberatively taken decisions also demands monitoring and accountability mechanisms. The implementation of the decisions both in France and the UK is not formally monitored. One could say that the monitoring of advertising is largely done by the public itself. In France the ARPP starts a new monitoring of specific issues every year. This is done officially as an exploration of a new advertising issue in order to report to the authorities, e.g. the reports on advertising and environment and advertising and female representation in 2007, on advertising and ethnic diversity in 2008 (ARPP 2009).

In the UK the monitoring task is performed directly by the CAP and BCAP; thus it is formally a self-monitoring by the industry. In a similar way to the ARPP in France, the monitoring surveys are carried out regularly on specific issues by *ad hoc* monitoring groups (CAP 2009).

4. To what extent do the deliberative processes constitute 'schools for democracy'?

Fung and Wright (2003: 32) argue that 'by seeing that cooperation mediated through reasonable deliberation yields benefits not accessible through adversarial methods, participants might increase their disposition to be reasonable and to transform narrowly self-interested preferences accordingly'. In fact all the experts interviewed agree that the governance experience within the advertising regulation bodies has positive effects on their perception of the media industry. Michel Bonnet notes how, since the inception of the CPP, every participant has been committed to actively listening to other positions and, even if there is a disagreement, the deliberations are based on the search of a 'best' common denominator.

However, Bonnet emphasizes how important it is for the civil society representatives to be trained regarding advertising issues. Without such training effective deliberation between advertising professional and non-professional would not be possible. The civil society representatives must know how the industry thinks and works in order to regulate advertising effectively. In this sense the ARPP as well as the ASA regularly offer staff training on the state of the art in the industry and on important legal and ethical problems related to different advertising content issues, both for civil society representatives and advertisers.

5. Are the actual outcomes of the entire process more desirable than those of prior institutional arrangements?

One must note that in neither country have there been major changes to how the advertising industry is regulated in recent decades. Nonetheless, the experts were asked about the benefits of such participatory governance approaches, especially from their perspective as civil society representatives. On the participation of civil society in the ASA, Neil Watts stated:

> It helps the councils to have a cross-section of society on its memberships. The representation of civil society within the ASA is excellent both in a gender and professional manner.

The self-regulation of the industry, too, is praised as a crucial feature for the success of the regulatory efforts. Jean Pierre Teyssier notes how important it is that the industry representatives maintain some form of control over the advertising codes. If they did not have this, the advertisers would not participate. Neil Watts, too, is convinced about the necessity of a self-regulating institution, because it brings a form of regulation that the media professionals are more comfortable with and over which they have a significant influence.

Teyssier points out that the accountability and transparency of the ARPP towards the government and the public are as crucial as the self-regulation of the industry. Accountability and transparency are guaranteed by public reports, which the ARPP publishes on his website, by the involvement of civil society organizations in the decision-making process and by the coverage that the mass media gives to the decisions of the ARPP.

Neil Watts summarizes the benefits of the regulation of advertising through the ASA as follows:

> The ASA gives confidence to society that if there is an advertisement which appears violent, racist, or generally advertising that should not be seen in the public arena, the public can take action. It also helps advertisers in the sense that it polices the industry by preventing others advertisers from using shock advertising. It keeps everybody (in the advertising industry) equal and gives consumers the right to complain, which is separate from the state and the law.

Asked about the potential transfer of the participatory approach from advertising regulation to other media regulation issues, all experts agree that it might be possible under specific conditions. The most important of these is the self-regulative nature of any media governance agreement. Without some form of self-regulation the media professionals and media companies may feel threatened in their freedom of expression or in their media freedom. All experts agree that we are moving towards greater self-regulation and are optimistic that their experience in participatory media governance institutions may become a school for media democracy.

From Media Regulation to Participatory Media Governance: Still a Long Journey

The growing complexity of media systems is often used as a rationale for the emergence of media governance, for the shift from top-down hierarchical political decision-making to more flexible and horizontal decision-making. But eventually a change within the decision-making structures reflects the need for a better approach to some political issues through some kind of regulation. Because, as we have seen, media governance is still regulation – from mandatory regulation to co- and self-regulation.

However, it should be noted that the academic discourse on media governance reveals only examples of the neglect of participation in the media policy process. This is regrettable, especially from a democratic point of view. In fact, if we are moving from top-down media policy to more horizontal and self-regulation processes, one could ask what about the democratic legitimacy of such processes? If the democratic state is going to step aside, who is going to replace the democratically elected politicians who participate in media politics as representatives of different constituencies? Freedom of the media should not mean freedom from regulation or freedom from democratic control. In fact, if the benefit of the governance approaches is a shift away from over-politicized media regulations towards multi-stakeholder approaches, then there should be more consideration for the neglected stakeholders, because as McQuail (1997: 511f) argued 'the principal dilemma faced is how to reconcile the increasing significance of media with the declining capacity to control them, on behalf of the general good.' In fact, allowing the media to regulate itself as an answer to the growing complexity of and the loss of control over media sytems would be absurd.

In order to answer the questions of how civil society can participate and how this participation is perceived, the governance approaches to advertising regulation both in France and UK are good examples of the involvement of civil society organizations in media governance institutions. With the analysis of the two governance institutions we have learned that:

- The deliberation process within the CPP and the ASA-Council is perceived as a benefit both to the advertising industry and the civil society organizations, which achieve a better understanding of the counterpart. This is a fundamental feature of participatory governance approaches, because it allows a conflict resolution based on achieving what seems reasonable and fair rather than pushing for as much as one can get. The governance experience and the deliberative processes within advertising regulation in the UK and in France should therefore be taken as good examples of the successful involvement of civil society organizations in the regulation of media matters. These two examples have shown that as a matter of fact civil society – through participation – can influence media policy.
- The advertising councils in the UK and France offer a platform where neglected stakeholders can assert their interests regarding media organizations and the state, which in this way may better assume their obligations, as Meier und Perrin point out (2007: 337). As the market alone may not be adequate in order to respond to the needs of the public, these governance institutions are seen as the right place for additional mediation and better mutual understanding. More information and interaction might even ameliorate the much-praised market mechanisms.
- Making the decision public is also a very important feature for the implementation of the decisions, not only as a discouraging 'name and shame' strategy towards the advertisers, but also as a form of accountability to the public. This publicity should be seen as an effective form of sanction, where the public is regularly informed about the shortcomings of the regulated actors. It is also a way of holding media companies accountable for their published content, which will be critically discussed in an open manner. Negative publicity resulting from a decision by the councils is perceived as an equally if not more efficient sanction than fines. On the other hand the extent to which some civil society organizations have a legitimate role in the governance institution remains unclear.
- The coexistence of self-drafted codes with an enforcement council where civil society interests are represented bridges the dilemma between media regulation and media freedom. In fact, the advertising industry seems to accept that non-industry representatives can judge the advertising content as long as the drafting of the regulatory code remains an initiative of the industry.

Despite the cooperative experiences in the advertising regulation, the way towards more democratic accountability of media companies is still a long one. Advertising governance is just a small step in the cooperation between the media industry and civil society in the regulation mostly of moral issues related to this pervasive form of communication. But media content is not only advertising. Democratic media governance, whether it is traditional media regulation or participatory media governance, should not be limited to advertising regulation, but expand to all issues related the production and consumption of media products. We are therefore concluding with three recommendations intended to foster democratic media governance in media sectors that are vital to the dissemination of political and social information:

(1) In order to achieve a more democratic regulation of media matters, the media companies should be firstly encouraged to adopt self-regulating codes, which must be open to public scrutiny and discussion in every sector, from media ownership to editorial policies.
(2) Following the deliberative experience of advertising regulation, various councils should be established in which civil society and media professionals' representatives can interact constructively. This would allow an open exchange of information that can help both sides.
(3) The state still has a role to play within this mediation process, especially by pressuring the media industry to adopt self-regulating codes and by fostering governance agreements where civil society organizations can participate as stakeholders. Moreover, the state should institutionalize some form of professional training for civil society organizations that are affected by mass media.

Participatory media governance could reinvigorate the democratic legitimacy of the mass media in civil society, firstly by giving organized interests within civil society some decision-making power, at least over the implementation of the codes, and secondly by assuring media companies that they are on the right path to satisfying the needs of their most important stakeholders, namely the public who buy their products.

Acknowledgements

This article is part of the research project 'From Media Regulation to Democratic Media Governance?' financed by the Swiss National Science Foundation.

References

ARPP (Autorité de Régulation Professionnelle de la Publicité) (2009), *Etudes ARPP*, http://www.arpp-pub.org/Etudes.html. Accessed 7 October 2010.

ASA (Advertising Standard Authority) (2009), *Advertising Under Control*, http://www.asa.org. uk/Regulation-Explained/Control-of-ads.aspx. Accessed 7 October 2010.

Benz, A. (2004), 'Governance – Modebegriff oder nützliches sozialwissenschaftliches Konzept?', in A. Benz (ed.), *Governance – Regieren in komplexen Regelsystemen*, Wiesbaden: VS, pp. 11–28.

Blomgren Bingham, L., Nabatchi, T. and O'Leary, R. (2005), 'The New Governance: Practices and Processes for Stakeholder and Citizen Participation in the Work of Government', *Public Administration Review*, 65: 5, pp. 547–558.

CAP (Committee of Advertising Practice) (2009), *Research and Surveys*, http://www.cap.org.uk /Resource-Centre/Research-and-surveys.aspx. Accessed 7 October 2010.

EU (European Union) (2001), *Governance in the European Union: A White Paper*, http://eurlex. europa.eu/LexUriServ/site/en/com/2001/com2001_0428en01.pdf. Accessed 7 October 2010.

EU (European Union) (2003), *Interinstitutional Agreement on Better Law-Making*, http://eur-lex.europa.eu/LexUriServ/LexUriServ.do?uri=OJ:C:2003:321:0001:0005:EN:PDF. Accessed 7 October 2010.

Freedman, D. (2008), *The Politics of Media Policy*, Cambridge: Polity Press.

Fung, A. and Wright, E. O. (2003), 'Thinking about Empowered Participatory Governance', in A. Fung and E. O. Wright (eds.), *Deepening Democracy: Insitutional Innovations in Empowered Participatory Governance*, London: Verso, pp. 3–42.

Grote, J. R. and Gbikpi, B. (2002), 'Introduction', in J. R. Grote and B. Gbikpi (eds.), *Participatory Governance: Political and Societal Implications*, Opladen: Leske + Budrich, pp. 17–34.

Hamelink, C. J. and Nordenstreng, K. (2007), 'Towards Democratic Media Governance', in E. De Bens (ed.), *Media Between Culture and Commerce: An Introduction*, Bristol: Intellect, pp. 225–240.

Held, T. (2007), 'Co-Regulation in European Union Member States', *Communications*, 32: 3, pp. 355–362.

Innes, J. E. and Booher, D. E. (2004), 'Reframing Public Participation: Strategies for the 21st Century', *Planning Theory & Practice*, 5: 4, pp. 419–436.

Kooiman, J (ed.) (1993), *Modern Governance: New Government-Society Interactions*, London: Sage.

Mayntz, R. (2005), 'Governance Theory als fortentwickelte Steuerungstheorie?', in G. F. Schuppert (ed.), *Governance Forschung. Vergewisserung über Stand und Entwicklungslinien*, Baden-Baden: Nomos, pp. 11–20.

McQuail, D. (1997), 'Accountability of Media to Society', *European Journal of Communication*, 12: 4, pp. 511–592.

——— (2003), *Media Accountability and Freedom of Publication*, Oxford and New York: Oxford University Press.

——— (2008), 'The Current State of Media Governance in Europe', in G. Terzis (ed.), *European Media Governance: National and Regional Dimensions*, Bristol: Intellect, pp. 17–25.

Meier, W. A. and Perrin, I. (2007), 'Media Concentration and Media Governance', *Communications*, 32: 3, pp. 336–343.

Pierre, J. and Peters, G. B. (2000), *Governance, Politics and the State*, Basingstoke: Macmillan.

Puppis, M. (2007), 'Media Governance as a Horizontal Extension of Media Regulation: The Importance of Self- and Co-Regulation', *Communications,* 32: 3 pp. 330–336.

Rosenau, J. and Czempiel E. O. (eds.) (1992), *Governance without Government: Order and Change in World Politics,* Cambridge: University Press.

Scott, J. and Trubek, D. M. (2002), 'Mind the Gap: Law and New Approaches to Governance in the European Union', *European Law Journal,* 8: 1, pp. 1–18.

Smisman, S. (2008), 'New Modes of Governance and the Participatory Myth', *West European Politics,* 31: 5, pp. 874–895.

Van Cuilenburg, J. and McQuail D. (2003), 'Media Policy Paradigm Shifts: Towards a New Communications Policy Paradigm', *European Journal of Communication,* 18: 2, pp. 181–207.

Van Kersbergen, K. and Van Waarden, F. (2004), '"Governance" as a Bridge Between Disciplines: Cross-Disciplinary Inspiration Regarding Shifts in Governance and Problems of Governability, Accountability and Legitimacy', *European Journal of Political Research,* 43: 2, pp. 143–171.

Notes

1   In France the interviews involved Jean-Pierre Teyssier, president of the Autorité de regulation professionnelle de la publicité (Advertising Regulation Authority) and former president of the European Advertising Standards Authority and Michel Bonnet, chairman of the Conseil Paritaire de la Publicité and representative of the civil society organization Famille de France.

2   In the UK the interviews involved Olivia Campbell, spokesperson of the ASA, and Neil Watts, a member of the Advertising Standards Authority and representative of the Association of School and College Leaders.

3   The ASA was established in 1962 with the main goal of ensuring that all advertisements that are published in the UK are both honest and decent (ASA 2009).

4   Fung and Wright specified six questions, but in the following of this evaluation only five questions are dealt with, as one of them relates to the transfer of knowledge to local units and there are no such units in either case study.

Chapter 21

Stepping Out of the Comfort Zone: Unfolding Gender Conscious Research for Communication and Cultural Policy Theory

Katharine Sarikakis

Introduction

Communication policy[1] research has seen an important growth in recent decades, undoubtedly partly because the processes and actions taken in the actual field of policy have increased in number and complexity, at national and international levels. Moreover, cultural policy has achieved an international level of acceptability and centrality because 'it has been identified globally as a source of value: it has adopted the tools linked to economic, technological [...] planning, and it has successfully been marketed by planners as a panacea for a range of social problems' (Beale 2008: 62). The intensified role the media are playing in everyday life and the centrality of culture as the realm of 'moral production' has placed communication and cultural policy on the agenda of public policy.[2] This book is testimony to the increased interest in and work on communication policy by scholars across Europe and to the avenues we take, in order to explore and understand developments in the field. It also attests to a glaring gap in the field and its coy relation with feminist analysis. My initial proposal was to discuss new notions of state and citizenship as conceptual and analytical axes for communication policy research, but then it became clear to me that no feminist theoretical or methodological piece was planned for this collection. I would therefore like to use this paper to (call on researchers to) *step out of the 'comfort zone' of communication policy research* and highlight the value and necessity of expanding our theoretical and methodological horizons in order to enrich and better our scholarship and field. My contention is that communication policy research as a field of study 'forgets' to ask enough questions about the *human*. It tends to treat the institutions and actors of policy-making, as well as the objects of policy, as semi-autonomous systems, of a neutral composition and objective, and of a technology- and evidence-based disposition. Moreover, communication policy research tends to focus on the micro level of particular policy cases but not on the macro level of policy impact. Hence our analysis of specific policy cases and objects focuses on their 'present,' whereas our attention on actors is largely monopolized by the assumption that institutions are abstract or neutral entities. Between these two poles, again, the *human* is invisible. Even studies that question the dominant meta-paradigm of 'objective,' 'neutral' technology-bound research have difficulty in integrating the 'human' factor into their questions and investigative tools.[3] Not surprisingly, a lot of policy research is under-theorized. Whatever theories are utilized – whether inspired by political sciences or communication and media studies – they are incapable of opening up the field to connect to research questions around the role of human actors in the policy continuum and the ways in which they are affected.

At present a large body of the mainstream and most widespread literature taught in higher education and produced by policy-makers is deprived of the perspective and scope that understands and recognizes the centrality of gender-based social stratification. With a very few specific exceptions, such as information-technology policy, the result is that the field of cultural and communication policy research largely continues to precipitate gender- (or sex-) blind accounts of the developments in the communication and cultural industries. Mainstream academic policy analysis and policy itself have yet to fully integrate feminist research and concerns, not because the subject matter of communication is gender-neutral but because of two intersecting patriarchal hegemonies: the normative and philosophical constitution of the State and the structural and normative construction of the academy. The effect of this rather surprising 'gap' is the perpetuation of 'some of the existing theoretical and political limitations of policy research' (Beale 2002: 199).

In the following pages, I am hoping to provide an impetus and framework for theory building and research in communication policy that is attentive to and curious about the human as a factor, a policy actor and an affected party. In particular, I am focusing on the common denominator of *gender* as a social category that at different points and in different contexts in time intersects with other categorizations, such as race, age and class. I will do so firstly by exploring the conditions of the manufacture of gender-blind analysis. Secondly, I will utilize feminist epistemological propositions to study policy in a way that puts the *human* back at the centre of research.

State, Policy and Gender

> A policy is a system of ultimate aims, practical objectives and means, pursued by a group and applied by an authority. Cultural policies can be discerned in a trade union, a party, an educational movement, an institution, an enterprise, a town or a government. But regardless of the agent concerned, a policy implies the existence of ultimate purposes (long-term), objectives (medium-term and measurable) and means (men [sic], money and legislation), combined in an explicitly coherent system. (Girard and Gentil 1983: 171f)

This definition rather successfully brings together the core elements in the realm of policy-making. Our scholarship has explored the organization of communicative and cultural expression, the control over and ownership of media and messages, of distribution systems and infrastructure. Given the enormous force with which the establishment of certain communication technologies has 'invaded' and ultimately defined the communication landscape – not without the support and facilitation of state policy and regulation – our research was attracted to the structures that technology uses to determine markets. As a review on the subject has shown, European communication policy research in the past decade has converged over issues largely defined by institutions, in particular those of the European Union, whereas its divergences relate to approaches to policy analysis that are dependent on national and cultural contexts (Sarikakis 2008). One important characteristic of communication policy research is that its objects of study are predominantly determined by the range of objects and issues in which the state makes policy. In other words, 'the attention of the state, in its various formations, on particular areas of communication and culture directly or indirectly steers the attention of policy scholars' (Sarikakis 2008: 295). Whether in a national or a supranational formation such as the EU or in an administrative organizational form, the state shapes the research agenda at least indirectly. Communication policy shapes the direction of the development and use of communication and culture, not only in their technological dimensions but also in the conditions of the cycles of production and consumption and generation of ideas, meanings and validation of knowledge. It constitutes the site for the 'production of cultural citizens'; it is the site of struggle for what Marx termed 'moral power,' where the cultural industries provide the representations of the world and the rationales for this moral power (Lewis and Miller 2003: 1). This almost inevitable flow acquires particular significance if one considers that the role of and notions about the state have shifted dramatically in the past three decades. Taking into account the structural changes in the organization of authority and the state, the current relations of power actors are now more accurately described as governance of communication. The legitimacy of governance is based upon normative justification and is sought through the control of the 'moral' realm (Sarikakis 2004). Our understanding and perhaps expectations of the state, the definition of its functions and *its relation to the citizenry*, have changed in parallel to the profound changes in the economic, political and administrative organization of our societies on a global scale. Indeed, the changing relations between state and citizens and state and markets have been paramount in the legitimizing of a new 'world order,' which is itself based on the gendered stratification of the state.

Neoliberalism has defined the terms of policy-making in nearly all domains of modern societies. It calls for state withdrawal from policy intervention, the privatization of services, spaces and resources, for global inter-industrial alliances and co-regulation with states and for the withdrawal of state support for publicly owned organizations and welfare. The emergence of international policy regimes consisting of a web of international organizations representing the most powerful states in the world, alongside global industrial alliances and the coexistence of regional, national and supranational policy systems, presents a complex dynamic between state and industrial power. Relatively recent moves aimed at including some form of citizen representation through the participation of civil society in international forums perhaps add another level of complexity in this constellation (Chakravartty and Sarikakis 2006; Harvey 2005; McLaughlin 2008). In the neoliberal, competition state (Cameron and Palan 2004), citizenship is highly privatized. Certain forms of citizenship are supported, in particular those that prioritize *self-reliance* and the *free market*. The competition state therefore favours policies that deal with 'privatized', depoliticized and consumption-defined subjects. The incorporation of communication rights as developed by civil society for debates at the World Summit on the Information Society points in the direction of the development of a framework that at its heart contains the normative and regulatory dimensions of the rights of citizenship, as understood in its economic, cultural, political and social expression. Feminist communication and cultural policy analysis utilizes a more intensified adoption and development of the concept of citizenship, as it has done with the concept of human rights. Although human rights offer the fundaments of minimum standards for universal adoption, they are also limited and do not connect comprehensively to a gender-sensitive framework. The notion of differentiated citizenship can offer the more *concrete and detailed framework* within which policy provision, implementation and evaluation can be analysed in order to promote a human and gender-sensitive agenda that treats women as subjects in their own right and not as a special-interest group (Meier and Lombardo 2008; Lister 1997; Young 1997; Yuval-Davis 1997).

Communication and culture have become the object of fierce competition among superpowers in debates that have been framed in an increasingly technologized manner. Gender is conspicuously absent in public policy – or at least it is absent in the debates among powerful actors, whereas it surfaces in areas of 'soft' policy, at a symbolic level and among less influential actors (Mazur 2002). Hence, although the 'playing field' seems to have become more open to diffuse interests as these are represented by civil society organizations, the range and shape of themes, discourse and areas included in the 'debate' has shrunk: cultural diversity, communication freedom, communication flow, access to information and access to the means of culture production have been framed in predominantly technological terms, culminating at the World Summit on the Information Society in 2003 and 2005 (Chakravartty and Sarikakis 2006; McLaughlin and Pickard 2005; Shade and Crow 2004). These dimensions in communication policy have strong gender implications, which are not adequately incorporated in 'mainstream' policy analysis, despite gender being a major organizing 'principle' in the social stratification of labouring, consuming and owning the media and culture industries. Women are located in specific positions on the ladder of wealth and power, which operates at a macro level of control of communication and a micro level of representation and visibility in public debate (Byerly 2004; Klaus 2009; McLaughlin 1993).

Historically, communication policy has served to maintain the gender status quo. Every major communication medium, from the cinema screen to telephone and from television and radio to the Internet, has been defined by institutions and actors whose organizational and ideological predispositions were gendered. Censorship of popular fiction on the cinema screen derived from gendered, moral concerns over the 'corrupting' influence of movies on women and children. Cinema's early days saw the transformation of society's socializing venues and habits, especially among lower classes, with women occupying public spaces such as cinema theatres, where romantic stories were thought to have a destabilizing influence on the gender order. As a result, the British Board of Film Censors was formed to define 'acceptable' content – and to avoid state regulation (Eldridge et al. 1997). At the beginning of the twentieth century, the process of domestication of the radio was shaped by policies aimed at re-establishing the gender order, after a brief period of its destablization in relation to technology. Initially, women were involved in the technological functions of the radio, assembling DIY radios as much as men did, because neither the state nor the industry had stepped in to 'frame' its use. Experimentation with radio technology was thus not gender bound. This period gave the women's movement the opportunity to popularize women's ability to interact with radio technology (through writings and cartoons). Conservatives, however, attacking women's organizations, combined their efforts with the media industries (advertising companies, magazines and radio) to generate and promote material such as advertisements compatible with conservative sentiments (Butsch 1998). Through the regulation of the frequency spectrum among other things, the governance of today's mobile technology gave control of the medium to those with 'specialized' knowledge and the political and economic elites – social groups that were and still are male dominated. As a result, women were pushed from a position of being active technologists into 'listening' audiences. In the regulation of the *digital* spectrum a century later, gender social relations underline policy directions for mobile communication, yet no international policy document acknowledges the gendered constructions of the use of mobile telephony and communication – except in the case of online pornography. Research is also very limited in the field, despite the fact that international policies prioritize the commercial use of mobile phones, which in turn restricts the innovative and emancipatory potential among women users (Crow and Shauchuk 2008). Moreover, in the governance of the spectrum, for example by the ITU and IEEE:[4]

> the gendered division of labour is relevant in terms of the individuals who make the decisions regarding spectrum policy, connected as it is to the transference of the skill sets required to create, produce, and distribute spectrum. In this communication chain, women are positioned as users and consumers, not as innovators, owners, or creators. (Crow and Shauchuk 2008: 99)

Hence, seemingly 'gender neutral' policies on the regulation of the media around technological, economic and social concerns have a strong gender dimension, which remains largely invisible in policy output. The lack of conscious acknowledgement of gender in policy making (and policy analysis), particularly in the media, reflects the assumption that objectivity equals gender-neutrality. As MacKinnon (1989:162) writes:

> Formally, the state is male in that objectivity is its norm. Objectivity is liberal legalism's conception of itself. It legitimizes itself by reflecting its view of existing society, a society it made and makes by so seeing it, and calling that view, and that relation, practical

rationality. If rationality is measured by point-of-viewlessness, what counts as reason will be that which corresponds to the way things are [...] neutrality is considered desirable and descriptive [...] the separation of form from substance, process from policy, role from theory and practice, echoes and re-echoes at each level of the regime its basic norm: objectivity.

Objectivity in policy-making is translated as non-policy-making with specific social groups in mind, which in itself *is* a form of decision to maintain the status quo. The problem of obscurity of the gendered character of communication and cultural policy lies in the fact that state and administrative bureaucracies, as well as mainstream academic enquiry, operate on the assumption that male normativity is an adequate reflection of the universal human experience. On the other hand, the feminization of certain sectors of bureaucracy and their fields of competence marks their lack of real power. Ferguson's (1984) research on administration and the state clearly demonstrates the way in which important policy actors identify with a system characterized by gendered structures, paths and cultures. Not only is genderness acute in the numbers of women appointed to influential positions but this is also the case in the organization of bureaucracies in hierarchies that are based on two functions: the prioritization of 'specialized' knowledge and the ability to reproduce the status quo. In other words, genderness depends on the mechanisms through which the system re/produces itself, with the obscuring of the very existence of genderness being inherent in this process.

Even when the state embarks on a feminist mission of corrective policy-making, such as in social policy cases or gender mainstreaming across a spectrum of social and public policy, the communication and cultural sectors prove resistant to any form of 'intervention.' I have discussed elsewhere how representative democratic institutions are closer to citizens and friendlier to diffuse interests. In the supranational 'state' scenario of the European Union the case of the European Parliament demonstrates that in unsympathetic environments of masculinized bureaucracies and neoliberal markets democratic supranational representation is capable of offering entry points for the representation of diverse interests, including women's interests (Sarikakis 2004). Much more than most national governments, the EU has adopted the strategy of *gender mainstreaming* in all aspects of political and social policy. This means that all policy areas include gender-conscious design, implementation and impact assessment. Despite the criticisms regarding the adequacy of gender mainstreaming,[5] when compared with the lack of gender-corrective strategies it is a vital tool in the hands of policy-makers and women's organizations. It is telling that communication and cultural policy domains have not permitted gender mainstreaming to be adopted and applied in the sector over the past 30 years of EU policy-making. Not only that, but virtually every political initiative to introduce gender problematization into the policy debate and output has been systematically and systemically undermined. On the one hand, in the industrialized world the segregation between ministries and committees dealing with 'soft' and 'hard core' policies has gone hand in hand with the feminization of the 'soft' arms of the state (Beale 2008; Sarikakis 2007). 'Culture,' as the 'soft' abstract policy domain that describes the arts and heritage – the domain of women – tends to occupy a different institutional territory on the policy map from that reserved for (tele)communications, the rather 'precise' and 'core' element of our modern societies: technology. On the other hand, a major objection to a gender-conscious policy in the case of content regulation has been the position that such a policy interferes with media freedom. There are numerous points in the legislative history of the EU where this has been the case. The most recent, as part of a legislative framework for employment, was the attempt by the Director General for Social Affairs to propose anti-sexism legislation at directive level banning the stereotypical representation of women in the media. The female socialist commissioner Anna Diamantopoulou was attacked fiercely by the media industry and by right-wing think tanks, including the US-based CATO Institute (EPC 2003; Pollock 2003). The draft directive was in essence a follow-up on numerous initiatives raised over the years by (female) MEPs in committee reports and parliamentary debates on the stereotypical representation of women in advertising and the media, the mainstreaming of pornography and the pornographic image, sexism in the professions, equal opportunities at work in the media and freedom of journalists (Sarikakis 2004). None of these issues were ever included in the Television Without Frontiers Directive and its audio-visual services follow-up in 2009. Moreover, gender mainstreaming never entered the agenda of policy negotiations. The reasons were manifold but, overall, communication policies have been dominated by corporate interests. Combined with unfriendly institutional structures and the DGs in charge of media and information, gender-conscious policy did not fit comfortably with deregulatory aims (Sarikakis and Nguyen 2009).

Definitional Dilemmas and the Policy Process

How do communication and cultural policies sustain a gendered system? This question points to the conditions of *political opportunity*, that is, the degree of gender-conscious concerns and input as well as the structural organization of the institutions·involved in the policy process. Moreover, as Beale and van der Bosch have argued (1998), the broader economic and social context of communication and culture plays an important role, such as in the funding of the arts, the protection of artists and media workers. As the privatization and liberalization of the industries has brought the casualization of work and the feminization of whole sectors of the industry – from the manufacture of microchips to telecentres and from public relations to education and 'voluntary' sectors – the retreat of the welfare state has accentuated existing polarizations (Beale 1998). The procedural character of policy regards gender as an *additional* rather than an *intrinsic* category of communication and cultural policy. Similarly, policy analysis that concentrates strictly on the procedural – and therefore 'measurable' object – produces 'detached' accounts of policy-making. The question is: 'who defines the problem' that policy is called upon to solve and what directs us to uncover power relations in the pyramid of hierarchy, not only of decision-making but also in the hierarchy of 'questions?' Bacchi (1998) asserts that meanings arise from power relations and institutions. Contending *interpretations* of the policy problem depend on representation of an issue:

> Traditional policy analysis is grounded in a narrow, falsely objective, overly instrumental view of rationality that masks its latent biases and allows policy elites and technocrats to present analyses and plans as neutral and objective when they are actually tied to prevailing relations of power. (Marshall 1997: 3)

If social relations are based on and traceable in communicative actions among social 'organisms', so the symbolic expression of these relations becomes the tool for hegemony. In the symbolic order, 'representation' in Bacchi's terms or 'language' (as a system of symbols and values) offers regenerative power, which is utilized in the definition of concepts, questions and treatments of the issues. Individuals and society present a plexus of social relations and the organization of experience into meaning and expression: professional discourses accompanying the introduction of the telephone in the US made it very clear that it was to be used in a 'serious' manner. 'Seriousness' of use was considered to be the domain of male usage, perceived to be for instrumental and business purposes and not for social use. In the former case, women were excluded (Rakow and Wackwitz 2004) while at the same time their patterns of usage (for social purposes) were ridiculed as not 'serious'. In the 1990s, *Wired*, the major magazine forum for debates on ICT, was entirely based on white masculine discourse. It is important to question the basis of the rhetoric of policy documents and the basis of the policy formulated through actions that do not need to be formally recognizable as such (Steward Miller 1998).

Discourses and representation, however, do not colour just the symbolic realm: policy understandings and the framing of policy problems are intrinsically dependant on available forms of representation. Institutional, procedural and political–economic structures integrate systems of representation when operationalizing directions in communication policy. Hence, discourses about consumer choice, pluralism of images and the free-market ideal have been utilized to support the relaxation of media ownership restrictions in the western world. As the media can be said to belong to men, the privatization of media spaces creates a strongly gendered landscape in terms of proprietary power (Byerly 2004; Klaus 2009). At the same time, if we expand the terrain of our investigation to include the impact on content, traditionally regarded as 'outside' the domain of policy analysis, other gendered dimensions emerge. Two striking examples from different socio-cultural parts of the world point to the need for more analysis. The first relates to the impact of media ownership and privatization policies in the shaping of a xenophobic and misogynistic media culture in the media of countries in eastern Europe. Moranjak-Bamburać et al. (2006) brought together a team of researchers who surveyed and analysed the attitude of the media to women politicians and the development of intolerant politics in Serbia and other countries in eastern and south-eastern Europe. On a separate yet evidently interlinked subject, Levande (2007) has identified the ways in which relaxation of ownership restrictions in the US, and especially the 1996 Telecommunications

Act, have resulted in loss of control over public service standards and the deterioration of values based on equity. Levande argues that the effects of cross-ownership and ownership concentration can be seen in the pornification of the image of female artists in the music sector. Moreover, ownership regulation has facilitated close connections between giant media companies that profit from adult entertainment, with the result that pornographic imagery is pushed into the mainstream and becomes omnipresent.

How can analysis integrate gender in areas where no apparent human factors are visible? For instance, how is it possible to even begin to talk about gender when dealing with satellite technology, technical standards or IT security? If the policy object, and consequently analysis, limits itself to a pre-defined conceptual framework (the 'representation' of the policy problem) then human subjects become 'irrelevant' in a highly technologized discourse. Once the process of the 're-humanization' of the policy object commences, analysis can address the under-problematized and invisible aspects of locating human subjects in the process. Only when the invisible or abstract – and marginal(ized) – gendered 'consumer', 'public', 'mass' is attended to will the analysis of communication and cultural policy be able to offer concrete statements about and for the human condition. Two fundamental tasks are vital to activate a *margins-conscious* course of study: self-analysis of one's own position and role in the possession and production of knowledge, and analysis of the knowledge base of the research/analysis tools. Here Hawkesworth's (1994) question is most relevant: 'what sort of knowledge is more useful – technical or political?' This is a question that the conscious researcher would need to ask in relation both to her/his work and to that of the organizations or documents being studied.

For Harding, the 'lives of those people upon whose exploitation the legitimacy of the dominant system depends can bring into focus questions and issues that were not visible, "important," or legitimate within the dominant institutions, their conceptual frameworks, cultures, and practices' (Harding 1998: 17). It is therefore through making the 'neutral' or 'objective' construction of knowledge *transparent* that the 'unaccepted/able' knowledge of the non-privileged can be juxtaposed to the historical lies, distortions and myths about the human condition. Policy analysis must therefore seek to uncover what Marcuse calls the 'political linguistics' of the bias concealed as objectivity and the stratification concealed as neutrality. At the same time, the conscious act of seeking out the material that only the experience of marginalization can provide attacks the proliferation of *false consciousness*, ideas and practices of the internalization of one's otherness, which prevents marginalized individuals and groups from questioning dominant ideologies. *Change* in social relations becomes possible through acknowledging unequal positions in the production of knowledge and making a critique of them. The role of 'specialized' knowledge and positions is crucial in policy-making. As such, a methodological politics and tool for policy theory and analysis can be developed to allow the researcher to identify and analyse power relations at the multiple levels of communication and cultural policy.

The first step in the analysis of communication and cultural policies, whether in documents or acts, interrogates the *validity* of the basis of the argument, which is the basis of its normative justification. In western democracies, discursive legitimacy is at the heart of state politics. Legitimacy manages conflict, hence the first task is to uncover the frames that construct policy problems (Bacchi 1999).

Secondly, historical study provides the contextual background that exposes the parameters of the gender-based factors of adequacy and internal consistency of theoretical presuppositions.

Thirdly, in order to maintain the relevance of critical abstraction and application, the standards of evidence, unspoken value statements and use of 'facts' need to be juxtaposed to the fundamental claim of the action and decision. Walker (2003: 263) warns:

> When a concept [...] is constructed by the process of 'moral ideology' it is detached from its grounding in the social relations in which events and activities take place and put through an abstract reorganization that conforms to the relevances of a particular or a number of discourses.

In order for the critic of policy to be able to dissect discourse or 'language' s/he may need to use this same 'language' or to contest it by providing the definitions closer to the most marginalized. This is also part of the profound dilemma of whom knowledge is being generated for – is it, for example, for those who will be most affected by decisions? (Bacchi 1999). In this process, the models of explanation utilized also need to be checked against their ability to account for propositions in regard to the shift of the power pendulum. The explanatory frameworks used should seek to disclose and correct bias and be able to refute a theory by showing that the practices it presupposes are in conflict with the practice it describes. In this instance, the role of the mainstream media, which maintains the dominance of patriarchal 'language' and 'representation' of women's issues, reinforces the broader extension of social relations as producers and products of psycholinguistic and cultural patriarchal relations. However, the hierarchy of sexes, which is tolerated and reproduced through culture, and the way in which one lives and knows further ensures the persistence of inequality through the failure to acknowledge its existence.

Concluding Remarks or the Question of Incessant Accountability

In this paper I have suggested that communication and cultural policy analysis must consciously include a gender-conscious agenda if it is to make useful theoretical and practical propositions and contribute to understanding the complexity of social and political worlds. I have not discussed race, age, sexuality or physical ability in this process, not because these are not crucial factors but because the one common underlying thread across all these 'othernesses' is that of sex or gender, and because the politics of social justice does not deny recognition of multiple expressions of inequality. However, even in progressive politics gender is sidelined as a secondary factor in this complexity. Feminist policy analysis is not only for feminists but also for the politics of human emancipation. I have argued that at the centre of communication and cultural policy analysis lies the question of power. If policy-making is categorized as three largely intersecting stages (problem-definition or agenda-setting, debate and analysis, and reaching a solution: proposition/decision-making) then two more procedural and structural determinants need to be addressed. The study of a policy object or set of actions should scrutinize the *participation and heritages* of those involved in the process of policy-making; in the same way, self-analysis is required from the researcher. Moreover, the work of policy analysis is never complete without the evaluation of the propositions and actions: in other words, the question to be asked is whether the policy output has the potential to *shift* to the power relations pendulum. Who are the groups for whom pro-active provision will make a difference, and is the gap closing between those with the means (voice, power, discourse, materiality) and those without it? Power is at the core of future-shaping, so communication and cultural policy analysis, rather than simply accepting the ideological position that there is a problem in the social world that is just waiting to be found, should scrutinize the role of power in determining its 'representation.' It should also locate the 'problem' in its material conditions that are favourable for its emergence and continuation. Here, control over the means where scrutiny and definition will take place are of equal importance. The role of the mass media in effectively silencing information related to international negotiations, such as intellectual property, ownership rules, cultural diversity, is deafening. How does the colonization of the public domain by private interests affect the treatment of the 'problem' and allow or prevent the intervention of marginalized voices? Given the nature of policy going hand in hand with power, power needs to be accountable at any given time.

A margins activated approach allows us to think of theoretical and methodological tools to maintain the process of accountability as a continual one. In its epistemological aim of locating truth and reality, it draws our attention to the necessity of bringing knowledge (and the seeking of truth) to politics and addressing the lived experience of surface relations (social relations), which co-determine the deeper level of experience, the self, and therefore consciousness. As such, the direct relation to a world experienced through our 'material' substance (body) relates to policies that address the reality of the conditions around us. How are these conditions shaped by policies in the communication and cultural domain? It would be difficult to imagine any of these at all if we were unable relate them to policies in other organizational domains. Here, questions of 'administration' of the cultural and communicative domain should entail the reflexivity and transparency as proposed by the theory. As a method and theory building, a human centred policy scholarship will seek to:

- Locate the gendered social relations maintained by the policy process.
- Analyse and learn from the politics of change within regulatory systems, organizations and cultures (i.e. traditions/rituals, ideologies and discourses).
- Locate and evaluate policy objects, agenda and normative justification by integrating a gender perspective.

- Evaluate the effect of policy implementation (or the impact of lack of policy) on the sustenance of the gendered status quo.
- Contextualize the surrounding system (social, political, cultural, economic) in its role in promoting an emancipatory cultural process.

Structurally, discursively and interactionally, communication and culture consist of social relations around the production, distribution and consumption of cultural goods. These sets of relations are subjects to and agents of structural and symbolic (or ideological, value-related and discursive/normative) determinants. With the exception of a few areas of affirmative action for the protection of content, communication policy is largely *negative* in that it promotes negative liberties and privileges while increasingly supporting the privatization of cultural activities. Our field needs proposals that provide more active and positive promotion of rights with the public interest at heart. However, the concept of public interest itself has proved to be vague and unhelpful, as authorities' rhetoric and practice differ. Indeed, the very rhetoric of public interest has sidelined women, especially when combined with un-libertarian state policies that base civil rights restrictions on conceptions of 'danger' and 'crisis,' such as terrorism and war (Jansen 2002). A policy approach that adopts the triumphant ideologies of neoliberal individualism is and must be critiqued on the basis of the impact of individualism on women's collective rights and for women as *social* individuals in and with socially embedded roles.

References

Andrew, C., Armstrong, P., Armstrong, H., Clement, W. and Vosko, L. F. (2003), *Studies in Political Economy. Developments in Feminism*, Toronto: Women's Press.

Bacchi, C. L. (1999), *Women, Policy and Politics. The Construction of Policy Problems*, London, Thousand Oaks and New Delhi: Sage.

Beale, A. (1998), 'Cultural Policy as a Technology of Gender', in A. Beale and A. van den Bosch (eds.), *Ghosts in the Machine. Women and Cultural Policy in Canada and Australia*, Toronto: Garamond, pp. 231–250.

—— (2002), 'Gender and Transversal Cultural Policies', in M. Raboy (ed.), *Global Media Policy in the New Millennium*, Luton: University of Luton Press, pp. 199–214.

—— (2008), 'The Expediency of Women', in K. Sarikakis and L. R. Shade (eds.), *Feminist Interventions in International Communication*, Lanham: Rowman and Littlefield, pp. 59–73.

Beale, A and van den Bosch, A. (eds.), *Ghosts in the Machine. Women and Cultural Policy in Canada and Australia*, Toronto: Garamond.

Butsch, R. (1998), 'Crystal Sets and Scarf-Pin Radios: Gender, Technology and the Construction of American Radio Listening in the 1920s', *Media, Culture and Society*, 20: 4, pp. 557–572.

Byerly, C. (2004), 'Women and the Concentration of Media Ownership', in R. R. Rush, C. Oukrop and P. Creedon (eds.), *Seeking Equity for Women in Journalism and Mass Communication Education. A 30-Year Update*, Mahwah: Lawrence Erlbaum Associates, pp. 245–262.

Cameron, A. and Palan, R. (2004), *The Imagined Economies of Globalization*, London, Thousand Oaks and New Delhi: Sage.

Chakravarrty, P. and Sarikakis, K. (2006), *Media Policy and Globalization*, Edinburgh: Edinburgh University Press.

Crow, B. and Shawchuk, K. (2008), 'The Spectral Politics of Mobile Communication Technologies: Gender, Infrastructure and International Policy', in K. Sarikakis and L. R. Shade (eds.), *Feminist Interventions in International Communication*, Lanham: Rowman and Littlefield, pp. 90–105.

Eldridge, J. Kitzinger, J. and Williams, K. (1997), *The Mass Media and Power in Modern Britain*, Oxford: Oxford University Press.

European Publishers Council (EPC) (2003), 'Sexism Directive Letter to Commissioner Diamantopoulou', http://www.epceurope.org/issues/epc-sexism-directive-letter-to-commissioner-diamantopoulou.shtml. Accessed 8 November 2010.

Ferguson, K. E. (1984), *The Feminist Case Against Bureaucracy*, Philadelphia: Temple University Press.

Freeman, B. M. (2001), *The Satellite Sex. The Media and Women's Issues in English Canada. 1966–1971*, Waterloo: Wilfrid Laurier University Press.

Girard, A. and Gentil, G. (1983), *Cultural Development: Experiences and Policies*, Paris: UNESCO.

Hafner-Burton, E. and Pollack, M. A. (2002), 'Mainstreaming Gender in Global Governance', *European Journal of International Relations*, 8: 3, pp. 339–373.

Harding, S. (1998), *Is Science Multicultural? Postcolonialisms, Feminisms and Epistemologies*, Bloomington: Indiana University Press.

Harvey, D. (2005), *The New Imperialism*, Oxford: Oxford University Press.

Hawkesworth, M (1994), 'Policy Studies within a Feminist Frame', *Policy Science*, 27: 2–3 pp. 97–118.

Jansen, S. C. (2002), *Critical Communication Theory. Power, Media, Gender, and Technology*, Lanham, Boulder, New York and London: Rowman & Littlefield.

Kilpatrick, D. G. (2000), 'Definitions of Public Policy and the Law', http://www.musc.edu /vawprevention/policy/definition.shtml. Accessed 8 November 2010.

Klaus, E. (2009), 'Media Systems, Equal Rights and the Freedom of the Press: Gender as a Case in Point', in A. Czepek, M. Hellwig and E. Nowak (eds.), *Press Freedom and Pluralism in Europe*, Bristol: Intellect, pp. 101–114.

Levande, M. (2007), 'Women, Pop Music, and Pornography', *Meridians: Feminism, Race, Transnationalism*, 8: 1, pp. 293–321.

Lewis, J. and Miller, T. (eds.) (2003), *Critical Cultural Policy Studies. A Reader*, Oxford: Blackwell.

Liebert, U. (2002), 'Europeanising Gender Mainstreaming: Constraints and Opportunities in the Multilevel Euro-Policy', *Feminist Legal Studies*, 10: 3, pp. 241–256.

Lister, R. (1997), *Citizenship. Feminist Perspectives*, London: MacMillan.

MacKinnon, C. (1989), *Toward a Feminist Theory of the State*, Cambridge: Harvard University Press.

Marshall, C. (1997), *Feminist Critical Policy Analysis: a perspective from post secondary education*, London: Falmer Press.

Mazur, A. G. (2002), *Theorizing Feminist Policy*, NY: Oxford University Press.

McLaughlin, L. (1993), 'Feminism, the Public Sphere, Media and Democracy', *Media, Culture and Society*, 15: 4, pp. 599–620.

McLaughlin, L. (2008), 'Women, Information Labor and the Corporatization of development', in K. Sarikakis and L. R. Shade (eds.), *Feminist Interventions in International Communication*, Lanham: Rowman and Littlefield, pp. 224–240.

McLaughlin, L. and Pickard, V. (2005), 'What Is Bottom-Up about Global Internet Governance?', *Global Media and Communication*, 1: 3, pp. 357–373.

Meier, P. and Lombardo, E. (2008), 'Concepts of Citizenship Underlying EU Gender Equality Policies', *Citizenship Studies*, 12: 5, pp. 481–493.

Moranjak-Bamburać, N., Jusić, T. and Isanović, A. (eds.) (2006) *Stereotyping: Representation of Women in Print Media in South East Europe*, Budapest: SEENPM.

Pollock, R. (2003), 'The New Europe Looks a Little Like 1984', http://www.cato.org/pub_display.php?pub_id=3157. Accessed 8 November 2010.

Rakow L. F. and Wackwitz, L. A. (2004), *Feminist Communication Theory*, NY: Sage

Sarikakis, K. (2004), *Powers in Media Policy. The Challenge of the European Parliament*, Bern: Peter Lang.

——— (2007), 'The Place of Media and Cultural Policy in the EU, *European Studies*, 24, pp. 13–22.

——— (2008), 'Communication and Cultural Policy Research in Europe: A Review of Recent Scholarship', in I. Fernandez Alonso and M. de Morragas i Spa (eds.), *Communication and Cultural Policies in Europe*, Barcelona: Generalitat de Catalunya, pp. 293–318.

Sarikakis, K. and Nguyen, T. (2009), 'The Trouble with Gender: Media Policy and Gender Mainstreaming in the European Union', *Journal of European Integration*, 31: 2, pp. 201–216.

Shade, L. R. and Crow, B. (2004), 'Canadian Feminist Perspectives on Digital Technology', *TOPIA*, 11: Spring, pp. 161–174.

Stewart Miller, M. (1998), *Cracking the Gender Code: Who Rules the Wired World?*, Toronto: Second Story.

Walker, G. (2003), 'The Conceptual Politics of Struggle: Wife Battering, the Women's Movement and the State', in C. Andrew, P. Armstrong, H. Armstrong, W. Clement and L. F. Vosko (eds.), *Studies in Political Economy. Developments in Feminism*, Toronto: Women's Press.

Young, I. M. (1997), *Intersecting Voices: Dilemmas of Gender, Political Philosophy, and Policy*, Princeton: Princeton University Press.

Yuval Davis, N. (1997), 'Women, Citizenship and Difference', *Feminist Review*, 57: 1, pp. 4–27.

Notes

1   I use the term communication policy to refer to a variety of policies whose object is not only the means of communication but also communicative processes. Here communication policy therefore refers to areas such as telecommunications as well as freedom of expression, and it also expands to characterize the policies affecting media, communication and cultural industries in their political–economic dimensions, and which might include labour relations, the relations of production and consumption and their effects on the political and socio-economic and cultural relations. Furthermore, communication policy

is understood as part of a broader 'set' of culture policy, which may intersect with areas we are accustomed to understand as 'high culture' (museum, arts, heritage policies).

2 'Public policy can be generally defined as a system of laws, regulatory measures, courses of action, and funding priorities concerning a given topic promulgated by a governmental entity or its representatives' (Kilpatrick 2000).

3 With the exception of user-type research, which however tends to enquire about the habits and behaviour of users within a given policy framework, i.e. without seeking to challenge assumptions on which the specific policy is based.

4 The International Telecommunications Union and the Institute of Electronics and Electronics Engineers.

5 Gender mainstreaming has been criticized due to its lack of legal enforcement, but, as Liebert (2002) argues, regulation alone cannot guarantee progress given the reluctance and resistance of policy makers. It takes legal measures, material incentives and knowledge-based inducements for a comprehensive, practical set of action. Liebert believes that the first two make little difference whereas the education of the public and decision-makers will be more effective. Moreover, a shifting of culture is necessary to fulfill some of the equality objectives. However, policies need to be based upon adequate resources and power of enforcement. For Hafner-Burton and Pollack (2002) the rhetoric of gender mainstreaming is more impressive than its implementation, an important case of the feminization of these specific bureaucratic sectors and their objectives. In their research on three major bureaucratic structures (UNDP, World Bank and EP), the authors found that structural factors and agents may strategically *frame* gender mainstreaming as a strategy in order to move away from agenda-setting to a more integrationist approach, to *include* gender in existing structures so that there is no need to shift the goals of the organizations.

Notes on Contributors

The Editors

Natascha Just is a senior research and teaching associate in the Media Change & Innovation division, Institute of Mass Communication and Media Research (IPMZ), University of Zurich, Switzerland. She is also a Fellow of the Stanford-Vienna Transatlantic Technology Law Forum (TTLF). She has an MA in communication science/romance philology (1997) and a Ph.D. in communication science (2001) from the University of Vienna (summa cum laude). She was the recipient of a three-year Hertha Firnberg Grant from the Austrian National Science Fund (Department of Communication, University of Vienna, Austria, 2005–2008), a visiting researcher at Stanford Law School (2007), a post-doctoral fellow on international communication at the ARNIC, Annenberg School for Communication, USC, Los Angeles (2004–2005); and a research fellow at the Austrian Academy of Sciences (1998–2004). Her current research centres on the transformation of statehood in the convergent communications sector with a special emphasis on changing governance structures, competition policy, market power control, and public service broadcasting. Her research has been published in journals such as *Media, Culture & Society*, *Telecommunications Policy*, *Communications & Strategies*, and *Knowledge, Technology & Policy*.

Manuel Puppis is a senior research and teaching associate at the University of Zurich's Institute of Mass Communication and Media Research (IPMZ) and the managing director of its 'Media & Politics' division. Additionally, he is a post-doctoral researcher at the National Centre of Competence in Research (NCCR) 'Challenges to Democracy in the 21st Century.' He has a Ph.D. (summa cum laude) from the University of Zurich. Currently he is a vice-chair of the ECREA's CLP Section and a co-chair of the Netzwerk Medienstrukturen. His work has been published in journals such as the *European Journal of Communication*; *Communication, Culture & Critique*; and the *International Communication Gazette*. He is also the author of the student textbook *Introduction to Media Policy* (in German). His research interests include media policy, media regulation and media governance, media systems in a comparative perspective, political communication and organization theory.

The Authors

Peter Bajomi-Lazar is senior research fellow with the Media and Democracy in Central and Eastern Europe project hosted by the Department of Politics and International Relations at the University of Oxford (http://mde.politics.ox.ac.uk/), professor of communications on leave at the Budapest Business School, and editor-in-chief of the Hungarian media studies quarterly *Mediakutato*. He earned his Ph.D. in political science at the Central European University in 2004. He has been teaching media sociology, media policy and media history at various higher educational institutions since 1999 and has been engaged in media policy research since 2001. He was granted the (Hungarian) Pulitzer Memorial Award in 2002.

Johannes L.H. Bardoel is Professor of Journalism and Media with the Radboud University of Nijmegen and a senior researcher with the Amsterdam School of Communications Research (ASCoR) at the University of Amsterdam. In 1976, he joined NOS (now NPO, Netherlands Public Broadcasting) where he worked as a senior policy advisor for the board of governors. In 1993, he started work at the Department of Communication of the University of Amsterdam. In 1997, he presented his Ph.D. thesis 'Journalism in the Information Society.' Bardoel's current research focuses on the evolution in the journalistic profession in the network society, on media governance and accountability, the future of public broadcasting and the changes in national and European media policies. Between 2002 and 2004 he was a member of the 'Broadcasting Review Commission' that advised politics on the future of public broadcasting and between 2006 and 2010 he was the chairman of the Media Commission of the Council for Culture, the official advisory body for the Netherlands Minister of Education, Culture and Sciences.

Lucia Bellucci is an assistant professor at the Università degli Studi di Milano, Law School. She holds a Ph.D. in law from the Université Paris 1-Panthéon Sorbonne and a Ph.D. in sociology of law from the Università degli Studi di Milano. In addition, she holds a post-graduate degree in economics and management of cultural industries from the Università Bocconi-SDA, and an undergraduate degree in law from the Università di Bologna. Her fields of research are media law in context (European, international and comparative with a focus on film law), and law and anthropology. She has published in both fields and presented papers at many international conferences and workshops. She teaches European media law in context, film production law in the EU and international and European media regulation. She has been a consultant for the Rizzoli Corriere della Sera (RCS s.p.a), New Businesses Division. She is now included in the list of potential experts selected to assist the Education, Audio-Visual and Culture Executive Agency, created by the European Commission, in the framework of EU programmes concerning international cooperation in higher education.

Jason Bosland is a senior lecturer at the Melbourne Law School, the University of Melbourne, Australia. He has a BA/LLB (Hons) and an LLM from the University of Melbourne. He also has an LLM (with distinction) from the London School of Economics and Political Science, where he was awarded the Stanley De Smith prize in public law. Prior to joining Melbourne Law School, Jason was a lecturer in law at the University of New South Wales. He is a joint editor (with Professor Andrew Kenyon and Professor Kathy Bowrey) of the *Media & Arts Law Review*.

Avshalom Ginosar is a senior lecturer at the Academic College of Emek Yezreel, Israel. His research interests are in media regulation and policy, advertising regulation, media ombudsmen, and journalism ethics. For more than 25 years, Avshalom has been a news editor both in a major newspaper (*Maariv*) and public radio stations in Israel. In addition, he was a director and chief editor of the local news in TV cable channels.

Peter Humphreys is a professor at the University of Manchester, where he has taught comparative European politics since 1986. He has published extensively on comparative media and telecommunications policy and regulation. His books include *Media and Media Policy in Germany* (Berg 1994) and *Mass Media and Media Policy in Western Europe* (MUP 1996). Since 1996, he has co-directed three large ESRC-funded research projects, each lasting three years, into different aspects of broadcasting and telecommunications policy. The latest project, recently completed, explored trends in audio-visual regulation in Canada, France, Germany, the UK and US, with regard to public service broadcasting and cultural policy in the audio-visual sector (http://www.esrcsocietytoday.ac.uk/esrcinfocentre/viewawardpage.aspx?awardnumber=RES-000-23-0966). This research is reported in a book he has recently co-authored with his Manchester colleague Thomas Gibbons, *Audiovisual Regulation under Pressure: Comparative Cases from North America and Europe* (Routledge, 2012).

Karol Jakubowicz Ph.D. worked for many years as a journalist and executive in the Polish media, including as Chairman of the Supervisory Board of Polish Television. He has held a number of posts in the field of media policy and regulation, including as Chairman, Intergovernmental Council of the Information for All Programme, UNESCO and as Chairman of the Steering Committee on the Media and New Communication Services at the Council of Europe. His scholarly and other publications have been published widely in Poland and internationally.

Kari Karppinen is a research associate at the Department of Social Research, University of Helsinki. He has published articles on democratic theory, the public sphere and media policy in a number of edited volumes and journals, including *Media, Culture & Society*, *Javnost/The Public* and *Nordicom Review*. His doctoral dissertation 'Rethinking Media Pluralism' (2010) deals with pluralism and diversity as contested concepts in European media policy debates.

Christian Katzenbach is a researcher and lecturer in media and communications studies at the Freie Universität Berlin. In his research and teaching, he focuses on media regulation and governance, online communication and social media, media change and innovation. He holds an MA in communication studies, philosophy and computer science and is currently working on his Ph.D. thesis on media technology and governance.

Andrew Kenyon is Deputy Dean, Professor of Law and a director of the Centre for Media and Communications Law in the Melbourne Law School. Andrew has law degrees from the universities of Melbourne and London, and is a member of the International Communications Association, the European Communication Research and Education Association and the Socio-Legal Studies Association. He researches in comparative media and communications law, including defamation, privacy, copyright, journalism and media policy. He is an editor of the international refereed journal, the *Media & Arts Law Review*, a network participant in the Australian Research Council Cultural Research Network and a former president of the Law and Society Association of Australia and New Zealand.

Ulrike Klinger is senior research and teaching associate at University of Zurich's Institute of Mass Communication and Media Research (IPMZ). She holds a Ph.D. in political science from the University of Frankfurt. Her doctoral thesis deals with media pluralism and the quality of democracy. Currently her research focuses on political communication and media politics.

Matthias Künzler is a senior research and teaching associate at the University of Zurich's Institute of Mass Communication and Media Research (IPMZ). He received his Ph.D. from the University of Zurich. His research interests and teaching activities include broadcasting liberalization, media history, media policy and media systems in a comparative perspective. Besides several articles in anthologies and various journals such as *Gazette* and *M & K – Medien und Kommmunikationswissenschaft*, he has both published a monograph on broadcasting liberalization in small European countries and a monograph on Switzerland's media system. In addition, he is the executive secretary of the Swiss Association for Communication and Media Research (SACM).

Michael Latzer is Professor of Communications at the Institute of Mass Communication and Media Research (IPMZ), University of Zurich, Switzerland, where he chairs the Media Change & Innovation division. He holds a Mag. rer.soc.oec. (MSc) in business informatics and a Ph.D. in political science from the University of Vienna and did his *Habilitation* [postdoctoral dissertation] in economics and politics of communication at the University of Vienna. Prof. Latzer is an expert on media convergence and European information society issues, eCommerce, the digital economy, telecommunications and media governance. For details, see www.mediachange.ch.

Maria Löblich is a research assistant in communication science at the University of Munich. She holds a Ph.D. from the University of Munich. Her research interests include media policy, Internet regulation and history of communication studies.

Jan Loisen is a senior researcher at the Media Policy Cluster of the research centre for Studies on Media, Information and Telecommunication (IBBT-SMIT) at the Vrije Universiteit Brussel (Free University of Brussels). He obtained his Ph.D. in 2009 with a dissertation on the WTO's impact on audio-visual policy. His research focuses on audio-visual and media policy in a multi-level governance context.

Martino Maggetti is a senior researcher and lecturer at the Institut für Politikwissenschaft (University of Zurich) and at the Institut d'Etudes Politiques et Internationales (University of Lausanne). He holds a Ph.D. in political science from the University of Lausanne. His research interests are mainly oriented towards the fields of comparative politics and policy analysis, with a special focus on: agencification and regulatory reforms, banking and financial regulation, democracy in deeply divided societies, policy diffusion, comparative research design and methodology.

Werner A. Meier is a senior researcher and lecturer at the University of Zurich's Institute of Mass Communication and Media Research (IPMZ). He also is the head of SwissGIS—Swiss Centre for Studies on the Global Information Society—at the University of Zurich and co-chair of the Euromedia Research Group. His research and teaching interests are media sociology, media policy and the political economy of media industries.

Hallvard Moe is an associate professor of media studies at the University of Bergen. His Ph.D. dissertation in 2009 was on 'Public Broadcasters, the Internet, and Democracy.' His work has appeared in journals such as *Media, Culture & Society*, *Television & New Media*, *Convergence* and *Javnost/The Public*. In 2010, Moe co-edited *The Digital Public*

Sphere: Challenges for Media Policy (Nordicom) with Jostein Gripsrud, *The Idea of the Public Sphere: A Reader* (Lexington) and *The Public Sphere vol. I–IV* (Sage) both with Jostein Gripsrud, Anders Molander and Graham Murdock.

Senta Pfaff-Rüdiger is a research assistant in communication science at the University of Munich. She holds a Ph.D. from the University of Munich. Her research interests include media use, media policy, children and media, qualitative methods and collective memory.

Pietro Rossi is a research associate at the University of Zurich's Institute of Mass Communication and Media Research (IPMZ).

Katharine Sarikakis is Professor of Communication sciences at the University of Vienna. Her research interests are in the field of European and international communication governance and in particular across two intersecting directions: the role of institutions in supra- and international communications policy processes and the implication of policy for the exercise of enlarged citizenship. She founded and led the Communication Law and Policy Section of the European Communication Research and Education Association and was elected as Head of the section twice. Sarikakis is also past Vice President of the International Association for Media and Communication Researchers and is serving now as an elected member of the International Council of IAMCR. Currently she is working on a research monograph on Communication and Control. Other books include: *Powers in Media Policy* (2004) and *British Media in a Global Era* (2004). She is the co-author of *Media Policy and Globalization* (2006) and the editor of *Media and Cultural Policy in the European Union* (2007). She is also the managing editor of the *International Journal of Media and Cultural Politics*.

Florian Saurwein is a research and teaching associate in the Media Change & Innovation division at the Institute of Mass Communication and Media Research (IPMZ) of the University of Zurich, Switzerland. He studied communication science and political science and holds an MA in communication science from the University of Vienna and a Ph.D. from the University of Zurich. Prior to joining IPMZ he was research fellow at the Research Unit for Institutional Change and European Integration (IWE) and at the Institute of Technology Assessment (ITA) of the Austrian Academy of Sciences. His current research interests focus on interrelations between media change and democracy. Research topics include the impact of media innovations on the formation of a European public sphere, multi-level governance and the implications of the increase of alternative modes of regulation (self- and co-regulation).

Seamus Simpson is a professor of media policy in the School of Media, Music and Performance at the University of Salford. His research interests are in European and global communications media policies, with a specific focus on a range of Internet, telecommunication and digital media convergence governance issues. Some of his recent work has focused on the EU as an actor in global Internet governance, critiques of the European Electronic Communications Regulatory Framework, next-generation communications media network policies at EU level and policy issues around private interest/hybrid public–private regulation in digital media environments. Work in these areas has recently appeared, or is shortly forthcoming in, among others: the *Journal of*

European Public Policy; Governance; Convergence; Information, Communication and Society; the *Journal of Common Market Studies;* the *European Journal of Communication* and the *Journal of Public Policy.* Seamus is also the author of *Globalisation, Convergence and European Telecommunications Regulation* (2005, Edward Elgar) (with Peter Humphreys) and *The New Electronic Marketplace: European Governance Strategies in a Globalising Economy* (2007, Edward Elgar; with George Christou).

Vaclav Stetka is senior research fellow with the Media and Democracy in Central and Eastern Europe project hosted by the Department of Politics and International Relations at the University of Oxford (http://mde.politics.ox.ac.uk/). He received his Ph.D. in Sociology at Masaryk University, Brno, where he then worked as a lecturer in the Department of Media Studies and Journalism between 2006 and 2009, teaching courses on media, modernity and globalization and methodology of mass media research. He has participated in several European comparative research projects, including the COST A30 action 'East of West: Setting a New Central Eastern European Media Research Agenda' (2007–2009) and EU Kids Online (2006–2009).

Miklós Sükösd is an associate professor at the Journalism and Media Studies Centre at the University of Hong Kong. He was academic director of the Centre for Media and Communication Studies at Central European University in Hungary, where he also taught as associate professor of political science. He served as chair of the COST A30 action 'East of West: Setting a New Central Eastern European Media Research Agenda' (2005–2009) and key expert in the EU project 'An Independent Study On Indicators For Media Pluralism in the Member States' (2008–2009). He has published over 20 books and several book chapters and articles about media and politics. His research and teaching interests include (post-)communism and the media in central and eastern Europe and China, media and the environment, and Buddhism and the media.

Julian Thomas is Director of the Institute for Social Research and Professor of Media and Communications at Swinburne University of Technology. His research interests are in new media, information policy and the history of communications technologies. His book *Framing Intellectual Property: Exhibition, Advertising and the Press, 1789–1918*, co-authored with Megan Richardson, will be published in 2011 by Cambridge UP. Julian is an associate editor of the website Australian Policy Online. He is a board member of the Foundation for Public-Interest Journalism, a member of the Consumer Consultative Forum of the Australian Media and Communications Authority and a member of the Australian Research Council Centre of Excellence in Creative Industries and Innovation (CCI).

Hilde Van den Bulck is a professor of communications studies and head of the Media, Policy and Culture research group at the University of Antwerp. Her expertise is situated in the complementary fields of media culture and media policy, focusing on public service broadcasting in diachronic perspective.

Marit Vochteloo is a senior policy advisor at the Media Department of the Ministry of Education, Culture and Science in the Netherlands. She completed an MA in (mass) communication science. Previously she worked as lecturer/researcher at the Communication Studies Department of the University of Amsterdam.